General Studies
for AQA A

Richard Hobson
David Walton
Victor Watton

An AS and A Level Course Text Third Edition

HODDER
EDUCATION
PART OF HACHETTE LIVRE UK

The Publishers would like to thank the following for permission to reproduce copyright material:

Photo credits p.11 Illustrated London News; **p.18** Joe McBride/Getty Images; **p.27** Science Photo Library; **p.40** Eric and David Hosking/Corbis; **p.51** *l* CAMR/A.B. Dowsett/Science Photo Library, *r* Steve Gschmeissner/Science Photo Library; **p.56** Tobias Schwarz/Reuters/Corbis; **p.64** Bettmann/CORBIS; **p.79** Patrick Ward/Corbis; **p.88** © Enigma/Alamy; **p.114** © Rachel Chapman; **p.123** Bridgeman Art Library, reproduced with kind permission of Coventry Cathedral; **p.129** Reuters/Corbis; **p.141** Alex Bartel/Science Photo Library; **p.149** William Conran/PA Archive/PA Photos; **p.159** © Ace Stock Limited/Alamy; **p.162** Francis G Meyer/Corbis; **p.167** Tony Kyriacou/Rex Features; **p.207** David Cheskin/PA Archive/PA Photos; **p.224** Michael Stephens/PA Archive/PA Photos; **p.231** Topham Picturepoint/Topfoto; **p.240** PA/PA Archive/PA Photos; **p.249** Chris Young/AFP/Getty Images; **p.260** © vario images GmbH & Co.KG/Alamy.

Acknowledgements Adherents.com for census facts on world religion; AQA material is reproduced by permission of the Assessment and Qualifications Alliance; BBC Design and Publications for the annual report and accounts table, Fig. 22.2; Cengage Learning Services for a diagram of the British Constitution from *Politics: An Introduction*, Barrie Axford (Routledge, 1997); Encyclopaedia Britannica for the definition of 'clone'; FDA Consumer Magazine for the gene therapy diagram, Fig. 6.1; Financial Times Syndication for the article 'Perks that go too far', adapted from Michael Skapinker, 25ᵗʰ September 2002; Guardian News & Media Syndication for an editorial (30 July 2000) and a letter (6 August 2000) from *The Observer*, and an extract from the article 'Faith in our schools', *Education Guardian*, 25ᵗʰ April 2000; Her Majesty's Stationery Office for census facts on religion in England and Wales, 2001, for tidal information reproduced by permission of the Controller of Her Majesty's Stationery Office and the UK Hydrographic Office (www.ukho.gov.uk), for the table 'Children looked after by local authorities by type of accommodation' (www.statistics.gov.uk), an extract from 'Do you feel British?' (www.statistics.gov.uk), table of ethnicity of UK population, Census 2001, table of employment rates by ethnic group (www.statistics.gov.uk), statistics on crimes recorded by the police with clear up rates in England and Wales (www.statistics.gov.uk), the DfES explanation of Citizenship from the DfES website, pie charts from the HM treasury and an extract from an advert (www.targetingfraud.gov.uk). Crown copyright material is reproduced with the permission of the controller of HMSO and the Queen's Printer for Scotland; Liberty for an extract from their mission statement, 2001; News International Syndication for an article 'Car makers miles away from green alternative', September 2000, 'Robbery statistics inflated by liars', 12ᵗʰ July 2002 and 'Globalisation crucial to creation of a just world', 12ᵗʰ November 2001; Dr Jane Nicklin and Rachel Chapman for the extract from the *Birkbeck College Magazine* (June 1999); Orion Publishing Group for an extract from *The Hidden Wiring*, Peter Hennessy (Victor Gollancz, a division of the Orion Publishing Group, 1996); Oxford University Press for the definitions of 'economics', 'religion', 'right' and 'science', from *Oxford English Dictionary*, 2ⁿᵈ edition edited by Simpson, John and Weiner, Edmund (OUP, 1989), and an extract from *British Politics* by Dennis Kavanagh, 1996; Penguin Group UK for the extract from *Ruling Britannia: The Failure and Future of British Democracy* by Andrew Marr (Michael Joseph, 1995) © Andrew Marr, 1995; Save the Children fund for an extract from the Save the Children mission statement, 2001; Adrian Searle for the extract from *The Guardian*, 11ᵗʰ December 2001; the Socialist Party for an extract from the Socialist Party's mission statement; Solo Syndication for letters to the *Daily Mail*, 4ᵗʰ October, 2000; US National Academy of the Recording Arts and Sciences for an extract from John Steinmetz's *Resuscitating Art Music*, 1993.

Although every effort has been made to ensure that website addresses are correct at time of going to press, Hodder Education cannot be held responsible for the content of any website mentioned in this book. It is sometimes possible to find a relocated web page by typing in the address of the home page for a webiste in the URL window of your browser.

Hachette Livre UK's policy is to use papers that are natural, renewable and recyclable products and made from wood grown in sustainable forests. The logging and manufacturing processes are expected to conform to the environmental regulations of the country of origin.

Orders: please contact Bookpoint Ltd, 130 Milton Park, Abingdon, Oxon OX14 4SB. Telephone: (44) 01235 827720. Fax: (44) 01235 400454. Lines are open 9.00–5.00, Monday to Saturday, with a 24-hour message answering service. Visit our website at www.hoddereducation.co.uk

Contents

The content of General Studies A and this book

Culture and society (AS unit 1 and A2 unit 3)

Themes	Study units
Understanding and appreciation of the changing nature and importance of culture	14, 20
Creativity and innovation	21
Aesthetic evaluation	19
Beliefs, values and moral reasoning	15 to 18
Religious belief and experience and connections between them	3, 15 to 18
Examination and appreciation of ideologies and values in society	25, 28
Media and communication	22, 23
Political processes and goals	29 to 31, 35
Relationship between law, society and ethics	26, 27

Science and society (AS unit 2 and A2 unit 4)

Themes	Study units
Characteristics of the sciences (physical, life and earth)	1, 4
Explanation and evaluation of human behaviour	8, 24, 25
Social and economic trends and constraints	32 to 36
Understanding of scientific methods, principles, criteria and their application	2, 3
Nature of scientific objectivity and question of progress	1, 2, 10 and 11
Nature of objectivity in social sciences	24, 25
Mathematical reasoning and its application	12, 13
Social, ethical and environmental implications of scientific discoveries and technological development	5 to 7, 9, 14
Moral responsibility of scientists	6, 18
Past and present relationships between technology, science and society	4, 5, 9, 14

Thinking, analytical and communication skills (all exam units)

Themes	Study units
Understanding the nature of knowledge, truth and belief and the distinctions between them	Introduction
Analysis of data, information, ideas, opinions and arguments	All units
Using the above to examine questions, form values, make judgements and draw conclusions	All units
Understanding of different kinds of knowledge, appreciating their strengths and limitations	Introduction
Use of language to impart knowledge and understanding and present opinions and argument	Practice questions in all units

Introduction

About the specification

The third edition of this book has been revised to support your studies of the new AQA General Studies A AS and A Level examination from 2008–09 onwards. The specification is divided into four units which are assessed in different ways. These units are shown in the table below.

The Four Unit Tests for AQA General Studies A	
Culture and Society	**Science and Society**
AS Unit 1	**AS Unit 2**
Passages for comprehension and analysis on themes in Culture and Society **Section A** 30 multiple choice comprehension questions (30 marks) **Section B** Three short extracts and three compulsory documentary source analysis questions (35 marks) <div align="right">1½ hours 65 marks</div>	**Passage and data for science comprehension and written questions on themes in Science and Society** **Section A** 30 multiple choice questions based on passage and data (30 marks) **Section B** One from three optional two-part questions on scientific and social themes (35 marks) <div align="right">1½ hours 65 marks</div>
A2 Unit 3	**A2 Unit 4**
Passage for evaluation and written questions on themes in Culture and Society **Section A** One compulsory source evaluation exercise (20 marks) **Section B** One from four optional essays on culture (25 marks) **Section C** One from four optional essays on society (25 marks) <div align="right">2 hours 70 marks</div>	**Case Study and written questions on themes in Science and Society** **Section A** Four short answer questions on Case Study materials, both pre-release and unseen (45 marks) **Section B** One from four optional science and society essays (25 marks) <div align="right">2 hours 70 marks</div>

The four assessment objectives for General Studies

These assessment objectives (AOs) outline the skills and abilities on which you will be assessed:

AO1   Demonstrate relevant knowledge and understanding applied to a range of issues, using skills from different disciplines.

AO2   Marshal evidence and draw conclusions; select, interpret, evaluate and integrate information, data, concepts and opinions.

AO3   Demonstrate understanding of different types of knowledge, appreciating their strengths and limitations.

AO4   Communicate clearly and accurately in a concise, logical and relevant way.

For each question in the examination there will be a number of marks allocated to some or all of these objectives according to the nature of the question and what it is intended to test. Up to sixty per cent of the assessment in AQA General Studies A is devoted to thinking and analytical skills and your understanding of the nature of knowledge (AOs 2 and 3). Further discussion of AO3 in particular is needed as there will be frequent reference to it when you come to the sample examination questions at the end of each unit.

Different types of knowledge

'Different types of knowledge' means in effect *different ways of getting knowledge*. We might get knowledge by fine measurement, and calculation. This gives us a degree of certainty. We might get it by observation, and by experiment. This gives us a degree of probability. Or we might get it by examination of documents and material remains, or by introspection – that is, by canvassing our own experiences and feelings. This gives us a degree of possibility. Knowledge, like most things, is a matter of degree.

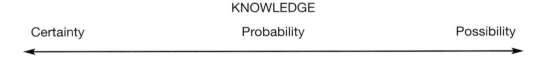

KNOWLEDGE

Certainty   Probability   Possibility

When we are talking about things, and the behaviour of things – of phenomena – we can be more or less certain. Our evidence is more or less *hard*, and we can be more or less *objective* about it. Thus, in the physical sciences, we can be confident enough to speak of *facts*, and laws.

As we begin to talk about species of being, and particularly when we talk about people, our evidence is *softer*, and – since we ourselves are people – more *subjective*. In the natural and social sciences we are obliged to speak rather of theories than of laws.

In the 'humanities', our evidence is softer still – though we may still be quite 'scientific' about how we get knowledge that is rather possible than certain. We are still looking for facts. Historians, for example, must base their interpretations of what happened on publicly attested facts. When they express *opinions*, they must make it clear that this is what they are doing – and we shall trust their opinions to the extent that they are supported by the facts that are available.

EVIDENCE

Hard/Objective   Subjective/Soft

← ── →

Facts   Opinions

Physical Sciences / Natural Sciences / Social Sciences / Humanities / Arts

It is a fact that:

- in the **physical sciences** energy travels in waves of varying lengths;
- in the **natural sciences** more than 95 per cent of all species that have ever lived have become extinct;
- in the **social sciences** 30 per cent of couples in one-family households, in 1998/99, had no children;
- in the **humanities** Robert Rauschenberg painted, and exhibited, an all-white canvas, and an all-black canvas.

But facts are not everything: physicists and biologists express opinions, too – and these may do as much to contribute to *truth*, to accordance with reality, as facts. For example: 'Genetically modified food is not harmful to humans.' Truth is so many-sided that we may never see all of its sides. We should be aware, though, that our *values* may influence our choice of facts, and colour our opinions. Values and *beliefs* are close cousins. The value that we attach to life may, for example, be expressed as a belief in the 'sanctity' of life. Such a belief may make us *partial*; it may *bias* our opinions, so that we disregard facts that are inconvenient to our point of view. Beliefs may have rather little to do with facts at all, and rather a lot to do with emotions.

Where AO3 is concerned therefore, the questions that we should address (in a particular context) are these:

- What are the *facts* in the case?
- Is the evidence *hard* or *soft*, *objective* or *subjective*?
- Are *opinions* well supported by facts?
- What *values* appear to influence the choice of facts and/or the opinions expressed?

Of course, we are all partial to a degree. We are all 'coming from' somewhere. There is nothing wrong with this: the important thing is to be aware of it, and to take it into account.

Here are some examples of 'second-order' (AO3) knowledge in the particular context of public and private transport:

- It is an *objective fact* that 61.2 per cent of all journeys made between 1996 and 1998 were made by car. (It can be shown by means of a reliable calculation/estimate.)
- It is a *theory*, based on quite *hard evidence*, that there is an inverse, direct relationship between car-ownership and access to public transport. (The greater the number of cars per head of population in an area, the less public transport is available.)
- It is an *opinion* that it is more convenient to travel by car than by long-distance coach.
- It is a *value*, shared by many on the left of politics, that investment in public transport is a social good.

- It is a *belief*, held by many on the right, that building roads makes for economic growth.

Political bias is one thing: preference for the private car over public transport may not be pro-social; but it isn't necessarily anti-social. A racial, ethnic, or gender bias is something else, because this is always, potentially, anti-social.

The 'limitations' referred to in AO3 have to do with the abundance or the scarcity of facts available in a case; and with the degree of objectivity that is possible. We know that the proportion of children's journeys undertaken on foot fell from 47 per cent to 37 per cent between 1985 and 1998. This is a hard, objective fact; but as evidence for an overall assessment of child health, it is limited. If a qualified paediatrician was to say:

> 'The fact that children are walking less now than they did in the past, is a powerful factor in a general decline in child health.'

we should treat this judgment with respect – but it is still limited. It does not tell us a lot; and it tells us nothing about physical activity other than walking. If a parent said:

> 'My child is safer strapped in the back seat of the car than walking on the pavement beside a busy road.'

we should respect the view – but it is a view limited by the parent's concern for one child, and perhaps by that parent's preference for driving over walking with the child.

Examination questions which are designed to test AO3 focus therefore on such matters as:

- Analysis and evaluation of the *nature* of the knowledge, evidence or arguments, for example, used in a text, set of data or other form of stimulus material.
- Understanding of the crucial *differences* between such things as facts, opinions and beliefs, and between objectivity and subjectivity in arguments.
- Appreciation of what constitutes *proof*; what is cause and effect, when conclusions are *valid and justified*; and what the *limitations* of these may be.
- Recognition of the existence of personal *values*, value judgements, partiality and bias in given circumstances.
- Awareness of the *effects* upon ourselves and others of different physical, emotional and cognitive experiences, and the limitations of feelings as a basis for knowledge.

Analysing an argument

You can use the flowchart in Figure 0.1 to help you determine whether an argument is valid and justified.

Types of argument

Deductive argument
This is where a conclusion can be deduced from the premises – i.e. it follows automatically. It argues from the general to the particular. For example, if the angles of a triangle equal 180 degrees (general statement) and in a particular triangle two of the angles equal 120 degrees, you can deduce the other angle equals 60 degrees.

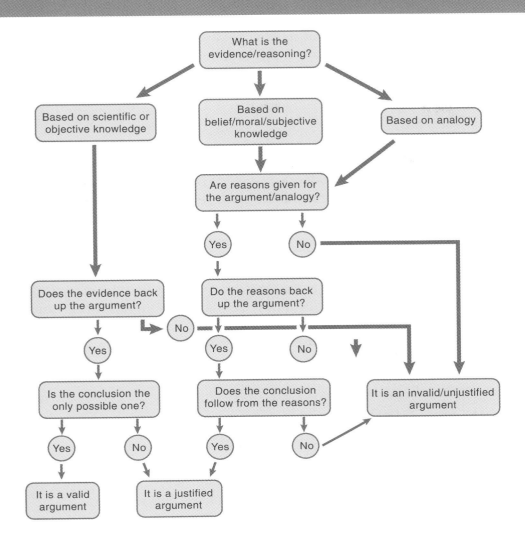

Figure 0.1 Is an argument valid?

Inductive argument

This type argues from the particular to the general, for example, each time I have boiled water it boiled at 100°C, therefore water always boils at 100°C. This argument will only be probable because it is based on experience, which we can never be certain about – for example, water boils at about 72°C on Mount Everest. Some inductive arguments are better than others, depending on the amount and reliability of the evidence.

Arguing from authority

This is claiming something is true because an important person or book says it is, for example 'Murder is wrong because the Bible says so'. This is a weak form of argument unless the authority is one that everyone recognises, for example 'Light does not travel in a straight line because Einstein said so'. By contrast, to claim murder is wrong on the authority of the Bible is not a valid argument unless you show why the Bible has moral authority and can give evidence that everything the Bible says is true.

Arguing from analogy

This is where someone quotes a similar case and argues from this that the same thing applies in a different situation. For example, William Paley argued that because a

Justified argument an argument
that has reasons which are
factually correct, and the
conclusion or interpretation
follows from the reasons, but is
not the only possible
conclusion. An example would
be the film *Shakespeare in Love*,
which interprets *Romeo and
Juliet* as a product of
Shakespeare falling in love. This
is a justified argument, but it is
not the only possible
interpretation

Valid argument this is either a
deductive argument or an
argument based on scientific or
objective knowledge, where the
conclusion or interpretation
follows from the evidence and
where the conclusion cannot be
doubted

watch is a complex mechanism that could not have been made by chance, the world, which is also a complex mechanism, could not have been made by chance either. However, for an argument from analogy to work, it must be shown that two things are the same, i.e. that the world has all the order of a watch and the watch has all the disorder of the world.

Arguing from lack of evidence

This is claiming that something is true because there is no evidence to say it is false. For example, no one has ever proven that fairies do not exist, therefore they must exist. This is a false argument because there has to be evidence upon which to decide whether something is true or false.

Truth

Philosophers have argued for the past 100 years about what truth is. Some philosophers argue that the truth is what corresponds to the facts, for example the statement 'swans are white' is true because it corresponds to the facts (this is known as the correspondence theory of truth). Others argue that what is true is what has not been falsified. It is not true to say that swans are white because Australian swans are black. However, it is true to say that most swans are white.

About the book

The book is structured into the three main areas of General Studies:

- Science, Maths and Technology (the scientific domain)
- Culture, Morality, Arts and Humanities (the cultural domain)
- Society, Politics and the Economy (the social domain).

These are then split into smaller units covering the subject content. Each unit includes:

- Key terms which define the key concepts relevant to the subject.
- Activities which give you practice and suggestions to deepen your subject knowledge and skills.
- Past exam questions from the AQA A specification (both AS and A Level questions) to give you exam skills practice.
- Examiner's advice to give you guidance on how to secure high marks.

Advice on how to tackle particular question types, and answers to the exam questions, are given at the end of the book.

Science, Maths and Techology

Scientific progress

In order to decide how scientific progress has been made, it is necessary to define what is meant by science. The *Oxford English Dictionary* defines 'science' as 'a branch of knowledge conducted on objective principles involving the systemised observation of and experiment with phenomena, especially concerned with the material and functions of the physical universe'. This could be further defined as:

- Observing regularities in nature, for example the way in which the seasons follow each other.
- Working out a rational theory to explain why these regularities happen, for example that the Earth moves round the Sun tilted at an angle and the seasons change as the Earth leans towards or away from the Sun.
- Formulating the theory into a formula that predicts what will happen, for example when the North Pole is tilted 23.4 degrees towards the Sun, the vertical noon rays are directly over the Tropic of Cancer.

Ideas about progress in science

Science has obviously made a lot of progress since the days when people thought that rain was caused by God opening windows in the firmament, but how has this change come about?

- The traditional theory is that science has grown gradually as scholars learned a little more in each successive generation and built on what they had learned from the previous generation.
- Another view is that progress in science depends on the nature of the society in which a scientist or scholar is living. If the society is changing rapidly or encourages people to think freely and to question traditional ideas, then there will be scientific progress. If a society is settled and has a system of authority where questioning traditions is punished, there will be little or no scientific progress (see Unit 14, 'The relationship between science and culture').
- Some scientists believe that progress in science depends on technology (making tools and instruments). For example, scientists could not have made discoveries about the planets without telescopes (see Unit 14).

Thomas Kuhn, an American historian of science, suggested in *The Structure of Scientific Revolutions* that scientific progress is made in sudden jumps. He argued that, in any society, scientists accept a *paradigm* given to them by their society. By a paradigm, Kuhn meant a view of what the world is like, how it works and how it can be investigated. He argued that the paradigm tells scientists what is important in science, what questions to ask and what problems are important. Change only occurs when scientists discover problems and contradictions in the paradigm. Eventually, this causes a crisis resulting in a new paradigm. This sudden change of paradigms is like a revolution in science and brings about progress because new ideas are needed.

In order for you to have sufficient information with which to answer a question on scientific progress, it is necessary to give a brief history of science.

A history of science

Early history
Archaeological evidence, such as cave paintings and scratches on bits of bone, indicates that humans have always been close observers of nature. Indeed, the whole of agriculture must be based on early humans observing the seasons and the way in which seeds grow in order to grow crops successfully. In the megalithic structures (such as Stonehenge) found in China, Central America, Mesopotamia, Egypt and Europe, there is evidence of knowledge of a number of mathematical principles, including that of the square on the hypotenuse equalling the sum of the squares on the other two sides in a right-angled triangle, almost 2000 years before Pythagoras.

Greek science
Euclid provided a mathematical basis for science by discovering the main theorems of geometry. Archimedes developed a method for manipulating scientific observations into a scientific law in mathematical terms – such laws can then be used to predict what will happen, for example Archimedes' own laws on levers and the displacement of water.

Aristotle developed the view that science is concerned with observation followed by theorising by asking questions such as 'What is the form of the object or process being observed?', 'How did it get that form?' and 'What is its purpose?' From these observations, Aristotle determined that the world is made up of four elements: earth, water, air and fire. Aristotle's view that the Earth is the centre of the universe (the *geocentric principle*) was finalised by Ptolemy, who devised a system of small circles on top of larger ones, that enabled astronomers to predict the movement of the Sun and planets while assuming that the Earth was stationary.

The great gift of the Greeks to science was their belief that the universe works on rational, natural laws discoverable by humans.

Medieval science
The Greek scientific ideas were developed by Islamic science, especially in the field of medicine, and by the Arab discoveries of the number system, algebra and chemistry. This Islamic science and the works of Aristotle were rediscovered in Europe when Spain was recaptured from the Islamic Empire. The medieval scientists were concerned with technology, discovering such things as the crank and gears, which enabled them to harness wind and water power for the beginnings of industry. They also used experiments to help to discover the natural laws.

The rise of modern science
Copernicus challenged the basis of much early science in 1543 when he suggested that the Earth goes round the Sun. This *heliocentric theory* was backed up when the

telescope was discovered and Galileo was able to show the phases of Venus and the moons around Jupiter (1610). Galileo's experiments on motion also showed that Aristotle's ideas were false.

Other seventeenth-century scientists built on Galileo's use of experiments and close observation. William Harvey discovered the circulation of the blood in 1628. Robert Boyle made various discoveries in chemistry, most famously Boyle's law of the compressibility of gas in 1662. Isaac Newton discovered the principles of gravity and motion in 1687.

It is generally thought that the basic principles of science were finalised by Newton (see Unit 2, 'Scientific method and its application'), but there is much argument as to whether the Copernican Revolution (as many historians call the change from an Earth-centred to a Sun-centred system) was simply a development of medieval science, the result of technology, or a new revolutionary idea.

You could use Unit 10 ('Transport issues'), Unit 4 ('Energy'), Unit 11 ('Computers') or Unit 9 ('Medical developments') to answer questions on scientific progress, but the subject of gravitational motion is a good way of doing so.

The progress of science as seen in gravitational motion

Early scientists did not realise that there was a connection between the way objects fall to Earth and the motion of the stars and planets. Aristotle claimed that the heavenly bodies were divine and in eternal, unchanging motion. As far as objects on Earth are concerned, they had a natural tendency to move towards the Earth's centre. These ideas led to a theory of motion that a body moving at a constant speed must have a constant force acting on it directly (i.e. interaction at a distance was impossible).

These ideas seemed to fit the facts as they were known. Indeed, the heliocentric theory causes problems. Galileo was asked why bodies do not fly off the Earth if it is spinning on its axis and circling the Sun. He was also asked why an object dropped from a tower falls to the bottom of the tower when the Earth has moved between it being dropped and it landing. Galileo's answer was that bodies do not fly off the Earth because, in revolutions per minute, they are not travelling very fast. Objects dropped from a tower share the Earth's rotation with the tower and so drop at the base of the tower. In his experiments of dropping objects, Galileo discovered that the distance a falling object travels varies as the square of the time.

Johannes Kepler (1571–1630) discovered that the planets move in ellipses rather than circles. He saw a great problem with planetary motion and suggested that the Sun emitted a magnetic force, which pushed the planets around it.

It was Newton who realised that it is the same force that makes objects fall to the ground and that makes the planets move in elliptical orbits. His law of universal gravitation states that there is a force of attraction between any two bodies that is proportional to the inverse square of their separation and the product of their masses ($F = GmM/d^2$). This law explains why objects of differing weights fall to Earth at the same speed and why planets have elliptical orbits.

Newton's laws were accepted until Einstein proposed that the elliptical paths of the planets were not caused by the gravitational effects of the Sun, but because the presence of a gravitational field caused a curvature of space-time. In the general theory of relativity, Einstein explained why objects fall and how the whole universe operates. His theory is generally regarded as having been confirmed at the eclipse of 1919, when scientists could see that light travels in curves rather than straight lines, and by the red-shift effect in light (which is also evidence for the Big Bang). This evidence came after the theory, but Einstein's theory is based on the mathematics of Bernhard Riemann (1826–66) about geodesics (the straightest curve possible in a curved grid). Some scientists also think that increased accuracy in telescopes showed that Newton's law was inaccurate in calculating Mercury's orbit before Einstein formulated his theory.

DID YOU KNOW?

Light, rain and rainbows
Medieval scientists investigated the nature of light in a rainbow by simulating the conditions under which the rainbows occur. Hollow glass balls filled with water were substituted for raindrops and light was passed through them. Conclusions about the behaviour of light could then be drawn without the huge difficulty of waiting for a rainbow to appear.

Figure 1.1 'The wonder is not that mankind comprehends the world, but that the world is comprehensible' (Einstein)

Activities

1. What is your paradigm?

2. Use the Internet to discover the scientific principles involved in: the building of Stonehenge; Archimedes' law of levers; Archimedes and the displacement of water; a water mill; a windmill.

3. What do you understand by Einstein's quotation about the world being comprehensible?

4. Thomas Kuhn argued that scientific advance is by a series of revolutionary jumps interspersed by long periods of relatively slow development. Critically discuss this model of scientific progress in reference to gravitational motion.

EXAM QUESTIONS

Consider the following passage and figures, and answer the multiple choice questions which follow.

Dating (Part 1)

(1) Henges are ceremonial sites from the Bronze Age. The most famous is probably Stonehenge on Salisbury plain. Seahenge in Norfolk was a remarkable ring of 55 oak timbers uncovered on a beach. This particular henge had a ring of timbers with an upturned oak stump in the centre. Using modern dating techniques, scientists have convinced the archaeologists that the ring is about 4050 years old. They can even say that the central oak was felled or died between April and June 2050 BC. The other trees were cut down in the spring of the following year.

(2) Two methods were used to date the find. The first was dendrochronology, which matches the growth rings in wood to known historical climate data. Rings are made of xylem. Pith is found at the centre of the tree stem followed by the xylem. Between the xylem and the rough bark is a layer of dividing cells (cambium), which form the xylem cells. Each year a new layer of xylem may be formed; thin-walled cells are formed as earlywood and thicker walled cells later in the year as latewood. The thicker walled cells appear as a darker band, before the next year's spring growth (Figures 1.2 and 1.3).

(3) An annual ring is from the beginning of the earlywood to the end of the latewood. Tree rings are never identical but the general patterns are similar. When the climate is particularly moist it will produce wide rings and in dry years narrow rings.

(4) Scientists use a crosscheck system to verify data. In order for this to be reliable four factors must be present:

- Species studied must produce only one ring per growing season or year.
- Only one dominant environmental factor can be the cause of reduced growth.
- The main environmental factor should be different each year, so changes are easily seen between different annual rings.
- The same pattern should be evident over a fairly wide geographic area, so comparisons can be made.

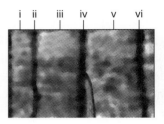

i ii iii iv v vi

Figure 1.2 Single locally absent ring:
- Bottom part of this photo has four full rings
- Top part of this photo has three full rings
- Wedging ring is 'locally absent' from that part of the sample
- This sample is cross-dateable, but not by mere ring counting.

Figure 1.3 Many locally absent rings:
- This photo of a coast redwood sample has many rings that are wedging out
- This sample is probably not cross-dateable
- Important point: not all tree-ring samples are cross-dateable.

(5) Factors which may affect tree-ring growth are slope gradient, temperature, snow accumulation, soil properties, sun and wind. In some years there may be no growth ring locally, due to severe weather (Figures 1.2 and 1.3).

(6) Figure 1.4 below shows how three samples can be compared to find the common overlap. From this the years that the tree was alive can be found.

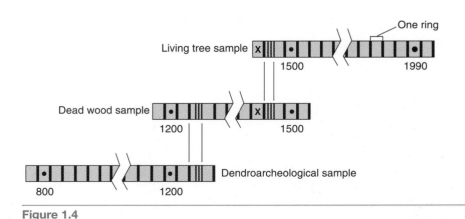

Living tree sample

One ring

1500   1990

Dead wood sample

1200   1500

800   1200   Dendroarcheological sample

Figure 1.4

After cross-dating, dendrochronologists can:

- Assign the true year of formation for every ring of each sample.
- Analyse past environmental and/or human events.

Cross-dated samples overlap in time. Using plotting this can be graphed out to find matching patterns.

Unfortunately, in the case of Seahenge's trees the oak rings matched many parts of Britain's weather spectrum.

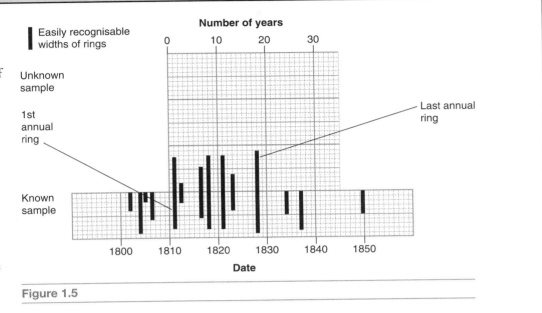

Figure 1.5

Source: AQA General Studies A, Unit 2, Question 1, May 2003

For the questions which follow, choose the answer A, B, C or D which you think fits best. Each of the questions is worth one mark.

1 Which of the following explains how scientists were able to tell that the central stump at Seahenge was cut down in late spring?
   A The middle ring had thin-walled cells.
   B The rings were unusually wide.
   C The outermost ring was incomplete.
   D The bark was still present.

2 Which of the following represents the order of tissues from the centre to the outer bark in a two-year old tree (paragraph 2)?
   A pith-xylem-pith-xylem-bark
   B pith-xylem-cambium-xylem-bark
   C pith-cambium-xylem-cambium-bark
   D pith-xylem-cambium-bark

3 In Figure 1.2, which of the labels show the earlywood (paragraph 2)?
   A i, ii, iii, iv
   B i, iii, v
   C i, ii, iv, v
   D ii, iii, iv, v

4 The term 'locally absent' (Figure 1.3) means
   A not in the area around the tree.
   B not on the same slope.
   C not found throughout the trunk.
   D away from the area.

5 Using Figure 1.4, which of the samples was alive when William the Conqueror invaded England in 1066?
   1 dendroarchaeological sample
   2 living tree sample
   3 dead wood sample

   Answer
   A if 1 alone is correct
   B if 2 alone is correct
   C if 3 alone is correct
   D if 2 and 3 only are correct

6 In Figure 1.4, in the dead wood sample, the ring X represents the year
   A 1494
   B 1495
   C 1496
   D 1505

7

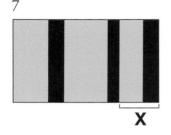

Figure 1.6 Diagram of rings in a sample

X

Which of the following conditions is most likely to have given rise to the ring at X?
A drier than average
B above average warm temperature
C above average sunlight
D moister than average

8

Centre ◄——————————————► Bark

Figure 1.7 Diagram of tree rings in a sample

Which of the following conditions represents the last two years' growth rings?
A year 1 moist; year 2 moist
B year 1 moist; year 2 dry
C year 1 dry; year 2 moist
D year 1 dry; year 2 dry

9 In Figure 1.5, the plots of the unknown sample show that it lived for
A 20 years.
B 19 years.
C 18.5 years.
D 18 years.

10 A series of tree rings for bristlecone pines extends back 9000 years. It is hoped that recently obtained samples will take this back 10,000 years. This will be interesting to scientists because
A it proves they are long-lived trees.
B it gives indications of past weather.
C it shows there has been no human interference.
D scientists like to gather trivial data.

EXAMINER'S ADVICE

- The passage and questions are similar to those which are set in Section A of AS Unit 2. In the exam proper there are 30 science comprehension questions based on a longer version of the passage. (See the next unit for the remainder of the passage and ten more multiple choice questions.)
- Check out the general advice on tackling multiple choice questions on page 266. The ten questions here are representative of those you will get in the exam and you should aim to complete them in, say, half an hour.
- You will note that some of the questions are about your understanding of the information and discussion in the passage and others about the scientific and mathematical principles involved. Some will test your knowledge and understanding of scientific facts and terms which you studied for GCSE. Any knowledge required beyond GCSE will be explained in the text. It is important to recognise that the test is not aimed at subject specialists.
- A few of the later questions (see next unit) will focus on your ability to distinguish between facts and opinions, confirmed results and unsubstantiated hypotheses. Generally, the questions become broader and more complex as you work through them, like Question 5 which has several options, and Question 10 which is about the purpose of science.
- The answers are given on page 271.

Scientific method and its application

Science is concerned with the phenomena of the universe, i.e. the physical things that happen in the universe. The methods used by scientists to explore the phenomena and come up with laws or theories to explain them are known as scientific method.

The scientific method

A seventeenth-century English scientist, Francis Bacon, worked out a formal method of scientific investigation based on studying empirical evidence ('empirical' means evidence that can be tested by the senses). This has been developed into the method that you probably use for GCSE science coursework.

All of science has to be *inductive* rather than *deductive* because it argues from a set of particular observations to a general law. However, what makes it scientific is that it is difficult to reject the conclusion without being irrational, and, more particularly, the experiments can always be repeated and will have the same conclusion (this is often called predictability – science can predict what will happen).

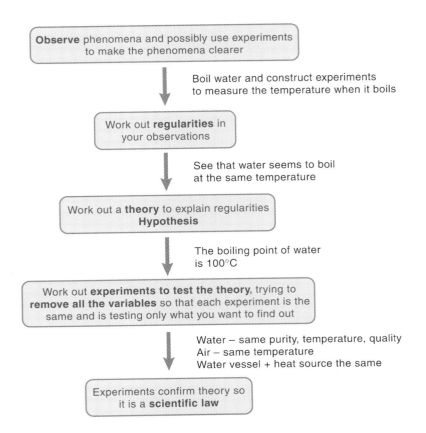

Observe phenomena and possibly use experiments to make the phenomena clearer

Boil water and construct experiments to measure the temperature when it boils

Work out **regularities** in your observations

See that water seems to boil at the same temperature

Work out a **theory** to explain regularities
Hypothesis

The boiling point of water is 100°C

Work out **experiments to test the theory**, trying to **remove all the variables** so that each experiment is the same and is testing only what you want to find out

Water – same purity, temperature, quality
Air – same temperature
Water vessel + heat source the same

Experiments confirm theory so it is a **scientific law**

Figure 2.1 The scientific method

Some philosophers of science follow Karl Popper and claim that the scientific method is based on *falsifying* rather than *verifying* ('verifying' – the use of scientific experiment to test whether a theory is true). They claim that science makes progress as scientists test theories or laws and find areas where they are false. Then they amend the law or theory to fit the new evidence (e.g. changing the air pressure and discovering that water does not always boil at 100°C and then devising the law that water boils at 100°C minus 1°C for every 300 m above sea level).

Using scientific method

The crucial points when trying to apply scientific method to any issue are to:

*   Use evidence that can be tested by the senses.
*   Work out a theory to explain the evidence.
*   Work out tests of the theory (experiments) that reduce the number of variables to as few as possible.
*   Decide whether the tests have given enough evidence to say that the theory is valid (true beyond reasonable doubt).

The application of scientific method – evolution

Some scientists would regard the most important theory in the biological sciences as evolutionary theory. Evolution means gradual change over the course of time and the theory is that life on Earth has evolved over 3–4 billion years, from very simple to very complex organisms, through modifications in each generation.

Observations

Naturalists such as Linnaeus (the first person to classify plants) and Lamarck had observed similarities between species in the eighteenth century. Linnaeus proposed that species could change, and Lamarck devised an evolutionary tree from tiny animals to human beings. Technological advances in canal and road building led to geological discoveries and fossils that seemed to show gradually changing life forms.

Charles Darwin, on his voyage to the Galápagos Islands on *HMS Beagle*, observed differences between species living on neighbouring islands and a similarity between living creatures and fossil remains in the same area.

The theory

In his *On the Origin of Species* (1859), Darwin proposed that life on Earth has evolved from the very simple forms of life seen in the earliest fossils to complex mammals such as humans through 'natural selection'. In each generation, more offspring are produced than can survive and some of the offspring have slight variations. The forces of nature (restricted food supply, disease, predators, etc.) destroy those less adapted to survive and those that do survive will pass on their successful variation to the next generation, so that over long periods of time, major changes will occur.

The evidence

Since Darwin's time, much testing of the fossil record has been possible. Discoveries in DNA have shown that the history of evolution is stored in the gene strands of DNA, and molecular biology is now able to trace some parts of the evolutionary process.

Conclusion

Scientists regard evolution in terms of organisms being related by common descent as a fact. There is so much evidence that it is irrational to doubt it. What is still regarded as theory is *why* evolution occurs.

The application of scientific method – plate tectonics

Some scientists would regard the most important theory in the Earth sciences as plate tectonics. This is a recent theory, which has been as revolutionary for Earth sciences as Copernicus was for astronomy and physics. It claims that all the geological processes of the Earth – mountains, oceans, volcanoes, earthquakes, etc. can be explained by the structure and behaviour of a small number of huge rigid plates, which form the outer part of the planet Earth (known as the lithosphere).

Observations

In 1911, Alfred Wegener claimed that observation of the early geological history of the Earth showed that there was once only one continent (which he named Pangaea). This was modified by du Toit in 1937 to the existence of two continents. Both these scientists had observed that the fossils in the pre-Cretaceous rock strata of Africa and South America (over 140 million years old) and the pre-Jurassic rocks of India, Australia, Madagascar and Africa (over 200 million years old) are so similar that they appear once to have been part of the same land mass. In the 1950s, it was observed that the magnetised remains in rocks indicate that the magnetic poles were at different places on the Earth at different periods in the Earth's history.

The theory

In the mid-1960s, the Canadian geologist Tuzo Wilson suggested that the regularities of the observations could be explained if the Earth's crust were made up of plates much thicker than the continents and the ocean floors. These plates cover the whole surface of the Earth, but where they meet each other, the nature of the plates either results in one plate going lower (creating oceans) or a collision (creating mountain ranges). Where two plates pass each other without subduction (one going lower) or collision, there is a fracture zone (for example, the San Andreas Fault in California). Wilson claimed that most of the Earth's seismic activity occurs along plate boundaries.

The evidence

Drilling of the ocean floors in the 1970s and 1980s confirmed that the ocean floors are less than 200 million years old, whereas the Earth itself is around 4.5 billion years old. Computer graphics have shown that at about 1000 m depth, the continents do match each other.

Isotopic dating has shown that the pre-Cambrian rocks in Africa and South America are the same in age and composition.

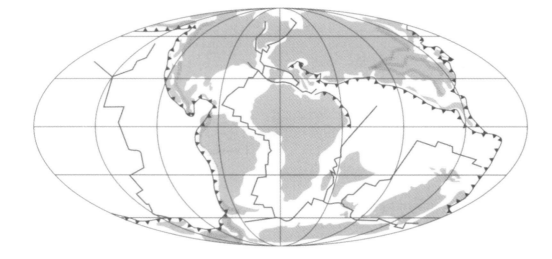

Figure 2.2 Continental distribution 80 million years ago

Activities

1. Look at the photo in Figure 2.3 and try to formulate a theory to explain the phenomena of people seeing UFOs.

2. Work out some experiments to test your theory and explain what would be needed for scientific proof of the existence of UFOs.

3. It has been claimed that left-handed people are more skilful at sports requiring hand–eye co-ordination than right-handed people. Explain how you would test this theory scientifically and how you would present your results.

Conclusion

Plate tectonics is still a theory rather than a fact because there are some pieces of evidence that do not fit the theory (e.g. the Rocky Mountains of North America cannot be explained by plate collision). However, the theory does seem to work and scientists are using the method suggested by Popper to adapt the theory to cover the exceptions.

Figure 2.3 Science fact or fiction?

EXAM QUESTIONS

Consider the following passage and figures, which are the continuation of those for the examination exercise at the end of the previous unit, and answer the multiple choice questions which follow.

Dating (Part 2)

(7) The second method is radio carbon analysis. There are three principal isotopes of carbon which occur naturally: Carbon-12 and Carbon-13 are both stable; Carbon-14 is unstable or radioactive. These are present in varying amounts.

Table 2.1

Type of Carbon	Percentage
12	98.89
13	1.11
14	1.0×10^{-10}

This means that one Carbon-14 atom exists in nature for every 1,000,000,000,000 Carbon-12 atoms in living material.

(8) The method depends on the rate of decay of the Carbon-14, which is formed in the upper atmosphere by cosmic ray neutrons acting on Nitrogen-14.

Nitrogen-14 + n => Carbon-14 + p where n = neutron and p = proton

The Carbon-14 is changed to carbon dioxide by reacting with oxygen. The carbon dioxide can then be taken up by plants in photosynthesis and converted to sugar. When animals eat the plants, the Carbon-14 is transferred to animals. The proportion of Carbon-14 in the living system is therefore the same as in the atmosphere.

(9) When the plant or animal dies, no more carbon dioxide is taken up but the tissue is

decayed by decomposing bacteria. However, where tissue is fossilised, it will contain the remains of the carbon which has not yet radioactively decayed.

(10) Libby, Anderson and Arnold first discovered that the radioactive decay of Carbon-14 occurs at a constant rate. They found that after 5568 years, half the Carbon-14 in the original sample will have decayed and after another 5568 years, half

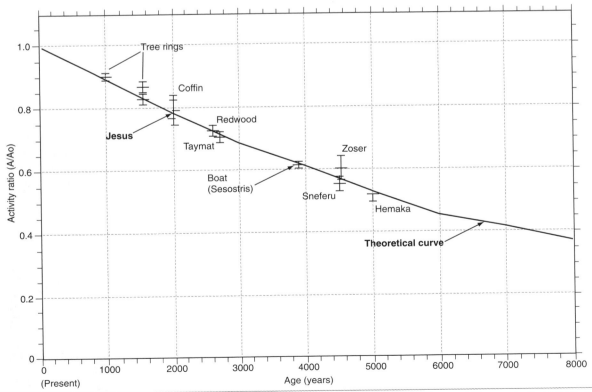

Figure 2.4 The 'Curve of Knowns' after Libby and Arnold (1949)

of that remaining material will have decayed. The half-life is the name given to this value, which was measured to 5568 years with an allowance for error of ±30 years. The Carbon-14 present in an unknown sample can then be compared with the Carbon-14 in similar oak tissue today. Then, by using the half-life, the age at which the fossilised remains died can be calculated. This can then be compared with the 'Curve of Knowns' (Figure 2.4).

(11) The new method was tested against radiocarbon dating of known age samples, mainly from Egypt. The Egyptian kings' names are given next to the corresponding ages obtained. The ages are shown as vertical lines. The theoretical curve was constructed using the half-life of 5568 years. The activity ratio plotted on the y-axis is the ratio of the activity of the sample (A) against modern activity (Ao).

(12) Later the half-life was adjusted to 5730 ± 40 years and this became known as the Cambridge half-life. Since then carbon dating has advanced to use better technology, where much smaller samples of the tissue are required. However, in tissue over 50,000 years old, the level of Carbon-14 would be too small to measure, so any item older than this needs to use other radioactive elements with longer half-lives.

(13) The modern standard is taken to be the measured Carbon-14 activity of oxalic acid in a crop compared to the absolute radiocarbon standard of 1890 wood. 1890 wood is used because it was growing before the fossil fuel effects of the Industrial Revolution. As the ratio of activity of the oxalic acid can be worked out compared to the 1890 wood, the oxalic acid can be used by scientists to compare an unknown sample to the activity in a sample of the oxalic acid.

(14) For the Seahenge timbers, even more complex statistical tests have been used to combine the dates for the dendrochronology and Carbon-14 methods to give the exact dates mentioned in paragraph 1.

Source: AQA General Studies A, Unit 2, Question 1, May 2003

For the questions which follow, choose the answer A, B, C or D which you think fits best. Each of the questions is worth one mark. For some of the questions you may need to refer back to the earlier part of the passage and figures on pages 12–13.

1   Which of the following represents the proportion of Carbon-14 in a plant (Table 2.1 and paragraph 7)?
    A   10,000,000,000 per cent
    B   1,000,000,000 per cent
    C   0.000,000,000,1 per cent
    D   0.000,000,001 per cent

2   Out of 300,000 atoms which is the best estimate of the number of Carbon-12 and Carbon-13 atoms (Table 2.1)?
    A 2.94×10^5
    B 2.99×10^5
    C 3.03×10^3
    D 9.99×10^2

3   Using the information in paragraph 8, in order to produce 10^7 Carbon-14 atoms, how many cosmic ray neutrons would be needed?
    A   70
    B   100,000
    C   1,000,000
    D   10,000,000

4   Using the information in paragraph 10, if Carbon-14 content was 5.5g, how much would remain after 16,704 years?
    A   0.055g
    B   0.69g
    C   1.38g
    D   2.75g

5   Using Figure 2.4, if a sample has an activity ratio of 0.5, its estimated age is
    A   younger than Hemaka.
    B   older than Zoser, younger than Hemaka.
    C   older than Hemaka.
    D   younger than Zoser and Sneferu.

6 Using Figure 2.4, if A = 0.7 and Ao = 1.15, then the age of the item would be
1   the same as the Boat
2   younger than the Zoser
3   younger than the Taymat
4   younger than the Hemaka

Answer
A   if 1 alone is correct.
B   if 1 and 3 only are correct.
C   1, 2 and 4 only are correct.
D   1, 3 and 4 only are correct.

7 During which time period was the Redwood living (Figure 2.4)?
A   2800–2000 BCE
B   2400–2300 BCE
C   1000–500 BCE
D   400–300 BCE

8 Tree rings from living specimens can be counted by boring into the tree and removing a narrow cylinder of wood. If the trunk is very thick it may not be possible to reach to the centre. Which of the following methods might best be used to estimate the age of the tree?
A   Match the ring pattern with those of younger trees.
B   Cut the tree down and count all the rings.
C   Work out average ring width and extrapolate from trunk radius.
D   Use Carbon-14 dating of the tree bark.

9 To establish the age of Seahenge, both tree-ring dating and Carbon-14 dating were used. Why were two methods needed?
A   to ensure that there was no contamination
B   in case one was wrong
C   because Carbon-14 is more accurate
D   because neither can give an accurate answer alone

10 A stalagmite recently found in a cave in Bermuda indicates that more than 20,000 years ago there were dramatic shifts in Carbon-14 concentration, which may mean that early dates are up to 5000 years out. This information means that dates earlier than 18,000 BCE
A   are all incorrect.
B   are probably inaccurate.
C   should be ignored.
D   are sufficiently correct to use.

EXAMINER'S ADVICE
- If necessary remind yourself of the points made at the end of the last unit about how to tackle questions like these.
- The answers are given on page 271.

3

Religion and science

As a working generalisation, it could be argued that science asks the question, 'Given that there is a world, *how* do things within it work?' Religion tends to ask the question, '*Why* is there anything at all?'

The nature of science

The modern age has often been described by historians and other thinkers as 'the age of science'. The value of science is that it provides us with accurate information about the world, which has been established by the most reliable methods available. Scientists produce an *hypothesis* – a starting point for future experiments and systematic observations that either confirm or refute the original assumption and then enable the observer to formulate a theory. This theory will be based on *repeatability* – the fact that the experiment has been repeated endlessly and has produced the same result given identical conditions – and *predictability* – the extremely high probability that the same result will occur in the future.

Science is useful because it helps us to explain and formulate rules about the way the physical world works and to control, adapt and survive in it, for example by:

- Producing a theory to explain tides in sea and rivers.
- Designing a steel bridge that will successfully cope with any future loads.
- Discovering that cyanide is poisonous to human beings.

The nature of religion

'Religion' can be defined as 'a particular system of faith and worship, usually involving recognition of a superhuman controlling power, such as a personal god or gods entitled to obedience and worship'. Unlike science, which is based on the *empirical* view that real knowledge comes to us by experience (i.e. via the senses), religion tends to claim that its knowledge comes from three sources:

- *Natural theology.* This is the view (particularly strong in the Roman Catholic tradition) that by the use of human reason, you can argue from evidence within the world to the existence of God. An example is the design argument, which was very popular during the eighteenth and nineteenth centuries. The complexities of a human eye or a butterfly's wing suggest a designer in the same way that the complexities of the world as a whole suggest a divine designer, rather than randomness.

- *Revealed theology.* God has revealed knowledge about himself to human beings through special writings such as the Bible or the Qur'an, through special creeds passed on by the Church or other religious institutions, and through special people such as Jesus of Nazareth or the Prophet Muhammad.
- *Personal or mystical experience.* Human beings can have intensely personal experiences of the divine, which may drastically change their lives and their understanding of the world.

The relationship between science and religion

Generally speaking, in the medieval period in the Western world, it was assumed that all knowledge would lead to God, who had created the world and whose mighty acts were described in the Bible. Knowledge was based on reason, authority and tradition:

- *Reason.* In general, this meant things which could be worked out by argument and logic, although Thomas Aquinas, the thirteenth-century theologian, also included evidence from the real world.
- *Authority.* This meant the Church's spiritual authority headed by the Pope.
- *Tradition.* This meant what had always been believed and taught by the Church and what was contained in ancient writings, for example, Aristotle's view of the universe, which was accepted by the Church.

Development of science and the modern outlook

In the Middle Ages, no philosophers or theologians would have imagined that the conclusions of faith and reason could diverge. What you could find out for yourself – *reason* – and what you believed – *faith* – both came to the same conclusion. In addition, there was what God might reveal to you, which was to be accepted even if you did not understand it. However, after the cultural developments of the *Renaissance,* which started in the fifteenth century, the growth of scientific method transformed what we know and our views about how we acquire knowledge. There was a fundamental shift from a God-centred world towards a human-centered one. Humans became the measure of all things. Eventually, this led to a divergence between scientific knowledge and the traditional teaching of the Church.

Period of transition

The seventeenth, eighteenth and early nineteenth centuries could be described as a transitional period. Most early scientists never doubted that their scientific examination of the world would reveal evidence of design, law and order, which would reinforce their belief in God as creator. Many sixteenth and seventeenth century thinkers, such as *Galileo, Descartes* and *Isaac Newton,* combined their belief in scientific method with more traditional beliefs. When Newton could not account mathematically for the irregular orbits of some of the planets, for example, he attributed their paths to the work of God.

Examples of conflict between science and religion

The trial of Galileo

Galileo has been described as the first scientist in the modern sense. In 1610, after his own observations using a telescope, Galileo published *The Message of the Stars*, in which he argued that the Earth went round the Sun, rather than the other way round. This view was condemned by the Church on the grounds that it contradicted the 'revealed truth' of scripture and the official Church view, based on Aristotle. But in 1632, Galileo supported the earlier astronomer, Copernicus, who had also argued that the Sun was the centre of the universe round which the planets revolved. Galileo was put on trial in 1633 and forced to withdraw his views by the Pope because he supported Copernicus's theory as a scientific fact, not just as a hypothesis. Galileo challenged the authority of established religion because:

- He based knowledge on the evidence of his senses – a modern empirical view.
- He claimed that the universe can be explained in terms of mathematical principles and in terms of cause and effect (Galileo himself thought that God could be seen both in the 'book of nature' and in the 'book of scripture' – they were complementary, rather than in conflict).

Charles Darwin and evolution

In 1859, based on his long research, including five years spent on *HMS Beagle* as a naturalist, Darwin published *On the Origin of Species*, in which he put forward several radical theories:

- Different species have evolved from one common ancestry.
- *Natural selection.* Natural genetic mutation produces some characteristics that help some individuals to survive better than others and they pass on these favourable characteristics to future generations over a very long period of time. Less favourable characteristics cause some species to die out.
- Human beings have evolved from earlier species, such as apes.

Darwin's theory, despite its imperfections, makes a fundamental contribution to the scientific view of the world. But it was furiously opposed at the time by many traditional religious believers, supported by others and criticised by some contemporary scientists. Darwin challenged the traditional views that:

- The world was created in 4004 BCE.
- Each species had been created separately by God and was distinct.

- Human beings were specially created by God and were different from other animals.
- The Genesis creation myths were a true historical account of how the world started.

Is it possible to believe in science and religion in the twenty-first century?

Some modern thinkers have suggested that the contrast between scientific thinking and religious thinking is not as great as has been claimed, and, indeed, that science still leads to God.

It is not true that everything is certain in science. In physics, light is sometimes described as waves, sometimes as particles. At one stage, the Newtonian view of fixed space and time was regarded as scientific fact, but now Einstein's theory of relativity, which argues that space and time can be affected by gravity, holds sway. In quantum physics, the behaviour of sub-atomic particles can only be predicted with probability, rather than certainty. At this level, scientists need the same powers of imagination, creativity and the ability to trust their judgement, which characterises religious belief.

The philosopher, Ludwig Wittgenstein, argued that we need to understand the context in which language is used in order to discover its meaning. Scientific language and religious language serve different purposes, and both are equally valid in their own situation. Religion asks questions such as, 'Who am I?' or 'What is the meaning of life?' Like general scientific theories (such as relativity), these questions are looking for truths that affect our lives, and they can be discussed rationally, but they produce answers that cannot be observed by the senses. This implies that science and religion are ways of looking at life that should be seen as complementary to each other, rather than in conflict.

Some scientists argue that the evidence for the Big Bang and evolution is also evidence for the existence of God. The fact that if the Big Bang had been a microsecond earlier the universe would have imploded and a micro-second later it would have exploded so fast that everything would have disappeared, implies that God determined the moment of the Big Bang. Some scientists also argue for the anthropic principle (that at the moment of the Big Bang, the nature of matter, the size of the bang and the laws of science made it inevitable that humans would be created) as evidence of God using science to create humans. Other scientists claim that the scientific coincidences necessary for life on Earth (stars being made out of hydrogen and helium to produce carbon and supernovae being needed to spread the carbon to planets like Earth) are so great that it could not have happened by chance, and so God must have caused it.

Some religious philosophers argue that the way we live our lives (and especially the way in which scientists conduct science) is based on the principle that everything has an explanation. The search for explanations has worked well in science and if everything in the universe has an explanation, it seems reasonable to accept that the universe itself must have an explanation. The only being who could explain the universe would be God, therefore it is reasonable to believe that God exists.

Extraterrestrial life

Given the size of the universe (there are at least 100 billion stars in our home galaxy alone and perhaps 100 billion galaxies of much the same size scattered throughout deep space) few scientists believe that the Earth is the only home of life. But, until quite recently, the field of exobiology – the study of extraterrestrial life also known as astrobiology – was almost defunct. It could come up with some interesting speculations but that was about all.

The robot planetary explorers that swept through the solar system in the 1960s and 1970s found no trace of life, or even potential life-supporting environments. Exobiology's most adventurous experiment – when the 1976 Mars Viking Lander tried to find biological activity in the soil of Mars – yielded discouraging results. The Mars disappointment was a low point for the hopeful new science. With the exception of the Earth, the solar system appeared to be barren. As for life beyond the solar system, the colossal distances involved made it simply unreachable, and in any case, no one knew for sure if other stars had planets at all, far less living planets.

Since those bleak days, exobiology's prospects have brightened enormously. A whole succession of discoveries has vastly increased the probabilities that life exists elsewhere in the solar system – as well as our chances of actually finding it.

Some of these discoveries have come from recent space probes and careful astronomical observation. For example, in the last few years, scientists have found evidence for planets around more than 60 nearby stars. The Galileo spacecraft has found what is almost certainly a liquid salty ocean beneath the surface of Jupiter's moon Europa. Mars most likely once had liquid water flowing on its surface. Scientists now believe that much of it is still there, locked beneath the surface.

The most vital discoveries of exobiology, though, were made right here on Earth. Biologists have learned that life is much more robust that most scientists believed 30 years ago. Earth micro-organisms have been found thriving in astonishingly hostile environments. Deep beneath the oceans, for example, near the volcanic vents known as black smokers, some microbes grow and multiply at temperatures above 110 degrees, and according to some scientists, perhaps as high as 170 degrees. Others thrive in acid conditions that would strip the skin from a human, while others still make a comfortable living in hot rocks kilometres below the ground. Some even prefer cold to heat: Antarctic life-forms can manage very well in what amounts to a permanent deep-freeze.

The existence of these so-called extremophile organisms radically changed our view of what might be called 'the necessities of life'. Extremophiles live happily without sunshine, without moderate warmth, without organic molecules to feed off and with no need for photosynthesis – many digest raw minerals and fuel themselves with basic chemical reactions.

Many share another fascinating characteristic, too. The genetic code of these creatures suggests that they are not recent adaptations that have moved away from 'mainstream life' into awkward niches shunned by their competitors. Instead, in evolutionary terms they are among the oldest living things on Earth, probably among the very first to appear.

The implications for life elsewhere in the solar system are huge. We know now that all life needs is liquid water – even a little dampness will serve – and some kind of energy source. Exobiology is back in business.

Mars remains the best candidate for the breakthrough discovery of an extraterrestrial organism. In the early solar system four billion years ago, it may well have offered better prospects for life than the Earth. In 1998, NASA scientists found what may have been fossilised ancient Martian bacteria in a meteorite blasted from the planet's surface by a cosmic impact. The Mars rock drifted through space for millions of years before eventually crashing down in Antarctica.

Exobiology will be a major element in the Mars missions of the first half of the twenty-first century. ESA's Mars Express arrived in Martian orbit in December 2003. The Aurora Programme is looking at plans for a sample return mission and even a human visit. Some of Earth's Antarctic life-forms could probably live on Mars today. Perhaps below the Martian surface, the corresponding native organisms are just waiting to be discovered.

KEY TERMS

Creationism the view that the 'Genesis' creation accounts are compatible with scientific evidence and are as equally valid as the theory of evolution

Fundamentalism the view that the Bible is entirely true and divinely inspired

General relativity the theory of Albert Einstein that time, space, mass and energy are related to one another so that space and time are affected by gravity

Natural theology the view that human beings can find evidence in the physical world to establish the existence of God

Quantum physics the study of the way in which sub-atomic particles behave

Figure 3.1 'Two things never fail to fill me with awe, the starry heavens above the Earth and the moral world within' (Immanuel Kant)

Europa, ten times more distant than Mars, is a more difficult proposition. But plans for Europa missions are on the drawing board, too. Exobiologists no longer restrict themselves to planetary environments. Comets, for example, are rich in organic material and certainly could be colonised by some kind of extremophile. Some theorists even think that life originated first in a cometary environment then reached Earth and, perhaps, other planets.

Religious implications

If extra-terrestrial life forms are found, this will be a challenge for traditional religions. The religions such a Judaism, Christianity and Islam will have to reconcile their traditional views that God made human beings in his own image so that we occupy a unique place in creation with the evidence that there may be untold millions of life-forms out there. Also, as space travel probes further into the cosmos it may well find more and more irrefutable evidence for the Big Bang theory. This will conflict directly with the creationist view that God created the universe in seven days.

EXAM QUESTION

This is an A2 Unit 4 essay question from the equivalent test set in January 2003. The themes draw on the discussion in the first three units of this section of the book.

Explain why there is conflict between Creationism and Darwin's Theory of Evolution.

A similar conflict between science and the establishment view was Galileo's defence of a heliocentric universe. Explain how the scientific method has encouraged acceptance of Darwin's and Galileo's accounts.

(25 marks)

EXAMINER'S ADVICE

- First of all check out the contents of the Unit 4 test on page 1 and also how A2 General Studies essays are marked on page 270. The same general mark scheme applies to all the essays you have to write in A2 Units 3 and 4.
- You should allow 40–45 minutes to plan and write your A2 essays and in Unit 4 you must show that you know some relevant science, as well as dealing with the more general issues in the question. Expect to write three to four pages for a good answer. In the exam proper you will have four different essay titles, from which you have to choose just one. In General Studies you cannot prepare for every topic, but you should revise a sensible range based on your knowledge and interests.
- Use the contents of the first three units of this book to prepare an answer to this question. First of all, make sure you know what followers of Creationism believe and what Darwin's theory proposes. This knowledge should constitute your answer to the first of the two questions, as it is self-evident from the details of each why they are in conflict.
- The second of the two questions asks for a judgement about why scientific method makes Galileo's defence of Copernicus and Darwin's theory more accepted. This requires an explanation of how scientific method was applied in these two areas and the principles and values that science sets out to represent.
- Compare your answer with the notes provided on page 271.

4 Energy

Energy is the capacity to do work. There are many forms of energy, such as *potential* (such as the string of a taut bow, which has the potential energy to fire an arrow); *kinetic* (the energy associated with movement, such as the movement of pistons in a car engine, which have the potential energy to move the car); *chemical* (the energy stored in food or fossil fuels); *gravitational* (the potential energy created when an object is raised above the Earth), etc.

In physics, *the law of conservation of energy* states that energy can neither be created nor lost, it can only be transferred or converted into another form. This can be seen in the process of creating electricity (see Figure 4.1). Another example of the conservation of energy is throwing a ball. When you throw a ball into the air, it rises according to the energy you have put into it. All the way up its trajectory, it is gaining gravitational potential energy. When all of your energy has been converted into gravitational potential energy, the ball begins to come down.

As far as humans are concerned, the conversion of energy into usable mechanical forms has been of huge importance. All animals convert the chemical energy of food

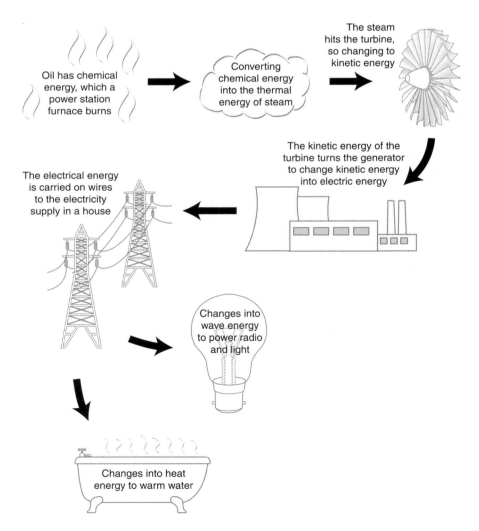

Figure 4.1 The creation of electricity: the law of conservation

into the kinetic energy of their bodies, but humans are the only animals who have managed to convert other forms of energy for their own uses, so being able to adapt their environment, rather than having to adapt themselves to their environment (for example, converting the heat energy of wood into the thermal energy of a fire enabled humans to live in cold climates).

Human energy conversion (the harnessing of energy)

As already stated, the first human conversion of energy was transforming wood and animal waste into fires so that the energy could be used for heating and cooking. By 5000 BCE, wood was changed into charcoal, whose greater heat was used for smelting metals. At first this process created bronze (a mixture of copper and tin, both of which occur naturally). Later, in about 1500 BCE, iron was produced from iron ore. This use of the energy of wood to make metals allowed humans to make tools and other implements necessary to produce other means of transforming energy. The first central heating systems were made by the Romans in about 100 BCE.

The first transfer of other energy into kinetic energy occurred in water mills, which first appeared in about 100 BCE as a means of grinding grain and olives. The Domesday Book of 1086 records a tidal mill operating at Dover (i.e. a water mill powered by the tides, rather than by a stream of water). Windmills first appeared in Iran in the seventh century. However, the great harnessing of energy did not come until the eighteenth and nineteenth centuries.

The inventions of Savery, Newcomen and Watt (see Unit 10, 'Transport issues') allowed the chemical energy of coal to change water into steam to produce the kinetic energy of a steam engine. This energy was used to drive machines (which allowed the creation of better metals, such as steel) and to revolutionise transport through the railways. In 1860, Lenoir of Belgium invented an internal combustion engine, which transformed coal into gas to move pistons. This discovery allowed Daimler to build the first petrol engine in 1883 for his motor car.

It was Faraday's discoveries in electricity, however, which led to the great changes of the twentieth century. Faraday invented an electric motor in 1821 and a transformer in 1831, from which all the inventions using electricity have been developed. So much of modern life depends on electricity that the major energy question of the twenty-first century is, 'What is the best way of transforming energy into electric energy?'

Methods of transforming energy into electricity

Non-renewable methods
Fossil fuels such as coal and oil have chemical energy, which can be transformed into kinetic energy to drive turbines, which make electricity.

Good points
- Very cheap to build, fairly cheap to run and very efficient.
- Easy to build near to centres of population.

Bad points
- Fossil fuels cannot be renewed, so they will run out.
- Cause lots of pollution (especially acid rain and the greenhouse effect).

Nuclear fission bombards uranium with neutrons releasing nuclear energy to transform water into steam to drive turbines (pressurised water reactor) or uses plutonium to create more atoms from the uranium which then heats sodium to produce steam to drive the turbines (fast breeder reactor).

Good points
- Fairly cheap to build, very cheap to run.
- No pollution.
- Very efficient.

Bad points
- Produces radioactive waste which has to be stored for thousands of years.
- Danger of leaks with huge health risks.
- Fuel can be used for nuclear weapons.

Natural gas (a fossil fuel produced in the same way as oil) is now used to fuel power stations.

Good points
- Cheap to build and run.
- Much less pollution than oil and coal.
- Very efficient.

Bad points
- A fossil fuel so it will run out.
- Transport dangers as the gas is highly explosive.

Semi-renewable methods

Geo-thermal energy uses the Earth's heat to create steam to drive turbines (some housing schemes use geo-thermal energy to provide hotwater).

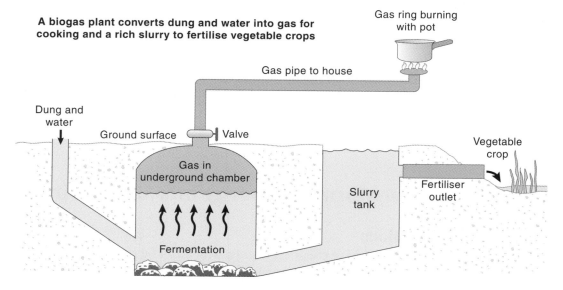

A biogas plant converts dung and water into gas for cooking and a rich slurry to fertilise vegetable crops

Figure 4.2 A biogas plant

Good points
- Fairly cheap to build, very cheap to run.
- No pollution.
- Very efficient.
- The heat will not run out for a long time.

Bad points
- Only creates small amounts of electricity.
- Production depends on special geological features so there are restrictions on where they can be built.

Energy from waste uses refuse which would be incinerated or put into landfill to power turbines to produce electricity.

Good points
- Cheap to build, very cheap to run.
- It gets rid of waste more effectively.
- Very efficient.

Bad points
- Produces carbon emissions, but not as much as coal and gas, and incineration produces it anyway.
- The more recycling there is, the less fuel will be available.

Biomass either uses the energy from chicken waste to turn water into steam to drive turbines or uses an anaerobic digester to produce methane gas from sewage or farm waste which can then drive a turbine.

Good points
- Cheap to build, very cheap to run.
- Gets rid of waste efficiently.
- Very efficient.
- The sewage and farm waste is virtually renewable.

Bad points
- Produces carbon emissions from the methane gases, but many of these would be produced any way from the decaying waste.

Fuel cells are like batteries which never run down. They produce electricity chemically when oxygen from the air and another fuel such as hydrogen are passed over the cells.

Good points
- Fairly cheap to build, very cheap to run.
- Little pollution.
- The oxygen is renewable.

Bad points
- Do not produce large amounts of power.
- Hydrogen needs other power to produce it and so is not renewable. The hydrogen used is often from oil refining which causes pollution.

Renewable methods
The most efficient renewable method is *hydroelectric power* (HEP), which converts the energy of flowing water into mechanical energy to drive turbines.

KEY TERMS

Atom the smallest part of a substance that can exist and still have the properties of a substance

Compound a substance whose molecules contain the atoms of at least two elements chemically bonded

Critical mass the minimum mass a substance needs to begin a chain reaction

Electrostatics like charges repel, unlike attract, e.g. a negatively charged rod and a positively charged rod will attract

Element a substance that cannot be split into simpler substances

Filament lamp a coil of tungsten wire in a glass bulb containing argon gas at low pressure – when an electric current goes through the wire it heats rapidly and gives out light

Fuel conservation a way of preserving non-renewable resources by making machines which use fuel more efficiently and so use less fuel, e.g. insulating houses

Galvanometer any device used to detect the presence of an electric current

Hypocaust Roman central heating system

Kinetic theory explains the behaviour of molecules, i.e. molecules that are closest together (solids) have the least energy, and those furthest apart (gases) have the most energy

Molecule the smallest particle of a substance (it can be one or many thousands of atoms, but each will have the atoms in the same arrangement)

Nuclear fission producing energy by splitting atoms

Nuclear fusion producing energy by giving nuclei sufficient energy for them to join together – it requires very high temperatures and, at the moment, can only be done in hydrogen bombs

Steel iron mixed with a small amount of carbon

Ultrasound sound made of ultrasonic waves above the sound of human hearing (20,000 hertz)

Activities

1. Investigate how much of your daily life is dependent on electricity.

2. Think of an example other than the power station to illustrate the law of conservation of energy.

3. If you could begin electricity generation from scratch, which methods of generating electricity would you choose, and why?

4. Explain, with illustrations, why energy can only be converted, not created.

Good points
- Very cheap to run.
- Very efficient.
- Causes no pollution.
- Fuel will never run out.

Bad points
- Very expensive to build.
- Can only be built in certain areas, well away from cities.
- Long lines of pylons are required to transport the energy to civilisation.
- Huge areas of land have to be swamped in order to fuel the plant.

Wind generators are now widely used to transform wave energy of wind into electricity. Hawaii now has a wind station producing 1500 megawatts, equivalent to a fossil fuel power station.

Good points
- Fairly cheap to build.
- Very cheap to run.
- Cause no pollution.
- Energy source will never run out.

Bad points
- Not very efficient – each set of blades only produces a small amount of electricity.
- Have to be built in wide open spaces and are a very prominent feature in the landscape.

Solar energy can be directly transformed into electricity using silicon or gallium arsenide cells. Other methods involve storing the heat and using it not only to produce electricity, but also to power heating systems, etc.

Good points
- Very cheap to run.
- Causes no pollution.
- Energy source will never run out.

Bad points
- Expensive to build.
- Need to cover a large area to produce a reasonable amount of power.
- More suitable for hot, sunny countries.

The *energy of the sea* can be converted into electricity through either tide or wave power stations. The Rance river estuary in France has a *tidal power station*, which drives turbines by damming the tide. In Japan there is an oscillating water column, which converts the *energy of the waves* to create an air turbine that drives a generator.

Good points
- Very cheap to run.
- Causes no pollution.
- Energy source will never run out.

Bad points
- Very, very expensive to build.
- Not very efficient yet.
- Can only be built in certain areas.

For the examination questions for this unit, go to the end of Unit 5.

Environmental issues

Environmental issues refer to the concerns raised by the way in which human beings have treated their surroundings and the long-term and possibly irreversible effects of such treatment. Most of these concerns are to do with two main interrelated areas:

- How we treat the natural world and its resources, for example, the use of fossil fuels, deforestation, acid rain and global warming.
- How we treat the animal world, for example, conservation, extinction and animal cruelty.

Modern ecologists have identified four important areas that are crucial to our understanding of the environment:

- *The ecosystem.* This refers to the way in which forms of life interact with each other, such as in food chains, which link different species and interlocking elements and chemical compounds (see Figure 5.1). This interconnection must be regarded as a system where a change in the delicate balance at one point can have

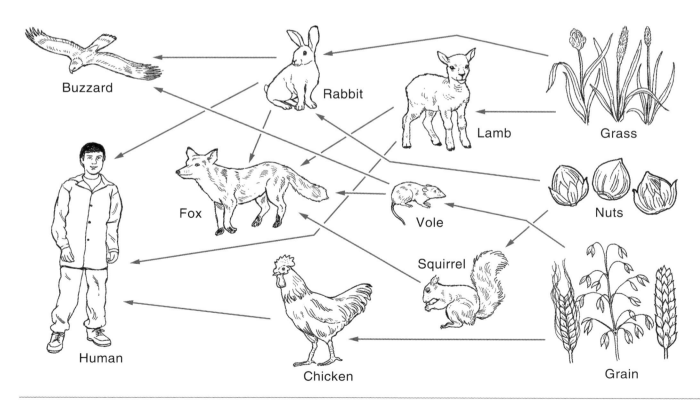

Figure 5.1 A food chain

far reaching effects in other parts of the system. For example, introducing rabbits to Australia, where there are no natural predators, led to them overrunning the continent and possibly led to the extinction of some native animals.

- *Growth.* The environment has a limited capacity. Modern scientists have recognised that there cannot be unlimited growth. Just as the animal population in its natural environment is limited by the availability of food, territory, mates and inter-species competition, so human beings must recognise that population, food consumption and pollution cannot increase indefinitely.
- *Ecological stability.* In the natural world, stability is maintained by a constant process of change and adjustment to continually changing conditions. Nature is never static. However, species with very small numbers of plants or animals are at much greater risk of extinction from disease, predators or changes in their food supply than species with large numbers.
- *The future.* Ecologists are concerned about the long-term effects of human intervention in nature. The natural environment needs continuity in order to flourish, so we need to consider what effect an activity carried out for short-term gain, such as chopping down trees for timber without an adequate system of replanting, may have on future generations. In relation to the age of the world as a whole, human beings have only been around for a few seconds, but the irreversible damage inflicted on the environment during that time has been immense.

Biological diversity

Diversity refers to the fact that the natural world contains at least 1.5 million different species. However, this figure only includes those that have been discovered so far. It is estimated that there may be between 5 million and 40 million more, including 500,000 plants and untold numbers of insect species. This diversity is essential for our own survival and that of the ecosystem as a whole for the following reasons:

- The more species there are, each with its own physical characteristics, the more chance there is of resistance to natural disasters.
- Half of all our medical cures, such as morphine and quinine, come from plants. Loss of species means a loss of important natural curative substances.
- Food and natural materials used as a basis for manufacturing are based on a wide range of natural species. Extinction means a loss of important food sources.
- The complex relationships within the whole ecosystem means that the loss of one plant, for example, can mean the possible extinction of a considerable number of other animals and insects.

Attitudes to the environment

Traditionally, Christianity has based its attitudes to the environment on the Creation myths in Genesis, Chapters 1–2. This suggests that the Earth was created by God for a purpose and that human beings, because they are superior to animals, have a responsibility or 'stewardship' over nature. However, this attitude was later modified by the idea that it is an individual's duty to work hard and make profits. The idea that nature is there to serve human need has led to its exploitation. This was further reinforced by the ideas of mathematicians and philosophers such as Sir Isaac Newton and René Descartes. Newton's mathematical laws explaining the way in which the physical world operated, led to a *mechanistic* view of nature as consisting of impersonal masses and forces operating according to deterministic laws. Descartes argued that animals are machines without minds or feelings. Also, the Industrial Revolution encouraged the view that the natural environment was merely an inexhaustible source of raw materials. The development of capitalism also led to the view that the need for private profit justified the damage to the environment caused by industrial technology. However, Charles Darwin's work on *evolution* emphasised:

- The way in which all natural living things, including human beings, are related to each other.
- The fact that nature is not static but constantly changing to survive.

Important environmental issues

Population
The population of the world is now six billion. It is estimated that it will grow by one billion every 11 years. This population explosion has mainly taken place in underdeveloped countries and continents and it has raised the following interrelated problems for the environment.

- *Pressure on land.* As more and more people try to live off the land, it becomes exhausted. Land that is overfarmed becomes desert. Two thousand years ago, large areas of North Africa supplied the Roman Empire with wheat. Much of this once fertile land is now desert, particularly in the Sahel region of West Africa. Poverty prevents the use of more 'eco-friendly' farming methods, such as the use of fertilisers, which might help to replenish the soil.
- *Deforestation.* This problem has various causes, of which population is one. During the past 30 years, huge areas of rain forest in South America and elsewhere in the world have been chopped down. This has taken place for a variety of reasons, including the need for firewood as a fuel by poor people, for timber, for paper making, to clear the land for agriculture and to get at valuable mineral deposits. This deforestation has led to desertification through the loss of topsoil, the loss of habitat for a large number of species, resulting in their actual or near extinction, and the loss of oxygen produced by jungle vegetation, which has contributed to global warming.
- *Urbanisation.* By 2030, it is estimated that 60 per cent of the world's population will live in urban areas. In poor areas, this leads to a drastic decline in local wildlife

and cultivable land and a large increase in environmental damage caused by sewage, industrial waste, transport systems and other forms of pollution.

Acid rain

This important example of pollution is mainly caused by the chemicals released by smoke from fossil-fuelled power stations, such as sulphuric and nitric acid, which change rainwater from pH5/6 to pH3, making it more acidic. In Sweden, which receives most of Britain's acid rain, some lakes and forests have been completely destroyed by the fall-out.

Ozone layer

The ozoneosphere is a region in the upper atmosphere, between 10 km and 50 km altitude, where there is much more ozone (O_3) than at lower levels. The presence of the ozone layer blocks all solar radiation of wavelengths less than 290 namometres from reaching the Earth's surface. If this did not happen, most living things would die. Ozone is formed by the reaction of short-wave ultraviolet radiation from the Sun on oxygen, but it is also destroyed by chlorofluorocarbons (CFC gases in aerosols) and nitrogen oxides (found in car and plane exhaust gases). The ozone layer is gradually being depleted, leading to an increase in the incidence of skin cancer in fair-skinned people. CFC gases have been banned by developed countries, but it is expensive for developing countries to stop using them.

Animal issues

Humans relate to animals in the following ways:

- as companions and working partners (for example, guidedogs and sheepdogs)
- as zoo animals for observation, research, conservation and enjoyment
- as food – worldwide, people eat about 140,000,000 tons of meat every year
- for medical or product research – over 200 million animals are used annually
- for hunting – animals are hunted for food, fashion, fun or for profit.

Recently, animal rights has become a widely discussed issue. It is no longer generally accepted that animals can be killed indiscriminately for pleasure or for profit. Poaching elephants for ivory or rhinoceroses and tigers for their horns and bones is now illegal in most countries. Causing animals pain for either medical or cosmetic purposes is now regarded by many as an infringement of basic animal rights. Many methods of animal rearing for food are now regarded as cruel (for example, factory farming and battery hens).

Global warming

The Arctic is warming rapidly, with the loss of polar ice projected to accelerate global warming as well as contributing to the sea level rising and flooding, according to a comprehensive four-year scientific study of the region conducted by an international team of 300 scientists that was released in 2004.

According to the scientists' most conservative estimates, about half of the summer sea ice in the Arctic is projected to melt along with a significant portion of the

Greenland Ice Sheet, as the region warms an additional 7°F–13°F by 2100. Rising sea levels are already observed and are predicted to accelerate as warming continues, according to the final report of the Arctic Climate Impact Assessment (ACIA).

The study confirms that the warming is human-caused, through heat-trapping emissions from the burning of fossil fuels. The United States is the largest world contributor of those emissions, yet has failed to enact limits.

The report comes out at a time of increasing pressure on the Bush administration to enact US emissions reductions. In November 2004, the Queen privately pressured Tony Blair to press the US on global warming policy, and she opened a 'climate change summit' of senior government officials from the UK and Germany to discuss the problem. Russian president Vladimir Putin signed the Kyoto Protocol, thus bringing the accord into effect worldwide.

'President Bush needs to change his approach to global warming in light of the damage already being seen in the Arctic,' said Dr Daniel Lashof, Science Director of the NRDC Climate Center. 'It is now clear we have to cut the pollution that causes global warming to prevent dangerous changes in the climate. The purely voluntary approach taken in the President's first term will leave the nation and the world in great danger from the threat of global warming.'

The assessment was commissioned by the Arctic Council, a ministerial inter-governmental forum comprised of eight nations, including the United States, and six Indigenous Peoples organisations; and the International Arctic Science Committee, an international scientific organisation appointed by eighteen national academies of science.

'The impacts of global warming are apparent now in the Arctic,' said Robert Corell, chair of the ACIA. 'The Arctic is experiencing some of the most rapid and severe impacts on Earth. The impacts of global warming on the region and the globe are projected to increase substantially in the years to come.'

Additional findings include:

- In Alaska, western Canada, and eastern Russia, average winter temperatures have increased as much as 4°F–7°F in the past 50 years, and are projected to rise 7°F–14°F over the next 100 years.
- Polar sea ice during the summer is projected to decline by 50 per cent by the end of this century with some models showing near-complete disappearance of summer sea ice. This is very likely to have devastating consequences for polar bears, ice-living seals, and local people for whom these animals are a primary food source. At the same time, the reduced extent of sea ice is likely to increase marine access to some of the region's resources.
- Warming over Greenland will lead to substantial melting of the Greenland Ice Sheet, contributing to global sea-level rise at an increasing rate. Greenland's ice sheets contain enough water to eventually raise sea level by about 23 feet.
- In the United States, low-lying coastal states like Florida and Louisiana are particularly susceptible to rising sea levels.
- Should the Arctic Ocean become ice-free in summer, it is likely that polar bears and some seal species would be driven to extinction.

KEY TERMS

Air pollution the release of harmful chemicals into the atmosphere by industrial processes, traffic emissions and incinerators, etc.

Biodegradable a substance that can be converted to simpler compounds by bacteria (most plastics are not biodegradable)

CFCs chlorofluorocarbons are manmade gases used in aerosols, refrigeration and air-conditioning, which are responsible for the increasing hole in the ozone layer

Composition of pure air 78 per cent nitrogen, 21 per cent oxygen, 1 per cent noble gases, 0.03 per cent carbon dioxide

Eutrophication an overgrowth of aquatic plants caused by an excess of nitrates coming into rivers from fertilisers, which causes a depletion of oxygen, which kills fish

Population explosion the huge increase in the world's population, mainly occurring in developing countries

Radiation the lethal fall-out produced by the use of nuclear power and weapons, with the highest potential to do long-lasting damage

Thermal pollution releases of warm water from power stations and factories – has the same effect as eutrophication

Activities

1. Find out about the Chernobyl nuclear power station accident in 1986. Make a list of effects of the accident, then discuss the view that the advantages of nuclear power outweigh the dangers.

2. What sort of immediate and/or long-term international measures would you like to introduce in order to reduce some of the damage being done by industrialised countries to the environment?

3. What reasons do you think could be used to support the use of animal experiments that involve the infliction of pain and/or death to the animals involved?

4. Should environmental considerations be more important than profit?

- Arctic climate changes present serious challenges to the health and food security of some indigenous peoples, challenging the survival of some cultures.
- Over the next 100 years, global warming is expected to accelerate, contributing to major physical, ecological, social, and economic changes, and the assessment has documented that many of these changes have already begun.

The assessment's projections are based on a moderate estimate of future emissions of carbon dioxide and other greenhouse gases, and incorporate results from five major global climate models used by the Inter-governmental Panel on Climate Change.

Conclusion

There has been a general realisation that the natural world is not a limitless, endlessly renewable resource. Human beings must learn to manage the environment so that the right of other species to life is protected and the damage caused by human pollution and activities is drastically reduced. Most countries took part in the UN sponsored meetings which resulted in the Kyoto Protocol. This is a legally binding agreement to reduce greenhouse gas emissions worldwide. It came into force on 16 February 2005. The UN called a conference in Bali in December 2007 to update, and check compliance with, the Protocol. However, the world's largest polluter (the USA produces 25 per cent of global emissions) signed but did not ratify the Protocol, and the two next largest polluters (China and India) were not involved in the Protocol.

Figure 5.2 Melting ice caps in the Arctic

EXAM QUESTIONS

Consider the following passage and figures, and answer the multiple choice questions which follow.

Global warming – facts or fallacies?

(1) As recently as 1975, reputable academics were publishing books and articles containing dire predictions of an imminent new ice age. Fifteen years later, climatologists warned of the danger of imminent overheating, leading to global catastrophe within a century. Doom-laden predictions of sea levels rising by as much as eight metres were put forward. The scientific prophets even knew the cause – rising carbon dioxide levels from the burning of fossil fuels and destruction of the tropical rainforests.

(2) How can these two diametrically opposed views have arisen in such a short time? Certainly in the 1980s there was a series of particularly hot summers, along with an increase in understanding of the now well-known greenhouse effect.

(3) The presence of certain gases in the Earth's atmosphere causes the greenhouse effect. These gases are transparent to solar energy in the wavelengths of visible light, which passes through the atmosphere and heats the surface of the Earth. The warmed Earth's surface re-radiates the heat at longer wavelengths in the infra-red part of the electromagnetic spectrum. This energy is absorbed by the greenhouse gases, trapping the heat within the atmosphere. It is thought that the greenhouse effect raises the temperature of the Earth by about 33°C. Without it, the average temperature would be about −24°C and life on Earth would be almost non-existent.

(4) It is very difficult to determine whether the Earth's climate has warmed significantly. Weather records have been kept for up to 200 years, but only in a few places. Information from tree rings can take us back to the beginning of this millennium but the data is inconclusive. In the Middle Ages the weather was relatively warm for an extended period; grapes were grown for wine-making in the North of England. From the sixteenth–nineteenth century, the 'Little Ice Age' saw an advance in the Alpine glaciers and ice fairs could be held on the frozen river Thames and on the Dutch canals (Figure 5.3).

(5) If 1860 is taken as a starting point, then global average temperatures have risen (Figure 5.4). At the same time global carbon dioxide levels have also risen, from the burning of fossil fuels.

(6) To draw more significant conclusions it is necessary to look over a very much longer period. It is possible now to deduce information about the weather of the distant past by examination of cores of snow from the Arctic and Antarctic snowfields, which never melt. The snow contains dissolved gases, found in the atmosphere at the time it fell. The proportions of different isotopes of oxygen and hydrogen present in this snow are sensitive to temperature and so can indicate the temperature at the time at which the snow fell. The ice-core data shows that the present warm period (the Holocene era) has lasted for around 11,000 years. It was preceded by an ice age approximately 100,000 years long, and that, in its turn, was preceded by an interglacial

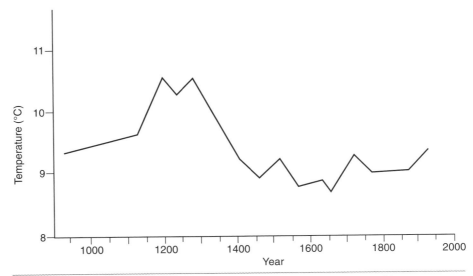

Figure 5.3 Average temperatures in Central England over the past 1000 years

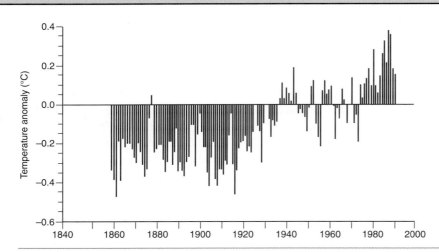

Figure 5.4 Changes in global average temperatures, 1860–1992, relative to the period 1951–80

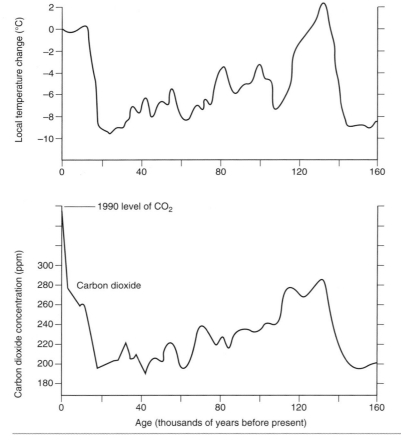

Figure 5.5 Temperature and carbon dioxide changes in Antartica over the past 160,000 years

period (the Eemian era) of around 20,000 years. Other data show that six or seven ice ages, with intervening inter-glacials, occurred during the preceding million years.

(7) Temperatures in the Eemian era reached a maximum 4°C higher than present temperatures and sudden warmings and coolings of up to 10°C occurred. Information from the ice cores show that levels of carbon dioxide in the atmosphere follow a similar pattern to those for temperature (Figure 5.5).

(8) The linkage between CO_2 levels and temperature found in the ice cores has led to carbon dioxide being suggested by some scientists as a dangerous greenhouse gas, causing 55% of global warming.

(9) Linkage, however, as any statistician will confirm, does not prove causation. The infra-red radiation leaving the Earth covers the range of wavelengths from 1–40 microns (1 micron = 1×10^{-6} m). Carbon dioxide absorbs infra-red waves very efficiently, but only at the wavelengths 4.3 and 15 microns. Another common gas, water vapour, absorbs IR over a much wider range of wavelengths than carbon dioxide does, and is present in much higher concentrations in the atmosphere than is CO_2. The percentage of water

vapour is, however, very variable (from 0–4 per cent). Because of this variability, tables of atmospheric gases usually show proportions found in dry air.

(10) When water vapour is brought into the calculations of global warming, it is found that it accounts for 97 per cent of the warming – for 32° of the 33°C – and carbon dioxide appears to contribute only about 1 per cent to the effect.

(11) The computer models of climate change used by the International Panel Climate Change (IPCC), have sought to forecast the effect of rising

carbon dioxide levels. They were based on the most accurate data available at the time that they were produced – the data from 1860–1988. The computer programs used were unable to make any allowance for cloud cover or for ocean currents, and water vapour was ignored. This has led to an over-estimation of the effect of the other greenhouse gases and particularly of carbon dioxide, which is the only one present in the atmosphere in readily measurable quantities.

(12) Despite the best efforts of scientists to find evidence of global warming by the use

of satellites which can accurately measure temperatures over the sea – and thus discount the urban heat island effect which causes false readings for much land-based temperature measurement – a study from 1979–1993 showed no increase in global temperatures during that period.

(13) The most recent pronouncements from the International Panel for Climate Change have suggested reduced future temperature rises and have agreed that the temperature change which has occurred in the last century is within

normal variation. It is possible that the theory that carbon dioxide is the major factor in global warming is the twentieth-century equivalent of the old notion that the Sun orbited the Earth.

[NB Since this passage and questions were set at the end of the 1990s, more progress has been made in measuring the causes and effects of climate change, which effectively challenge the conclusions drawn here. There is now a much greater consensus that global warming is taking place, although the problems of measuring and evaluating the implications remain just as valid.]

Source: NEAB A Level General Studies, Paper 1, Question 3, 1998

For the questions which follow, choose the answer A, B, C or D which you think fits best. Each of the questions is worth one mark.

1　Which one of the following centuries had the highest average temperature in Central England (Figure 5.3)?
   A　11th
   B　12th
   C　13th
   D　14th

2　Which one of the following temperatures represents the average temperature in Central England in 1150 AD (Figure 5.3)?
   A　9.2°C
   B　9.6°C
   C　10.1°C
   D　10.4°C

3　Assuming the trend shown since the beginning of this century continues, what is the predicted average temperature for Central England for the year 2000 (Figure 5.3)?
   A　8.5°C
   B　9.0°C
   C　9.5°C
   D　10.0°C

4　In how many years between 1960 and 1980 was there a lower global average temperature than the average for the period 1951–1980 (Figure 5.4)?
   A　2
   B　4
   C　6
   D　8

5 Approximately when were the first significant weather records kept in Britain (paragraph 4)?
 A at the beginning of the seventeenth century
 B at the end of the seventeenth century
 C at the beginning of the eighteenth century
 D at the end of the eighteenth century

6 Which one of the following observations led researchers to believe that there was a danger of the onset of a new ice age (Figure 5.4 and paragraph 1)?
 A There was a very cold winter in 1962–3.
 B Global temperatures were high from 1860–1970.
 C Global temperatures were low from 1940–75.
 D Average temperatures in Central England fell below 9°C in the 1970s.

7 Burning fossil fuels and the destruction of tropical rainforests increase the amount of carbon dioxide in the atmosphere because
 A only fossil fuels release carbon dioxide when burned.
 B the carbon dioxide is produced faster than it is used up in photosynthesis.
 C fossil fuels are inefficient heat producers.
 D fossil fuels release more carbon dioxide than other fuels for the amount of heat they produce.

8 For approximately how many past years can tree rings be used to provide climatic data (paragraph 4)?
 A 10^2
 B 10^3
 C 10^4
 D 10^6

9 Which one of the following describes 'an inter-glacial' (paragraph 6)?
 A a cold period during an ice age
 B a warm period between two ice ages
 C a period during which glaciers form
 D a period when there are no glaciers

10 Using Figure 5.5 and paragraph 6, which one of the following was the CO_2 concentration in p.p.m. at the beginning of the Eemian era?
 A 180–195
 B 210–220
 C 220–240
 D 260–285

11 Which one of the following describes the situation in Antarctica 130 000 years ago compared to the present (Figure 5.5)?
 A Temperatures were higher, but carbon dioxide levels were lower.
 B Temperatures and carbon dioxide levels were the same.
 C Temperatures were the same, but carbon dioxide levels were higher.
 D Temperatures were lower and carbon dioxide levels were lower.

12 Which of the following hypotheses might be suggested from the similarity of the shapes of the graphs for change in temperature and change in carbon dioxide levels in Antarctica (Figure 5.5)?
 1 Increases in atmospheric carbon dioxide cause temperatures to rise.
 2 Rising temperatures cause increased atmospheric carbon dioxide.
 3 An unknown factor causes both increased atmospheric carbon dioxide and a rise in temperature.
 4 Atmospheric carbon dioxide and temperature are unconnected.

Answer
 A if 4 alone is correct.
 B if 1 and 3 only are correct.
 C if 2 and 4 only are correct.
 D if 1, 2 and 3 only are correct.

13 Which one of the following properties of carbon dioxide is the principal reason it is regarded as a greenhouse gas?
 A It reflects ultra-violet radiation.
 B It absorbs infra-red radiation.
 C It reflects long-wave radiation.
 D It absorbs ultra-violet radiation.

14 Which one of the following reasons explains why scientists from the IPCC were unable to include levels of water vapour in the air in their computer simulations of the climate (paragraph 11)?
 A Levels of water vapour in the air cannot be measured.
 B There are too many readings of levels of water vapour in the air.
 C There are too few readings of levels of water vapour in the air.
 D The level of water vapour in the air is too variable.

15 Which one of the following most accurately describes the urban heat island effect (paragraph 12)?
A Towns and cities are usually warmer than the surrounding countryside.
B Urban islands are warmer than mainland towns and cities.
C Towns and cities are warmer than islands.
D Towns and cities have more smog than the countryside.

16 Which one of the following pairs of statements is implied by the final sentence of the passage (paragraph 13)?
A Carbon dioxide is the major Greenhouse Gas; the Sun orbits the Earth.
B Carbon dioxide is the major Greenhouse Gas; the moon orbits the Earth.
C Carbon dioxide is not the major Greenhouse Gas; the Sun orbits the Earth.
D Carbon dioxide is not the major Greenhouse Gas; the Earth orbits the Sun.

17 Which one of the following conclusions does the author of the passage wish the reader to reach?
A Scientists are always predicting disasters.
B Scientists invariably make mistakes.
C Scientists may change their opinions.
D Scientists are usually right.

18 Cloudy skies have two contrasting effects on the temperature of the air beneath them. Which one of the following statements describes the reason for the contrasting effects?
A Clouds reduce light energy entering and reduce infra-red energy leaving the air beneath them.
B Clouds reduce light energy entering and increase infra-red energy leaving the air beneath them.
C Clouds increase infra-red energy entering and increase light energy leaving the air beneath them.
D Clouds increase light energy entering and reduce infra-red energy leaving the air beneath them.

19 Figure 5.5 shows that, compared to the average for the 20th century, the temperature in Antarctica 20,000 years ago was
A 8.5°C higher.
B 9.5°C higher.
C 10.5°C lower.
D 9.5°C lower.

20 The conflicting theories described in paragraph 1 show that
A scientists ignore vital evidence.
B no scientists can be believed.
C contradictory conclusions can both be true.
D selective use of data can support differing conclusions.

EXAMINER'S ADVICE

- If you have not already done so, check out the general advice on tackling multiple choice questions on page 266 and for Unit 2 as a whole on page 1. The 20 questions here are representative of the 30 you will get in the exam and you should aim to complete them in, say, 40 minutes.
- In this set of questions, quite a few (e.g. Questions 1–4) require you to analyse and apply the data to produce some conclusions, Questions 12 and 14 to think about how sound and reliable scientific conclusions can be drawn, and Questions 17 and 20 are general questions about the nature of the scientific process itself.
- The answers are given on page 271.

6

Genetic engineering

Genetic engineering refers to the techniques and consequences associated with the technology of altering the information carried by genes. Genes are the basic building blocks of life and they contain all the information required to enable cells to replicate themselves. They have an increasingly important and controversial role to play in the scientific observation and plotting of diseases usually referred to as *genetic screening*.

Human genetic engineering

Various techniques have been developed to try to alter the genetic structure that gives rise to such diseases.

Somatic-cell therapy

This technique is based on the fact that, although, in theory, every cell in a human body carries all the information needed to grow that whole human body, it can block off the information not needed for its specialised function in a particular part of the body. This *somatic* or body cell can reproduce itself exactly and then divide. Somatic-cell change involves replacing faulty cells where the genes do not work properly with cells containing genes which do, although these new cells will themselves need renewal.

For example, with the disease of cystic fibrosis (CF), faulty CF genes, which failed to control the passage of salt and water in and out of the body's cells in the lungs, were replaced with normal ones successfully.

Germ-line therapy

Somatic-cell therapy cannot be passed on from one generation to another by sexual reproduction because the cells involved are not connected to the *gametes* or reproductive cells. In germ-line therapy, new DNA is introduced in order to *recombine* with DNA in the reproductive cells. This results in the possibility of changing the genetic profile of a child of parents who carry a genetically based disease. Once the new gene is recombined, it can be reproduced over many generations.

Cloning

A clone can be defined as 'an individual organism that was grown from a single body cell of its parent and that is genetically identical to it' (*Encyclopaedia Britannica*).

Gene cloning can be used for all sorts of purposes. *Plasmids* (small rings of DNA) are inserted into a bacterium to produce a specified protein, so that an endless supply of copies will then be created. Such cloning is being used to produce insulin and hepatitis B vaccine, among other proteins.

The first successful, but controversial, clone of an adult animal was carried out by a team of scientists at the Roselin Institute in Edinburgh. The nucleus of a cell from the mammary gland of an adult sheep was implanted into the embryo of another sheep's unfertilised egg, from which the nucleus had been removed. An electric current was passed through and the egg began to divide, so becoming an embryo, which was implanted into the uterus of another sheep. The lamb – Dolly – was a clone of the sheep whose mammary gland was used.

The Human Genome Project

Rapid technological advances pushed the completion date of the Human Genome Project to 2003, having started in 1900. Aims included:

- entire human genetic blueprint
- storage of databases
- discussion of legal, ethical and social issues.

What is a genome and why is it important?
A genome is the complete make-up of DNA in an organism, including its genes. Genes carry information for making all the proteins required by all organisms. The particular form which a genome takes up is based on a unique chemical base and determines its make-up as a plant, fish, mammal, etc.

Genomics
A genome map helps scientists navigate around the genome. Like road maps, a genome map is a set of landmarks that tells people where they are, and helps them get where they want to go. The landmarks on a genome map might include short DNA sequences, regulatory sites that turn genes on and off, and genes themselves. Often, genome maps are used to help scientists find new genes. Most everyday maps have length and width, latitude and longitude, like the world around us. But a genome map is one-dimensional – it is linear, like the DNA molecules that make up the genome itself.

What is the difference between a genome map and a genome sequence?
Both are portraits of a genome, but a genome map is less detailed than a genome sequence. A sequence spells out the order of every DNA base in the genome, while a map simply identifies a series of landmarks in the genome. Many animal 'genome projects' currently underway, such as those that focus on the dog and the horse, aim to map the genomes of these species. This will help scientists learn more about the biology of these species, without the enormous resources required when sequencing a genome. Genome maps help scientists find genes, particularly those involved in human disease.

Genes for cystic fibrosis, Huntington's disease and many other inherited diseases have been identified by this method. But it's a time-consuming, laborious process.

Several million base pairs are still a lot of DNA, and a region of the genome that size may contain dozens of genes for scientists to sort through.

In the future, researchers hope that more detailed genome maps will help them find genes faster, leading them straight to each gene the way you can look at a road map and determine the sequence of streets that will take you exactly where you want to go. A more detailed map would also help scientists study complex human diseases and traits that involve many genes – for example, cancer, heart disease, and personality.

In addition to helping in the search for genes, genome maps are useful in the day-to-day activities of molecular biology laboratories. In the lab, the human genome lives in the form of 'clones' – chunks of DNA that have been chopped up and spliced into the DNA of bacteria or other cells. This method keeps each chunk of the genome separate from the others and available in many copies for easy experiment and study.

Genome maps also help scientists find and learn about other important parts of the genome, such as the regulatory regions that help control when genes are turned on and off. Maps help scientists keep track of which colleagues are studying nearby or related parts of the genome, so they can learn from each other and don't duplicate each other's work. They illuminate the overall structure of the genome – places where several related genes are clustered together. Also, maps enable scientists to compare the genomes of different species, yielding insights into the process of evolution.

What is gene therapy?

Genes, which are carried on chromosomes, are the basic physical and functional units of heredity. Genes are specific sequences of bases that encode instructions on how to make proteins. Although genes get a lot of attention, it's the proteins that perform most life functions and even make up the majority of cellular structures. When genes are altered so that the encoded proteins are unable to carry out their normal functions, genetic disorders can result. Gene therapy is a technique for correcting defective genes responsible for disease development.

How does gene therapy work?

In most gene-therapy studies, a 'normal' gene is inserted into the genome to replace an 'abnormal', disease-causing gene. A carrier molecule (called a vector) must be used to deliver the therapeutic gene to the patient's target cells. Currently, the most common vector is a virus that has been genetically altered to carry normal human DNA. Viruses have evolved a way of delivering their genes to human cells. Scientists have tried to take advantage of this capability and manipulate the virus genome to remove disease-causing genes and insert therapeutic genes.

Target cells, such as the patient's liver or lung cells, are infected with the viral vector. The vector then unloads its genetic material containing the therapeutic human gene into the target cell. The generation of a functional protein product from the therapeutic gene restores the target cell to a normal state. See Figure 6.1 showing this process.

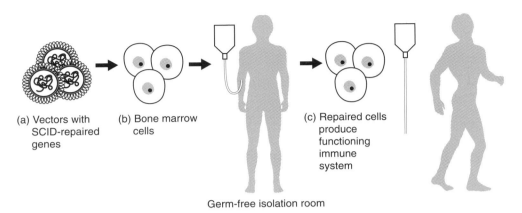

(a) Vectors with SCID-repaired genes

(b) Bone marrow cells

(c) Repaired cells produce functioning immune system

Germ-free isolation room

Figure 6.1 The process of gene therapy (Source: *FDA Consumer Magazine*, August 2000)

Some of the different types of viruses used as gene-therapy vectors are:

- Retroviruses – a class of viruses that can create double-stranded DNA copies of their RNA genomes. These copies can be integrated into the chromosomes of host cells. Human immunodeficiency virus (HIV) is a retrovirus.
- Adenoviruses – a class of viruses with double-stranded DNA genomes that cause respiratory, intestinal, and eye infections in humans. The virus that causes the common cold is an adenovirus.
- Adeno-associated viruses – a class of small, single-stranded DNA viruses that can insert their genetic material at a specific site on chromosome 19.
- Herpes simplex viruses – a class of double-stranded DNA viruses that infect a particular cell type, neurons. Herpes simplex virus type 1 is a common human pathogen that causes cold sores.

Besides virus-mediated gene-delivery systems, there are several non-viral options for gene delivery. The simplest method is the direct introduction of therapeutic DNA into target cells. This approach is limited in its application because it can be used only with certain tissues and requires large amounts of DNA.

Another non-viral approach involves the creation of an artificial lipid sphere with an aqueous core. This liposome, which carries the therapeutic DNA, is capable of passing the DNA through the target cell's membrane.

Therapeutic DNA also can get inside target cells by chemically linking the DNA to a molecule that will bind to special cell receptors. Once bound to these receptors, the therapeutic DNA constructs are engulfed by the cell membrane and passed into the interior of the target cell. This delivery system tends to be less effective than other options.

Researchers also are experimenting with introducing a 47th (artificial human) chromosome into target cells. This chromosome would exist autonomously alongside the standard 46 – not affecting their workings or causing any mutations. It would be a large vector capable of carrying substantial amounts of genetic code, and scientists anticipate that, because of its construction and autonomy, the body's immune systems would not attack it. A problem with this potential method is the difficulty in delivering such a large molecule to the nucleus of a target cell.

What is the current status of gene therapy research?

The US Food and Drug Administration (FDA) has not yet approved any human gene therapy product for sale. Current gene therapy is experimental and has not proven very successful in clinical trials. Little progress has been made since the first gene-therapy clinical trial began in 1990. In 1999, gene therapy suffered a major setback with the death of 18-year-old Jesse Gelsinger. Jesse was participating in a gene-therapy trial for Ornithine Transcarboxylase Deficiency (OTCD). He died from multiple organ failures four days after starting the treatment. His death is believed to have been triggered by a severe immune response to the adenovirus carrier.

Another major blow came in January 2003, when the FDA placed a temporary halt on all gene therapy trials using retroviral vectors in blood stem cells. FDA took this action after it learned that a second child treated in a French gene-therapy trial had developed a leukaemia-like condition. Both this child and another who had developed a similar condition in August 2002 had been successfully treated by gene therapy for X-linked Severe Combined Immunodeficiency Disease (X-SCID), also known as 'bubble baby syndrome'.

Gene therapy is a novel method of treating some of the hitherto untreatable diseases. It involves the introduction of a functional gene to replace the activity of a resident defective gene so that biologically active proteins can be synthesized within the cells whose function is to be altered. Introduced as a concept about two decades ago it has become a reality today. A variety of DNA delivery systems have been developed involving biological, physical and chemical agents. Gene therapy was initially thought to be a treatment technique for inherited single gene defects. However, it has also found applications in acquired diseases. Its use is being studied in the treatment of cancer, immunodeficiency diseases, cardiovascular, metabolic and neurological disorders; hormones and blood factors deficiencies. It is also being developed as a 'gene' vaccine against influenza and malaria. Recently attempts have been made for its use in treatment of HIV infection. Gene therapy, although still in the infant stages of development offers the possibility for major advances in prevention and treatment of these diseases. Since 1990, there have been over 300 human gene therapy trials with well over 3,000 patients enrolled, and this number is steadily growing. For terminal systemic disorders such as paralysis or Parkinson's disease, gene therapy has had limited success.

What factors have kept gene therapy from becoming an effective treatment for genetic disease?

- *Short-lived nature of gene therapy.* Before gene therapy can become a permanent cure for any condition, the therapeutic DNA introduced into target cells must remain functional and the cells containing the therapeutic DNA must be long-lived and stable. Problems with integrating therapeutic DNA into the genome and

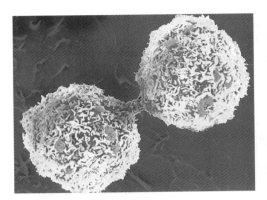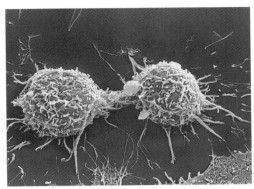

Figure 6.2 Dividing cells. Left: healthy liver cells; right: cervical cancer cells.

the rapidly dividing nature of many cells prevent gene therapy from achieving any long-term benefits. Patients will have to undergo multiple rounds of gene therapy.

- *Immune response.* Any time a foreign object is introduced into human tissues, the immune system is designed to attack the invader. The risk of stimulating the immune system in a way that reduces gene-therapy effectiveness is always a potential risk. Furthermore, the immune system's enhanced response to invaders it has seen before makes it difficult for gene therapy to be repeated in patients.
- *Problems with viral vectors.* Viruses, while the carrier of choice in most gene therapy studies, present a variety of potential problems to the patient – toxicity, immune and inflammatory responses, and gene control and targeting issues. In addition, there is always the fear that the viral vector, once inside the patient, may recover its ability to cause disease.
- *Multigene disorders.* Conditions or disorders that arise from mutations in a single gene are the best candidates for gene therapy. Unfortunately, some of the most commonly occurring disorders, such as heart disease, high blood pressure, Alzheimer's disease, arthritis, and diabetes, are caused by the combined effects of variations in many genes. Multi-gene disorders such as these would be especially difficult to treat effectively using gene therapy.

Important issues raised by genetic engineering

- Germ-line therapy cannot be recalled. Recombinant DNA becomes a living part of the host body and its successors.
- Like natural DNA, it becomes liable to random mutation, so that its future behaviour could be dangerously unpredictable.
- Genes tend to interact in their effects. There is no way of knowing how the introduction of one gene may affect all the others.
- If insurance companies or employers got hold of the results of someone's genetic screening, they might use the information to discriminate against them in terms of insuring or employing them.

DID YOU KNOW?

Genetics
One human cell may contain up to 100,000 genes. Most of the pioneering work in genetics was done by an Austrian monk called Gregor Mendel (1809–84), who did thousands of experiments with pea plants to work out how characteristics were transmitted from one generation to another. In 1953, in Cambridge, Francis Crick and James Watson discovered the double helix shape and the chemical bases of DNA, for which they received the Nobel Prize.

KEY TERMS

Amniocentesis prenatal screening of a foetus to look for genetic abnormalities

DNA deoxyribonucleic acid, the chemical inside molecules that contains genes

Chromosomes lengths of DNA containing genes, which can make proteins

Mutation damage to part of a genetic code which, if occurring in gametes, may result in new physical characteristics (e.g. an albino squirrel)

Somatic-cell change altering the behaviour of non-reproductive cells by the introduction of new genetic material

Activities

1. 'There is something fundamentally unacceptable about any institution, corporation or individual having ownership over part of a human being' (Alistair Kent, Director of the Genetic Interest Group). What reasons could be given for this view? (See Unit 17, 'The need for morality and the nature of ethical theories'.)

2. What evidence might be used to support the view that the advantages of genetic screening outweigh the disadvantages?

3. Is there a difference between searching for a defective gene that causes muscular dystrophy and searching for one that causes homosexuality? Split into small groups and produce arguments to defend your point of view.

- The ability to identify the sex of or possible genetic abnormalities in a fetus means that some parents might opt for abortion in order to fulfil their expectations of a perfect child.
- In the past, *eugenic programmes* aimed at improving society have involved the selection of certain favoured human physical or mental characteristics and the deliberate destruction of those considered to be inferior. The possibility of genetic manipulation may increase this danger.
- Genetic research is very expensive and tends to be carried out by large multinational medical corporations who will 'own' the results of their research. This will give them very powerful monopolies.
- The cost of genetic treatment may result in a two-tier society, consisting of those whose parents could afford to 'improve' their offspring and those who may well be regarded as inferior.

Other ethical and religious issues

- Some critics have argued that all human genetic engineering is 'tampering with nature' – it is a violation of the principle that 'nature knows best'.
- Another religious view is that there is a permanent, universal '*natural law*', which reflects divine intentions and that genetic engineering is against what God intended.
- Other concerns have been expressed about the economic implications. Rich countries, which can afford both genetic research itself and the results of that research, will benefit the most. This will increase the gap between wealthy and poor countries.

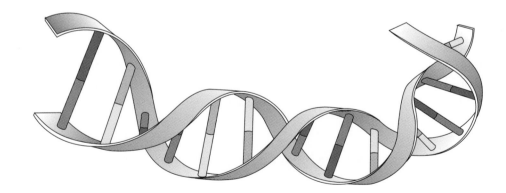

Figure 6.3 The structure of DNA

EXAM QUESTION

This is an A2 Unit 4 essay question from the equivalent test for January 2004. The topic could also be set in Section B of AS Unit 2. See page 1 for details.

'Human cloning is ethically unacceptable.' Discuss the extent to which you agree or disagree with this statement.

(25 marks)

EXAMINER'S ADVICE

- This question could turn out to be the biggest ethical dilemma of the twenty-first century and is one that you can be expected to know and have thought about. Remember also that this is a science essay question, and although it is specifically about the ethical aspects of human cloning, you cannot discuss it properly without some relevant general scientific knowledge. You should therefore include this wherever it is appropriate to support your arguments – it will gain you marks.
- The reason why human cloning represents such a huge dilemma is that there are arguments *for* developing some aspects of the relevant technology. You should include some of these in your discussion, even if you ultimately disagree with them, for example the use of stem cells to cure particular diseases or aid infertility problems. It is important to show that you are aware of different sides to an argument. The same applies if you are in favour of their use – you should acknowledge the potential problems and say why you think the benefits outweigh negative aspects.
- This is also an important issue because it raises the ethical responsibilities of scientists in a general sense – the extent to which scientific research should be restricted because it could be put to 'bad' use is a difficult question. Who should decide and by what means? Similar arguments apply to such activities as weapons research.
- When you have attempted your answer, compare your points with those made on pages 271–272.

Agriculture and food production

Introduction

Throughout history, human beings have tried to find new ways to produce more and better food. Our ancestors learned by trial and error how to breed and domesticate a wide range of animals, how to develop improved varieties, and found ways of processing and preserving raw foods. Successful experiments by plant breeders also to led to the introduction of more disease-resistant and higher yielding crops. For example, the average wheat yield in the UK in 1900 was two tonnes per hectare. Now it is eight tonnes per hectare.

The crucial problems facing world agriculture are:

- Whether the increased use of bio-technology – the *gene revolution* – will be sufficient to feed and sustain a world population which will grow by two billion over the next 30 years.
- Whether the disadvantages associated with the use of pesticides, fertilisers, genetically modified crops, etc. are outweighed by the benefits resulting from increased production.

Hunger

One in five of the population in developing countries suffers from *malnutrition*. This is 30 per cent of the total world population. Hunger is both a violation of human dignity and an obstacle to social, political and economic progress. Apart from the purely physical issues related to the production of food, there is also a political dimension. International law recognises that everyone has the fundamental right to be free from hunger and thirst. National governments have a duty to do everything possible to make sure that people have the physical and economic access to enough safe and nutritious food to lead healthy and active lives.

Violations of the right to food include blocking access on the grounds of race, sex, language, age, religion or political belief. In societies where civil and political rights are recognised, there is far less likely to be famine than in countries run by dictators and/or extreme religious or political factions. In Africa, for example, millions of people have died from starvation and related diseases caused by the deliberate destruction and neglect of crops and harvest and the diversion of large amounts of monetary aid into the pockets of corrupt political leaders and government officials.

In Rwanda, during the civil war, three out of four farmers were forced off their land and the harvest was halved. Similarly, in Afghanistan as the result of prolonged armed conflict, 700 square miles of arable land were sown with landmines which continue to kill or injure 300 people a month.

Major problems facing agricultural development

- The last World Food Summit set a target of reducing world hunger by half by 2015. Apart from the diseases which malnutrition leads to, such as anaemia, vitamin deficiency, stunted growth, blindness and shortened life expectancy, those suffering can rarely work to normal capacity because of chronic lethargy.
- Other problems include natural occurrences such as floods, drought, locusts, the AIDS epidemic, over-fishing and the misuse of land in order to make quick profits as seen in deforestation.
- In order to guarantee access to the results of agricultural development for all who need it worldwide, the world trading system would have to be restructured so that the rich developed countries no longer had the power to control prices, dictate to less developed countries what they should grow, exploit cheap labour and/or adopt restrictive practices towards foreign goods.

Significant developments in agriculture

The challenge facing world agriculture in the twenty-first century is to develop programmes which are sustainable and which will achieve the following objectives:

- Increase yields.
- Reduce costs.
- Protect the environment.
- Improve the reliability of food delivery.
- Improve the material welfare of those engaged in farming.
- Reach international agreement on such issues as the use of dangerous chemicals.

Biotechnology
The Food and Agriculture Organisation, a United Nations Agency concerned with the development of all aspects of agriculture and food production, has argued that there are controversial areas such as the use of genetically modified crops and transgenic experiments involving the cloning and organ transfer of animals. But in other areas such as vaccination, the development of high-yield, salt-water-resistant and disease-resistant crops and breeding programmes, biotechnology has already produced significant benefits.

Genetic modification (usually referred to as GM)
Genes control the traits that are passed from generation to generation, for example, the colour of a flower's petals or a child's eyes. A plant can have up to 50,000 genes.

In many cases, scientists can now identify the individual gene that governs a desired trait, extract it, copy it and insert the copy into another organism. That organism (and its offspring) will then have that trait. This process is known as *genetic modification* and enables desirable traits to be transferred between different species of micro-organisms, plants or animals which normally could not breed with each other.

> **DID YOU KNOW?**
>
> Approximately 850 million people worldwide are malnourished. Children are the most visible victims of malnutrition. Malnutrition plays a role in at least half of the 10.9 million child deaths each year.
>
> Vitamin A deficiency can cause night blindness and reduces the body's resistance to disease. In children, vitamin A deficiency can also cause growth retardation. Between 100 million and 140 million children are vitamin A deficient. An estimated 250,000 to 500,000 vitamin A-deficient children become blind every year, half of them dying within 12 months of losing their sight.
>
> The world produces enough food to feed everyone. World agriculture produces 17 per cent more calories per person today than it did 30 years go, despite a 70 per cent population increase. This is enough to provide everyone in the world with at least 2,720 kilocalories (kcal) per person per day. The principal problem is that many people in the world do not have sufficient land to grow, or income to purchase, enough food.

Figure 7.1 Greenpeace activists set up a mock corn-on-the-cob field in front of Berlin's parliament building in 2003 to protest against genetically modified corn

KEY TERMS

Bio-technology any technological application that uses biological systems, living organisms or derivatives thereof, to make or modify products or processes for specific use. For example, the use of genetic engineering techniques to clone sheep or to produce higher yielding crops through genetic modification

FAO Food and Agriculture Organisation the United Nations Agency which is particularly concerned with the improvement of food production worldwide through the funding of research into crop disease, irrigation systems, and more efficient use of land

Sustainability the idea that agricultural development and practice has to consider the effects of its actions so that the environment is not damaged. It means that cultivation of land, for example, has to avoid soil erosion through over-intensive farming or toxic damage caused by chemicals. It is about long-term food production in harmony with the environment

Although the insertion of new genes into the cells of a crop plant is relatively straightforward, there is an enormous amount of work involved in identifying, isolating and characterising the gene, and years of trials are necessary to develop commercial varieties. Even so, it is much quicker than the traditional method of trial and error.

Genetic modification is a major advance in biotechnology. It is seen by some as offering great benefit to agriculture and food production. Others, however, see it as potentially very dangerous with the possibility of catastrophic consequences. For example, the accidental transference of the herbicide-resistant trait developed in a variety of wheat to a nearby actual weed, could result in a plant that could not be controlled.

Organic farming

An alternative approach is *organic farming* which claims that its methods tend to support and preserve those parts of the environment which intensive farming methods tend to damage. Organic farming emphasises environmental protection, animal welfare and the use of sustainable resources. The amount of land now converted to organic farming in the UK has increased significantly during the last 20 years.

Organic farming is a system which excludes the use of artificial fertiliser and most pesticides and growth regulators. It relies on crop rotation, the use of recycled organic material in the form of animal and green manures and the natural resistance which healthy plants have to predators. A small number of naturally occurring pesticides and simple chemical ones are permitted in some circumstances. The disadvantage of organic farming is that it requires more land to produce a given amount of food than intensive farming does using a full range of fertilisers, etc.

At the present time, 50 per cent of the organic crops consumed in the UK are home grown.

Those in favour of organic farming argue that it does the least harm to the environment, enhances animal welfare and produces healthier more natural tasting products. However, current research has not yet shown any significant difference in terms of nutritional value or food safety.

Sustainability

One crucial issue facing world agriculture is the problem of producing food in such a way that non-renewable natural resources are not depleted beyond recovery. The irreversible damage to local flora and fauna caused by contamination from powerful chemical fertilisers and pesticides is one example. Deforestation caused by ruthless timber extraction without replanting is another.

Food preservation

Food preservation is the treatment of food to prevent or delay spoilage and stop growth of harmful organisms (e.g. bacteria and moulds) which would make the food unsafe. Throughout history humans have applied scientific concepts and engaged different technologies to help preserve food, and as a consequence improve food safety. Through scientific discovery, automation and technological innovation, traditional methods of preservation, such as sun drying and pickling, have been supplemented with pasteurisation, canning and freezing, and more recently high-pressure treatment, high electric field pulses and bio-preservation.

The basic principles of food preservation can be summarised as:

- The use of low temperatures (e.g. chilling or freezing) to retard growth of micro-organisms and inhibit enzyme activity, e.g. frozen pizza, frozen meat and fish.
- The use of high temperatures, e.g. heating food to destroy micro-organisms and prevent enzyme activity, e.g. pasteurised milk, canned foods.
- The use of substances to slow down growth of micro-organisms. This may include placing the food in a sugary or salty solution to make water unavailable to micro-organisms (e.g. jam) or changing the acid/alkaline environment, e.g. pickled onions.
- Controlling the atmosphere and restricting access to oxygen. For example, keeping food in airtight containers to deprive micro-organisms of oxygen and prevent further contamination, e.g. canning; modifying the atmosphere in the packaging of a food product, e.g. vacuum packing.
- The use of dehydration to make water (which is essential for growth) unavailable to micro-organisms, e.g. drying grapes to form raisins.
- The use of physical methods, e.g. irradiation (only limited use currently permitted).
- The use of fermentation to produce food products with extended shelf life, e.g. using milk to produce cheese.

Activities

1. 'Many people talk about the poor, very few actually talk to them' (Mother Teresa). Discuss the meaning of this statement with your fellow students. What actions could be taken to avoid this criticism in future?

2. 'Charity begins at home.' What arguments could be used to support or refute this point of view?

3. Research the work of one major charitable organisation and describe in detail one recent project with which it has been involved.

4. Identify one major world problem and organise a committee with the aim of making some practical contribution towards helping some of its victims.

Food additives

Additives are substances added to foods to perform a range of specific functions. They may be natural, nature identical or artificial.

- Natural additives are substances found naturally in a foodstuff and are extracted from this food to be used in another, for example beetroot juice with its bright purple colour can be used to colour other foods such as sweets.
- Nature-identical additives are manmade copies of substances that occur naturally. For example, benzoic acid is a substance that is found in nature and is made synthetically and used as a preservative.
- Artificial additives are not naturally present in foods and are made synthetically. An example is azodicarbonamide, a flour improver that is used to help bread dough hold together.

Their range of functions includes:

- keeping food wholesome until it is eaten
- making the food look or taste better
- ensuring that the food is convenient to store or use
- keeping the price of the food competitive
- making the food healthier (higher in vitamins or lower in fat)
- aiding in the processing and manufacture.

Additives can be grouped by their main function:

Antioxidants – decreases the chance of oils and fats in foods from combining with oxygen and changing colour or turning rancid. Rancid fats smell and taste unpleasant and are a health risk. Antioxidants are also used in fruits, vegetables and juice to extend their shelf life. Vitamin C (ascorbic acid) is one of the most widely used antioxidants.

Colours – are used to make food look more appetising. During the processing of some food, colour can be lost so additives are used to restore the original colour, for example canned marrow fat peas. Colour additives can also be used to make the existing food colour brighter, for example, enhance the yellowness of custard. Colours are either natural (e.g. curcumin (E100) is a yellow extract of turmeric roots), nature-identical or artificial. Some colours are also vitamins (e.g. riboflavin and beta-carotene) and these are the only colours allowed in baby foods.

Flavour enhancers – are used widely in savoury foods to make the existing flavour in the food stronger. Monosodium glutamate is an example of a flavour enhancer.

Sweeteners – are either intense or bulk. Intense sweeteners (for example saccharin and aspartame) are many times sweeter than sugar and so are only used in tiny amounts. This makes them suitable for use in products such as diet drinks, which are very low in energy. Bulk sweeteners (such as sorbitol and sucralose) have a similar sweetness to sugar so are used in similar amounts.

Emulsifiers, stabilizers, gelling agents and thickeners – emulsifiers help mix together ingredients like oil and water that would normally separate; stabilisers prevent them from separating again. They are used in foods such as ice-cream. Gelling agents are used to give foods a gel-like consistency while thickeners increase the viscosity of foods.

Preservatives – as described in the previous section.

All additives are assessed for safety before they are permitted for use, and they are only then permitted to be used in a limited range of products. Approved additives are given a number and some are also awarded an 'E'. An E shows the additive has been accepted as 'safe' for use within the European Union. Even when an additive has been approved, regular repeat testing is required to maintain its status as 'approved'.

However many health specialists around the world are becoming increasingly convinced that the additives in processed foods are linked to an apparently significant rise in children's allergies and conditions such as 'hyperactivity'. Particular attention needs to be paid to infants' and children's products because their immature organs are less efficient at removing such toxins from their systems.

Detailed food labelling gives information about most additives present so that consumers can make informed choices, but sometimes not all contents are listed.

Healthy eating

A good diet is important for good health. A healthy and varied diet can help to maintain a healthy body weight, enhance general well-being and reduce the risk of a number of diseases including heart disease, stroke, cancer, diabetes and osteoporosis.

A healthy diet is a diet based on breads, potatoes, and other cereals and is rich in fruits and vegetables. A healthy diet will include moderate amounts of milk and dairy products, meat, fish or meat/milk alternatives, and limited amounts of foods containing fat or sugar. No single food can provide all the essential nutrients that the body needs. Therefore, it is important to consume a wide variety of foods to provide adequate intakes of vitamins, minerals and dietary fibre, which are important for health. The balance however between carbohydrate, fat and protein must be right for us to remain healthy. Too little protein can interfere with growth and other body functions, too much fat can lead to obesity (a growing problem in the Western world) and heart disease. Adequate intakes of vitamins, minerals and dietary fibre are important for health, and there is growing evidence that a number of bioactive plant substances (also termed phytochemicals) found in fruit and vegetables are also important in promoting good health.

The Government's *Eight Tips for Eating Well*, published in October 2005, are:

1. Base your meals on starchy foods
2. Eat lots of fruit and vegetables
3. Eat more fish
4. Cut down on saturated fat and sugar

5. Eat less salt – no more than 6g a day
6. Get active and aim for a healthy weight
7. Drink plenty of water
8. Don't skip breakfast

7

EXAM QUESTION

This is an A2 Unit 4 essay question from the equivalent test for June 2004. The topic could also be set in Section B of AS Unit 2.

What is genetically modified food? Considering the health and environmental effects, discuss the safety of genetically modified food.

(25 marks)

EXAMINER'S ADVICE

- There are at least two or three parts to this question depending on how you treat it. The first requires you to explain what genetically modified food (GMF) is. As this is a science essay question, you should include as much relevant science as you can, but for General Studies you should aim it at the 'intelligent general reader', i.e. not too technical.

- The second and third parts of the question require you to discuss the safety of GMF from both a health and environmental point of view. These may overlap but there are different amounts of knowledge to cover and issues which arise. Make sure that you discuss both elements if you can.

- This is quite difficult territory because of the shortage of 'hard' and sustained evidence. Many people have intuitive views on the issue and valid concerns about possible long-term effects which cannot be known, but you should acknowledge that much amounts to speculation. You should attempt to set this against the best-informed scientific opinion you can muster.

- When you have attempted your answer, compare your points with those made on pages 272–273.

Human and animal behaviour

Psychology is the science of the mind. The human mind is the most complex machine on Earth. It is the source of all thought and behaviour. Even if we were to split open the skull of a willing volunteer and have a look inside, we would only see the gloopy grey matter of the brain. We cannot see someone thinking. Nor can we observe their emotions, or memories, or perceptions and dreams.

So how do psychologists go about studying the mind? In fact, psychologists adopt a similar approach to scientists in other fields. Nuclear physicists interested in the structure of atoms cannot observe protons, electrons and neutrons directly. Instead, they predict how these elements should behave and devise experiments to confirm or refute their expectations.

Although we cannot observe the mind directly, everything we do, think, feel and say is determined by the functioning of the mind. So psychologists take human behaviour as the raw data for testing their theories about how the mind works. Since the German psychologist Wilhelm Wundt (1832–1920) opened the first experimental psychology lab in Leipzig in 1879, we have learned an enormous amount about the relationship between brain, mind and behaviour.

Psychology and other disciplines

Psychology lies at the intersection of many other different disciplines, including biology, medicine, linguistics, philosophy, anthropology, sociology, and artificial intelligence (AI). For example, *neuropsychology* is allied with biology, since the aim is to map different areas of the brain and explain how each underpins different brain functions like memory or language. Other branches of psychology are more closely connected with medicine. *Health psychologists* help people manage disease and pain. Similarly, *clinical psychologists* help alleviate the suffering caused by mental disorders.

A good example of the link between psychology and other disciplines is the notion of freedom. You can discuss this from the political, sociological, physiological, etc. points of view and they are all equally valid. Any attempt to explain why humans think and behave in the way that they do will inevitably be linked to one or another branch of psychology. These include *behavioural psychology*, *cognitive psychology*, *social psychology*, *biological psychology* and *psychodynamic psychology*.

What all these different approaches to psychology have in common is a desire to explain the behaviour of individuals based on the workings of the mind. And in every area, psychologists apply scientific methodology. They formulate theories, test hypotheses through observation and experiment, and analyse the findings with statistical techniques that help them identify important findings.

The psychology of memory

Why do we have different ways of remembering things? Memory underpins every thought we have and everything we have learned, from how we walk and talk, through to recognising our favourite movie stars in a magazine.

Memory is at the heart of cognitive psychology, the branch of psychology that deals with mental processes and their effects on human behaviour. Most of us take memory for granted until the point when it fails and we forget something.

Psychologists talk about different kinds of memory: *sensory memory, working memory* and *long-term memory*. When we have to remember a new phone number without the help of pen and paper, we are using our working memory. When it comes to words, we can only keep fresh as many words as we can say in about two minutes. People who speak very quickly tend to have a high working memory capacity because they can pack more words into those two minutes than slow talkers.

Even information in working memory will fade unless it is transferred to the permanent store known as long-term memory. But once it is there, we cannot always get it out. We have all had trouble recalling someone's name or the answer to an easy quiz question.

Psychologists have found that new memories can interfere with old ones, making us believe that something happened when it never actually did. This finding is of great importance in criminal prosecutions, when witnesses try to recall events of critical importance. It also has implications for cases of recovered memories, where adults who previously thought they had had a normal childhood begin to recall traumatic events such as sexual abuse.

Developmental psychology

Researchers in developmental psychology are interested in processes of change. They want to know how babies learn and grow to become mature adults with a sophisticated knowledge of the world. Newborn infants appear to be the most helpless of all mammalian offspring, but it has been discovered that they come into the world already equipped with abilities that provide the springboard for future growth. Babies do maths: adding and subtracting. For example, even four-month-old babies seem capable of rudimentary counting. Of course, they cannot count out loud, because infants do not speak their first words until they are about one year old. But psychologists can gain an insight into what babies know by presenting them with impossible events, a bit like magic tricks or illusions. If babies show surprise, we can be fairly sure that their expectations have been violated. And their expectations are based on what they know about the world.

The psychology of animal behaviour

In the past century, animal behaviourists have discovered a great deal about what makes animals behave in the way that they do.

Animals carry out behaviours in response to situations that they come across in their environment. There are all sorts of ways in which an animal can organise a response when faced with a particular situation. Some require no 'thought' at all, while others are extremely complex and only open to a few species.

Reaction to stimuli

The simplest behaviour is one in which a single factor, known as a stimulus, is perceived in some way (seen or heard or smelt or tasted or felt) and an automatic behaviour is triggered in response.

Hard-wiring

There are a whole host of reactions like this, and they are called innate or hard-wired behaviours. The circuits are laid down before birth, and cannot be controlled in any conscious way. Some animal behaviours that appear to require a lot of thought are actually innate behaviours. For example, Egyptian vultures use stones to break open eggs. At first glance this looks like an example of an animal that has learnt to use a tool – one of the cleverest things that animals do. But vulture chicks hatched in isolation do the same behaviour from a young age – the behaviour is innate. When Egyptian vultures see an egg, they respond automatically by throwing stones at it, and there's no 'thought' involved.

Habituation-poking and sea slugs

A slightly cleverer version of this hard-wired system is one in which the response can be switched off if there's no advantage in doing it. This is called habituation, and it was first demonstrated in the simple sea slug.

Sea slugs have floppy, vulnerable gills that they retract with the slightest touch. But if they are poked repeatedly, and nothing bad happens, they switch off the retraction behaviour because it's a waste of energy.

Learning and Pavlov's dogs

A breakthrough happened when our understanding of memory evolved. In essence, memory is the ability of a nervous system to grow new connections. This means that an individual animal could learn from their experiences by adjusting or adding to its hard-wiring.

The simplest learning is when animals swap one stimulus for another. A Russian researcher, Ivan Pavlov, did a famous experiment with a dog in which the dog came to associate the ringing of a bell with the arrival of food. In the end, the sound of the bell alone was enough to bring about a behavioural response – the dog began drooling. Though Pavlov didn't know it at the time, he had encouraged new connections to grow in the dog's brain that linked perception of the bell with the production of saliva.

It sounds hideous, but this sort of learning happens all the time in the wild. It makes sense for an animal to be able to learn new cues within the environment that tend to lead to food.

Figure 8.1 Pavlov and his staff demonstrating their behavioural response work

Trial and error learning

This involves trying out different patterns of behaviour until a successful one, i.e. one that brings a reward, is discovered and adopted. This process lies at the heart of all animal training. The animal learns to behave in a way that will win it a reward. It looks like 'thinking', but really it's just learning to respond in a suitable way. There's a popular technique called *clicker training* in which the animal performs trained behaviours in order to hear the sound of a 'click'. These animals have been previously trained to associate the click sound with a reward, just as Pavlov's dog thought that the bell meant food, so they'll do anything for a 'click'.

Problem-solving

This is a step up from trial and error learning. Here, when faced with a situation, an animal tries out various responses that it's done before in its head. This involves firing off various nerve cell networks in the brain without doing the behaviour itself, and using a sophisticated brain 'tool-kit' to predict the outcomes of their actions. Running these 'what-ifs' is extremely clever and relies on a detailed understanding of the real world.

It is argued that animals of several species are capable of solving a range of problems that involve abstract reasoning. In 1914, Wilhelm Kohler carried out some experiments with nine chimpanzees. Their pen contained a variety of objects, including boxes, poles, and sticks, with which the primates could experiment. Kohler constructed a variety of problems for the chimps, each of which involved obtaining food that was not directly accessible. In the simplest task, food was put on the other side of a barrier. Dogs and cats in previous experiments had faced the barrier in order to reach the food, rather than moving away from the goal to circumvent the barrier. The chimps, however, presented with an apparently analogous situation, set off immediately on the circuitous route to the food. Kohler concluded that chimpanzees were capable not only of problem solving with training, but also of *insight* – grasping the solution to a new problem without help.

Insight

To use insight an animal must be in a situation it has never encountered before and be able to try out responses they've never done before in their heads before coming up with the solution. In this way, they've solved a problem without referring to any of their memories. It's a sort 'penny drops' type of thinking. Using a lifetime of memories, the animal can draw upon the results of the behaviours it has used before.

Behaviourism

Burrhus Frederic Skinner (1904–90) was an American psychologist and author. He conducted pioneering work on experimental psychology and advocated behaviourism, which seeks to understand behaviour entirely in terms of physiological responses to external stimuli. He also wrote a number of controversial works in which he proposed the widespread use of psychological behaviour modification techniques (primarily operant conditioning) in order to improve society and increase human happiness.

His research suggested that punishment was an ineffective way of controlling behaviour, leading generally to short-term behaviour change, but resulting mostly in the subject attempting to avoid the punishing stimulus instead of avoiding the stimulus that brought about being punished. A simple example of this is the failure of prison to eliminate criminal behaviour. If prison (as a punishing stimulus) were effective at altering behaviour, there would be no criminality, since the risk of imprisonment for criminal conduct is well established. However, individuals still commit offences, but attempt to avoid discovery and therefore punishment. The punishing stimulus does not stop criminal behaviour. The criminal simply becomes more sophisticated at avoiding the punishment.

Biological psychology

This works on the principle that, ultimately, human behaviour depends on physiological activity, i.e. what the body does.

Neurophysiology is a branch of biological psychology which is particularly concerned with the role of the brain in behaviour, thinking and feeling. It investigates such activities as sleeping and dreaming and it would assume that any unusual characteristics in these functions are caused by chemical changes in the brain.

Sleep

For many years, sleep researchers have known as absolute fact that sleep loss is associated with progressive impairment of alertness. On the other hand, we have had to say that we do not know the vital biological function or functions of sleep.

DID YOU KNOW?

Social engineering
Skinner is popularly known mainly for his books *Walden Two* and *Beyond Freedom and Dignity*.
Walden Two describes a visit to an imaginary utopian commune in 1950s America, where the productivity and happiness of the citizens is far in advance of that in the outside world due to their practice of scientific social planning and operant conditioning of children.
Beyond Freedom and Dignity advances the thesis that obsolete social concepts, like 'freedom' and 'dignity', are threatening the survival of the human species and, again, advocates widespread operant conditioning of human beings to ensure productive and happy citizens.

Sleep homeostasis

When we need continually to maintain a constant level or flow of something in our bodies, it is called *homeostatic*. An example of such a process is the regulation of body temperature to maintain it close to 98.6 degrees Fahrenheit. When our prior nocturnal sleep time has been reduced, our tendency to fall asleep the next day increases, and we tend to sleep more deeply the next night. When we obtain substantial 'extra' sleep, we are less likely to fall asleep or become drowsy on the next day, and we may not sleep as deeply the next night. The obvious purpose of this homeostatic process is to ensure that each of us will obtain a certain amount of sleep as a daily average.

Sleep need

Each of us needs a certain amount of sleep which, if obtained on a daily basis, will maintain our homeostatic equilibrium. When we have lost a great deal of sleep and are feeling very sleepy and extremely miserable, it may seem that we would become extremely ill and even die if the sleep deprivation continued. In addition, the homeostatic regulation of a process ensures that a vital function is strongly protected, for example, fluid intake and food intake. We are not absolutely certain that sleep is vitally necessary, but the intense desire to sleep after only a night or two without sleep, points in that direction.

Long-term sleep deprivation studies have been carried out mainly in human beings and rodents, primarily laboratory rats. In the case of rats, total sleep deprivation is fatal in 16–20 days without exception. At this point, the direct cause of death in the rodents appears to be huge numbers of live bacteria in the blood stream and body tissues.

The function of sleep

The question of whether sleep is vitally necessary for humans would be relatively easy to answer if there were an easy, non-stressful method to maintain very prolonged wakefulness. However, the increasing strength of the sleep drive and the increasing difficulty of preventing sleep make prolonged sleep-deprivation studies in humans very difficult. After a few days without sleep, methods that are considered dangerous and unethical would be required.

So, what does sleep do for us? It might not be vitally necessary, but sleep is certainly helpful to human existence. Human beings evolved as a day active species and are highly dependent upon vision to interact with their environment and are pitifully helpless in the dark. Accordingly, one huge advantage of the homeostatic drive to sleep is to force the human species to seek a safe place in which to sleep during the nocturnal hours. Not only are human beings drawn towards day activity by their highly developed visual senses, but also the timing mechanisms of the circadian system have evolved such that the biological clock promotes wakefulness and activity during the daylight hours. Another huge adaptive advantage of sleeping every night is the substantial reduction in energy expenditure. If human beings were fully active 24 hours a day, they would need many more calories and their food requirement would be perhaps 50 per cent higher, creating a vulnerability to food shortages.

There have been several reports of studies of individuals who appeared to need very small amounts of sleep, as little as one hour in some cases. It is not clear, however, if these individuals were fully alert in the daytime. Presumably they were normally alert, but tests to demonstrate this were not undertaken.

The restorative function of sleep

Some evolutionary psychologists have argued that sleep is necessary to fully restore some physiological functions. Certain vital chemicals essential for cell growth, the production of hormones and neuro-transmitting cells vital for internal brain communications can only develop during sleep.

Aggression

Aggression is the intentional harming of another who is trying to avoid the harm. The study of aggression is considered an important one in psychology as it deals with a major social problem. In 1980, one out of every 180 Americans was a victim of a violent crime – murder, robbery, rape or assault. Furthermore, while the incidence of some crimes has dropped in recent years, violent crime hasn't by the same amount. In the USA, the number of murders doubled over the ten years from 1970–80, but has declined slowly over the 20 years from 1980–2000.

What are the origins of aggression?

Ethological approach – Konrad Lorenz

This approach suggests that humans are the most dangerous of animals, not only in terms of danger to other species but also to their own species. This is because we have not evolved any mechanisms that inhibit intra-species aggression. Other animals have lengthy rituals during fights – baring teeth, making loud noises, and adopting aggressive postures – and often these alone will prevent a fight with one animal backing off. If a fight starts then a submissive posture will often signal the end of the fight and the stronger animal will let the loser live. There is also lots of ritualised fighting where animals go through the motions but avoid any serious injury, this is good for the survival of the species.

Humans, however, are relatively weak and harmless when it comes to fighting. We have no fangs, claws, venom, etc. with which to kill an opponent. As a result, we have not developed ritualised aggression inhibiting mechanisms to ensure the survival of the species. However, our superior intelligence has led us to be able to overcome our weakness. An old weak lion with bad teeth can not kill a healthy strong rival, but an old weak man can kill a strong fit young man – all he needs is gun. For this reason, man is considered a very dangerous animal.

Furthermore, it is suggested that humanity's social evolution has led to a situation where an individual's aggression builds up and is not released through everyday activity. We no longer have to hunt for food, etc. and so have to expend very little energy just staying alive, warm and dry. In addition, Lorenz suggests that there are far

---

KEY TERMS

Behaviourism approach to psychology which emphasises scientific method, is primarily concerned with observable human behaviour rather than internal emotion, and which believes that virtually all human behaviour is learnt through either positive or negative experiences referred to as 'conditioning'

Dreams seem to be a way for the subconscious mind to sort out and process all the input and problems that are encountered in waking life. According to Freud, dreams are the result of subconscious thoughts and desires. Other psychologists consider dreams to be random 'noise' in the neurons without special meaning

MRI (Magnetic Resonance Imaging) process which produces a detailed image of sections of the brain. This can be used by neuropsychologists to establish whether a particular illness is caused by some physical damage to the brain itself

Psychodynamism type of psychology which argues that our present feelings and behaviour are heavily influenced by previous events, particularly unpleasant ones. Many of these pressures are deeply rooted in our subconscious so that we are completely unaware of them. Sigmund Freud (1856–1939) is most famously associated with this approach

Psychology the science of mind and behaviour

Sublimation according to Freud, this is the transformation of unwanted impulses into something less harmful – a defence mechanism. For example, many sports and games are sublimations of aggressive urges

Territorial instinct a defensive response which occurs when one animal invades the space of another of the same species (including humans), e.g. sticklebacks turn red and puff out their chest

Activities

1. Investigate the views of B. F. Skinner, the behavioural psychologist. Explain why you think he called one of his books *Beyond Freedom and Dignity*. Why do some people regard his views as rather sinister?

2. In small groups, make a list of significant positive and negative experiences which you may have had. Keeping the views of Sigmund Freud in mind, discuss how far you think that those experiences may have affected your current behaviour, feelings and attitudes?

3. Should employers be allowed to give prospective employers sophisticated psychological tests? Are these a useful tool or an invasion of privacy? Discuss.

more things in society to be unhappy about, and that we have far more time to think about them. This means that we build up aggression that can be released in physical activity – physical activity that we are not undertaking. This is the theory of catharsis, and it suggests that if people undergo physical activity they can reduce their levels of aggression and therefore reduce the likelihood of aggressing toward others. However, the research in this area has produced mixed findings.

Why do people aggress?

Frustration always leads to aggression. Aggression is always a product of frustration. This hypothesis assumes that the relationship between these two is basically a result of innate predispositions, and that aggression will follow more or less automatically from feelings of frustration. It is proposed that frustration is anything that blocks your goals, or interferes with goal-orientated behaviours.

Survival of the species

It was not until the 1930s that a serious attempt to conduct research on animal behaviour from evolutionary and selectionist perspectives was begun. Konrad Lorenz (1903–89) grew up on his family's estate near Vienna with dogs, cats, chickens, ducks, and geese. In this setting, his observations of animal behaviour led to the founding of the field of *ethology*, defined as 'the comparative study of behaviour', which applies to the behaviour of animals and humans all those questions asked and methodologies used as a matter of course in all other branches of biology since Charles Darwin's time.

By extending Darwin's theory of natural selection to behaviour, Lorenz posited a genetic basis for specific behaviours that was subject to the same principles of cumulative blind variation and selection that underlie the adapted complexity of biological structures. In the case of the greylag goose, goslings that maintained close contact with the first large moving object they saw (usually the mother goose) would be in a better position to enjoy her protection and nurture. Consequently, they would be more likely to survive and to have offspring that would similarly show behavioural imprinting. Those goslings that lacked this behavioural characteristic would be less likely to survive to maturity and reproduce. In much the same way that we understand how a tree frog can become so well-camouflaged over evolutionary time through the elimination by predators of those individuals who are less well-camouflaged, we can also understand how instinctive behaviour can be shaped through the elimination of individuals whose behaviours are less fit to their environment.

EXAM QUESTION

This is a two-part question taken from the Section B of 2007 Specimen Paper for AS Unit 2. The first of the two questions (a) relates to the subject content of Unit 7 of this book.

SIR – As young people in today's 'fast-moving, hyper-competitive culture', we feel that an all-out assault on junk food, as proposed by Jamie Oliver, is the wrong path. Banning junk food will only make it more desirable and children will go to further lengths to ensure they can taste this 'forbidden fruit'. Making sure children can differentiate between 'junk food' and 'real food' is far more important.

As to the matter of exercise, even if children did turn to the type of play that some writers may fondly remember, these children would be reprimanded for causing a disturbance. Parents are under pressure to make sure their children get exercise and play outside but leaving them without supervision is criticised. The problem is not parents being overly protective: it is, instead, the fault of meddlers.

Source: Adapted from a letter written by a group of sixth formers, *The Daily Telegraph*, 20 September 2006

(a) For what social and scientific reasons is a varied and balanced diet beneficial to all individuals?

(17 marks)

(b) Discuss the difficulties involved in improving the diet of many young people and increasing their amount of exercise.

(18 marks)

EXAMINER'S ADVICE

- This question is from Section B of the AS Unit 2 paper. Check out the full details for this paper on page 1. In Section B you have a choice of one from three two-part written questions like this and approximately 45 minutes to read the short prompt and answer the questions. That is, about 20 minutes on each question including thinking and planning, as well as writing time.
- In this type of question, the emphasis will be mostly on scientific aspects in the first part (a) and social ones in the second (b). So for the first part, what are the scientific reasons for maintaining a varied and balanced diet? Think of the various nutritional elements that a healthy body needs, e.g. carbohydrates, protein, minerals, etc. and the various food groups that can provide these, e.g. fruit, vegetables, meat, dairy products and so on. These lists should be as extensive as you can make them. Then you should consider the benefits of variety and balance – not too much of any one type, such as

what can happen if you consume too much fat, sugar, salt or alcohol. That possibly takes us into the social aspects of the question.
- The second part of the question is rather more open-ended and reliant on knowledge and experience of yourself, your peers and those younger than yourself. You should make as much use as you can of the prompts in the brief article accompanying the questions. It mentions the pace of life, 'junk' food, exercise and play, parental supervision and interference (by the state/public authorities). What are the differences between 'real' food and junk food? What factors can influence the kind of foods young people eat and the exercise they take? Parents and personal preferences obviously, but how might these be influenced by advertising and marketing, lifestyle and leisure choices, school meals, access to facilities, for example.
- Compare your answers with the points given on pages 273–274 and the general mark scheme for this type of question on page 269.

Medical developments

The application of scientific method and technology to the problems of the human body has led to enormous advances in the capacity of medicine to deal with life-threatening diseases, both in terms of prevention and cure. Many once fatal or dangerous conditions can now be treated successfully. Diseases such as smallpox have been eradicated in most of the world. Tuberculosis and diphtheria, for example, no longer kill enormous numbers of people, particularly children, in many developed countries. National health systems, which utilise *vaccination programmes*, have led to continuing improvements in public health so that diseases such as rickets, measles, poliomyletis and whooping cough no longer represent the same threat to the quality of life or to life itself. Other important medical advances, often interrelated, have been made in such areas as

- genetics
- embryo and reproductive technology
- immunology
- neurology and scanning techniques
- surgery and transplants, including cosmetic surgery
- life extension
- obesity.

Genetics (see Unit 6 'Genetic engineering')

Arguably, genetic research was the most spectacular and far-reaching area of medical development in the twentieth century. Genetic screening, which examines human beings for malfunctioning or defective genes, could soon be as commonplace as blood tests and could become linked to procedures that can replace or repair genetic damage. The successful completion of the *Human Genome Project*, which was set up to map all the genes in the human body, has not only enabled the identification of differences in genetic make-up in different ethnic populations, but will also help to identify possible causes of various diseases and conditions. *Germ-line gene therapy* will enable genetic changes to be made to those cells that transmit information from one generation to another, thus enabling permanent changes to be made. Diseases already identified as having genetic components include asthma, leukaemia, sickle-cell anaemia, Huntington's disease, diabetes and cancer.

Developments in genetic technology have also led to the possibility of *cloning*. (See also Unit 18 'Ethical issues'.) This involves the exact duplication of one human being's genetic code in order to reproduce an identical person. In 1998, the Human Genetics Advisory Committee argued that cloning in order to produce 'spare parts' such as kidneys or livers should be allowed but that the cloning of complete human beings should be banned. One of the advantages of cloning human tissues is that they would not be rejected by the human being from whom they were originally cloned.

Embryo and reproductive technology

Medical advances in this area now mean that infertility no longer automatically leads to childlessness. There are now 13 different ways to have a baby other than through sexual intercourse, including:

- *In vitro fertilisation.* This was first developed in the 1960s by the British gynaecologist Patrick Steptoe and involves the removal of an egg from a woman's womb, which is then fertilised by the husband's sperm in a test tube or culture dish. The process has partly depended on the ability to remove eggs successfully from the womb, to store them at freezing temperatures and to re-implant them.
- *Surrogacy.* Infertile couples now have the possibility of genetically related children through surrogacy. This involves the implantation of an embryo into the womb of a woman who is not genetically related but who will carry the embryo until the child is born and then return it to the real parents. Embryos can also be created in the test tube for research purposes but may only be used for up to 14 days after fertilisation.
- *Fertility drugs.* These have been developed as an aid to overcoming infertility and to increase the chance of a woman conceiving. They often involve '*superovulation*', which results in the production of more ripe eggs than would normally be produced. This can lead to the problem of multiple births, which may damage rather than enhance the possibility of survival of embryos.

Immunology

Immunology is 'the study of resistance to disease in humans and animals'. Great developments took place in this field in the second half of the twentieth century, particularly after the discovery that the body's immune system is based on the activities of various types of white blood cells, found in blood, lymph vessels and tissue fluids. The main centres of activity are the *thymus*, *spleen* and *lymph nodes*. An immune response is triggered when the body detects the presence of a foreign body. By 1900, medical technology had already identified serum defence and developed vaccinations and antitoxins against such killer diseases as cholera, rabies, bubonic plague and typhoid. Important work on blood cells was done by *Karl Landsteiner* (1868–1943), whose experiments led to the possibility of blood transfusions. Further immunological research has led to a greater understanding of why transplanted organs are rejected by the host body and this has saved thousands of lives. In the 1970s, *molecular biology*, *cell biology* and *immunochemistry* have shared spectacular interconnected results, in particular, a greater understanding of the way cancers and human immuno-deficiency (HIV) develop, although there are as yet, no certain cures.

Superdrugs and superbugs

Antibiotic resistance is the ability of a microorganism to withstand the effects of an antibiotic. It is a specific type of drug resistance. Antibiotic resistance evolves naturally via natural selection through random mutation, but it could also be engineered. Once such a gene is generated, bacteria can then transfer the genetic information in a horizontal fashion (between individuals) by plasmid exchange. If a bacterium carries several resistance genes, it is called multiresistant or, informally, a superbug.

In the United States and globally, many other infectious germs, including those that cause pneumonia, ear infections, acne, gonorrhea, urinary tract infections, meningitis, and tuberculosis, can now outwit some of the most commonly used antibiotics and their synthetic counterparts, antimicrobials. According to the Mayo Clinic in Rochester, Minn., drug resistance may have contributed to the 58 per cent rise in infectious disease deaths among Americans in recent years.

Antibiotic resistance isn't a new problem; resistant disease strains began emerging not long after the discovery of antibiotics more than 50 years ago. Penicillin and other antibiotics, which were initially viewed as miracle or super-drugs for their ability to cure such serious and often life-threatening diseases as bacterial meningitis, typhoid fever, and rheumatic fever, soon were challenged by some defiant strains.

Antibiotic resistance is a consequence of evolution via natural selection. The antibiotic action is an environmental pressure; those bacteria which have a mutation allowing them to survive will live on to reproduce. They will then pass this trait to their offspring, which will be a fully resistant generation. If let untreated, the victim will quickly die. Several studies have demonstrated that patterns of antibiotic usage greatly affect the number of resistant organisms which develop. Other factors contributing towards resistance include incorrect diagnosis, unnecessary prescriptions, improper use of antibiotics by patients, and the use of antibiotics as livestock food additives for growth promotion.

Neurology and scanning techniques

Following on the work of several seminal researchers in the late nineteenth century, particularly in relation to the minute electrical charges produced by certain functions of the brain, scanning techniques have been developed that have helped us to understand how the brain works. Specific 'brain waves', produced by impulses emanating from the cerebral cortex and reflecting states of consciousness, external stimuli and 'mental' operations, can be used to diagnose malfunctions such as epilepsy. Further work on these brain waves has helped with the diagnosis of psychiatric disorders, migraine and blood pressure, as well as contributing to sleep research. Recent developments in scanning technology have helped scientists to build up a far more accurate picture of the central nervous system and the damage done to it by strokes or Alzheimer's disease. Neuroscientists such as the Nobel prize-winning *Gerald Edelman* have developed sophisticated maps to show how flexible and adaptable the brain actually is. To a certain extent, some parts of the brain can take over functions damaged elsewhere. This research has also led to a greatly increased ability to diagnose and cure a wide range of psychiatric and personality problems.

Surgery and transplants

Advances in surgery have been driven partly by the need to treat dreadful wounds received during wartime. Up until the Second World War, many surgeons believed that a wide range of medical conditions could be cured by the 'knife', including tumours, tuberculosis, throat cancer, hernias, etc. However, it took a long time before many of these operations developed a high success rate, based on improved sterilisation and increased understanding of how internal organs and cell growth actually work. Enormous strides have been made in heart surgery. In 1931, Werner Fossman, injected a radio-opaque substance via a catheter into his heart, thereby allowing the first heart X-ray to take place. This was followed by the technique of forcing a tiny balloon through a constricted artery in order to clear it and allowing the heart to function properly. By 1939, surgeons were able to suture and repair damage to the walls of the heart without a strong risk of infection. The development of the heart-lung machine, which takes over the functions of these organs, has led to the replacement of blocked arteries leading to the heart and the use of artificial valves and pacemakers.

Transplants

In modern times, the emphasis in surgery has changed from *excision* – cutting and removal – to *replacement* and *plastic surgery*. This can include:

- cosmetic surgery
- removal of skin tumours, cleft palates and cleft lips
- skin grafts to repair burn damage and scars – these techniques were significantly improved by *Archibald McIndoe*, who developed reconstructive and plastic surgery in response to the horrific burns suffered by young Air Force pilots in the Second World War.

Organ transplants involving the replacement of lungs, liver or spleen and particularly kidneys have drastically increased success rates because of:

- a greater understanding of how immune reactions work
- the recognition that the tissue types of the organ being transplanted have to be matched exactly with those of the recipient
- the development of immunosuppressive drugs such as cortisone and cyclosporine.

Life extension: science fact or science fiction?

Recent discoveries in genetics have lead to an increased interest in *gerontology* – the science of ageing. Some scientists have argued for the existence of genes which are responsible for how long we live. Theoretically, it may be possible to manipulate these genes so that human life could be extended to a lifespan of 150 years.

KEY TERMS

Acquired immuno-deficiency syndrome (AIDS) a usually fatal breakdown in the body's immune system caused by a virus which destroys white blood cells

Angioplasty a surgical technique that clears a blocked artery by inserting a tiny balloon in order to clear away obstructions

Antibodies protein molecules produced to combat microbial infection and provide immunity

Electrocardiograph a machine that records the minute electrical currents produced by the heart

Immunisation the artificial creation of immunity to disease by vaccination

Scientists studying certain worms and fruit flies have found several genes that seem to control how long these creatures live. By making a change in just one of these genes, they have almost doubled the average lifespan of both fruit flies and one type of worm. Others looking at longevity have shown that one particular gene, already shown to control how fast yeast cells age, may do the same thing in mice. This gene is also present in humans.

Genes alone, however, are only a part of the reason that some people live a long time. How people live, their lifestyle, may be more important. For example, does someone smoke? Do they exercise? Are they under a lot of stress? What do they eat? Some scientists think what people eat and how much they eat can lead to a longer life. Caloric restriction is one area of research on ageing. A calorie-restricted diet has 30 to 40 per cent fewer calories than a normal diet, but it has all the needed nutrients. This diet seems to extend the life of almost every animal type in which it is studied. It has worked in protozoa (very small, one-celled organisms), fruit flies, mice, and rats. However, scientists are not sure why this works.

The chemical approach

Antioxidants are natural substances in foods. It may be possible to strengthen the way in which they help to protect the body from the accumulative effects of stress, smoking, strong sunlight and heart disease, for example. Other scientists have argued, however, that there is no 'magic pill' and no real evidence that any of the chemicals tested really work. Some of the more common dietary supplements include ginkgo biloba, ginseng, saw palmetto, echinacea, and St. John's wort. Although there may be a lot of hype about these supplements, we don't have scientifically proven facts about their effects. However, dietary supplements are widely available. Each year, people spend billions on these vitamins, minerals, herbs, and hormones. They are hoping for more energy, stronger muscles, better memory, protection from disease, and maybe even a longer life.

Conclusion

Many of these recent developments in medicine have saved thousands of lives and made the lives of the chronically ill or disabled far more bearable. However, the technology involved is hugely expensive. National Health Service hospitals with limited resources have to make 'life and death' decisions such as who should have access to a kidney dialysis machine, or whether such scarce resources be 'wasted' on the old. The desperate shortage of organs such as hearts and livers means that difficult decisions have to be made about who should have them. Progress in medicine brings with it complex ethical issues.

EXAM QUESTION

This is an A2 essay question taken from Section B of the Unit 4 Specimen Paper in 2007.

Considerable progress has been made in the transplantation of organs in the last 40 years and now even face transplants are becoming possible.

Explain the medical and scientific concerns that doctors may have about different forms of transplant surgery.

Examine the issues that might be important to organ donors, their families and those who receive transplants.

(25 marks)

EXAMINER'S ADVICE

- This is a standard A2 essay question and, after the introduction which briefly sets the scene, there are two main parts to the question which you must address – first the medical and scientific concerns and then the ethical perspectives, relating to doctors, donors and recipients, of a range of organ transplants. Some forms of transplant may raise more issues than others.
- Internal organ transplants developed slowly with kidney transplants in the 1950s and the first transplants (especially of hearts after 1967) were greeted with plenty of protests and reservations. Now they are broadly accepted, certainly in the scientific and medical community.
- The first partial face transplant took place in France in 2005 when Isabelle Dinoire received the lips, nose and chin of a donor after being savaged by her pet dog. Professor Peter Butler has now received permission from the Royal Free Hospital's ethics committee to undertake a full face transplant although there is no agreement yet for the NHS to fund this and there is no date for such an operation to take place.

- A full-face skin transplant opens up a new area of controversy because it is a new procedure. A number of surgeons are opposed to face transplants because they feel there are too many 'unknowns', perhaps involving considerable risks. A disfigured face, though extremely distressing, is not necessarily life-threatening. Should priorities be to save life rather than improve it? For others, quality of life is equally important.
- The UK has one of the lowest donor-transplant rates in Europe (partly because of a series of scandals such as Alder Hey and Bristol Royal Infirmary involving organs being kept without relatives' consent). Some 7,000 people are waiting for transplants but only 3,000 will get one at present within a year. Fifteen per cent of patients die on the waiting list. There are many pressures on all concerned.
- Build these and other ideas from the unit into your arguments and compile lists of the arguments for and against. When you have thought about the topic and assembled some details for your answer, spend no more than 30–40 minutes writing out your answer. Then compare your ideas with the notes on pages 274–275.

Transport issues

The history of transport

As transport until the nineteenth century was dependent on the horse, it is sometimes argued that the key event in transport was the domestication of the horse, which occurred sometime around 1500 BCE. However, others would argue that the greatest influence was the invention of boats, enabling goods to be carried along rivers and across seas. The earliest boat discovered so far is a pine canoe dating from around 7000 BCE and found in Holland. Nevertheless, all modern forms of land transport rely on the invention of the wheel which was probably invented between 4000 and 3000 BCE. The wheel enabled carts, chariots and carriages to be built which allowed one horse to carry several people and considerably more goods.

Steam

A huge advance in transport came with the invention of the steam engine. The first steam engine was built by Savery in 1698, followed by Newcomen's 1712 engine – the first proper steam engine using a piston. However, it was not until James Watt introduced a condenser and gears that it became possible to use a steam engine for transport. Several steam locomotives were designed at the beginning of the nineteenth century, and George Stephenson's *Locomotion* hauled the first public passenger railway between Stockton and Darlington in 1825. So began 'the Railway Age' and between 1825 and 1914, railways were built across all countries and continents, revolutionising not only transport, but also the development of suburbs and communications (newspapers and the telegraph).

Cars

The invention of the internal combustion engine (Karl Benz, 1885) and Henry Ford's mass production methods (Model T Ford, 1908) made cars the most popular form of transport. The car puts the individual in charge of their transport. The popularity of the car led to the need for a modern road system. The first motorways were built in Germany before the Second World War (autobahns) and from the beginning of the M1 in 1959, Britain developed an interconnected motorway system completed by the London Orbital Motorway (M25).

Planes

The first flying machine of the Wright Brothers (1903) had little effect on ordinary people's lives. However, after the First World War, the USA used aircraft for mail routes, and after the Second World War, the development of jet airliners (Comet, 1959, Jumbo Jet – Boeing 747 – 1969, Concorde, 1969) made flying faster, more comfortable and cheaper. Travel between continents, which had taken days or weeks on ships, now takes hours.

Space travel

Space travel began when the Russian Yuri Gagarin made an orbit of the Earth in 1957. By 1969, space travel had developed rapidly enough for the Americans

Armstrong, Aldrin and Collins to land *Apollo 11* on the Moon. Although space travel has been mainly used for exploration (for example, of Mars), research (for example, the Hubble Telescope) and satellite communications, it is beginning to be used for tourism as the Russian space centre now sells flights into space.

Science or technology?

There is often argument as to whether the advances in transport have been made by science or technology. Cayley worked out the three basic principles of flight (lift, thrust and control) in 1804, but it was another 100 years before the technology was developed to make aircraft.

Frank Whittle patented his theory of the jet engine in 1930, but it was 1939 before the German firm *Heinkel* built the first jet plane. The whole theory of electricity was discovered before Faraday invented the first electric motor (1821), but it was 1879 before an electric motor big enough to drive a vehicle was invented (Siemens' electric train).

However, the development of the steam engine seems to have been more affected by changes in technology, such as better iron and steel making and the needs of industry. Savery, Newcomen, Watt and Stephenson were all engineers with little knowledge of science. Even so, they must have developed theories, of the power of steam, for example, in order to think of a steam engine.

It appears that science and technology have always been intertwined, with some scientific discoveries requiring developments in technology (for example, particle accelerators to make discoveries in atomic physics) and some developments in technology requiring scientific theories (for example, space travel and the Earth's gravitational pull).

Transport issues

Public or private?

Public transport refers to the types of vehicle which can transport a large number of people with one means of propulsion (railways, buses, trams, ferries, planes for which tickets can be bought) whereas private transport is transport which is owned by an individual for their own use (for example, cars, private jets and yachts).

In the 1980s, the Conservative Government privatised the public transport system. Local bus services, which had been run by councils, were opened to competition with different companies competing with each other on the same routes. Councils were allowed to pay subsidies to private bus firms for routes which were not profitable. British Rail (which had run all rail services) was abolished and RailTrack (a private company) took over the tracks. After the Hatfield rail crash caused financial troubles to the company, Network Rail (a not-for-profit company responsible to the Department of Transport and the Office for Rail Regulation) took over control of the tracks. Train services were provided by private companies awarded franchises for a set period by the Department of Transport.

Arguments in favour of privatisation	Arguments against privatisation
1. Competition is the best way of ensuring efficiency and there can only be competition if there are private transport companies. 2. Since the privatisation of the railways, there has been a great increase in the number of passengers travelling by rail. 3. Theoretically, the financial cost of maintaining and developing the railways has been taken from the government. 4. Competing private bus companies should provide more services, so making buses more attractive to travellers. 5. Private companies will be trying to get more passengers, and be run more efficiently, so they will offer cheaper fares.	1. The countries with the most efficient public transport systems (e.g. Japan and Switzerland) are publicly owned. 2. On railways, dividing ownership of the tracks from ownership of the trains will lead to conflict and inefficiency (e.g. if there is a delay caused by the track, the rail company claims compensation from the track authority). Any competition is going to be artificial unless there are separate tracks. 3. Competition among bus services has almost died out as large companies like Stagecoach have divided up the routes among themselves rather than competing. 4. The government is now paying four times more in public transport subsidies than it did before privatisation. The rail companies received £6.3 billion in subsidies in 2006 compared with £5 billion in fares.

Cars or buses and trains?

Traffic congestion has been a problem for cities at least since Roman times. In the first century BCE, Julius Caesar banned wheeled traffic from Rome during daylight hours. In several European cities parking restrictions and one-way streets were introduced in the seventeenth century to deal with the congestion. The arrival of railways as a faster means of transport reduced congestion, but the age of the car has led to massive problems.

In the UK there are now around 30 million vehicles on the roads. On occasions the centres of cities experience gridlock (a traffic jam affecting a number of intersecting roads so that nothing can move). A small accident on the busiest motorways sometimes causes traffic queues of up to 25 miles.

Several solutions have been proposed:

- Banning cars from city centres, or charging for access to city centres (this seems to be working in Central London, but requires an expansion of public transport).
- Making petrol and car tax so high that people give up their cars (this also requires a big expansion of cheap public transport, otherwise people will just pay the extra to keep their cars).
- Making bus lanes to give rapid transit for public transport (intersections, however, are a major problem as it is impossible to keep buses and cars separate).
- Forcing freight onto the railways and waterways, as in much of Europe (however, rundown rail and waterway systems means there are insufficient facilities to expand).

- Introducing computerisation from a traffic control centre (automatic vehicle-control system) where a vehicle is checked into a control station, gives its destination and is put into a traffic lane with its spacing to the vehicle ahead controlled by an on-board computer (it is estimated that this could increase traffic flow from the current maximum of 2000 vehicles an hour to at least 10,000 vehicles an hour).
- Encouraging people on to public transport with schemes such as 'park and ride' and 'save as you travel' where the bus or train company allocates a portion of the ticket cost to a savings account for the traveller so that the more public transport is used, the greater the saving.

All of these measures (especially the expansion of public transport) will require a large Government investment (which could be funded by using increased car taxes). The Government published a transport White Paper in 2004 requiring local authorities to produce five-year plans to make it easier to walk or cycle than to drive and to integrate buses and rail in their area. It also set out the ways in which the Government would take a more direct role in the running of the railways.

Air travel arguments

There has been a massive increase in air travel since 1990, partly due to the rise of low-cost airlines like EasyJet and Ryan Air. More than 200 million people take low-cost European flights from the UK every year. Forecasts are for a doubling of air travel by 2015. In 2003, 131 million passengers used UK airports. This could rise to 400 million by 2020, the equivalent of four new Heathrows. However, this is now being contested because:

Figure 10.1 One horsepower will move 150 kg by road, 450 kg by rail and 3600 kg by canal

- Aircraft cause massive amounts of pollution as kerosene emits more greenhouse gases than petrol. It is estimated that airlines are responsible for 7 per cent of man-made pollution.
- Over 300,000 people suffer noise pollution from living near Heathrow.
- Motorists pay around 75 per cent tax on every litre of petrol meaning petrol costs around 96–102p per litre whereas airlines pay no tax on fuel and they pay around 20p per litre. Even though Britain now has taxes on passengers (£20 per passenger for shorthaul, £40 per passenger for longhaul, and twice this for business class), these still make air travel much cheaper per mile of fuel used than car travel, even though it is more polluting.

Some transport experts believe that short haul flights should be banned as trains are as quick and cause much less pollution. They also believe that there should be no car parks at airports to force passengers to use public transport (much of the congestion on the M4 and M25 is caused by passengers travelling to and from Heathrow and Gatwick).

Pollution and new methods of propulsion

Almost all land and air transport use fossil fuels (mainly oil) which cause pollution and are likely to run out. This has led to the development of new forms of propulsion:

- Car manufacturers have tackled pollution by fitting catalysers, using unleaded petrol, improving fuel consumption and recycling steel, plastic, batteries, etc. Some cars are now made of 75 per cent recycled materials and it is estimated that it would take 50 small cars produced in 2000 to cause the same pollution as one small car produced in 1976. Car manufacturers are aiming to reduce the total tonnage of pollution caused by cars by 75 per cent in the year 2010 compared with 1992.
- Some firms are now producing cars powered by the hydrogen from water. Ford and BP are working together on hydrogen-powered vehicles. Hydrogen is most likely to be the fuel of the future. It holds the possibility of ending the dependency on oil in the long term, and of producing cars with totally green exhausts. A hydrogen-powered car emits nothing but droplets of pure water. Ford is part of a gigantic global research effort into hydrogen cars. But no one will buy such machines until they know they can get the fuel. So BP is building a series of hydrogen filling stations. Ford and BP are responding to a US-government initiative to put hydrogen cars and vans on the road and get people to drive and refuel them in everyday conditions.
- Rolls-Royce is making marine gas turbine engines which are more fuel efficient and emit much less SO_2 and NO_2 than diesel marine engines (SO_2 and NO_2 from ships are linked with acidification of soils and sea and freshwater systems).
- The *Firebird* is a new type of helicopter which uses hydrogen peroxide to produce superheated steam to give the upward thrust using jets on each end of the rotors rather than having a conventional engine.
- The European Space Agency is developing a new type of rocket propulsion known

as solar-electric propulsion which converts sunlight into electricity via solar panels and uses it to electrically charge heavy gas atoms which propel the spacecraft at very high velocity. These are also known as ion engines and have successfully lifted the *Artemis* satellite into orbit.

Safety

Death and serious injury from road accidents has gone down from 80,132 in 1985 to 37,215 in 2003, despite an increase in road traffic from 300 billion kilometres in 1985 to 500 billion kilometres in 2003.

There are many reasons for this, most of which have come from science and technology:

- The use of cameras, radar and videos has led to a greater adherence to speed limits.
- The building of more roads with carriageways separated by a crash barrier.
- The use of 'soft' signs and lamp-posts and guard rails around objects such as bridge piers.
- Improved car safety features such as seat belts, collapsible steering column, air bags, side impact bars, improved brakes and tyres.
- The breathalyser to reduce 'drink' driving.
- MOT tests for older cars to keep unsafe vehicles off the road.

More improvements to safety could come from onboard computers, which could reduce speeds, warn drivers of approaching hazards, stop drivers from falling asleep, etc.

Activities

1. Visit a local car showroom for information on safety and pollution improvements.

2. What scientific methods would you use to test a new fuel that is claimed to be pollution-free?

10

EXAM QUESTION

Read the following article and answer the question which follows.

Extract from a case study on *Transport*
Car makers still miles away from a clean green alternative

For Tony Appleton from Essex, the answer to the fuel shortage was sitting in the back of his garage: a Sinclair C5 electric car that had been unused for a decade, *writes Deborah Collcutt*. Like other attempts to overtake the internal combustion engine, the C5 was a brave failure. But it may be only a matter of time, and dwindling oil stocks, before a viable alternative to petrol and diesel has to be found.

This week, Sinclair said that he intended to bring out a new range of battery powered vehicles. 'I am going to launch a new light-weight electric car and an electric scooter,' he said. 'I always knew a fuel crisis would come. With even better commercial timing, Toyota launched a hybrid petrol/electric car, the *Prius,* on Friday. It already has a rival in a hybrid model from Honda, called the *Insight*. General Motors (GM) has plans for a fully functioning family saloon that has a small normal engine supplemented by batteries. And at this year's Birmingham motor show, Ford will be exhibiting an electric car called *Th!nk*.

In reality, however, electric cars will not be seen on a widespread basis for many years because they still cannot deliver high enough speeds and because the infrastructure needed for motorists to 'plug in' for recharging is costly.

Natural gas is another possibility. The supermarket chain Safeway already has seven distribution lorries that run on natural gas. But in the longer term, the same problems as with other fossil fuels apply.

Other, more complex technologies are being researched at vast expense, with fuel cells seen as one of the most promising. In a fuel cell system, an energy source such as natural gas or methanol is broken down to generate hydrogen, which is combined with oxygen to generate electricity. A fuel cell does not run down or require recharging in the same sense as a conventional battery. It will produce energy as long as fuel is supplied.

Without mass production, however, the system does not come cheap. The first production fuel cell cars – due on the roads by 2003/4 – are likely to cost substantially more than petrol or diesel vehicles. In the medium term, fuel cells and natural gas vehicles are likely to prove more suitable for commercial vehicle operators – particularly municipal bus operators or refuse collection services – than for private motorists. For fleet vehicles, the infrastructure obstacles can be overcome by establishing central fuelling depots, and could offset initial capital costs.

Despite the difficulties, even traditional car makers and oil companies acknowledge that the future of the internal combustion engine is limited. Ford has teamed up with BP Amoco to explore environmentally friendly road transport. GM has joined forces with Exxon on research into fuel cells.

For the moment, however, the problem is that, despite the European fuel protests, in the world's largest car market, petrol is still cheap and the incentives for pushing alternatives are limited. In America, a gallon of petrol still costs between £1.10 and £1.25 – less than a bottle of mineral water. Most industry analysts believe the real pressure to develop an alternative will have to come from tougher emissions controls in America. California has drawn up the country's stiffest emissions legislation and other states have introduced regulations dictating the use of alternative fuels in government vehicles.

But even before newer, cleaner engine technologies arrive, there may be other measures introduced with the aim of cutting petrol driven congestion and pollution in Britain. More effective than high levels of duty on petrol, say experts, are charges for those who use busy roads at peak times. 'Congestion charging could be a powerful tool for raising revenue and managing traffic demand.' said Professor David Begg, Head of the Government's Commission on Integrated Transport. 'Satellite technology that will allow congestion charging is already here, which eliminates the need to stop drivers at toll booths. If congestion charges were linked to reductions in fuel duty, suddenly a driver in the Highlands whose car trip has less environmental impact might be paying lower fuel charges, lower car tax and low congestion charges. As it is, some poorer rural Scottish households spend up to 60% of their travel budget on fuel.'

Source: The Sunday Times, September 2000

Discuss to what extent new technologies offer a
solution to the United Kingdom's transport problems.

(11 marks)

EXAMINER'S ADVICE

- This is an A2 Unit 4 question based on a case
  study on *Transport* set in June 2002. It is one of
  four questions for extended writing on issues
  raised in a series of documents mostly released for
  you to study in advance. See page 1 and pages
  267–268 for more information and details about
  Unit 4.
- The question is worth eleven marks, so you
  should write 250–300 words (about a page of
  your answer book) and make at least eleven
  supported points or arguments.
- This is a 'to what extent' question and these are
  very common in General Studies. It allows you to
  give your own opinions and evaluation of the
  issues but requires you to consider a range of
  points both for and against a proposition – to
  what extent do new technologies offer a solution?
- In this case you should look at the range of
  possibilities mentioned in the passage and evaluate
  how effective each is or could be, taking into
  account their strengths and limitations. If you
  have some additional knowledge and ideas of your
  own, include it as long as it is relevant, but a
  degree of balance in your answer is probably quite
  important for such a difficult and intractable set
  of problems. There is perhaps a useful clue in the
  title of the passage for some sort of overall
  statement at the end.
- Note that the article was written in 2000.
  Consider to what extent it might be out of date in
  some aspects. Are there now newer
  technologies/fuels, being developed? A quick
  internet search might help here.
- When you have written your answer check out the
  notes on page 275 to see how your points match
  up.

---

11 Computers

A computer is an electronic machine that can store and perform calculations and process data at very high speeds. Computers require programs (a sequence of operations) by which the computer can process the data to produce the intended outcome. For example, if a manufacturer wants a business to be able to input all its billing data so that the computer can output individual bills, the programmer has to work out every step of the process and write each step into a command performable by the computer. Since their invention, computers have revolutionised many aspects of life and now affect everyone.

The history of computers

It is generally accepted that Charles Babbage designed the prototype computer in 1834. It was a machine that could both perform and store the results of calculations. However, it was too complicated to build. Howard Aitkin of Harvard University succeeded in building on Babbage's idea, with a combination of the technology of IBM and Harvard, producing the *Automated Sequence Control Calculator* in 1944. The first electronic digital computer, the *Electronic Numerical Integrator and Calculator*, was built at the University of Pennsylvania in 1946. Although it was progammable and could store problems, it occupied 1500 square feet of floor space and could only process one program or problem at a time.

It was the invention of the *transistor* (a miniature device to amplify electronic signals) and the *printed electronic circuit* (replacing the copper wires used for carrying the electric current with a small board) that allowed the building of the first computer, the *Manchester Mark I*. The first computer to be sold commercially was the *Ferranti Mark I* in 1951. In 1958, Texas Instruments produced integrated circuits on a silicon chip. The major breakthrough in computing came in 1969 when Hoff of the USA developed the *microprocessor* by placing all the circuits that do the work of a computer onto a single silicon chip. The era from 1970 to 1999 is often referred to as the Microprocessor Revolution, similar in impact to the Industrial Revolution of 1750–1850.

Early computers were huge, but the invention of the microprocessor allowed the development of much smaller computers and the first personal computers (PCs) that could be used in homes. The first PC was the *Altair*, marketed in 1975, which never achieved great success because it came in kit form and had to be assembled at home. The first successful PC was the *Apple II*, which was small enough and cheap enough to be used in small businesses, schools, offices and homes. In 1981, IBM introduced their PC, which was no faster than the Apple, but used the Microsoft Corporation's operating system MS-DOS, which became the industry standard so that any competitors had to market their equipment as 'IBM compatible'.

During the 1980s and 1990s, operating systems and microprocessors developed to give greater speed and memory, but the next big development was the CD-ROM, which allowed computers to use digital sound and video images, so becoming 'multimedia'. However, the most important computer development of the 1990s was the *World Wide Web* (WWW) and the connected *Internet.* The Web was released to the public in 1992 and by 1999 there were millions of users worldwide.

Types of computer

Although most people are only likely to use PCs, there are many different types of computer. The largest are called *supercomputers* which are mainly used by groups of scientists in research e.g. the particle laboratory in Geneva. Next are *mainframe computers* which are normally used as a central repository for a mass of data which can then be accessed via workstations and PCs. Next is the *minicomputer* which can be used to power a small network or for scientific researchers who require a powerful computer. Slightly less powerful than the minicomputer is the *workstation*, which is used in scientific research, engineering and business. *Personal computers* (PCs) are the least powerful computers and come in four types. The largest PCs are not portable and are known as *desktop computers.* Large portable PCs are known as *laptop computers*, smaller portable PCs are known as notebook computers. The smallest PC is known as a *palmtop* or *PDA (Personal Digital Assistant)* and can be held in the hand. Palmtops can be incorporated into a mobile phone known as a *blackberry.*

Computer networks are collections of computers (or terminals equipped with microprocessors such as supermarket tills) interconnected by telephone lines or other high speed communication links to exchange data or process information. The network can be a national one (such as those connecting shops with credit card centres), or a local one (known as a LAN – local area network) restricted to an area or an organisation or even to a building. Networks connected by telephone lines require a *modem* (modulator/demodulator) to convert the digital impulses from the computer into the analogue impulses required for telephone lines. Broadband networks either upgrade phone lines or use fibre optic cables for fast data transmission.

Uses of computers

Computers began as an aid to scientific research and to the defence industry, but are now used in every area of business and life. In industry, computers are used for flexible manufacturing systems (FMS) and computer-integrated manufacturing (CIM).

CIM begins with the design of a new product, and this can be done much more efficiently using CAD (computer-aided design) than it could by hand. The designer creates a drawing of the product (as a draughtsman would), then stores the drawing and uses various pieces of software to test the effects of heat, pressure, etc. on the new product. The results of these tests can then be incorporated into the design and detailed drawings drawn by the computer, so that the production team can make a prototype, which has already undergone many tests and adjustments without the time and expense of making products.

After the design, computers are used to formulate the best method of manufacture (computer-aided manufacturing, CAM). If there is a continuous manufacturing process, computers can be used to control the whole process. A computer will measure the important process variables such as temperature, flow rate and pressure. Then it works out the best manufacturing strategy and operates the devices (switches, valves, furnaces, etc.) in the manufacturing process to achieve the strategy. Finally, the computer produces management reports on production performance, product quality, etc. If there is no continuous process, the computer will plan the processes required for the most efficient production of the product.

Computers will then be involved in the business system: ordering raw materials and organising stock control, customer orders, employee payroll, customer service, etc. All this use of the computer is aimed at achieving the optimum product and profit for the company. Most companies use computers to operate a 'just in time' stock control system that saves considerable money on stock holding.

FMS is based on machine tools being linked together by a *material handling system* controlled by a computer. The computer system works out which machine should be doing what and organises the materials for them. This should result in the system being able to operate at maximum performance – whether a machine breaks down, there is a shortfall of supplies or whatever – but it requires the firm to invest in machine tools that can be computer controlled.

Banks are able to use their own networks to reduce the need for cash being moved around the country. The bank computerisation that affects most workers in the country is the BACS system, which enables firms to pay wages into individual workers' accounts without cash being used.

Networking has also made it possible for businesses to encourage their employees to work from home using a PC connected to a network. This saves the company a considerable amount of money in providing the office space for that worker.

The Internet

The Internet is a network connecting many computer networks based on a system called *transmission control protocol/Internet protocol*. It was established in 1983 to enable academics at universities around the world to share research with each other. The original uses of the Internet were electronic mail (e-mail letters sent immediately to another computer anywhere in the world) and newsboards or bulletin boards giving information. However, the development of the World Wide Web in 1989 by Tim Berners-Lee and colleagues at CERN, a European scientific laboratory researching the nature of matter in Geneva, transformed the Internet.

The Web converts documents into hypertext and then stores them so that they can be accessed through a word in the text. It also allows hypermedia documents (documents featuring images, sounds and moving pictures) to be accessed. The Web was made available to the public as part of the Internet in January 1992, and since then many companies have set up *Internet service providers* (ISPs) to allow individuals and businesses to use the Internet and the World Wide Web. The main ones are AOL (America On Line) and Microsoft Network. Obviously, the fees for using the Internet are mainly determined by the company owning the connecting cables. In the UK this is mainly BT, though some cable telephone/television companies are installing Internet cables, for example NTL. Companies like Yahoo and Google provide search engines which act as topic/index locators.

So many Internet businesses have been established, that in 1999 it was possible for a man isolated in a room with access only to the Internet, to be able to obtain all the food, drink, clothes, furniture, etc. he needed simply by clicking his mouse button. Most firms now have a website to advertise their business or to enable orders to be made by e-mail. Many Internet companies have been established to provide special Internet services. For example, it emerged in January 2000 that there is an Internet company that will provide addresses of people who have ex-directory telephone numbers (some unknown person used this service to discover Jill Dando's address). The Internet also allows small companies to advertise worldwide for a very small cost – some such companies, such as specialist cheese manufacturers, are finding their sales rocketing.

Many Internet companies have been established to provide special Internet services such as chat lines, research and entertainment. Interactive multi-media sites mean that films, computer games, television, music and radio can be accessed by an individual at a PC. MP3 enables Internet users to download music from the Internet onto MP3 players (the iPod being the most popular brand of these). This is revolutionising the media industry (it is thought to be the reason behind the merger between AOL and Time Warner, in January 2000, which created the world's largest company). AOL's Internet connections can now use all the films, cartoons, television programmes, music and magazine articles of Warner Brothers. It also has access to television stations to advertise itself, and use new technology to allow Internet access through cable and digital television. Digital television and radio makes it possible for the viewer/listener to take control through interactive links.

The Internet's major revolution has been *freedom of information*. It is impossible to censor the Internet as there is so much going on that no one would know where to start. Even in 1995, when the number of Internet subscribers was only about 25 million, the volume of information exchanged on 'the Net' was enough to fill 30 million books of 700 pages each!

The future

The phenomenal changes during the last ten years mean that no one can tell what will happen in the future.

Some, such as the science fiction novelist William Gibson who invented the term, believe that *cyberspace* will arrive. This means an artificial environment created by computers. People will work and be entertained via their PC.

Others believe that work patterns will be changed by networking and that the Internet will take over a lot of shopping. However, people will still be required to process orders made via the Internet, to deliver goods ordered by the Internet, to produce the goods ordered by the Internet, to make the music and television programmes downloaded from the Internet, and so on. There is already some evidence

KEY TERMS

Algorithm a set of rules used for calculation or problem solving

Analogue using signals or information represented by a continuously variable quantity, such as spatial position or voltage (the US form is analog)

Bit a unit of information expressed as a choice between two possibilities (also called a digit binary)

Byte a group of eight bits operated as a unit

Clients programs that request documents from a server as users ask for them

Database a structured set of information held in a computer, which can be accessed in different ways, e.g. a list of customers and suppliers

Desk-top publishing using a desk-top PC's word-processing, images, charts, tables, etc. together

Digital using signals or information represented by digits (regarded as more efficient than analogue)

Floppy disk a disk that can be put into a computer to store information outside the computer

Hard copy a printout on paper

Hard disk the part of the computer that stores information

Hardware computers and peripheral machines like printers

Megabyte a million bytes (technically, 1024 kilobytes)

Memory how much data can be stored by a computer

Server computers or programs that store and transmit data to other computers on the network

Software programs and systems that are put into a computer

Figure 11.1 Mobile phone company O$_2$ claims to have sold 'tens of thousands' of iPhones in the first weekend of sales

Activities

1. Ask a computing teacher how companies make money from the Internet.

2. Look in the business pages of a quality newspaper to see what is happening to computer companies.

3. Make a list of how your life is affected by computers, and what effects you think computers will have on your life over the next ten years.

that people do not want to work at home. Part of the value of work is the social element, meeting different people, forming friendships, gossiping, etc. and people do not want to give these up. Also many people find it difficult to work at home – there are distractions such as the family, and temptations such as daytime television!

There are also other problems. The very freedom of information on the Net means that parents can only exercise control by being in the room all the time their children are online. The much publicised cases of paedophile Internet stalking have led some parents to decide that the safest way to bring up children is to have no Internet connection. Some people are worried that they have to give credit card or bank details to shop on the Internet and that their details can be hacked into. This fear has been increased by the reaction of some banks to *phishing* (criminals using online bank accounts and pretending to be the bank to get confidential details from customers so they can use the account) – they have refused to reimburse customers losing money through giving out their details.

However, whatever individual complaints might be, there is no doubt that computers will continue to play a greater and greater part in industry and business, and so in everyone's lives.

EXAM QUESTION

This is an A2 essay question taken from Section B of the Unit 4 Specimen Paper in 2007.

> The growing use of CCTV cameras, computerised health records, the police DNA database, the monitoring of e-mails at work are just a few examples of the move towards what is sometimes called 'a surveillance society'.
>
> Explain the contribution of technology to the process of growing surveillance.
>
> Discuss the extent to which such technology is beneficial or excessively intrusive to the individual and society.

(25 marks)

EXAMINER'S ADVICE

- The first part of the question requires some (but not necessarily detailed and highly technical) commentary on areas such as Closed Circuit TV cameras, the highly ambitious National Health Service plans to computerise patients' health records, the police DNA database, monitoring of personal use of e-mails and the Internet by employees at work, as given in the question. The second part of the question requires a discussion about the concept of 'a surveillance society' – the benefits that this has brought about set against fears of a '*1984/Brave New World*' threat. In November 2006, Richard Thomas, the watchdog appointed by the government to protect people's privacy, warned that Britain is 'waking up to a surveillance society that is all around us'.

- Evidence for this is the 3.5 million profiles held on the national DNA database along with 6 million fingerprints; 4.2 million CCTV cameras (more than the rest of the EU put together), some fitted with zoom lenses and listening devices, 50 per cent of population of UK have a loyalty card; 8 million criminal record checks for jobs since 2002; 35 million vehicle number plates currently read every day; any individual may be captured on camera up to 300 times a day; 2 million motorists caught by speed cameras in 2004.

- DNA was discovered in the 1950s but the police DNA database (increasingly used to investigate 'cold cases') is a comparatively recent development. Everyone arrested (even if not subsequently charged) has to provide a DNA sample and, once on the database, samples cannot be removed. By April 2007, it was estimated that there were 3 million profiles on the police database, 20 per cent of these belonging to people of African-Caribbean origin.

- A key question to consider and on which you will have to have a view is how much surveillance is needed. People watch over each other for mutual care and protection, but the extent to which this might intrude on an individual's rights to privacy, by exposing personal information in an unauthorised or discriminatory manner is the issue. (e.g. American Muslims in particular may become subject to racial profiling and find it more difficult to obtain access to air travel).

- When you have thought about the issues and what ground you intend to cover, allow yourself no more than 30–40 minutes to write out your answer. Then compare your ideas with the notes provided on pages 275–276.

The application of maths

Much of the Maths you need for General Studies is based on what you learnt for GCSE. This unit gives you some of the basic techniques you will need. The focus in General Studies is on application and reasoning.

Mean, median, mode and range

The following were the scores in a golf tournament: 72, 86, 67, 94, 76, 82, 76, 69, 74, 76.

You find the *mean (average)* for the golf scores by adding together all the figures and dividing by the number of figures. This is 770 divided by 10 (the number of scores), giving a mean of 77. If you are given a table of statistics that gives the frequency of classes, you find the mid-value of each class (by halving it) and multiply by the frequency, add all those results together and divide by the number in the sample (see Table 12.1).

You find the *median* by putting the numbers into order of size, dividing the number of figures by 2 (essentially the middle value) and the median is the middle number. The golf scores put into order of size are: 67, 69, 72, 74, 76, 76, 76, 82, 86, 94. The fifth number is the middle number, so the median is 76.

The *mode* is the figure that occurs most frequently. In the golf scores, 76 occurs three times, but all the others only occur once, so the mode is 76. Sometimes a question will ask for the modal group rather than the mode, but it means the same.

The *range* is the difference between the lowest number and the highest number. In the golf scores, the highest number is 94, the lowest is 67, so the range is 27. Often you will need to find the interquartile range on a cumulative frequency graph (a graph where the frequencies of a statistics are added together as you go along). You do this by dividing the frequencies by 4 and plotting one-quarter and three-quarters. The interquartile range is the range between these.

There are some ideas you need to know about when interpreting these concepts. The bigger the range (especially the interquartile range), the more unreliable the mean is likely to be. If the range is large, the median is likely to be a more reliable figure than the mean. If the range is small, the mean is the most reliable figure. Interpreting statistics also requires you to think about who is using the figures and what they want them for, for example a shoe manufacturer will be more interested in the mode of shoe sizes than the mean (they will need to gear their production of shoes to the popularity of sizes).

Example

The table below illustrates the distance between home and the town centre of a group of 75 students and shows how to work out the mean distance.

Table 12.1 Mean distance between home and town centre for a group of 75 students (km)

Distance in km (d)	No of students (frequency, f)	Mid-interval value (MIV)	f × MIV
1 km or less	6	0.5	3.0
$1 < d \leq 2$	7	1.5	10.5
$2 < d \leq 3$	15	2.5	37.5
$3 < d \leq 4$	18	3.5	63.0
$4 < d \leq 5$	10	4.5	45.0
$5 < d \leq 6$	10	5.5	55.0
$6 < d \leq 7$	7	6.5	45.5
$7 < d \leq 8$	2	7.5	15.0
Total	75		274.5

Mean = 274.5 (mid-interval value frequency added together) ÷ 75 (total no. in sample) = 3.66 km.

Example

The graph below illustrates how to draw a cumulative frequency graph and calculate the interquartile range using the figures from example 1.

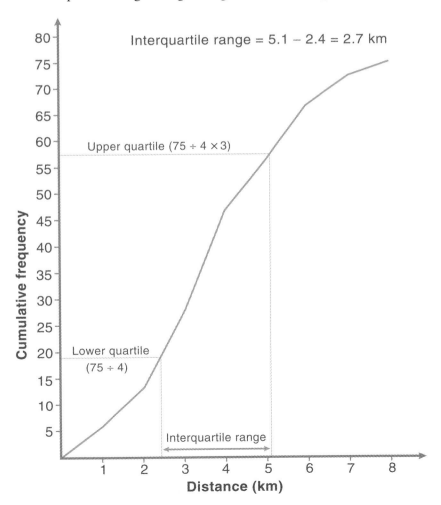

Figure 12.1 Cumulative frequency and calculation of the interquartile range

Scatter graphs

A scatter graph is a graph that simply records a set of results without putting them into classes or groups. If you can draw a line of best fit through the results, there is a correlation in the results. The *line of best fit* is a straight line that is closest to the majority of points on the graph. If the line of best fit goes up, there is a *positive correlation* (if one variable rises, the other does as well). If the line of fit goes down, there is a *negative correlation* (if one variable goes up, the other will go down). If you cannot draw a line of best fit, there is no correlation.

Lines of best fit can be used to predict what will happen on the other variable (see the example below).

Example

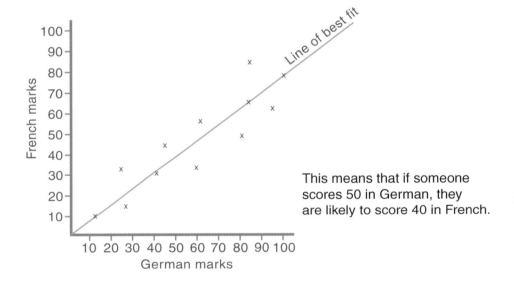

This means that if someone scores 50 in German, they are likely to score 40 in French.

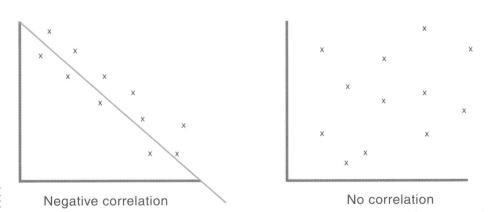

Figure 12.2 Lines of best fit

Negative correlation

No correlation

Calculating percentages

1 You are likely to be asked what percentage is represented by one of the figures in the tables. To do this, you work out the total number, then apply the formula:

$$\frac{(\text{figure you need} \times 100)}{\text{total number}}$$

For example, the percentage of golfers scoring 76 is: $\frac{3 \times 100}{10} = 30\%$

2 You may be asked to find a percentage difference. To do this, you work out the difference, multiply by 100 and divide by the original amount.

For example, a shopkeeper buys soap powder at £10 for five packets and sells it for £2.75 per packet. What is his percentage profit?

1000 ÷ 5 = 200 pence (the amount he pays for one packet),
275 − 200 = 75 (the profit per packet) × 100 ÷ 200 = 37.5%.

3 You may be asked to remove part of a percentage. To do this, you add the percentage you have to remove to 100, divide by the total and multiply by 100.

For example, if a computer costs £1175 including 17.5% VAT, what would be its price without VAT?

100 + 17.5 = 117.5; 1175 ÷ 117.5 × 100 = £1000.

4 You may be asked to find an original amount when a percentage has been taken off. To do this, you subtract that percentage from 100, divide the current amount by your answer and multiply by 100.

For example, a Playstation costs £76 in a 20% off sale. What was its price before the sale?

100 − 20 = 80; 76 ÷ 80 × 100 = £95.

5 You may be asked to work out compound interest. To do this, you add 100 to the annual interest, divide by 100 and store this in the memory of your calculator, then multiply by the capital (amount invested). You then keep multiplying by the stored number for the number of years of interest.

For example, what would £5000 be worth after 5 years if invested at compound interest of 6.5% per annum?

This is what you do on your calculator:

100 + 6.5 ÷ 100 STO M+ × 5000 × RCL M+
× RCL M+ × RCL M+ × RCL M+ = £6850.43.

If you are asked for the amount of interest, you simply subtract the amount invested from your calculator answer.

6 If you are asked to calculate depreciation, it is a very similar calculation to compound interest. You subtract the percentage depreciation from 100 and divide the answer by 100, store this in the memory, multiply by the initial value, then multiply by the stored number for every year of depreciation.

For example, if a car bought for £15,000 depreciates at 10% a year, what will its value be after five years?

This is what you do on your calculator:

$$100 - 10 \div 100 \text{ STO M+} \times 15\,000 \times \text{RCL M+} \times \text{RCL M+}$$
$$\times \text{RCL M+} \times \text{RCL M+} = £8857.35.$$

Calculating probability

Any probability can be written as a decimal between 0 and 1 where 0 is impossible and 1 is certain. You work out the probability by dividing the chance by the total.

For example, the probability of throwing a six when you throw a die is 1 in 6 (there are six numbers and only one six); $1 \div 6 = 0.17$ probability.

When you have two possible outcomes you multiply the relevant outcomes to find the probability.

For example, Rebecca has a 2 in 3 chance of winning the darts competition and a 3 in 4 chance of winning the dominoes competition. What is the probability of her winning both competitions?

$$2 \div 3 \times 3 \div 4 = 0.5.$$

What is the probability that Rebecca will win only one of the competitions? She has a 2 in 3 chance of winning the darts and a 1 in 4 chance of not winning the dominoes; she has a 3 in 4 chance of winning the dominoes and a 1 in 3 chance of not winning the darts. So what are her chances of only winning one event?

What you put into your calculator:

$$(2 \div 3 \times 1 \div 4) + (3 \div 4 \times 1 \div 3) = 0.4167.$$

Calculating volumes

The basic formula for calculating volume is height × length × width. However, prisms cause problems because the volume is the area of the cross-section multiplied by the length.

The *volume of a cylindrical prism* is worked out by multiplying the area of the circle at the end of the cylinder by the height of the cylinder:

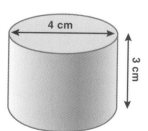

Volume = 2×2 (radius squared) $\times \pi \times 3 = 37.699$ cm^3 (cubic centimetres).

This means that, if you are given the volume and radius, you can work out the depth. For example, how deep is the water in a cylinder of diameter 4 cm if there is 37.699 ml of water in the cylinder?

$$37.699 \div (2 \times 2 \times \pi) = 3 \text{ cm, so the depth is 3 cm}$$
$$(1 \text{ ml} = 1 \text{ cm}^3 \text{ and } 1000 \text{ cm}^3 = 1 \text{ litre}).$$

The *volume of a triangular prism* is worked out by finding the area of the cross-section triangle and multiplying by the length.

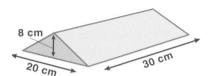

Volume = 10×8 (half the base of the triangle multiplied by the height to get the area of the triangle) $\times 30$ (the length) = 2400 cm³.

Mass is the weight of an object, *density* is the weight per item of length.

$$Mass = \text{volume density}$$
$$Density = \text{mass volume}$$
$$Volume = \text{mass density}$$

Conversions

Imperial measures	Metric measures
1 lb = 454 g	1 kg = 2.2 lbs
1 ton = 1 tonne	1 tonne = 1 ton
1 inch = 2.5 cm	1 cm = 0.4 inches
1 foot = 30 cm	1 metre = 1.1 yards
1 yard = 0.9 m	1 km = 0.625 miles
1 mile = 1.6 km	1 litre = 1.75 pints
1 pint = 0.5625 litres	1 litre = 0.22 gallons
1 gallon = 4.5 litres	

To convert imperial to metric:

- If you are given the imperial chart, multiply the imperial by the metric. For example, how many litres are there in 3 pints of beer? Answer: 1.6875 litres (3×0.5625).
- If you are given the metric chart divide the imperial measure by the imperial equivalent. For example, how many metres are there in 3 yards? Answer: 2.73 ($3 \div 1.1$).

To convert metric to imperial:

- If you are given the imperial chart, divide the metric by the metric equivalent. For example, how many pints are there in 3 litres? Answer: 5.33 ($3 \div 0.5625$).
- If you are given the metric chart, multiply the metric by the imperial. For example, how many yards are there in 3 metres? Answer: 3.3 (3×1.1).

The same processes can be used in converting currencies.

Exchange rate: £1 = 1.9358 dollars, 1.4464 euros, 198.36 yen

Using the above exchange rate:

How many pounds would you get for 30 dollars? Answer: 30 ÷ 1.9358 = £15.50

How many euros would you get for £30? Answer: 30 × 1.4464 = 43.39 euros

How many dollars would you get for 500 yen? Answer: convert the yen into pounds (500 ÷ 198.36), then convert the answer into dollars (2.52 × 1.9358) = 4.88 dollars

Ratio

Ratios are best thought of as fractions – the ratios are the numerators and the numbers added together are the denominators.

For example, Jamie, Sunita and Alice are in a lottery syndicate. Jamie buys 3 tickets, Sunita buys 2 tickets and Alice buys 5 tickets. If they win £100,000, how much will each receive? Answer: Jamie will receive 3 ÷ 10, Sunita 2 ÷ 10, Alice 5 ÷ 10, so dividing by the denominator and multiplying by the numerator gives £30,000 for Jamie, £20,000 for Sunita and £50,000 for Alice.

If the question asks for one ratio in terms of another, then you use the ratio given and divide by it, then multiply by the ratio you need.

For example, concrete is made by mixing sand, gravel and cement in the ratio 2:3:1. If I use 20 cubic metres of sand, how much gravel will I need? Answer: 20 ÷ 2 = 10, 10 × 3 = 30 cubic metres of gravel

Scale

Scale is the same as ratio. It is used to make drawings or maps of large things. To make a scale drawing, you have to work out a ratio based on the same measurements. This means that you have to change metres and kilometres into cms. There are 100 cm in 1 metre and 100,000 cm in 1 kilometre.

To work out how many cm there are in the drawing by looking at the real, you make the real into cm and then divide by the largest ratio.

For example, on a scale of 1:50,000 1 km is 2 cm (100,000 divided by 50,000 = 2).

To work out the real from the drawing, multiply the cm by the larger ration and then divide by 100 to change to metres or 100,000 to change to kilometres.

For example, how far is it from Sydney to Perth? Answer:

The distance on the map is 16.5 cm, the scale is 1:20,000,000

20,000,000 divided by 100,000 = 200 therefore 1 cm = 200 km.

200 × 16.5 = 3300

So the distance from Sydney to Perth is 3300 km.

Bearings

Bearings are based on 360 degrees in a circle.

North is	000
East is	090
South is	180
West is	270

You always write bearings as three numbers, so if the number is less than 100, you use 0 or 00 at the beginning. Whenever you work out the bearing, you make sure you are facing North.

For example, you are standing on the end of a pier when you spot a boat on a bearing of 123 degrees, your friend is standing 6 kilometres due South of you and sees the boat on a bearing of 065 degrees. Draw an accurate scale drawing showing this information.

Answer:

- Choose an appropriate scale of 1 cm per kilometre.
- Draw a vertical 6 cm line labelling the top, self, and the bottom, friend (due South of you).
- Use your protractor to measure 123 degrees from the top point and draw a line along that measurement.
- Use your protractor to measure 65 degrees from the bottom point and draw a line along that measurement.
- Label the point where the two lines cross, boat.

Inequalities

Inequalities are based on the signs:

>	greater than
<	less than
>=	equal to or more than
<=	equal to or less than

Therefore:

$-5 > x < 0$ means that x is -1 or -2 or -3 or -4

$3 >= x <= 5$ means that x is 3, or 4, or 5

If you are asked to solve an inequality, you treat it as a normal algebra equation until you write your answer.

For example, solve the inequality $15x - 2 <= 11x + 14$.

Answer: $15x - 11x = 14 + 2$, $4x = 16$, $x = 4$

So x is equal to or less than 4.

3. Scarlett Rousers and Grace Ox make clothes together. The probability of Scarlett producing a sub-standard item is 0.1 and the probability of Grace producing a sub-standard item is 0.3.
   (a) What is the probability that they will both produce a sub-standard item?
   (b) In a consignment of 900 garments produced by them both, how many will have flaws?

4. A firm wants to start manufacturing televisions. This involves the following activities:
   (a) order components
   (b) order packing
   (c) manufacture parts
   (d) set up testing procedures
   (e) assemble sets
   (f) test sets
   (g) pack sets
   (h) despatch sets to the wholesaler.
Draw a critical path network for this process.

Networks (critical path analysis)

This is a way of diagramming a process (such as manufacturing a product or organising an event) so that you can work out things such as the shortest time it will take for the product to reach the shops (critical path). It is based on nodes (a stage in the process), prerequisites (what has to happen before a node is reached) and activities (paths between the nodes).

For example, a firm wants to start manufacturing MP3 players. This will involve the following activities as shown in Figure 12.3:

A   order components
B   components delivered
C   manufacture sets
D   set up testing procedures
E   test sets
F   pack sets
G   deliver sets.

If each activity after A takes two days, what is the soonest that the MP3 players can be in the shops? Answer: Ten days (setting up testing procedures is off the critical path).

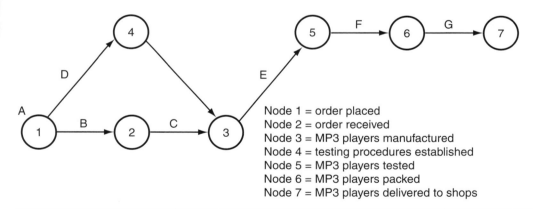

Node 1 = order placed
Node 2 = order received
Node 3 = MP3 players manufactured
Node 4 = testing procedures established
Node 5 = MP3 players tested
Node 6 = MP3 players packed
Node 7 = MP3 players delivered to shops

Figure 12.3 The critical path of the manufacture of MP3 players

For the questions which follow, choose the answer A, B, C or D which you think fits best. Each of the questions is worth one mark.

1   A mobile phone company used to have a tariff which charged customers 25p per minute for the first two minutes of calls of any one day, and 15p per minute for any further use that day. Calls were charged by the second. What was the cost for using the phone for 4 minutes 20 seconds on one day?
   A   65p
   B   66p
   C   83p
   D   85p

2   The charge for one day's use was £1.76. How long was the phone used for on this day?
   A   8 min 40 sec
   B   10 min 24 sec
   C   10 min 40 sec
   D   11 min 44 sec

3   A type of pyramid is made of blocks as shown so that there are 2 blocks on the top layer, 6 blocks on the second layer, 12 blocks on the third layer, 20 blocks on the fourth layer and so on.

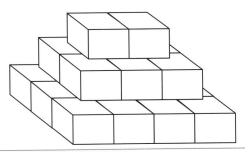

Figure 12.4

Continuing the same pattern, how many blocks will be in the nth layer?
   A $2n$
   B $4n - 2$
   C $n^2 + n$
   D $2n^2$

4   The figure shows a gate made from metal rods. The gate measures 1.2 m by 85 cm.

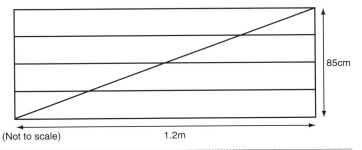

(Not to scale)   1.2m

Figure 12.5

The length of metal, correct to the nearest 10cm, needed to make the gate is
   A   7.7 m
   B   9.1 m
   C   9.2 m
   D   9.9 m

5   After taking part in a competition, each contestant was given a grade from 1 (the lowest) to 6 (the highest). The table shows the results of the competition.

Grade	1	2	3	4	5	6
No. of contestants	10	15	25	20	15	5

What is the probability that a randomly chosen contestant achieved a grade higher than the modal grade?
   A $\frac{4}{9}$
   B $\frac{1}{2}$
   C $\frac{5}{9}$
   D $\frac{13}{18}$

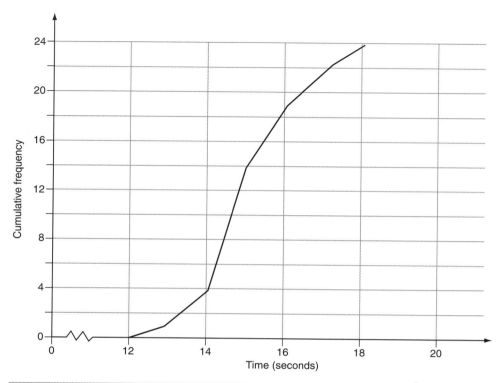

Figure 12.6

6 The cumulative frequency graph (Figure 12.6) shows the time taken by each pupil in a class to run 100 metres.

Which time interval includes the result for the slowest member of the class?
A   11–12 seconds
B   12–13 seconds
C   17–18 seconds
D   23–24 seconds

7 What is the approximate value for the interquartile range of the times?
A   1.5 seconds
B   3 seconds
C   6 seconds
D   12 seconds

8 Statement 1
The median time of the fastest 12 students is approximately half the median time for the whole class.
Statement 2
The range of times for the fastest 12 students is approximately half the range of times for the whole class.

Which of the above statements is/are correct?
A   Both 1 and 2
B   1 only
C   2 only
D   Neither 1 nor 2

9 A tourist went to Australia with £1000 to spend. The exchange rate was £1 = A$2.681. He spent A$1500. He then went to New Zealand where the exchange rate was £1 = NZ$3.217. The number of NZ$ he had to spend was
A   367
B   984
C   1417
D   3799

10 The volume, V, of a sphere of radius r is given by
$V = \frac{4}{3}\pi r^3$

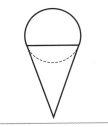

Figure 12.7

The volume of ice-cream needed to fill a cone is modelled by a sphere of diameter 5 cm. The number of such cones which can be filled from 1 litre of ice-cream is approximately

A 2
B 15
C 65
D 520

11 On a ride at a theme park a car performs a vertical loop as shown below.

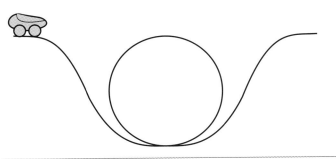

Figure 12.8

Which graph in Figure 2.9 best shows the speed of the car during the ride?

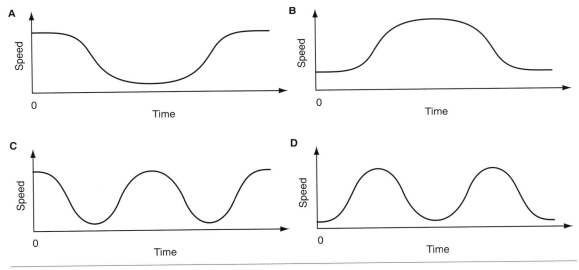

Figure 12.9

12 The times 60 customers spent waiting in the queue for the ride are shown in the table.

Time in queue	Number of customers
Up to 10 minutes	2
10 minutes up to 20 minutes	7
20 minutes up to 30 minutes	18
30 minutes up to 60 minutes	33
Over 60 minutes	0

The best estimate of the mean waiting time is

A   25 minutes.
B   30 minutes.
C   35 minutes.
D   40 minutes.

EXAMINER'S ADVICE

- All these questions are taken from Section 2 of the AQA AS Unit 2 test for May 2003. In the new exam from 2009 onwards the mathematical questions will be included as part of the science comprehension in Section A of Unit 2. They will only cover the kind of mathematical application relevant to the topic chosen for the test. (See the exam questions for Units 1, 2, 4 and 5 for the science questions from the same paper.)
- The 12 questions here are representative of the range you might get in the exam and you should aim to complete them in about 15 minutes.
- Many of the questions are about your understanding of a range of mathematical principles and techniques which you studied up to GCSE (like Question 4 where you need to use Pythagoras' theorem). Some of the key topics are covered earlier in the unit but it is important to recognise that the questions are not aimed at subject specialists and many are just about your ability to carry out calculations correctly in a logical manner (like Questions 1, 2, 8), to analyse a problem or process systematically (Questions 3 and 11) and to draw logical conclusions (Question 12).
- The answers are given on page 276.

Mechanical and spatial relations

The skills involved in mechanical and spatial relations are those needed in everyday life when trying to make sense of an IKEA furniture flat pack instruction sheet, finding a safe way off the moors, adjusting a lawn mower blade, rewiring a house, placing a water feature in the garden or even for those rare gifted individuals such as Galileo who tried to make sense of the motion of Jupiter's moons, or Eratosthenes who extrapolated from his knowledge of the Sun's shadow to find the measurement of the Earth's circumference. Unfortunately, as far as we know, neither man had the benefit of General Studies, but they were obviously supreme problem solvers and it is an aim of the examination to produce good flexible problem solvers in life.

Galileo and astronomy

Galileo may be familiar to you. He made a telescope in Venice in 1609 with an improved magnification and turned it on the stars. He did, for the first time, what we think of as practical science. He built the apparatus, did the experiment, and published the results in a book called *The Starry Messenger*. He was able to show, to anyone who cared to look, that the Ptolemaic heaven simply would not work. Ptolemy was an ancient Greek astronomer who proposed that the Sun and planets circled the Earth – a view which was not challenged until Renaissance figures such as Tycho Brahe, Nicholas Copernicus and Galileo appeared on the scene.

Eratosthenes and astronomy

It was Eratosthenes, whose sieve for prime numbers you may remember from Key Stage 3 Mathematics, who as director of the great library in Alexandria in Egypt 2200 years ago, read about a place called Syene at the first cataract of the Nile. He read that at Syene on 21 June each year, the longest day of the year or the summer solstice, vertical sticks cast no shadows. A reflection of the Sun could be seen at the bottom of a deep well there. The Sun was directly overhead! Eratosthenes was a scientist and his thoughts changed the world. He wondered if a stick in Alexandria would cast no shadow at exactly the same moment as a stick in Syene. He found that a stick in Alexandria cast a substantial shadow at noon on 21 June. If there had been no shadow, might he have reasonably concluded that the Earth was flat? He decided that the Earth must be curved. The clue was to realise that the Sun's rays could be considered to be parallel because the Sun was so far away. The angle between the direction of sunlight and the stick at Alexandria was seven degrees and the distance from

DID YOU KNOW?

Naismith's Rule?
Naismith was a prominent engineer who walked in Scotland in the late 1800s and who was aware that a method of estimating walking time was needed.

His formula was *three miles per hour plus half an hour for every thousand feet climbed.*

This involves the concept of average walking speed applied to hilly terrain. It has been converted to SI units as follows:

Allow between *two and five kilometres per hour and add one minute for each ten metres climbed* (contours are usually shown in ten-metre gaps). This is the sort of idea that might be applied in a series of questions about a map.

From a personal navigation point of view, you ought to be aware of your average walking speed. If not, see how long it takes you to walk a mile and use eight kilometres as equivalent to five miles to convert to SI units. Also, how many paces do you take to walk one hundred metres on the flat? Use your school/college athletics track to find out. This is information you might need using your map to keep track of your whereabouts in a mist.

Activities

1. Ask your teacher if you could open up a manual gearbox to see how it works, but be careful! It could be messy if the oil is not removed first.

2. Many primary schools make cam-operated toys as part of technology education. If you missed this activity, ask a DT teacher to explain what cams are. Try making some yourself!

3. There is a three dimensional form of the game *Connect Four* or *Four in a Row*. Play it with a friend and it will help you to think in three dimensions and to think strategically.

4. Browse the website www.howstuffworks.com This has many explanations of how devices work with some wonderful and helpful animated sequences.

5. You are not too old to play with technical Lego or Meccano sets.

6. Read a map. Try and visualise the lie of the land from the map before seeing the reality. Convert map distances to actual distances. How do you know whether you are climbing or descending?

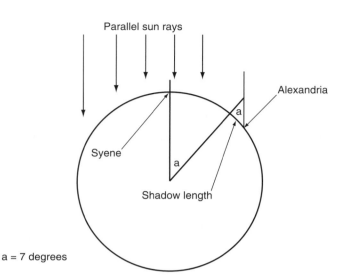

a = 7 degrees

Figure 13.1 Eratosthenes' calculation

Alexandria to Syene was 800 kilometres – Eratosthenes hired a man to pace it out. So, the calculation of the Earth's circumference is a straightforward piece of geometry:

$$\frac{7}{360} = \frac{800}{C}$$

This gives a value of C of approximately 40,000 km. Remarkably, this is 'correct' to within a few per cent.

The examination

From a spatial point of view, the skills that are needed cover the extent to which you are able to visualise and interpret two- and three-dimensional representations such as geometrical shapes and solids, maps, weather charts, contours, engineering or technical drawings, perspective views and photographs.

Mechanically, the relationship between moving parts in simple devices such as levers, gears, pulleys, pumps and other simple mechanisms and machines is sought. Where underpinning or related knowledge is needed, it will be assumed that you are familiar with the content of the GCSE Double Science. Any additional knowledge will be given in the question. For *spatial* items, concepts such as scale, similarity, congruence, reflection, line and rotational symmetry, plan, elevation and net will be assumed and for *mechanical* items, you should know about concepts such as force, moment of a force, velocity, acceleration, angular speed, pressure, energy, work and power. Due to the widespread use of digital clocks students today may not be as familiar as their elders with 'clockwise' and 'anticlockwise' but these terms are likely to appear in questions.

Preparation

It is difficult to teach this unit in practice and the best way to prepare for the examination is to look at papers from previous years in conjunction with the examiner's report and to try and work out why a particular answer is correct. You will note from the examples given that it may be possible to improve your chances by sensible elimination of some of the four options given. Also, some activities are suggested in the activities box that may help you to develop your thinking in an appropriate way.

Acceleration the rate of change of the velocity of a moving body. Of particular note is a body moving at constant speed in a circle. The direction of the velocity is changing continuously, the magnitude is constant, so there is an acceleration towards the centre of the circle

Angular speed in a circle. As radial distance from the centre increases the linear speed increases proportionately

Clockwise and anticlockwise need a little care as it depends where you are looking from. Someone inside the clock looking out will see it differently from someone outside looking in!

Congruence exists between objects when they are exactly the same shape and size

Elevation is similar to a plan but the viewing point this time is from the front, side or back of the original

Energy the capacity for doing work. Mechanical – kinetic, gravitational potential. Electrical, chemical, light, thermal are different forms of energy

Force any influence that changes the velocity of an object. It is a vector quantity having both magnitude and direction. Its SI unit is the newton

Moment of a force a measure of the turning force or torque produced by a force acting on a body. It is equal to the product of the force and the perpendicular distance of its line of action to the pivot. Its SI unit is the newton metre. *The Principle of Moments* states that anticlockwise moments equal clockwise moments when a body is in equilibrium – think of a see-saw

Net is a plane shape composed of individual common geometrical shapes showing how they can be folded to make the original solid

Plan is a two-dimensional view of a solid as if viewed directly from above. Edges between plane (flat) surfaces which can be seen from above are shown as straight lines in the plan and hidden edges are shown as dotted lines

Power the rate of doing work and measured in joules/second which is equivalent to a watt

Pressure the force acting normally per unit area exerted by a fluid or gas. Atmospheric pressure at sea level is due to the weight of the air above

Reflection occurs when each point of a shape or object is mapped to a corresponding point that is an equal distance from, and at right angles to, a mirror line for shapes or a mirror plane for three-dimensional objects

Scale a fixed ratio that represents the relationship between a drawing or model and the real object. For example a map scale of 1:50,000 shows that 1 mm on the map represents 50,000 mm in reality – this is the same as 2 cm to 1 km

Similarity exists when objects are the same shape but different sizes

Symmetry exists when a shape can be halved or turned in such a way that it fits exactly onto itself. Line symmetry is when a shape can be halved, e.g. a butterfly or the letter A and rotational symmetry is when the shape can be turned to fit exactly onto itself, e.g. a rectangle has rotational symmetry of order two, an equilateral triangle is of order three

Velocity speed of an object in a given direction. It is a vector quantity since its direction is important as well as its magnitude or speed

Work a measure of the result of transferring energy from one system to another to cause an object to move. The product of a force and the distance moved by an object in the direction of the force. The SI unit of work is the joule

Practice – 1950s jukebox

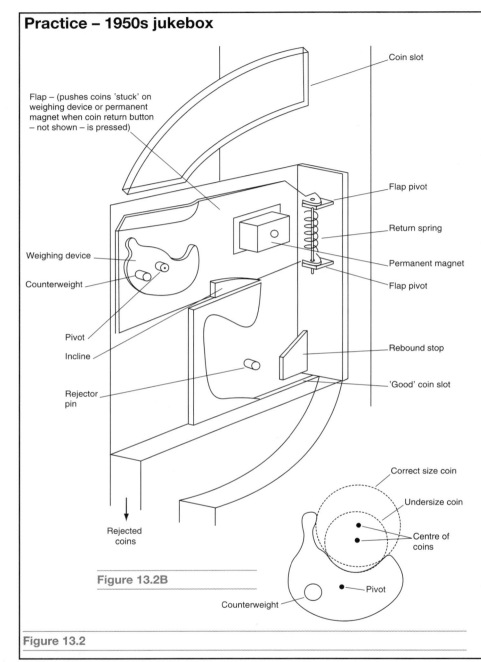

Flap – (pushes coins 'stuck' on weighing device or permanent magnet when coin return button – not shown – is pressed)

Weighing device

Counterweight

Pivot

Incline

Rejector pin

Coin slot

Flap pivot

Return spring

Permanent magnet

Flap pivot

Rebound stop

'Good' coin slot

Rejected coins

Correct size coin

Undersize coin

Centre of coins

Pivot

Counterweight

Figure 13.2B

Figure 13.2

When a coin is deposited in the machine a series of tests is conducted to see if it is counterfeit. Modern devices have more sophisticated discrimination and can even give change, but a 1950s jukebox would have a separate slot and corresponding set of checking mechanisms for each type of coin allowed. In a 1950s machine the first check is at the slot itself which disallows coins of excessive thickness or diameter. A weighing device will tip only if the coin is of at least the correct weight. Any undersize coins that have the right weight will fail to tip the device (Figure 13.2B) because the moment of its weight will not be large enough and it will be rejected when the coin return button is pressed. The effect of pressing this button is to swing the side flap to one side and push any coins caught by the weighing device into a coin return channel. After the weight check, the coins runs through the field of a permanent magnet which will retain the coin or let it pass depending on its composition. Retained coins here are released when the coin return button is pressed. The final check is literally a hurdle. A valid coin will have just the required kinetic energy to jump the rejector pin and get into the 'good' coin slot. Coins which are too slow or too fast at this point will be rejected.

1 After testing the thickness and diameter, the correct order of testing coin properties is
   A weight, kinetic energy, composition.
   B density, composition, kinetic energy.
   C weight, kinetic energy, density.
   D weight, composition, kinetic energy.

2 An undersized coin of the correct weight will fail to tip the weighing mechanism device (Figure 13.2B) because
   A its kinetic energy is insufficient.
   B its linear momentum is insufficient.
   C its centre of gravity is too close to the pivot.
   D its density is insufficient.

If a counterfeit coin is put into the machine it will be rejected for one of the following reasons:
A   it fails to tip the weighing device.
B   it is attracted to the magnet.
C   it does not roll fast enough to clear the rejector pin.
D   it is rolling too fast as it approaches the rejector pin.

Taking into account the order of testing, select the reason from A–D above, to explain why a counterfeit coin, of the same thickness and diameter as a valid cupronickel coin, would be rejected if it were made of

3   lead (which is denser than cupronickel).
4   iron (which is less dense than cupronickel).
5   a steel alloy (which has the same density as cupronickel).

Practice – elevation, section and contours

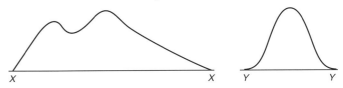

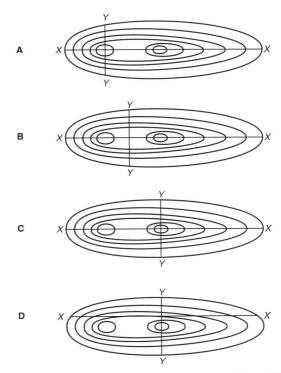

Figure 13.3

> **EXAMINER'S ADVICE**
> * Question 1. The fact that three of these begin with 'weight' might suggest you ignore B. A glance at the text and diagram tells us that kinetic energy is the last test so you can further ignore A and C leaving D as the correct key.)
> * Question 2. Kinetic energy and momentum are features of moving bodies and if we assume that this is a statics problem as shown in Figure 13.2B, we are left with either C or D as the correct answer. Density is not relevant – it is the weight of the coin that is important here. The problem is whether the moment of the coin's weight is enough to tip the device, so this leads you to C.
> * Question 3. The lead coin has the correct volume but it will be heavier than a valid coin so it will tip the weighing device; it is not magnetic so it will reach the rejector pin but its gravitational potential energy will be too high as it rolls down the incline giving it a kinetic enery which will be too high as it reaches the rejector pin leading to D as the correct answer.
> * In Question 4 the iron coin has the correct volume but will be too light to tip the weighing device, so A is the correct answer.
> * In Question 5 the coin will tip the weighing device but it is magnetic and will not get passed the magnet, so B is the correct answer.)

> **EXAMINER'S ADVICE**
> Figure 13.3 shows a question from the AQA January 2003 paper that is obviously spatial in nature, combining the ideas of elevation, section and contours. The four optional answers are plan views showing contours of the two hills whose elevations are shown as sections at right angles to each other. In Answers A and B the Y–Y section is too tall which leaves C or D as the correct answer. Answer D would not show the twin peaks needed for the X–X section, so the correct answer is C.

Practice – gears

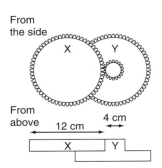

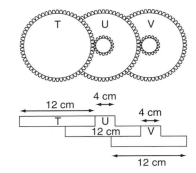

For every one rotation of gear X, gear Y rotates three times. The gear ratio of the train is 3:1 (Diameter of X: Diameter of Y).

Figure 13.4 A gear train of two gears

From the side

From above

For every one rotation of gear T, gear U rotates three times and gear V rotates nine times. The gear ratio of the train is 9:1.

Figure 13.5 A gear train of three gears

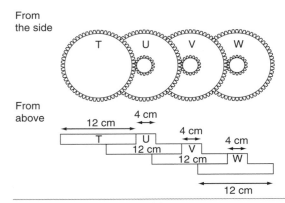

Figure 13.6 A gear train of four gears

1 The gear ratio of the four-gear train is
A   3:1.
B   9:1.
C   27:1.
D   81:1.

2 If the speed of rotation of Gear U is 20 revolutions per minute (rpm), the speed of gear W will be
A   20 rpm.
B   60 rpm.
C   180 rpm.
D   360 rpm.

3 The number of rotations of gear T needed to make gear V turn 144 times is
A   8.
B   16.
C   32.
D   64.

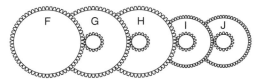

Figure 13.7 A gear train of five gears

4 If gear H is rotating clockwise then
A   all gears are rotating clockwise.
B   F is anti-clockwise.
C   F and J are anti-clockwise.
D   G and I are anti-clockwise.

EXAMINER'S ADVICE

Figures 13.4, 13.5 and 13.6 give information on gears, obviously a mechanical topic, from the AQA June 2002 paper. Question 1 follows on from the information given alongside Figures 13.4 and 13.5 giving a gear ratio of 27:1 so answer C is correct. Question 2 follows a similar line of reasoning to give a speed multiplier of 9 with an answer of 180 rpm – answer C. Question 3 is based on a speed multiplier of 9 giving an answer of 144/9 = 16 which is answer B. Finally, use the knowledge that adjacent cogs rotate in opposite directions – so the answer is D (G and I).

EXAM QUESTIONS

13

Here are some spatial questions from the AQA June 2004 paper on *Tides*. Note that Question 2 is of a slightly different type where a combination of options is required for the correct answer.

Figure 13.8 and Table 13.1 were obtained from the website of the UK Hydrographic Office.

Every 12 hours or so, the sea falls in a low tide then rises again in a high tide. Tides are caused by the way the moon's gravity pulls the water in the ocean into an egg shape around the Earth, creating a bulge on each side of the Earth.

High/Low Waters (The figures are for the tides at the mouth of the Tees.)

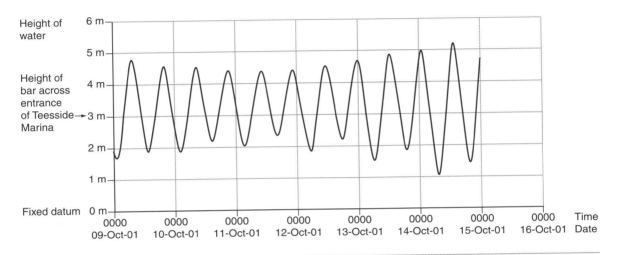

Figure 13.8 River Tees Entrance

09 Oct 2001		
	time	height
high	07:33 20.03	4.7 m 4.6 m
low	01:21 13.44	1.7 m 1.9 m

10 Oct 2001		
	time	height
high	08:40 21.13	4.5 m 4.4 m
low	02:18 14.50	1.9 m 2.2 m

11 Oct 2001		
	time	height
high	10:05 22.35	4.4 m 4.4 m
low	03:41 16.27	2.0 m 2.3 m

12 Oct 2001		
	time	height
high	11:05 23.46	4.5 m 4.6 m
low	05:30 17.50	1.7 m 2.1 m

13 Oct 2001		
	time	height
high	12:45	4.8 m
low	06:38 19.04	1.5 m 1.8 m

14 Oct 2001		
	time	height
high	01:02 13.42	5.0 m 5.2 m
low	07:39 20.00	1.0 m 1.4 m

15 Oct 2001		
	time	height
high	01:55 14.30	5.4 m 5.5 m
low	08:30 20.48	0.6 m 1.1 m

Table 13.1 River Tees entrance. From midnight local time

1   Using the data in Table 13.1, 15 October would look like which of the following?

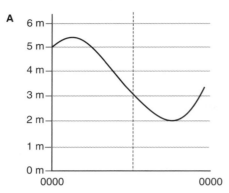
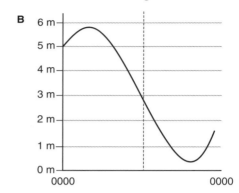
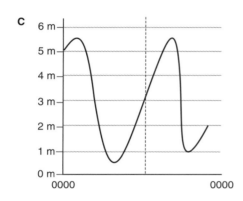
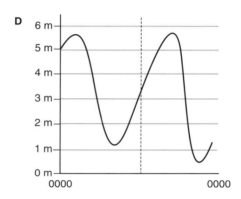

Figure 13.9

2   During the week, which of the following trends were observed?
   1   The heights of successive high tides were gradually decreasing and then increasing.
   2   The heights of successive low tides were gradually increasing and then decreasing.
   3   The heights of the first low tide of the day were gradually increasing then decreasing.
   4   The heights of the second low tide of the day were gradually increasing then decreasing.

   Answer
   A   if 1, 2 and 3 only are correct.
   B   if 2, 3 and 4 only are correct.
   C   if 1, 3 and 4 only are correct.
   D   if 1, 2 and 4 only are correct.

3   The morning high tide at the River Tees Entrance on 16 October would be at approximately
   A   1.00 a.m.
   B   3.00 a.m.
   C   9.00 a.m.
   D   11.00 a.m.

4   There is only one high tide on 13 October because
   A   the cyclical time between successive high tides is greater than 12 hours.
   B   the moon is new.
   C   this is a characteristic feature on 13th day of every month.
   D   an off shore wind is forecast.

5   An underwater barrier, a bar, at a height of 3 metres
(Figure 13.8) is built across the entrance to the
Teesside Yachting Marina to stop each of the
following **except**
    A   dangerous currents entering the marina.
    B   yachts with large keels entering the marina.
    C   trawling for fish on entering or leaving the
        marina.
    D   yachts becoming grounded when the tide goes
        out.

6   The tidal flow of water slows down the Earth's
    rotation.

    The day length is increasing ⅟₁₀₀₀ seconds every
    century.

    If slowing down continues at this rate, days will be
    twice as long in $60 \times 60 \times 24 \times 100 \times 1000$
    A   seconds.
    B   hours.
    C   days.
    D   years.

7   The diagram (Figure 13.10) shows how we always
    see only one side of the moon from Earth because
    the moon goes around its orbit once every 27⅓ days.
    A moon day (the time from one sunrise to the next)
    lasts
    A   one Earth day.
    B   27⅓ Earth days.
    C   one Earth year.
    D   forever.

8   Tidal charts are vital for mariners for which of the
    following reasons?
    1   assessing risk of grounding when anchored
    2   weather prediction
    3   avoiding reefs
    4   clearing the bar when entering a marina

    Answer
    A   if 1, 2 and 3 only are correct.
    B   if 1, 3 and 4 only are correct.
    C   if 1, 2 and 4 only are correct.
    D   if 2, 3 and 4 only are correct.

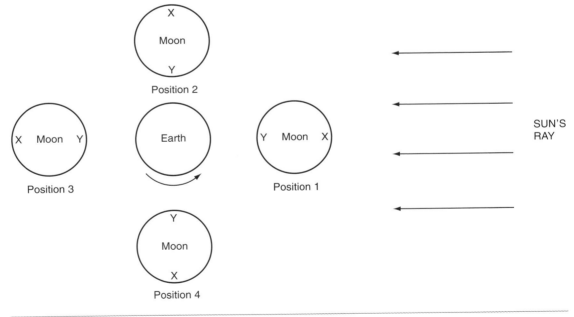

Figure 13.10

EXAMINER'S ADVICE

- In the new exam from 2009 onwards these questions will be included as part of the science comprehension in Section A of Unit 2. They will only cover scenarios relevant to the topic chosen for the test, so there will not be many of them in any one test.
- You should aim to complete the eight questions here in about 20 minutes, allowing 10 minutes to study the data and just over 1 minute per question.
- Most of the questions test simply your analytical, logical and problem-solving powers. In this particular case, they are testing your ability to extrapolate data in Question 1, to move from data in one form (graph) to another (descriptive language or table) in Questions 2 and 3, to make deductions and draw logical conclusions in Questions 4, 5 and 8, and occasionally to perform relevant calculations, as in Question 6. Other sorts of questions test your ability to move from two to three dimensions and back or to envisage how a system would actually work in practice (Question 7 is a typical example of this).
- Many of these questions appear more complicated and challenging at first sight than they actually are. Generally, the scores are quite high and the important thing is not to give up on them. Perseverance is definitely rewarded, even if it makes your brain hurt a bit.
- The answers are given on page 276.

The relationship between science and culture

Examples of the relationship

Printing

One of the most important impacts of technology on culture has been printing.
Printing enabled the rise of literature (especially novels) and such developments as
newspapers. It can be argued that printing was the major development of the second
millennium, as it allowed ideas and information to spread rapidly. When books had to
be written by hand, it was easy to prevent information from spreading, but it was
almost impossible after the invention of the printing press. The Reformation could
not have happened without printing, and it is possible that the scientific revolution
would not have occurred either.

Music

Science has had some major effects on music, not only in such things as the invention
of the piano (around the middle of the eighteenth century), but also such things as
amplifiers, electronic instruments, synthesisers, etc. Perhaps the major effect was the
invention of the gramophone. This was the musical equivalent of printing. Prior to
the record, people could only hear live performances where audiences would be
measured in thousands at most – after the record, audiences were measured in
millions. Of course, the music industry has also been affected by the invention of
radio, television and video – what effect has the invention of video had on the
promotion of popular music?

Theatre, opera and ballet

Theatre, opera and the ballet have all been affected by scientific advances in
construction, lighting and design, which enable a much wider range of staging and
special effects (the special effects that science has given to the cinema, for example *Star
Wars* and the Bond films have been adapted for use in theatres). It was thought that the
scientific inventions of film and television would kill off live theatre, but this has not
been the case. In fact, just as television has improved and popularised film (investigate
how many great British films have been produced by Channel 4 television), so both
television and film encourage people to go to the theatre. (How many TV soap stars
appear in Christmas pantos at the theatre?) All theatres and live music shows now use
computers, especially to control the lighting and other special effects.

Art

Art has always been affected by science. It was the discovery of oil paints that led to
the great revolution in painting in the fifteenth century. The invention of

Rotten science?

Many artists see aesthetic value in the discoveries of science. A sculptor, Rachel Chapman, and a microbiologist, Dr Jane Nicklin, worked together in 1999 to create a living work of art. 1,040 agar-filled petri dishes were filled with mould cultures commonly found growing on domestic foodstuffs and arranged to create a palette of textures and colours. The moulds were grown in the biology labs of Birkbeck College, London University and timed to be incorporated into the sculpture so that the colours were in artistic order, yet constantly changing. They called their work of art, Sapros.

The exhibition was very successful. Of the relationship between science and the arts, Rachel Chapman said, 'A lot of the things you do as an artist are science-based, but most artists have no understanding of it at all. Physics and chemistry come into play when we manipulate the composition of paints or the reactions of materials under different stimuli.' Dr Jane Nicklin said, 'The more I understand art, the more comfortable I feel with some of the other things I do. In both ecology and physics, balance and the beauty of an idea are important concepts.' (*Birkbeck College Magazine*, June 1999).

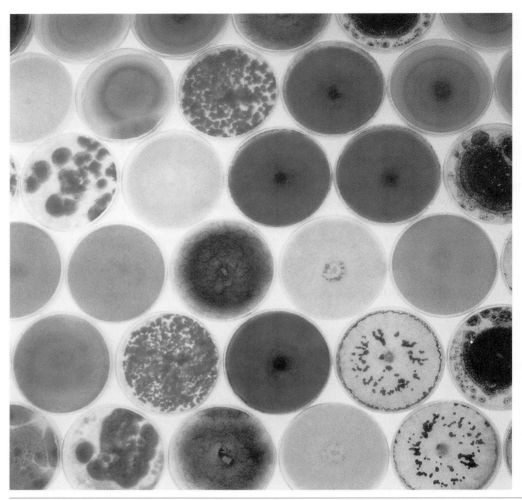

Figure 14.1 Sapros (Source: *Birkbeck College Magazine*, June 1999)

photography led to changes in painting in the nineteenth century as people became less interested in portrait painting so that Impressionism could develop. Sculpture has been affected by new tools and, particularly over the past 50 years, by welding and discoveries in metallurgy. Computers enable designs and graphics to be developed by artists in different ways. Artists have now much more chance of a commercial career through such things as cartoon films and computer games.

The impact of science on religion is dealt with in Unit 3 and should be included in any essay on the impact of science on culture.

The impact of science on society

Science has had tremendous effects on society. The units in this book on transport, energy and information technology should be used for any examination questions. The changes made to society by the inventions of railways, steam ships, cars and planes are not confined to having holidays abroad. Newspapers, the growth of suburbs where workers can live away from their factories, the possibility of all types of goods being transported round the world (until the growth of air freight, such fruits as strawberries could only be eaten in June and July) are all the product of scientific advances. The inventions of electricity, telephones, radio, television, film, records have revolutionised the ways in which humans can communicate. They have also revolutionised society. Entertainments that would have only been available to the very rich are now available in everyone's living room.

When combined with the effects of computers and the development of the Internet and e-mail, science has changed society from small communities in small nation states into what is now called 'the global village'. This term means many things:

- That what happens in one area of the world is immediately known elsewhere in the world, that finance and commerce are so worldwide that everyone is interdependent (see Unit 34 'Economic theories').
- That the same things can be bought anywhere in the world (for example, McDonalds).
- That there is a similar culture and set of values throughout the world.
- That work can take place anywhere in the world (for example, British firms having their call centres in India).
- That people can holiday anywhere in the world, so that there can no longer be communities unaware of other types of people.

There are those who argue that there is no such thing as a global village as there are so many differences between societies. However, one of the best indicators of how science has led to the world becoming a global village was the way in which the millennium was celebrated around the world, especially in countries such as Japan and Pakistan, where the indigenous culture has a different dating system. The effects of the scientific revolutions in transport and communications have been that all societies are now using the western dating systems, as such things as the Internet require common dating and time zones. For this reason the AD and BC letters (identifying the system as Christian) are being replaced by CE (Common Era) and BCE (Before the Common Era), so that the system can be used by anyone whatever their religion or culture.

Perhaps the greatest effect that science has had on society has been the way in which science has replaced religion or the government as the basic authority behind society. The fact that science is now the source of authority has also required the advance of democracy. Science requires that everyone has to have equality of opportunity, as ability and truth are the only criteria for someone's ideas to be accepted. Science can only thrive in a free society where thinkers can exchange ideas.

Some historians claim that science was the cause of the fall of the Soviet Union in the Cold War. The communist countries and NATO countries never actually fought each other, but kept developing more and more advanced weapons so that there was mutually assured destruction, resulting in the Star Wars programme (weapons in space which could block an opponent's missiles). This bankrupted the Soviet Union, leading to the collapse of communism.

Ampère (André) a French scientist who discovered the connection between electricity and magnetism

Babbage (Charles) English mathematician who invented the first, very basic, computer

Baird (John Logie) Scottish inventor of television

Bell (Alexander) Scottish-American inventor of the telephone

Benz (Karl) German inventor of the first petrol-driven car

Biro (Joseph) Hungarian inventor of the ballpoint pen

Crick (Francis) and Watson (James) English and American scientists who discovered the double helix structure of DNA

Daguerre (Louis) French inventor of photography

Edison (Charles) American inventor of the record player and the light bulb

Hertz (Heinrich) German scientist who discovered radio waves

Gutenberg (Johannes) German inventor of the printing press

van Leeuwenhoek (Antonie) Dutch inventor of the microscope

Linnaeus (Carl) Swedish scientist who developed the system for classifying plants

Lippershey (Hans) Dutch inventor of the telescope

Lumière brothers (Auguste and Louis) French inventors of the motion-picture camera (cinematographe)

Marconi (Gugliemo) Italian inventor of the radio

Nobel (Alfred) Swedish scientist who discovered dynamite and established Nobel prizes

Nuclear weapons weapons based on nuclear fission or fusion whose tremendous energy can cause massive destruction

Nuclear deterrent the idea that if a country has nuclear weapons, it will deter any other country from attacking them because of the horrendous consequences

The impact of culture and society on science

In the same way that science has had great effects on culture and society, so society and culture have had effects on science.

There are thinkers who argue that without the Reformation, modern science would not have been able to develop. Galileo was silenced by the Inquisition, but in countries such as England, Holland, Scotland and the Protestant German states his ideas were able to flourish. Indeed, Descartes moved to Holland so that he could have the freedom to publish his ideas. There is also a great connection between the rise of capitalism and the rise of science. Capitalism led to industrialisation and the two together encouraged scientists as new inventions were going to lead to greater profits for the capitalists. Capitalism also requires freedom (scholars such as Weber and Tawney have argued for a connection between Protestantism and the rise of capitalism) and so capitalist societies had the necessary freedom of thought for the rise of science. Science has often been funded by capitalism, either through research carried out in industry or through university research funded by capitalism. You need to ask such questions as whether some scientific advances, such as genetically modified crops or cloning, would have been developed if capitalism was not offering great profits to the scientists.

Perhaps the other great effect of culture and society on science is that some scientific advances have been halted or altered because society's values are opposed to the changes. For example, the generally accepted ethic is that life is sacred (even atheists accept that human life should be treated as a gift, even though not a gift from God). Consequently, scientific attempts to clone humans or to develop brain transplants have been stopped by society's culture. Clearly, there has always been a tension between society's culture and values and the free advance of science. Synoptic questions may focus on whether there should be any limits put on science by culture and society (all the information in Units 5, 10, 16 and 17 is relevant here). It might also be a good idea to use some of the arguments for and against censorship (Unit 19) to apply to science as well as the arts.

Activities

1. Choose an area of culture in which you are interested (e.g. pop music) and investigate how far it has been affected by science and technology.

2. Investigate your own life (home, school, entertainment) to see what effects science and technology have on you.

3. Choose an area of design (e.g. a new car) and assess how far culture has had an effect on the science and technology involved.

4. Evaluate the scientific, economic, political and moral arguments that could be used to argue for and against a greater privatisation of the National Health Service.

EXAM QUESTION

This is another two-part AS extended writing question taken from Section B of the Unit 2 Specimen Paper in 2007.

A recent survey by the broadband information company Point Topic suggested that there were more than 5.4 million people in the UK who work from home. Of those, nearly 2 million are self-employed freelances, about 1.6 million work for an employer with a separate office base, and only 300,000 are running a business that has employees.

But it doesn't suit everyone because it's all too easy to get distracted. Sarah Jackson, chief executive of Working Families, a pressure group that campaigns for work-life balance, has a word of warning. 'Anyone thinking of working from home should think hard about their personality,' she said.

Source: Adapted from Andrew Taylor, 'The ups and downs of working at home',
The Sunday Times, 23 July 2006

(a) For what reasons has the number of people doing paid work from home increased considerably in the last ten years?

(17 marks)

(b) Discuss the potential disadvantages of this form of work for some individuals.

(18 marks)

EXAMINER'S ADVICE

- Like the question at the end of Unit 8, all these two-part questions from Section B of Unit 2 are very similar in structure and you have a choice of doing one from three. The first part (a) of these questions is designed to test your knowledge and understanding of some aspect of general science and technology and the second (b) the social issues which arise or relate to it. They carry almost equal marks, so you should aim to spend approximately 20 minutes on each, which includes thinking and planning as well as writing time.
- Homeworking is not new although now it is often known as teleworking. Typically, prior to the ICT revolution, homeworkers were often unskilled and female, forced to work at home for very low pay because of family responsibilities.
- There has been a dramatic change in the structure of industry in the last two decades with the decline of manufacturing and the rise of the tertiary sector with homeworking growing rapidly as more people become accustomed to it and publicity grows. Over 8 per cent of the workforce operates from home (compared to nearly 7 per cent in Germany and 4.6 per cent in France) with some estimates suggesting that 16 per cent of the workforce will be working wholly or partly from home by 2020.
- Your answer to the first question will almost certainly focus on a range of developments in ICT, which have now made it possible for many types of work to become far less 'location-specific'. List as many of these developments as you can covering both specific equipment and types of software. In this part of the question some technical knowledge of how things work will score you good marks.
- Even though ICT is most likely the main reason, it might not be the only one for people choosing to work from home. Try to develop some other possible reasons as well.
- As with all these two-part questions the second part is more down to your own personal ideas and preferences. Note that the question says 'for some individuals', so you have to try and put yourself into someone else's 'shoes'. List some of the possible advantages from going to a place of work each day, as well as some possible negatives from staying at home.
- When you have written your answers, compare your ideas with the notes provided on pages 276–277.

Culture, Morality, Arts and Humanities

15 The nature of religion

Religion is one of the oldest of human activities. As far back as anthropologists (people who study the origins of humanity) can go, they find evidence of the existence of religion.

According to the *Oxford English Dictionary*, 'religion' is:

1. the belief in a superhuman controlling power especially in a personal God or gods entitled to obedience and worship
2. the expression of this in worship
3. a particular system of faith and worship.

Major world religions

When most people use the word 'religion' they tend to use it in the third sense as the Christian religion, the Jewish religion, etc. You should be aware of the basic beliefs of each of the major world religions. All the religions have groups within them that have different interpretations or emphases (such as Catholics and Protestants in Christianity).

Buddhism

Buddhism was founded by an Indian prince, Siddhartha Gautama, known as the Buddha (the Enlightened One), in the seventh century BCE. It is based on the Four Noble Truths, which say that life is suffering and that humans are stuck on a wheel of life – they live, they die, they are reborn. Humans keep being reborn, and so suffering, because they crave life. The way out of suffering and rebirth is to follow the way of the Buddha in the Noble Eightfold Path, which, by meditation, ends craving and leads to *nirvana* (paradise). Buddhism does not necessarily involve belief in God or worship, though many Buddhists do both. The teachings of Buddhism are found in three holy books known as the *Tripitaka*.

Christianity

Christianity was founded by a Jewish teacher, Jesus of Nazareth, known as the Christ (God's Anointed One), in about 30 CE. It is based on the belief that Jesus was the Son of God who showed humans what God is like. Christians believe that humans fall short of what God wants them to be and so at the end of life (Christians do not believe in reincarnation), they will not go to heaven as God wants them to. However, if they follow the Christian way of love of God and love of neighbour set out by Jesus they will spend eternity in paradise as shown in the life and resurrection of Jesus. The teachings of Christianity are found in the *Bible*, especially in the *Gospels* of the *New Testament*, which contain the life and teachings of Jesus.

Hinduism

Hinduism originated in India around 1500 BCE. Many Hindus say there is no such thing as Hinduism, only Hinduisms, as there are so many variations of belief. Nevertheless, there are certain beliefs that most Hindus have in common. All Hindus believe in reincarnation and karma (the law of cause and effect which states that what you do in this life determines what you will be born as in your next life). They also agree that the aim of life is to escape from rebirth into *nirvana*. Different Hindu groups teach different ways to gain this freedom from rebirth, known as *moksha*. It can be achieved through fulfilling your duty as a member of a caste and so moving up the castes from the *shudras* to the *brahmins* and then to *nirvana*; through knowledge of God, through devotion to God, or through the way of yoga. Hindus believe in one universal spirit, Brahman, who is seen by humans in many different forms such as Shiva, Vishnu and Krishna. The teachings of Hinduism are found in the *Vedas*, *Upanishads*, *Ramayana* and *Bhagavad Gita*.

Islam

Muslims believe that Islam was the original religion founded by the prophet Adam at the beginning of creation, which was distorted and then given back its original form by the Prophet Muhammad in the seventh century. Muslims do not believe in reincarnation. They believe that there is only one God (who is referred to as *Allah*, the Arabic for 'the one God'). They feel that the purpose of life is to look after the world as stewards (*khalifah*) of God's creation by following the way of Islam as set out in the *Qur'an* (the word of God given directly by God to Muhammad) and in the *Sunnah* (example and sayings of Muhammad, as recorded in the *Hadith*). This way of life is the Five Pillars (belief, prayer, charity, fasting, pilgrimage) and the *Shari'ah* (the laws of Islam, which cover every aspect of life). If this way of life is followed, God will reward Muslims with paradise after death.

Judaism

The fathers of Judaism are Abraham (1500 BCE) and Moses (1200 BCE). Jews believe in one God, who they call the Almighty because the name of God is too holy to say. They believe that God chose the Jewish people and gave his laws to the Jews so that they could be God's holy nation and bring the rest of the world to true worship of God. The laws are in the *Torah* (the first five books of the Bible) and are explained in the *Talmud* and the teachings of the *rabbis*. Jews do not believe in reincarnation. They believe that if they obey the commandments of God they will go to heaven.

Sikhism

Sikhism is based on the teachings of ten *gurus* (teachers) and especially the first *guru*, Guru Nanak (1469–1539). It is the youngest of the world religions and began in the Punjab area of India, where Hindus and Muslims were fighting each other. Sikhs believe that humans are self-centred rather than God-centred, and that this causes them to be reborn. So Sikhs believe in reincarnation, but they also believe that by becoming a Sikh you will not be reborn. By following the Sikh way of life of service and equality (there are no castes and no differences between men and women in Sikhism) and devotion to God, you will go to heaven. The teachings of Sikhism are found in the holy book, the *Guru Granth Sahib*.

Conclusion

This brief run-down has provided a summary of the major world religions, using 'religion' in its main dictionary sense (definition 3 page 120). All the religions except Buddhism believe in a supreme being, God, who has created the universe (definition 2 page 120). They all believe that there is a purpose in life and that by following certain rules and teachings (definition 1 page 120), humans will have eternity in paradise.

Sociologists study religion and look at how it operates in society. Functionalist sociologists (see Unit 24, 'The nature of society') give a definition of religion in general, which can be useful in answering questions about the importance of religion. They claim that the key feature of religion is to answer the major and ultimate questions of a society (for example, 'What is the purpose of life?') and to establish a value system that unifies the members of the society. Although such a definition can be criticised because religious groups are often at the forefront of trying to change society's attitudes (for example, Christians and the antislavery movement), it does seem that people are attracted to religion because it offers answers to the ultimate questions and gives a sense of belonging.

Symbolism and ceremony in religion

As religion is concerned with the intangible (things that cannot be tested by the senses), it uses symbolism to express ideas and beliefs that are difficult to express in straightforward language.

Some of the symbolism is in language. For Christians, the word 'father' symbolises the creativity, care and concern of God for his children; it also symbolises the relationship existing between humans and God. The word 'love' symbolises the care of God for humans, the emotions Christians should feel for God, the care and concern Christians should have for their neighbours, the relationship of God to Jesus and through Jesus to the world, etc. Some religious thinkers believe that all words used in religion are symbolic because it is impossible for anyone to describe God using human language.

Religious beliefs are also expressed symbolically in religious ceremonies and rituals. In the Christian service of the Eucharist (Holy communion), the main symbolism is the bread and wine, representative of the body and blood of Jesus. They are used to make worshippers aware of the presence of Jesus, who is regarded as an eternal spirit. The rituals of prayers and actions in a Eucharist service are intended to help the worshippers in their lives (for example, confessing and being forgiven for sins) and to bring them into a closer relationship with God (for example, through taking Jesus into their body through the symbols of bread and wine).

Figure 15.1 Coventry Cathedral Sutherland tapestry. What symbols can you see and what meaning might they have?

KEY TERMS

Agnostic someone who is not sure whether God exists

Atheist someone who believes that God does not exist

Benevolent the belief that God is all-loving and forgiving

Ecumenical Movement a Christian movement to bring the different Christian churches (denominations) together (Christian unity)

Gurdwara a Sikh place of worship

Immortality the belief that humans have a soul that lives on forever after the death of the body

Inter-faith understanding the attempt by religious people living in multi-faith societies to bring different religions together by understanding each other and working together

Mandir a Hindu place of worship

Monotheism the belief in one God

Mosque a Muslim place of worship

Omnipotent the belief that God is all-powerful

Omniscient the belief that God is all-knowing

Polytheism belief in many gods

Religious fundamentalism the belief of certain groups in many religions that: their basic beliefs cannot be adapted or changed; the teachings and customs set down in the scriptures must be strictly maintained; all other religions are wrong

Resurrection the belief that the body will come back to life at some point after death

Secularism the belief that religion and religious belief are unimportant and should not affect society's institutions

Synagogue a Jewish place of worship

The effects of religion on everyday life

Holding a religious belief is likely to have a huge effect on the way a person lives their life. However, it should always be remembered that people have different levels of commitment to their faith, and different members of the same faith regard different beliefs in the religion as more and less important.

Consider the influence that religion has on the everyday life of a Muslim. Muslims believe that there is only one God who gave Muhammad the *Qur'an* in a form that can never be changed. This means that Muslims must do everything the *Qur'an* says. Also, as there can be no prophets after Muhammad, Muslims must follow the example of Muhammad as set out in the *Shari'ah* (Muslim holy law). So Muslims should:

- pray five times a day
- go to mosque every Friday lunchtime
- refrain from food and drink during daylight hours in Ramadan
- give two per cent of their wealth to the poor every year
- only eat halal food
- not drink alcohol
- not gamble
- neither pay nor receive interest on loans and many, many more things.

Clearly these are major effects symbolising that Islam means submission to God and a Muslim is one who has submitted to the will of God. However, not all Muslims do all of these things. Some feel that God cannot expect all of them to be followed, so they decide what are the most important and follow only this selection.

Freedom of religion

Many religious believers feel that it is their basic human right to educate their children in their religion. Consequently they feel that the Government should fund faith schools which teach the National Curriculum from a particular faith point of view. This already happens with Church of England, Catholic and a few Jewish schools (due to the political origins of the English state education system). Muslim, Hindu and Sikh groups are now seeking similar state funding for their schools. They also argue that faith schools produce better results and more moral school leavers.

However, others argue that in a multi-faith society such as Britain, faith schools are socially divisive. They argue that children in a multi-faith society should be educated in all religions, not just one, and that children should not be segregated according to religious belief. Many would claim that religiously segregated schools have exacerbated the problems in Northern Ireland. There is also the issue of religious freedom for other people. What of an atheist whose only available state schools are all religious? Their religious freedom has been removed by faith schools.

Read the passage below about religious education and faith schools in the United Kingdom and answer the multiple choice questions which follow.

Faith in our schools

(1) The parable of the Good Shopper is what children learn in their French and German lessons, argues Allison Farnell of the Stapleford Centre, a Nottingham-based Christian educational trust that recently began publishing secondary school textbooks. 'When you learn French in a school, you learn what to say in a café, or a railway station, or a market,' she says. 'The whole content of foreign language teaching in England assumes you are a tourist, or a spender or a consumer.'

(2) The Stapleford Centre's new GCSE textbooks for French and German are rather different: 'We do all the same grammar, but we set it in a different context. We look at the faith and beliefs of people in France and Germany. We look at light as a symbol of hope. We look at the way people held candles when the Berlin Wall came down. Our French books show how to buy bread in a patisserie, but they also show bread as a symbol in Christianity and in Islam.'

(3) The centre, which links with St John's Theological College in Nottingham, now publishes GCSE-level textbooks in science, maths, French, German and English. They cover the material required by the national curriculum, but from a spiritual point of view. Ordinary GCSE maths books often teach percentages by asking children to work out how much interest they will gain on money deposited in a bank. Stapleford's maths book asks children to calculate the percentage of their future income they might give away.

(4) Since 1992, schools have been under a legal obligation to 'promote spiritual and moral values throughout the curriculum'. The demand for the Stapleford books is a direct result of this, says Alison Farnell. 'Our books enable teachers to bring out spiritual and moral issues. They are not for use in teaching RE; they are for languages, or maths, or science with a spiritual and moral dimension.'

(5) Spirituality throughout the curriculum is only one of several religious obligations on state schools. What most schools call 'assembly' is actually defined in law as 'daily collective worship', compulsory for all pupils (unless their parents withdraw them) up to the age of 18. This must be 'wholly or mainly of a broadly Christian character'.

(6) In England and Wales all state schools must also provide religious education for all pupils up to the age of 18. This includes 14–16 year-old pupils who drop other subjects. It is possible for some pupils to replace science and languages with vocational-style courses, for example, but they must study RE unless their parents withdraw them from it.

(7) All these regulations apply to the three-quarters of state schools that have no official link with any religion. In the other quarter, the schools that are affiliated to particular denominations, and for which the state pays 85–100% of the running costs, religion will be more overt still. Several governors of these schools will be chosen by the church or other religious groups. Children may be offered or denied places on the basis of their parents' religion and/or attendance at services.

(8) Eric Goodyer lives in the village of Hathern in Leicestershire, where the local Church of England primary school is the only one in the village. Included in the school's aims is the phrase 'to promote Christian values'. Goodyer has protested at this, and at the requirement for parents to support it in the home–school agreement. In a one-school village he cannot exercise his right to freedom of religious expression which, from next year, will be his under European and English law.

Source: edited from 'Faith in our schools', *Education Guardian*, 25 April 2000

For the questions which follow, choose the answer A, B, C or D which you think fits best. Each of the questions is worth one mark.

1 A 'parable' (paragraph 1) is always
   A illustrative.
   B fictional.
   C religious.
   D humorous.

2 Each of the following is regarded in the passage as a strength of the Stapleford books (paragraph 3) **except**
   A they comply with government legislation.
   B they offer a moral dimension for a wide range of subjects.
   C they are specifically produced by Christians.
   D they promote spiritual and moral values.

3 The approach taken by Stapleford described in the last sentence of paragraph 3 is best described as
   A capitalist.
   B ethical.
   C profitable.
   D religious.

4 In paragraph 3 the author identifies two approaches to teaching a subject. These are best described as
   A subjective versus objective.
   B practical versus theoretical.
   C materialistic versus spiritual.
   D outdated versus innovative.

5 The Stapleford Centre's main concern (paragraphs 1 to 3) is that
   A national curriculum subjects concentrate on the pupil as a consumer.
   B materialistic values endorsed in textbooks are unacceptable.
   C national curriculum textbooks are too balanced.
   D there is a lack of spirituality in many textbooks.

6 School assembly (paragraph 5) must include
   A a religious element.
   B all religious denominations.
   C prayers.
   D every pupil.

7 The denominational schools mentioned in paragraph 7
   A have identical regulations to state schools.
   B have all their running costs paid for by the state.
   C have specific requirements covering admissions.
   D are wholly controlled by religious governors.

8 Paragraph 8 suggests that a major legal clash is likely because
   A of the existence of both Muslim and Jewish schools.
   B of the New European Human Rights legislation.
   C the state is anxious to reduce its educational costs.
   D the Church is likely to involve ecclesiastical laws.

9 Eric Goodyer's complaint in paragraph 8 is essentially that he
   A rejects Christian values.
   B cannot afford to send his child to private school.
   C does not approve of home–school agreements.
   D has no choice over the education his child receives.

10 According to the author in paragraphs 1 to 8 each of the following is compulsory by law in English education **except**
   A daily religious assembly.
   B provision of Church schools.
   C promotion of spiritual and moral values.
   D religious education.

EXAMINER'S ADVICE

- The passage and questions are taken from the AQA AS Unit 1 test for May 2003. In the exam proper there are 30 questions based on a longer version of the passage, followed by three questions for documentary source analysis (see the question at the end of the next unit).
- Check out the general advice on tackling multiple choice questions on page 266 and for Unit 1 on page 1. The ten questions here are representative of those you will get in the exam and you should aim to complete them in, say, half an hour.
- You will note that some of the questions are about the meaning of words, some about the arguments in a paragraph and some about the passage as a whole. Generally, the questions become broader and more complex as you work through them.
- The answers are given on page 277.

Why people have religious belief

It is one of the remarkable characteristics of all human beings that they claim to have religious beliefs. The word 'belief' itself can have several different meanings:

- 'Belief' might mean trust or confidence in something, for example believing in a person or believing in justice.
- 'Belief' might mean accepting that a particular state of affairs is actually the case, for example believing that there are tigers in India.

Religious beliefs, which can be defined as any belief that is distinctive to members of a particular religious group or denomination, are often a mixture of both types, for example:

- 'Belief that' something is true, for example a factual proposition such as, 'Jesus was a messenger from God'.
- 'Belief in', which is to do with the trust and commitment people experience in their relationship with God.

Often these beliefs are interdependent. You cannot believe *in* God in the sense of trust and commitment, for example, unless you first believe *that* his existence is a fact.

Problems with religious beliefs

One of the fundamental beliefs common to most religions is the belief in some divine being or beings. In the modern world this belief raises serious problems. How can someone claim that some special knowledge or message that he or she believes they have received from God is real knowledge? How do we know, for example, that *Mother Teresa* or *St Francis of Assisi* were not mistaken about their belief that God spoke to them? We cannot prove the existence of God by either rational or empirical means – the two generally acceptable methods of establishing proof of the existence of something.

Types of knowledge

Particularly since the work of *René Descartes* (1596–1650), a *rationalist* philosopher, there has been a strong tradition arguing that to know something is to be able to prove it: to reach a conclusion by logical inferences from self-evident premises. In practice, this means proving things by using your reason, for example proving that 2 + 2 = 4 or proving Pythagoras' theorem. However, *rational knowledge* cannot tell us anything about the real world. *Empirical knowledge*, however, is based on sense-experience, our perceptions of the real world. But the problem with sense-experiences is that they may be mistaken. For example, railway lines appear to converge in the distance even though they are actually parallel. So rational knowledge is certain knowledge, but it is only about logic, and empirical knowledge is about the real world, but it may be mistaken. Religious believers usually claim that their religious beliefs are *real* but are not simply matters of logic or ideas, or mistaken sense-impressions.

Where do religious beliefs come from?

There are various answers to this question including the religious, the sociological and the psychological.

Religious explanations for religious belief

Many religious believers would claim that their religious belief is based on a *religious experience* which led to their *conversion*. Conversion often involves a dramatic change of attitude, beliefs and behaviour. The best known example of this is *Paul* on the road to Damascus, who changed suddenly from being a persecutor of the early Christian Church into its greatest missionary after experiencing a blinding light and hearing a voice.

Other religious experiences might take the form of an appearance by a saint or a divine figure, hearing voices or experiencing some strange phenomena, such as:

- Moses and the burning bush
- the Virgin Mary appearing to Bernadette of Lourdes
- the angel Gabriel appearing to the prophet Muhammad.

The problem for religious believers is that, although they are usually certain about their beliefs, it is difficult to establish the authenticity of these events by the usual methods. Also, the claim that a particular experience is an experience of God may simply be self-deception. The experience may be self-generated, i.e. arise in the imagination of the person having the experience, rather than having been caused by a source outside.

Peter Sutcliffe, '*the Yorkshire Ripper*', claimed that God told him to murder 13 women. Joan of Arc claimed that the saints spoke to her and told her to save France. It is extremely difficult to prove or disprove the authenticity of these claims as they are intensely personal, private, 'inner' experiences, which, by their very nature, cannot be shared.

Some religious believers claim that their belief is based on a religious book, such as the Bible or the Qur'an. This raises several problems:

- Some passages in these religious texts seem to contradict each other.
- It is often not clear whether particular passages have divine or human origins, despite the claims made by some believers that their scriptures are inspired by God (see 'Did you know?' box on page 131).

- Most religious texts reflect the social/cultural conditions of their own time and it can be difficult to see how they can be the basis of religious faith 2000 years later.
- Only one religious book can be true and there is no way of deciding which it is.

Sociological explanations for religious belief (see also Unit 17)

Sociological theories tend to assume that the explanation for religious belief lies in society itself, rather than in the idea that there is some external divine reality responsible for the experiences that believers claim to have had. Sociologists are interested in *belief systems* rather than individual beliefs, because most religious believers have an interlocking set of beliefs, rather than individual ones. They are also interested in the way in which religious beliefs reflect and are part of the *culture* of a particular society. Indian children are more likely to be Hindus than European children because their religious beliefs have been learnt within a Hindu culture. In 1912, the French sociologist *Emile Durkheim* offered a *functionalist* analysis of religion in terms of what purposes religion serves in society. These include:

Figure 16.1 Hindus bathing in The Ganges – many religions see water as purifying sin and bringing people closer to God

- *Social solidarity.* Social life is impossible without shared values and moral beliefs. Religion reinforces those values and collective religious worship is a way of bringing people together so that they can integrate and strengthen the moral values that unite them.
- *Reverence for society.* Durkheim argued that when people have the experience of standing before the divine or some greater power, what they are really doing is worshipping society itself. People use religious ideas as a symbol of what they hold most sacred, which is the tribe or clan and its values and customs to which they belong.

There are other functions of religious belief identified by sociologists:

- *Crisis management.* Religious belief and ritual helps people to deal with life crises such as birth, puberty, marriage and death. The religious services surrounding such events help people to cope with the disruption of their lives caused by such things as death and to support each other. This support helps to reintegrate society and to provide solidarity.
- *Meaning of life.* Religion also helps people to cope with uncertainty in life. It helps them to answer difficult questions like why there is evil and suffering and whether there is life after death.
- *Continuity.* Religious ceremonies help to maintain a sense of history and link together different generations.

Critics have pointed out, however, that if religious belief is merely a reinforcement and reflection of the values of society as a whole, it is hard to see where revolutionaries or prophets come from in the first place. If religion were no more than a reflection of society's values, the ability to criticise the values of the society in which they have grown up or to develop a more universal perspective on life would never have developed.

Psychological explanations for religious belief

Sigmund Freud (1856–1939), the originator of psychoanalysis, regarded religious beliefs as 'illusions, fulfilments of the oldest, strongest and most insistent wishes of mankind'. He regarded them as a mental defence against the more threatening aspects of nature, floods, death and disease, etc. According to Freud, human beings project onto the universe the memory of their father as a great projecting power in order to cope with the threat of these natural forces. Although much of Freud's explanation is rejected by modern critics, his view of religious belief as a kind of 'psychological crutch' is accepted by many religious thinkers as a true description of some aspects of religion.

Karl Marx (1818–83) described religion as 'the opiate of the masses'. As an atheist, he argued that there is no God except the God that man creates for himself. Religious belief encourages human beings to put up with intolerable conditions and obscures the fact that history is controlled by human interests and desires. Religion does not help human beings, but chains them.

Religion and terrorism

Modern terrorism is increasingly motivated by extremist religious rather than political points of view. The most worrisome example is the worldwide *Jihad* phenomenon. There are two main trends in modern terrorism. The first is the tendency toward higher-casualty attacks, and the second is a far-reaching change in the motivation behind terrorist attacks. Today's terrorist is much more likely to be driven by extremist religious beliefs than by a wish to gain political concessions – the Islamic extremist al-Qaeda network is a prime example of this. The aim of such groups is to win converts among potential supporters, to intimidate potential enemies, and to punish actual enemies.

The rise of religiously-motivated terrorism has been accompanied by a rise in suicide attacks. This is particularly true of extremist Islamist terrorism, where the image of the suicide bomber, or '*Shahid*', carries great power and prestige.

The vast majority of Muslims are hospitable, compassionate and tolerant, with very little hatred in their hearts. During the past century, the mass of suffering that the West has inflicted on Muslims, especially the Arabs, has given them reason to hate. Yet, only a few have developed blind hatred.

There appears to be three schools of Muslim thought on the subject of the relationship between Islam and other religions. The majority group believes that it is the sacred mission of Islam to rule the world by use of the sword if necessary – the Jihad or holy war mentality. Another group accepts cohabitation with other religions as long as Islam is the world's pre-eminent religion. A third group, the moderates, advocates co-existence primarily because of the economic benefits it brings.

Many Arabs hate the United States because of its military and political support of modern Israel, a state which was created after the Second World War in response to the need for a homeland for displaced Jews. This involved, however, the loss of statehood and the actual homes of thousands of native Muslim Palestinians who have been fighting for justice ever since. Until very recently, most Arab countries have refused to recognise the State of Israel. Wars have been fought in 1948–49, 1956, 1967 (The Six Day War), 1973–74 (The Yom Kippur War), and 1982 between Israel and the Arab states.

The religious backdrop to the situation is heavily mixed with anti-US sentiment, where the US is seen as supporting Israel only because of American oil interests. Further, the US is seen as being responsible for militarising the region (the Middle East is the most militarised region in the world) and propping up corrupt Arab governments in order to guarantee secure oil supplies. The US is accused of double standards because it uses the support of freedom and democracy as justification to invade some countries such as Iraq but ignores the suffering of the Palestinians.

Islamic groups which simply hate Israel and want to destroy it include *Hamas, Hezbollah*, the *Popular Front for the Liberation of Palestine*, and the *Palestinian Liberation Front*. The *Palestine Liberation Organisation* (PLO) is the co-ordinating council for all Palestinian organisations, founded in 1964 at the first Arab summit meeting. The dominant group is *Al Fatah*, until recently headed by Yasser Arafat who formed a group of warriors known as *fedayeen*, and became chairman of the

DID YOU KNOW?

Osama Bin Laden
A multi-millionaire who runs a private terror network from a hideaway in Afghanistan or parts unknown. Born into a wealthy Saudi family in 1957 as the seventh of 50 children, he joined the Afghan Mujahedin in 1979, one of many Arabs trained by the Americans to overthrow the Russian backed Afghanistan government. During the Gulf War, he became incensed that Saudi Arabia allowed American troops on its soil, and later came to blame the U.S. for the problems of Palestine. In 1996, he issued a fatweh, or religious decree, to kill American soldiers, and in 1998, announced that all dutiful Muslims should consider killing American civilians and their allies, including women and children, as their legitimate, sacred duty. He has masterminded many acts of terrorism including the destruction of the World Trade Centre on 9/11. Bin Laden represents a view which hates everything American but which presents its opposition in religious terms.

Activities

1. Research the life of Jackie Pullinger in Hong Kong or Camillo Torres in Colombia. What effect do you think their religious beliefs have had on their lives?

2. 'Religious beliefs are an essential part of a society's culture.' What evidence is there to support or oppose this point of view?

3. 'Religious beliefs do not have to be true. They just have be important to the believer.' Evaluate this statement, giving reasons for your answer.

PLO in 1968. Since its founding, the PLO has been committed to the destruction of Israel, and over the years has been involved in acts of terrorism. It toned down its rhetoric and acts of terrorism in 1974 when it received UN recognition as a government in exile.

EXAM QUESTION

This is a two-part documentary source analysis question taken from Section B of the AS Unit 1 Specimen Paper in 2007. It is the first of three compulsory questions in this section of the paper.

Britain's race watchdog has said the Labour Minister, Jack Straw, was 'completely right' to express his concerns about Muslim women wearing veils. Trevor Phillips, chairman of the Commission for Racial Equality, added 'It is not a matter of public policy, but a question of social etiquette and good manners'. Mr Phillips also said that he believed the wearing of veils for religious reasons should not override school-uniform policies, providing they have been arrived at properly.

Harriet Harman, the Constitutional Affairs minister, delivered the strongest attack on veils by a government member when she said: 'If you want equality, you have to be in society, not hidden away from it. How can you stand as an MP when men's faces are on posters, and voters can't see yours? The veil is an obstacle to women's participation, on equal terms, in society.'

Source: Adapted from NIGEL MORRIS and SARAH CASSIDY, 'Race equality head backs Straw on wearing of veil', *The Independent,* 12 October 2006

(a) Using your own words, give *three* reasons *from the Source* in favour of removing religious veils.

(4 marks)

(b) Using your own knowledge, give *three* reasons against removing religious veils in certain circumstances.

(4 marks)

EXAMINER'S ADVICE

- Check out the requirements for Section B of AS Unit 1 on page 1. You are required to answer three compulsory source analysis questions, each based on a short source like the one here, for a total of 35 marks and you have about 45 minutes in which to complete them. This first question is the shortest and simplest and is worth eight marks, which means that you should aim to complete it in no more than ten minutes.

- Part (a) asks for *three* reasons *from the source*, using your own words. The mark scheme says 'Award one mark for each reason, up to a maximum of three, plus one mark for accurate communication, predominantly in own words.' The question is an exercise in quickly picking out key points in a text and communicating them mostly in your own words. Here your answer should consist of three simple sentences (ideally one per point) and you should use only points or arguments made in the source.

- Part (b) requires you to think of arguments *against* those made in the extract and here you have to use your own ideas and knowledge. Refer back to the previous two Units 15 and 16 if you fall short of the three points you need to make. Once again your answer should consist of three simple sentences, for which you stand to gain one mark for each valid point made, plus one overall for accurate communication.

- When you have written your answers, compare your points with those given on page 277. For comparison there are similar questions at the end of Units 28 and 30.

The need for morality and the nature of ethical theories

Why morality is important

Human beings are gregarious – they like to be with other people and they like to live in groups or societies. If you live in a society, then you need to know how other people are likely to act, and you need some method of balancing one person's self-interest against the self-interests of others.

A set of moral principles is known as a moral code. Sociologists sometimes call this 'a shared value system'. They feel that any society needs to have shared values if it is to survive, because without shared values there will be conflict.

As societies have come together and changed, there can be several value systems at work and this is why there is now debate about moral issues. There are no longer shared values about issues such as cohabitation (living together without being married), divorce, abortion, fighting for your country, etc.

Even though there are such differences about what is right and what is wrong, we all make moral judgements saying, 'this is right' or 'that is wrong'. In fact, we have to do this. If you are offered drugs, if your boyfriend/girlfriend wants to sleep with you, you have to make a moral choice. If you are a scientist cloning sheep, or a doctor killing human embryos in order to give a couple a baby through IVF, you are making a moral decision. Studying ethics should help you to make informed moral choices and moral judgements.

Ethical theories

There are many different theories on what makes an action right or wrong. You should use at least some of these theories when you are answering questions on ethical issues in the exam.

Utilitarianism

This is the view that you decide whether an action is right or wrong by looking at the consequences. If you have a choice of actions, you should choose the one that will produce the most happiness or the least suffering to the people who will be affected by the action. For example, if you had to decide whether to ban smoking in public places, you would weigh the suffering caused to the smokers by having to wait for a cigarette against the suffering caused to non-smokers by passive smoking (lung cancer,

Amoral outside morality, or having no moral principles

Conscience an inner feeling about good and bad, which makes you feel you ought to do the good and makes you feel guilty if you do the bad

Consequential an ethical theory, which says that what makes an act good or bad is the effects or consequences of the action

Deontological an ethical theory based on rules rather than the effects of an action, which says some things are absolutely right and others are absolutely wrong

Duty following your conscience by doing what you feel you ought to do

Immoral having moral principles, but going against them

Objective morality an ethical theory based on outside facts, which are independent of an individual

Shared values the idea that for society to function, members of that society must share similar ideas on what is right and what is wrong

Subjective morality an ethical theory based on the ideas of an individual

heart disease, bronchial problems, etc.) and decide that the least suffering would be caused by banning smoking.

This theory is associated with *Jeremy Bentham* (1748–1832) and *John Stuart Mill* (1806–73) and the phrase 'a good action is one that brings about the greatest happiness of the greatest number'.

Religious morality

Almost all religions argue that it is God who decides what is right and what is wrong and that humans discover how to behave from finding out God's will. Christians believe that this comes from the teachings of the Bible and the decisions of the Church. Muslims believe that God's will was revealed through the *Qur'an* and the Prophet Muhammad, and from these Muslim lawyers have worked out the *Shari'ah*, a holy law covering every aspect of life. So, if Muslims are faced with a moral choice, they find out what the *Shari'ah* says. Orthodox Jews consult the laws of God found in the *Torah* (the first five books of the Old Testament). Buddhists would look at the moral precepts laid down by the Buddha. In all these cases, there is no looking at consequences, what makes something right or wrong is decided by God.

So, if faced with the issue of whether homosexuals should be allowed to marry, Christians would look at the Bible and say that homosexuality is condemned, therefore homosexuality is wrong and there can be no marriage. A Muslim would make a similar statement, based on the teachings of the *Qur'an*.

However, not all religious people would make moral decisions in this way. Many feel that the consequences must be looked at and that some of the laws in the holy books were only intended for the time when they were written. If two people love each other and want to commit themselves to each other in marriage, then allowing them to do so is the most loving thing, so homosexual marriage should be allowed.

Activities

1. Make two lists of arguments for and against cloning animals. Read the key terms definitions, then go through your lists and work out which of your arguments are deontological and which are consequential. Do you think your lists make you agree or disagree with cloning?

Figure 17.1 Making moral decisions

Natural law

Thomas Aquinas (1224–74) used the earlier work of Aristotle to claim that just as there are natural laws of science, so there is a natural law of morality. Just as scientists can study the world and find the principles on which it is based, so moral philosophers can study humans and society and find out what is the 'natural' form of behaviour, which will lead to a perfect society if everyone follows it.

Aquinas believed that God created everything with a final cause or purpose and that discovering this tells you what is right. For example, the final cause of sex is the creation of children, so any form of sex that does not involve the creation of children is wrong. Those who follow natural law today tend to relate behaviour to the place of humans in the world and the basic requirements for humans to survive.

To take another example, if making a decision about homosexual marriage, they would say that heterosexuality is natural because it is a basic requirement for humans to survive and so homosexuality must be wrong and homosexual marriage cannot be allowed.

Social contract theory

This is a view first put forward by Plato, but very much connected with *Thomas Hobbes* (1588–1679) and *Jean-Jacques Rousseau* (1712–78). It claims that laws and morals are a human invention upon which we agree to make life better for ourselves. As Hobbes said, 'Life without laws would be nasty, brutish and short.' Rousseau claimed that if governments or rulers do not make life better for their subjects, then the subjects have a right to overthrow the government.

If making a decision about homosexuality, social contract theorists would say, 'What would be the impact on society? Is it something like adultery, which we can't have laws about without being too restrictive on people's freedom?' They would then probably agree to homosexual marriage because it will make the couple more stable and therefore make society more stable.

'There is an inescapable sense that events are somehow influenced by human choice. Without that, there would be no sense of morality' (Mel Thompson, *Teach Yourself Ethics*).

Activities

2. Make a list of the morals and laws you would put forward if you were in Rawls' 'original position'. Are they similar to those Rawls suggests? Write down what you think of Rawls' ideas and why.

3. Read through the ethical theories in this unit again. Using the key term definitions, work out which theories are objective and which are subjective. Then work out which theories are deontological and which are consequential. Decide which theory you would find most useful in making a moral decision and why.

4. Use the Internet to identify a country with a high population growth. Also find out its gross national product (GNP) and per capita income. Then use the ethical theories and your own ideas to discuss whether the country should adopt a policy of compulsory sterilisation for couples after they have had one baby.

5. On the basis of all the work you have done, answer the question 'Is it ever justifiable to break the law?'

EXAM QUESTION

This is an A2 essay question taken from Section C of the Unit 3 Specimen Paper in 2007.

What do you understand by the term 'terrorism'?

Discuss, with reference to recent or ongoing conflicts, if terrorism can ever be justified.

(25 marks)

EXAMINER'S ADVICE

- This is a standard A2 essay question in two, but not equal, parts.
- The first part requires a definition, or an explanation, of what you understand by 'terrorism'. It might be useful to think of recent terrorist acts, e.g. 9/11, the Bali nightclub, Madrid train, and London Underground bombings, and to think about the essential characteristics of these acts that distinguish them from other acts of aggression, such as wars. How do 'terrorist' organisations tend to operate?
- After this, the main requirement is to examine the question of whether any form of terrorism might ever be justified. In strictly moral terms this is a very difficult question. Usually it is history or the justness of a cause which determine whether violent acts can be justified – using one form of evil to fight another? Do the 'ends ever justify the means'?
- The most important element of this part of the question however is to show that you know something about some of the conflicts across the world that have spawned terrorist acts. The history of Northern Ireland might be a good place to start, or South Africa during Apartheid, or the conflicts between Palestinian groups and Israel.
- Some key figures who were deemed to be terrorists in the past have become national leaders when circumstances have changed, e.g. Nelson Mandela, or a number of Israeli leaders.
- Use the discussion in this unit and the previous one to build up your arguments and compile some illustrations which will support them. This is not a topic where the examiner is expecting a single right answer and you are well within your rights to argue both sides, according to individual circumstances and personal belief.
- When you have thought about the topic and assembled some material for your answer, spend no more than 30–40 minutes writing it out. Then compare your ideas with the notes on page 277.

Ethical issues

One of the major characteristics of modern society is the way in which our existence is dominated by technology. The beneficial effects of this can be seen in such areas as housing, transport and the media. However, this technology often brings with it very difficult ethical questions. This is particularly true in the field of medicine where inventions such as life support or kidney dialysis machines give doctors apparent power over life and death. Two particularly controversial areas are cloning and abortion.

Cloning

To clone is simply to make an exact genetic copy of an existing organism. It happens naturally in many plants (if you bury a potato it sprouts clones of itself), and even a few animals. Significantly, it does not normally happen in mammals and humans, except for 'identical' twins, whose condition is due to a natural genetic aberration. Dolly, on the other hand, was a sheep created by taking cells from the udder of a ewe and 'reprogramming' them to create a new embryo, by a process known as nuclear transfer, and implanting the embryo in another ewe.

This was a biological revolution as it had been thought impossible to grow a mammal from body tissue. Also it raised the daunting question about the possibility of cloning human beings, particularly since cattle and mice had recently been cloned. Cloning raises a fundamental question about the relationship between technology and society. The fact that something is possible does not mean that it is necessarily desirable. Other factors have to be taken into account, particularly in relation to the amount of benefit and/or harm using a technology might produce.

The overwhelming reaction from most people is not just that it should not be done, but also a fear that someone might try. Statements opposing cloning human beings have issued from numerous national and international organisations, including the UN, the European Parliament, and the United Kingdom Human Fertilisation and Embryology Authority.

Ethical concerns
*   Cloning runs counter to the evolutionary need to maintain a basic level of genetic diversity and variety in nature. It appears to attack the fundamental idea of individuality. Cloning selects the genetic composition of some existing individual and then takes part in an intentional, controlled act to produce an identical copy. The crucial point is not the genetic identity but the human act of control of it. The most fundamental ethical case against human cloning is that no human being should have their complete genetic makeup pre-determined by another human. We can reject their upbringing, but we cannot change our genes.
*   In most of the recent controversial cases, for example the failed attempt to clone a young boy in order to provide a compatible donor for his own bone marrow (see 'Did you know?' box on the next page), the person cloned would appear to have been created not as an end in themselves but rather as a means of benefiting someone else.

- No one knows the psychological effects of discovering that one was the twin of a parent or sibling. Would that person simply be a copy of someone else who already exists and not really an individual in their own right? Since we have no sure way of knowing in advance, we surely do not have the right to inflict, knowingly, that risk on another person.
- There is the physical risk in the light of the animal cloning experience. It took 277 attempts and 29 implantations to produce one healthy Dolly. Significant pregnancy difficulties have been a common feature of cloning work in sheep and cattle, involving deformation and premature ageing. In addition, while the production of cloned human embryos may provide stem cells which can reproduce themselves and replace those that cause Parkinson's disease or premature ageing, for example, the medical procedures used have the potential to become mere 'spare part surgery'. Embryos would be discarded if surplus to requirements, and they might come to be valued merely as collections of usable organs rather than as potential human beings.

Abortion

This is a highly emotive and controversial subject. There are three issues central to the abortion debate:

- Should a woman have the right to do what she wants with her own body?
- Does a fetus have the same rights as someone who is already living independently?
- Is a fetus a person?

Most religious and moral codes agree that, in principle, human life is sacred. However, they differ in how far they are prepared to put aside this principle in particular circumstances. The Roman Catholic Church, for example, would not allow abortion on the grounds of rape or incest, but would allow it if it were clear that the mother would definitely die otherwise. This is the *natural law position* – the idea that human life is sacred and that pregnancy and the creation of human life are natural processes and ultimately part of God's will.

Objections to abortion often seem to concentrate exclusively on the act of abortion itself and to ignore the circumstances in which an abortion was considered. This raises the question of whether actions should be judged by the result they produce or by the motives from which they were done. This can be difficult to decide. For example, how would you assess the result of an abortion if it took away the life of the unborn child but made the mother happy?

Some Churches and other organisations would allow abortion in cases of rape, incest or where bringing the pregnancy to full term would seriously damage the health or threaten the life of the mother, or where the deformity of the fetus precludes any chance of survival.

Competing rights

Many moral issues seem to centre on the problem of competing rights. Those opposed to the *1967 Abortion Act* have argued amongst other things, that the phrase 'risk to the physical or mental health of the mother' is too vague and allows abortions to be granted for trivial and irresponsible reasons. If abortion involves the taking away of human life, then the argument that the mother doesn't want the child, or can't support it, is not sufficient to justify it. There are far more couples waiting to adopt newborn babies than there are babies available for adoption. This argument implies that the risk to the health of the mother is not equal to the death of the baby. In terms of rights, what is being said is that the right of the mother to decide to have an abortion in these cases is not as great as the right of the unborn child to live. Many of those opposed to abortion see themselves as defending the rights of a fetus which cannot defend itself.

From the moral point of view, it is usually agreed that rights and responsibilities go together. Some people have argued, for example, that a couple or a single person leading a totally promiscuous lifestyle, who ignore readily available contraceptive techniques, should not be allowed to choose an abortion which involves the death of a human being and the use of expensive, hard-pressed NHS resources.

Exercising the right to choose an abortion denies the right of a fetus to live. So the freedom to make decisions carries with it the responsibility to make these decisions carefully and sensitively, as human life is involved.

Is a fetus a human being in the same sense that we apply the term to human beings outside the womb?

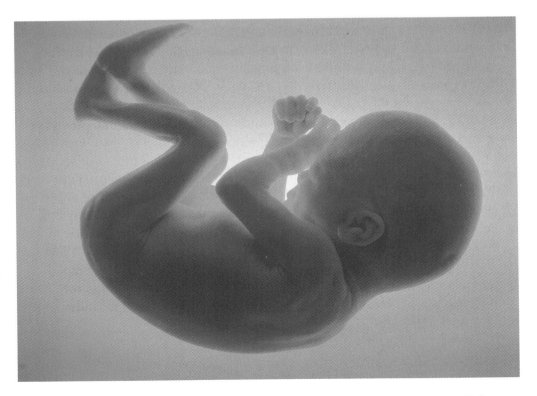

Figure 18.1 A fetus at 20 weeks

KEY TERMS

Active euthanasia a positive action that brings about death – it can apply to all three types of euthanasia mentioned above

Disproportionate treatment treatment that may involve so much invasive surgery, cost or pain that the possible benefit is insignificant in proportion

Embryo the organism between 14 days and the eighth week of gestation

Fetus the developing human being between 14 weeks and birth

Involuntary euthanasia ending someone's life when they have not given consent but were able to do so

Non-voluntary euthanasia ending the life of someone who cannot choose for themselves

Passive euthanasia a lack of action, which will bring about death – may also apply to the three types of euthanasia mentioned above

Personhood consciousness, the ability to feel pain, a developed capacity for reasoning, the ability to communicate and self-awareness (Dr Mary Warren)

Pro-choice the term used by those who consider that a woman's right to choose is absolute

Pro-life the term used by those who argue that a fetus is an innocent human being, who should never be killed

Viability the term used to describe the independent survival of a fetus outside the womb

Voluntary euthanasia helping someone to die at their own request

Zygote the cell formed by the union of sperm and ovum

Fetuses rarely survive *ex utero* (outside the womb) before 22 weeks. (The fact that some do survive at this early stage has been important evidence in favour of the recent amendment to the 1967 Abortion Act, passed by parliament in 1990, reducing the maximum time for an abortion from 28 weeks to 24 weeks.)

Euthanasia

Euthanasia is a compound of two Greek words – *eu* and *thanatos* – meaning literally 'a good death'. The word is generally understood today to refer to the 'mercy killing' of a person by another, either with or without the person's consent. There are two important features to remember about euthanasia:

- It involves taking someone's life.
- It is done for the claimed benefit of the person whose life is being taken, usually because he/she is suffering from an incurable or terminal illness.

Historically, all civilised societies have moral principles about the taking of human life, but there have been considerable variations concerning when it is permissible. Infanticide and suicide were all accepted and widely practised in Greek and Roman times. However, the growth in influence of Judaism and Christianity in the western world led to the view that human life was sacred and that only God had the power to take it.

The legal position

At the moment, euthanasia is illegal in this country. Despite fairly recent bills debated in the House of Lords in 1969 and 1976 in support of it, the bills were defeated, mainly on the grounds that it seemed to be too difficult to draw up adequate safeguards to protect a possible recipient of euthanasia from unfair pressure or abuse. However in 1993, the Dutch parliament made law certain guidelines under which doctors could carry on administering lethal injections to consenting, terminally ill and suffering patients without fear of prosecution – a practice in which some Dutch doctors had already been engaged for several years.

Modern life-support systems make such decisions very difficult. The initial positive decision by a doctor to place someone on a life-support machine in order to improve the chances of survival, may become a more controversial issue under the following circumstances:

- removing someone when there is no possibility of improvement
- removing someone when life is only being maintained by the machine, for example a serious brain-stem injury
- removing a seriously deformed and/or very premature baby.

Without modern life-support machines, the question of survival for the examples mentioned above would not arise. However, a doctor can now be sued for switching off a machine, an action which is seen as life-threatening or life-taking. On the other hand, without the opportunity of being on the machine in the first place, the patient would certainly have died. Medical ethics often discusses these issues in terms of *proportionality*. This involves balancing the amount of benefit accruing to the patient in relation to the amount of pain, suffering, cost, inconvenience, etc.

About death

A modern philosopher, Peter Singer, has argued that the growth of our capacity to keep people alive has forced us to reconsider what we mean by 'the sanctity of life' and what we mean by death. It is now generally accepted that *brain-stem death* (when there is no chance of the brain recovering the use of its functions) is real death. This means that bodies that appear to be warm, pulsating and breathing can be technically dead, and may be given no further medical support, but may be kept functioning until vital organs can be removed for transplants.

Case studies

Baby John was born prematurely at 27 weeks with an infection and breathing difficulties and placed on a ventilator, initially for a month. However, he remained very ill and handicapped, suffered from convulsions and breathing problems, which did not improve. His long-term prospects for a reasonable quality of life were described as non-existent. He was severely brain-damaged, blind and deaf and in constant pain.

In a court case, the judge ruled that the baby should be treated with antibiotics for his chest infection but that his doctors were not obliged to put him back on the ventilator. This decision was based on two principles:

- It would not serve the child's best interests to give him treatment that would prolong his suffering and produce no benefit.
- There is a difference between normal care (i.e. antibiotics) and extraordinary care (i.e. life-support machines).

In September 1992, Dr Cox was found guilty of deliberately killing a 70-year-old patient, Mrs Boyes, who was terminally ill with rheumatoid arthritis, in terrible pain and who had asked Dr Cox to help her die. Mrs Boyes could not be relieved from her pain or cured and the injection given to her by Dr Cox was deliberately designed to end her life.

The court ruled that Dr Cox's action was illegal because it was 'deliberately designed to take a life'.

Tony Bland was in 'a persistent vegetative state' from 1989 until 1992, after the Hillsborough football disaster. His body continued to function but there was no possibility of the recovery of consciousness because of his severe brain damage.

The court ruled that doctors could discontinue ventilation, nutrition and hydration by artificial means.

According to Michael Keeling, a writer on Christian ethics, these three cases raise many of the difficult questions surrounding euthanasia, for example, deciding which of the following actions is legally or morally permissible:

- Withdrawing sustenance, which will inevitably lead to death (Tony Bland).
- Not using 'extraordinary' or disproportionate care to keep a baby alive where the cost or difficulty of the care outweighs the possible benefit (Baby John).

Arguments for euthanasia

- Mature human beings should have the right to choose what to do with their own lives.
- Human beings should have the right to end a life that may consist only of pain, incurable illness, loss of dignity, dependence on others and loneliness.
- Euthanasia avoids the situation of being a constant physical, emotional and financial burden on others.

The points mentioned above refer to *voluntary euthanasia*, where the patient can choose for him/herself. When a patient is in a coma, so seriously ill that they are incapable of making a decision, or in the case of an incurably sick baby in an incubator, then someone else has to choose to terminate their life. This is known as *involuntary euthanasia*. This raises the problem that the responsibility for the death now lies with someone else and also the problem of how you stop a helpless patient from being murdered by greedy relatives who then claim that they were carrying out the wishes of the victim. In Holland, they have introduced the idea of 'a living will', a legal document prepared in advance, which states clearly what is to be done if the patient becomes incapacitated.

Arguments against euthanasia

- Voluntary euthanasia has been condemned by many church and civil organisations, including the *World Medical Association*.
- Where euthanasia is legal, compulsory termination of life has been used by some governments, such as Nazi Germany, to remove those who embarrassed the state, either through political opposition or because of so-called racial, mental, physical or social deficiencies.
- The practice of euthanasia would undermine the trust that patients have in the medical profession to always act in the interests of preserving life.
- If you allow exceptions to the principle that human life is sacred, you weaken the principle itself.
- The evidence gained from *the hospice movement* in the past few years has also shown that people can experience terminal illnesses in a context of love, dignity and painlessness, surrounded by their family. This evidence attacks the view that euthanasia is preferable to letting a terminal illness take its natural course.
- Many religious people would argue that because the right to life is God-given, the value of human beings is constant, whether rich or poor, strong or weak, handicapped or normal. No human life can be sacrificed merely for the economic or political welfare of either states or individuals. However, individuals may decide to sacrifice themselves in exceptional circumstances. It is never permissible to take innocent life.

Activities

2. Using an example from any recent television series you may have watched, discuss the difficulties faced by someone thinking about abortion.

3. Why is abortion described as an issue about competing rights?

4. What arguments would you use to defend/oppose the actions of the doctors in the cases described in the above case studies?

5. Discuss the view that the legalisation of euthanasia would put unfair pressure on doctors and incurably ill elderly patients.

6. Should the decision to end someone's life be a medical or a moral decision and who should be involved?

EXAM QUESTION

This is an A2 Unit 3 Section B essay question from the equivalent test in January 2002.

'The taking of human life is never justified.' Discuss this proposition in the light of dilemmas faced in such situations as war, euthanasia, capital punishment and where taking a life may save the lives of others.

(25 marks)

EXAMINER'S ADVICE

- The issues in this question overlap with those in the question at the end of the previous unit. The same sort of thinking and values apply, so use the material in both units to help formulate your answer.
- Here you have the option to agree or disagree strongly with the proposition or to reserve your position, recognising that certain situations may present us with genuine moral dilemmas, as suggested in the prompts. You should use some of the suggested examples in the question to develop your viewpoint(s), although in the timescale of the examination you might struggle to cover all the aspects fully in 45 minutes.
- It may also be possible to hold a different view according to the circumstances, for example accepting that people will kill or be killed in a war which you think it is necessary to fight, whilst at the same time rejecting the principle of euthanasia, i.e. because you feel that the arguments in each case are different.
- Abortion is another relevant topic to this debate, but be careful not to argue too narrowly and limit your answer as a consequence. If you are seeking to argue a one-sided agreement with the proposition, you should nevertheless explain in as much detail as you can what your position would be in a war or in a situation where your life or that of someone you loved was threatened. How would you or should other people deal with this kind of dilemma?
- When you have attempted your answer, compare your points with those made on pages 277–278.

19 Aesthetic evaluation

Aesthetics is the study of what makes something beautiful, what makes something valued as a work of art. In a sense, aesthetic evaluation is a matter of taste. We say someone has good taste or bad taste in areas such as choice of furniture, interior design, clothes, hairstyle, garden ornaments, etc. In the same way, people have good taste or bad taste in culture and the arts. However, there is more to aesthetic evaluation than taste alone. There is a connection between aesthetic values and moral values. Someone can have terrific style and taste in all the other areas previously mentioned and be thoroughly evil without it affecting their taste. However, a work of art that is evil cannot be regarded as a great work of art. Works of art are not just concerned with beauty, they are concerned with human behaviour, the nature and meaning of life, the concepts of good and evil.

Some critics have challenged this view and claim that aesthetic evaluation is solely concerned with the form of a work of art and the effect it has on the person experiencing it. They suggest that it is impossible to know what the artist had in mind when creating the work of art, so all that matters is its effects on the person experiencing it. Some critics, such as Cleanth Brooks, have gone as far as to say that nothing can be said about a work of art; it can only be experienced.

Although it is true that great works of art from the past still function for us as great works of art, even though we have no idea of their creators' reasons for creating them (e.g. pre-historic cave paintings, Greek sculptures), such a view seems to ignore many factors. If works of art can only be experienced, what is the point of their existence? Can there be no greater value in Beethoven than in Sir Cliff Richard? Great art can shock, challenge, even change the lives of those who experience it. People have lost their faith in God through reading books such as Dostoevsky's *The Brothers Karamazov*. People's attitudes to the Spanish Civil War were changed by Picasso's painting, *Guernica*, which was based on an incident in the war. Dictators such as Hitler and Stalin tried to keep firm control of the arts because they saw them as dangerous in provoking criticism and questioning of the regime. The Nazis burnt books whose ideas they disagreed with and censored any art form to make sure that it was promoting the ideals of the regime. All of which indicates that there is something about the arts that can be evaluated. It is possible to draw up a set of criteria to be used when trying to determine whether something is a great work of art and whether one piece of art is better than another.

Criteria for aesthetic evaluation

1. Form
This means the method of production which varies in different art forms. The first issue is craftsmanship – is the painting well painted, is the novel well written?

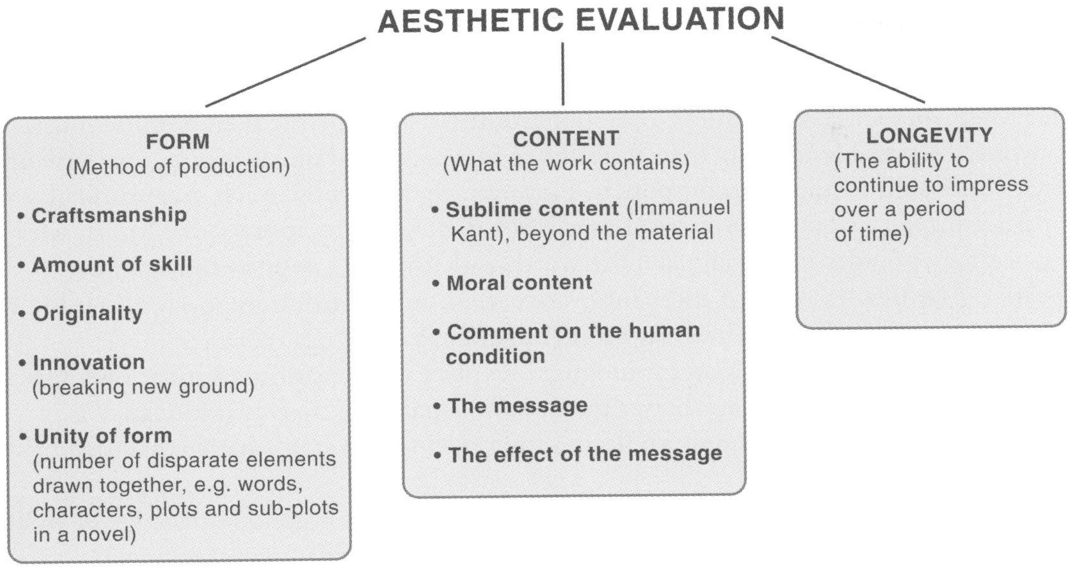

AESTHETIC EVALUATION

Figure 19.1 Elements within aesthetic evaluation

FORM
(Method of production)

- **Craftsmanship**

- **Amount of skill**

- **Originality**

- **Innovation**
(breaking new ground)

- **Unity of form**
(number of disparate elements
drawn together, e.g. words,
characters, plots and sub-plots
in a novel)

CONTENT
(What the work contains)

- **Sublime content** (Immanuel
Kant), beyond the material

- **Moral content**

- **Comment on the human
condition**

- **The message**

- **The effect of the message**

LONGEVITY
(The ability to
continue to impress
over a period
of time)

Connected with this is the amount of skill needed to produce the form, for example a symphony. A great work of art should also be original. Copying needs craftsmanship and skill, but it is not original. Connected with originality is innovation. Often the greatest works of art break new ground in the field rather than just following the tradition. Finally, the work needs a unity of form. Any work of art must bring together a great number of disparate elements (for example a novel needs good choice of words, characters, plots, sub-plots, etc., a symphony brings together lots of different instruments and even more musicians). It is often said that the more disparate elements an artist manages to unite into one work of art, the greater the work is.

2. Content

This means not only what the work contains, but also what its message and effect is. A great work of art must have some content which Kant called 'the sublime'. Something which makes the viewer/reader aware of the transcendent – the feeling that there is something beyond the obvious material world. It may be an awareness of God, or, with atheistic artists, an awareness of the wonder of the human spirit. Great works of art will also have some moral content, making the viewer/reader aware of the battle between good and evil in life. Novels, poems, plays and films will also say something about the human condition (what life is like, what it could be like and what it ought to be like).

3. Longevity

A great work of art should continue to impress people over a long period of time. This will possibly be more true of painting, sculpture and music than novels, etc. because language changes over the years. Nevertheless, great literature such as Shakespeare continues to impress even though much of the language is now unused.

Using aesthetic evaluation

The criteria for aesthetic evaluation can be used in a wide range of situations. In deciding whether classical music is more beautiful or worthwhile than popular music, it would be possible to show that, in terms of form, classical music is better because of the greater skill required to compose it. However, there may be much more difficulty in determining whether the classical music of Salieri (a contemporary of Mozart, who was equally popular in his day) is more worthwhile than the popular music of the Beatles. The Beatles were far more innovative, their music had more to say about life, and their music is likely to have far more longevity than that of Salieri.

The criteria can also be used for judging one piece of art against a similar one, for deciding whether a live play is better than a film, a painting by David Hockney is better than a painting by Rembrandt, or a song by one pop star is better than one by another.

Whenever you use the criteria, however, you should have a good knowledge of what you are applying the criteria to, and an awareness of the difficulty of drawing a boundary between popular culture and high culture (see Unit 20).

Price and value in art

There is often argument about the price paid for a work of art (particularly a painting) in auctions and whether this price reflects the true value of the work. In 1979, a painting by Modigliani could not fetch its reserve price (the minimum price the vendor is prepared to accept) of £325,000, but when it was auctioned at Sothebys, New York, in November 2004, it set a record of £17 million for any painting by the artist. At the same auction, a painting by Gauguin, which would have fetched very little 50 years ago, fetched £21.3 million.

There are several reasons why a work of art becomes more valuable:

- The artist dies, so there will be no more such works coming onto the market and they gain a rarity value.
- It is easier to see the value of an artist's work in retrospect. The originality, innovation and longevity of the artist's work cannot be fully assessed until around 50 years after their death.
- An original piece of great art is something many people would like to own, including many new public art galleries around the world. The more people there are bidding, the more the price will go up.
- Investors with no interest in art know that any work by a dead, great artist is going to increase because the value is in the work of art and so will not change. The evidence of the twentieth century was that a great painting was the most secure investment of any type, as all great paintings increased in value far more than inflation plus interest.

Clearly, works of art, just like footballers, are worth what people are prepared to pay for them. It appears that some modern art such as 'installation art' (see Unit 21) may only be fetching high prices because it is a fashion accessory for super-rich people, and fashion certainly plays a part in what is regarded as valuable. Nevertheless, just as in clothes, architecture, etc. for art to be fashionable, it must have some of the criteria for form and content.

Government sponsorship of the arts

Arts such as opera, classical music, ballet, serious theatre, and even serious film, would not survive without government funding. The Arts Council of Great Britain receives government grants to support the Arts. In 1992, the Arts Council received £215 million, in 2007 they received £412 million. In 1992, museums and art galleries received £259 million, by 2007 this had increased to £468 million as a result of the Labour Government making entry to museum and art galleries free. Large sums are also given to the arts by the National Lottery.

The arguments for government sponsorship of the arts

- High culture is a vital part of a nation's culture. Popular culture can survive without subsidy precisely because it can command large audiences, but high culture is expensive to maintain and cannot be financed by the smaller numbers who attend performances.
- The arts are a sign of a society's civilisation. They give the members of the society an opportunity to think about the meaning of life and to experience great beauty. Arts such as sculpture and architecture make the environment more pleasant.

Figure 19.2 The refurbished Royal Opera House, Covent Garden, London

KEY TERMS

Baroque seventeenth- and eighteenth-century style in the arts based on extravagant design and exuberant decoration

Blank verse unrhymed poetry using iambic pentameters (a special form of rhythm based on short and long syllables)

Chamber music classical music not intended for a full orchestra or soloists, e.g. string quartet

Expressionism a style of art, music, etc. that subordinates realism to expressing the artist's inner feelings

Impressionism a style of art, music, etc. intended to convey the general effect, rather than elaborate detail

Lieder song form of the Romantic era, especially associated with Schubert

Oratorio a work for singers and orchestra (usually with religious connections) to be performed as a concert, rather than an opera

Pas de deux dance in ballet for two persons (usually the male and female leads)

Quality drama plays or films that have most of the criteria for aesthetic evaluation

Romanticism a movement in the arts that emphasised the theme and feelings of a work of art, rather than its form (e.g. Beethoven in music, Wordsworth in literature, Turner in painting)

Sonnet poem of fourteen lines with ten syllables to a line

Stream of consciousness a form of novel writing depicting a continuous flow of a person's thoughts and reactions to events rather than telling a story

Surrealism a movement in art and literature expressing the subconscious through dreams

19 Aesthetic evaluation

Activities

1. Re-read the novel you studied for GCSE English and use the aesthetic evaluation criteria to explain why it is/is not a great work of art.

2. Choose an area of popular music you enjoy and explain why you enjoy it.

3. Choose a painting, piece of classical music, play or film that is considered to be a great work of art and use all the information in this unit to discuss whether it really is a great work of art (argue the points for and the points against).

4. 'Only the rich enjoy the arts so the arts should not be subsidised by government taxes.' Examine the validity of this statement. (This means just the same as discuss!)

5. 'The arts are only entertainment, and, although enjoyable, they are of no use to society.' Discuss this view with reference to more than one art-form.

- The arts can make money for the country. Although the domestic performances of the Royal Shakespeare Company require subsidies, their tours abroad make a profit. More importantly, many tourists come to Britain to experience our wide range of cultural activities. Their money makes a substantial contribution to Britain's exports (money spent by tourists in Britain is an export; money spent by British tourists abroad is an import).
- The popular arts such as music and theatre depend on the training given by high culture. Many of the production teams and backing groups for pop stars have a classical music training. Actors in popular theatre and television have often had a classical training.
- There is no clear division between high culture and popular culture, and it could be that a society without high culture would also lose much of its popular culture.
- Market forces can lead to a serious downgrading of culture. The argument about the BBC being funded by licence rather than advertising (a form of subsidy because there are people who buy a licence but never watch the BBC's programmes) is usually based on a comparison between BBC programmes and those on the satellite and cable channels, which are solely determined by market forces. If quality television requires subsidy, then quality arts should also receive subsidy.
- All governments now subsidise the arts, so that if Britain stopped doing so, all the best artists would go overseas.

The arguments against government sponsorship of the arts

- The people who want high culture and who go to the opera, etc. are relatively well off, and are able to pay the market price for their seats (a French survey of the arts showed that less than ten per cent of audiences at serious theatre, opera and symphony concerts were working class).
- Most government subsidy is spent on the arts in London, which is unfair to people in the regions.
- In every other area of life, workers are paid the market rate and if their industry cannot compete it has to reduce wages and costs. The same economics should apply to serious theatre, opera, etc. Wages and costs should be reduced until subsidies are not needed.
- Writers of serious literature survive without subsidy and many serious films make profits.
- The people who decide on arts sponsorship are people from within the arts industry. Subsidies should be organised by ordinary people and the arts industries wanting the subsidy should have to justify their claims for subsidy.
- There are much more important things to spend hundreds of millions of pounds on than the arts – such as the homeless, world poverty or the National Health Service.

19

Read the passage below about art music and answer the multiple choice questions which follow.

Resuscitating Art Music

(1) Today, art music – whether by Bach or Coltrane or Shankar or Philip Glass – sometimes seems like a species on the verge of extinction. Those of us who have been moved, nourished, and inspired by art music find it hard to believe what's happening: symphony orchestras are collapsing, artist managers are going out of business, presenters are reducing their chamber music offerings, newspapers are cutting back on coverage, audiences are greying, and funds are drying up. What's going on? How did things get this way? Is there anything we can do about it?

(2) I once tried an experiment with a music class of mine. We listened to two pieces of music: one a song that was popular in the music charts at the time, and the other a fourteenth-century love song. Predictably, most of the class liked the modern, popular piece, but they all hated the fourteenth-century love song. One said that he disliked the fourteenth-century piece because the music wasn't in English. Another said that she didn't like anything that sounded like 'that stuff my parents listen to – you know, Pavarotti

and all that'. One student answered, 'I like rock music because even if I'm doing something else, even in a different room, I can still get it. I can still tell where the beat is.' Then he said something I've been thinking about ever since. 'I like rock music because you don't have to pay attention in order to get it.' He really seemed to resent it that the fourteenth-century music required him to do something, to pay attention. I think that in these modern times the ability to pay attention has become endangered. As a result, art forms that require the audience's attention are endangered, too.

(3) Art music isn't the only institution suffering right now. General Motors is in trouble. IBM is in trouble. Atmospheric ozone is in trouble. Even Japan is in trouble. Is it any wonder that art music is in trouble, too? Sometimes, in my more optimistic moments, I think that all this trouble – GM's problems, music's problems, the national debt, the ozone hole, all of it – is really great. This is evolutionary pressure, forcing us human beings to learn to do things better. Look at General Motors:

until recently it didn't matter that many of GM's management practices were stupid and wasteful. They still made tons of money. Now, if GM wants to survive, it will have to do its job better. Art music is in a similar situation.

(4) Until recently, art music could be presented in thoughtless or inefficient ways without harming itself. It didn't matter if we put on performances that baffled the audience and bored the musicians. It didn't matter if we gave youth concerts that turned young people off. It didn't matter if we performed only for a white middle class audience. It didn't matter if we ignored new listeners and didn't help them learn how to pay attention. We still had audiences. We still had plenty of money. We still had lots of people who cherished the medium. Now, rather abruptly, all those things that didn't matter have become crucial. Art music is under pressure to do its job better. But what is so special about this music and why should it survive?

(5) When I talk about art music, I mean any music that you have to pay attention to

in order to reap its rewards. I don't care so much about preserving any particular style of music, so my definition doesn't describe the music at all; it describes the listeners. What I want to keep alive are the qualities of attention, the kinds of human interactions, and the ways of knowing and experiencing that are found in the practice of art music, and indeed all forms of serious art. So let's simply say that art music requires conscious attention and some experience in order to be properly understood. This music rewards such devotion with multiple, complex layers of meaning and feeling.

(6) You can see right away that many different styles of music fit my definition: jazz, Indonesian gamelan music, and South Indian classical music are only three of the many kinds of music that can be just as artistic in this sense as European classical music. And some European classical music probably doesn't qualify as art music at all. The key message is that if you think your favourite music fits, include it; but make sure it fulfils the vital criteria for genuine art music.

Source: adapted from John Steinmetz, 'Resuscitating Art Music', *Journal of the US National Academy of Recording Arts and Sciences*, Summer 1993

For the questions which follow, choose the answer A, B, C or D which you think fits best. Each of the questions is worth one mark.

1 When the author states that audiences are 'greying' in paragraph 1, he means that they are
   A becoming bored.
   B being disregarded.
   C growing older.
   D reducing in size.

2 In paragraph 1 the author's tone is mostly one of
   A anger.
   B surprise.
   C resolve.
   D denial.

3 The main point made by the author in paragraph 3 is that
   A art music is experiencing more problems than most.
   B inefficient businesses can still be profitable.
   C as things evolve, problems are bound to arise.
   D problems should lead to improvements.

4 In paragraph 4, the author refers to each of the following criticisms of art music **except** that it was
   A unprofitable.
   B elitist.
   C difficult to understand.
   D unwelcoming.

5 From what the author says in paragraph 5, his statement in paragraph 6 'And some European classical music probably doesn't qualify as art music at all', implies that this music is
   A too simple.
   B too religious.
   C unmusical.
   D too complex.

6 The **essential** point being made by the author in paragraph 6 is that
   A art music is international.
   B European classical music varies in quality.
   C music from outside Europe can be of high quality.
   D art music is a matter of personal taste.

7 Which of the following characteristics are implied in the definition of art music given in paragraphs 5 and 6? It
   1 embraces different styles.
   2 is emotionally rewarding.
   3 is intellectually stimulating.
   4 disregards the audience.

   Answer
   A if 1 and 4 only are correct.
   B if 3 and 4 only are correct.
   C if 1, 2 and 3 only are correct.
   D if all of them are correct.

8 Based on this article, which of these statements could be said to be true of the author? He
   1 has a low opinion of popular music.
   2 is worried about the decline of certain kinds of music.
   3 believes that young people are incapable of appreciating good music.
   4 regards any kind of music as art music.

   Answer
   A if 1 only is correct.
   B if 2 only is correct.
   C if 2 and 3 only are correct.
   D if 1, 3 and 4 only are correct.

9 The main purpose of the author in writing this article is best described as to
   A show young people the benefits of classical music.
   B argue the case for more subtle appreciation of art forms.
   C criticise modern popular music.
   D improve education in the arts for all.

For Question 10 you are given an assertion followed by a reason. Consider the assertion and decide whether, on its own, it is a true statement. Then consider the reason and decide if it is a true statement. If, and only if, you decide that both the assertion and reason are true, consider whether the reason is a valid or true explanation of the assertion. Choose your answer as follows.

	Assertion	Reason	Argument
A	True	True	Reason is a correct explanation of assertion
B	True	True	Reason is **not** a correct explanation of assertion
C	True	False	Not applicable
D	False	True	Not applicable

10 **Assertion:**   The author is arguing the case for art music . . .

   Reason: . . . because art music needs careful attention to be properly understood.

EXAMINER'S ADVICE
- The passage and questions are taken from the AQA AS Unit 1 test for January 2004. In the exam proper there are 30 questions based on a longer version of the passage, followed by three questions for documentary source analysis.
- Check out the general advice on tackling multiple choice questions on page 266. The ten questions here are representative of the type and range you will get in the exam and you should aim to complete them in, say, half an hour.
- Generally, the questions become broader and more complex as you work through them. Note that Questions 7 and 8 require you to select a combination of answers, so you have to accept or reject each of the numbered options in turn. There are also several stages to work through for Question 10. These types of questions are usually harder than the rest.
- The answers are given on page 278.

The nature of culture

Culture can be defined in a variety of ways, but it is generally agreed that culture means human beliefs, knowledge and behaviour, which form a distinctive pattern or system. Each society has its own culture based on such things as a separate language, a separate history, different rituals and customs (for example, French culture, Scottish culture, Maori culture). This idea of culture has led to stereotyping, so that Scottish culture is often seen in terms of associations such as the kilt, the bagpipes, haggis, Burns' Night and tossing the caber.

However, in the second half of the twentieth century, cultures began to mix much more and the old monocultural idea (where each society has only one culture, which everyone accepts and lives by) has been displaced, as most societies have become multicultural. In a multicultural society, there may be groups living according to a variety of ethnic cultures, but there will also be some subcultures such as teen culture, urban culture, rural culture, pop culture, mass culture, high culture. Sociologists now accept that the culture into which an individual is born may have a much smaller influence than it used to have. Individuals now have the opportunity to choose their own culture, in the sense that in a multicultural society any individual will be influenced by several cultures.

In order to help you to answer questions on culture, this unit will explain some of the more common types of culture.

Western culture

Western culture is the basic culture of Europe and the USA and has a major effect on most other cultures in the world. Much argument about culture is based around whether it is inevitable that all cultures will eventually become subcultures of western culture and whether western culture has a good or bad effect. Japan is a typical example of this argument. Its economy and media are thoroughly western culture, but Japanese culture still dominates many people's personal lives (attitudes towards and rituals concerning birth, marriage, death, festivals and so on).

The main features of western culture are:

- A concern for individual rights – free speech, freedom to choose or reject religion, free choice of marriage partner, freedom for an individual to move from the bottom to the top of society, freedom from arbitrary arrest (if arrested, people must be brought before an open court within a short length of time).
- Equality of opportunity – free education available to everyone, all jobs (especially government jobs) open to anyone, legislation against racist or sexist bias.
- Protection of the poor – healthcare and payments to the unemployed, the sick and the old through taxation.
- Democratic systems of government.

- The arts following certain forms (see 'High culture' and 'Popular culture' below).
- Dress and lifestyle based on the individual, rather the group.
- Festivals and holidays based on Christianity (for example, Christmas and Easter).
- Moral values based on Christianity (respect for monogamy, honesty, loving one's neighbour, etc.).
- The media reflecting the lifestyles and arts (especially popular culture) and having great importance in people's lives.

Many people would not accept all these features, and some critics of western culture see its key features and symbols as jeans, Coca-Cola, McDonalds and pop music, which they also see as destroying the indigenous cultures of the world.

High culture

Many people link culture with the arts and use the term 'cultured person' to refer to someone who appreciates, and is knowledgeable about, classical music, opera, ballet, great literature, poetry, serious theatre and film, painting and sculpture. It is claimed that this type of culture is a sign of civilisation because these arts speak to us about the meaning of life, speak to 'the human spirit' and pass on human values.

Classical music

This includes music written either for a symphony orchestra or for groups of instruments from the orchestra. A symphony orchestra is made up of strings (violins, violas, cellos, double bass), woodwind (clarinets, oboes, bassoons, flutes, cor anglais, piccolos), brass (horns, trumpets, trombones and tubas) and percussion (drums, cymbals, etc.). The main types of music played by a symphony orchestra are symphonies, concertos (solo instrument and orchestra) and overtures. However, symphony orchestras can also be used to accompany choirs in major choral works such as Handel's *Messiah*, Bach's *St Matthew Passion* and the great masses such as the *Requiems* of Mozart and Fauré. The first great concertos were written by J. S. Bach (*Brandenburg Concertos*) and Vivaldi (*The Four Seasons*); the first great symphonies were written by Haydn (*London Symphonies*), Mozart (*Jupiter Symphony*) and Beethoven (*Eroica Symphony*). Classical music did not end with Beethoven. Mendelssohn, Lizst, Brahms, Mahler, Stravinsky, Rachmaninov, Elgar and Britten continued and evolved the tradition. There are many composers still writing classical music, such as John Taverner, whose *Requiem* was played at the funeral of Diana, Princess of Wales.

Opera

This can be defined as 'drama set to music where the music is essential to the drama'. The first operas were performed in Italy (Monteverdi's *Coronation of Poppea*) and developed by Glück (*Orpheus*) and Mozart (*Don Giovanni, The Marriage of Figaro, The Magic Flute*). Opera depends on the plot as well as the music, solo singers who act the main parts, often a chorus of singers and a symphony orchestra (though this is often smaller than a full orchestra). Many people see opera as the highest form of culture because it combines classical music with theatre and art in the sets and costumes. This also makes opera the most expensive art form to perform. The most popular operas today are those by Mozart, Verdi (*Nabucco, Aida, Il Traviata*), Wagner (*Die Meistersingers, The Ring*), Bizet (*Carmen, The Pearl Fishers*), and Puccini (*La Boheme, Madame Butterfly, Tosca*). Opera singers such as Caruso, Maria Callas and Luciano Pavarotti can achieve as much fame and money as great pop stars.

Ballet

This is a form of dancing to classical music that has been popular in many cultures for centuries. Ballet began in France in the late seventeenth century, with the work of the French composer Lully. Much of modern ballet developed in the nineteenth century in France, but some of the great changes to modern ballet occurred in Russia, under Diagilev, just before the communist revolution. Famous female ballet dancers include Isadora Duncan, Maria Pavlova and Margot Fonteyn. The two most famous male ballet dancers were both Russian: Vaclav Nijinsky and Rudolph Nureyev. The most popular ballets today are probably those with music by Tchaikovsky (*The Nutcracker, Swan Lake, Romeo and Juliet*), Delibes (*Coppelia*) and Stravinsky (*Petroushka, The Rite of Spring, The Firebird*). The ballet requires a symphony orchestra and so is often staged in opera houses. In England the Royal Ballet and the Royal Opera both use the New Covent Garden Opera House.

Great literature

This refers to novels or short stories that have a message about the meaning of life and say something about human nature through their characters (though their storyline may or may not stand up to scrutiny). The novel you studied for GCSE English literature will be termed as 'great literature'. The first great piece of English literature can probably be regarded as *The Canterbury Tales* by Chaucer. Novels did not evolve until the eighteenth century, when *Joseph Andrewes* by Henry Fielding and *Robinson Crusoe* by Daniel Defoe were written. The greatest nineteenth-century British novelist was Charles Dickens (*David Copperfield, Great Expectations, Oliver Twist*), though some would claim that it was Jane Austen (*Pride and Prejudice, Sense and Sensibility*) or the Brontë sisters (*Jane Eyre, Wuthering Heights*). Twentieth-century novelists such as D. H. Lawrence (*Sons and Lovers, Women in Love*), James Joyce (*Ulysses*), John Braine (*Room at the Top*) have tended to be more working class than in previous centuries. There are many contemporary novelists writing what may be considered 'great literature' such as William Trevor, Salman Rushdie (*Midnight's Children, Satanic Verses*), Martin Amis and Margaret Forster. You should be aware of great world literature such as *War and Peace* by Leo Tolstoy (about Russian aristocratic families during and after the Napoleonic Wars), *The Brothers Karamazov* by Fyodor Dostoevsky (about murder and the existence of God) and *A La Recherche du Temps Perdu* by Marcel Proust (about the decline of a group of French aristocrats at the beginning of the twentieth century).

Poetry

It is often said that 'a poem can say in a page what it takes a novel 300 pages to say'. It is also said that poetry is 'the best words in the best order'. From this it can be

CULTURE, MORALITY, ARTS AND HUMANITIES

seen that poetry is about putting forward ideas about the meaning of life, and also about using words in special ways to give a beautiful sound, as well as a deep meaning. There is a close connection between poetry and other forms of literature. Shakespeare wrote poems as well as plays (mostly sonnets). Thomas Hardy, who wrote great novels such as *Tess of the d'Urbervilles* and *Jude the Obscure*, also wrote much poetry. One of the great periods in English poetry was the Romantic period of the early nineteenth century, whose writers included Wordsworth (*Daffodils, Upon Westminster Bridge*), Keats (*Ode to a Nightingale, Endymion*), Shelley (*Ozymandias, To a Skylark*) and Coleridge (*Kubla Khan, The Rime of the Ancient Mariner*). You will probably have studied twentieth-century poetry for GCSE English. Try re-reading some of it to see whether your views about it have changed.

Film and performing arts

This is probably the part of high culture which has the most impact on ordinary people. Although many would think only of the theatre when they think of 'performing arts', and going to the theatre to see serious drama is a minority activity, more than 50 per cent of the population is likely to come into contact with the performing arts through television drama and films.

The performing arts aim to bring imaginary situations to life so that the audience becomes involved in the situation and, through a successful portrayal, begin to look at life in different ways. Clearly the performing arts are almost totally reliant on literature through dramatists or scriptwriters.

Not many young people would go to see the RSC performing *Romeo and Juliet* for pleasure, but Baz Luhrmann's film version set in 1990s America with Leonardo di Caprio as Romeo brought Shakespeare to millions of young people worldwide. Certainly the updating made many young people think more deeply about Shakespeare's theme of institutionalised violence bringing tragedy to those who are most loved.

It is not only through performances of famous serious dramatists, such as Shakespeare, Beckett and Pinter, that the performing arts make people think deeply. Television dramas (such as *The Second Coming* about Jesus returning to contemporary society) and films (such as *Mona Lisa Smile* about feminism in the late 1950s) can enable the performing arts to encourage a lot of people to think more deeply about serious issues.

The adaptation of serious literature for film or television (or even in the case of Victor Hugo's *Les Miserables* for a musical) is a genre which does more than simply 'bring a book to life'. BBC1's adaptation of *North and South* by Elizabeth Gaskell gave a twenty-first-century interpretation of the book, helping people today to see the major problems caused to both employers and employees by the Industrial Revolution.

Of course, the performing arts do not have to be serious, Shakespeare wrote comedies. Films such as *Bend it Like Beckham*, *Bruce Almighty* and *Knocked Up* were box office hits seen by millions of people, but they brought serious issues to life in a less serious way.

KEY TERMS

American dream the alleged basis of American culture, that any individual can do anything they want and achieve the lifestyle they desire through using market forces

Booker Prize the most important British literature award for newly written serious novels

Elitism the belief that a small, select group (e.g. advocates of high culture) is superior to the rest of society

Cultural norms standards of a culture, e.g. the norms of western culture are individual rights, equal opportunity, etc.

Cultural values what is regarded as important in culture (very similar to cultural norms)

Ethnic originally connected with race, it is now used to refer more to a cultural group, which may have certain racial characteristics (e.g. gypsies, Sikhs)

Grand opera opera in which there is no spoken dialogue; everything is set to music

Indigenous culture the culture that is native to the area (e.g. the culture of the native Americans is the indigenous culture of the USA)

Monoculture a society based on only one culture

Multiculture a society with several different cultures

Multiethnic a society with different races and cultures connected with those races

Pop art serious art based on popular culture and the mass media, e.g. Andy Warhol's painting of a can of Campbell's soup

Turner Prize the most important British award for contemporary art

Whitbread Prize a British award for the best book of the year

Youth icon an object of admiration reflecting what is regarded as important by young people

Painting and sculpture

These have been part of human life from prehistoric times. Some of the earliest examples of human culture are cave paintings, the most famous being those from northern Spain and southwest France, dating from over 40,000 years ago. The Egyptian civilisation is remembered both by its sculpture, such as the huge statues of pharaohs, and by the intricate paintings on the walls of the tombs and on the sarcophagi (coffins of the mummies). Of course, painting and sculpture is joined together in architecture, which often reflects the spirit of an age. The most famous ancient sculptures come from Greece (*Venus de Milo*), where sculptures began to be made from bronze as well as marble. In western Europe, most art took the form of architecture until the Renaissance, when painting and sculpture enjoyed a rebirth. Michelangelo is famous not only for the paintings on the ceiling of the Sistine Chapel (frescoes depicting Christianity from Adam to the final judgement), but also great sculptures such as *David* and *Pieta*. After the Renaissance, there have been several different periods and styles: Baroque (Bernini, El Greco, Carravaggio, Rembrandt), Rococo (Canaletto, Watteau), Romantic (Goya, Turner), Impressionist (Renoir, Degas, Monet, Cezanne), Expressionist (Van Gogh, Roualt, Munch and abstract expressionist in Jackson Pollock), Surrealist (Klee, Magritte, Dali). The most famous sculptors of these periods have been Bernini, Rodin and Henry Moore.

Popular culture

Popular culture is often used in a derogatory sense to indicate the type of culture that is less educated and less valuable than high culture. However, each area of high culture has a corresponding feature in popular culture. Music is perhaps the easiest example, where popular music is a major business worldwide. Groups and popstars can attract massive audiences at concerts almost anywhere in the world and their records sell millions of copies. Closely connected with popular music are a variety of dance forms, from ordinary people dancing in a nightclub to professional dancers in modern dance shows. Popular literature ranges from thrillers and romances to biographies of sports and pop stars. Theatres and cinemas make their money from the popular shows and films they put on. Andy Warhol developed a form of painting that he called pop art, but no painting can ever be popular in one sense because only the rich can afford to buy original paintings. However, most homes will have some cheap reproductions of famous paintings, which may reveal that paintings are often more a part of popular culture than high culture, e.g. Constable's *Haywain*. Many modern sculptures are publicly funded and can become popular because they are in places frequented by the public. *The Angel of the North* in Gateshead seems to be more popular with ordinary people than with those who consider themselves 'cultured', and as such is perhaps an example of popular sculpture.

This sculpture also identifies a major problem with trying to make a division between high culture and popular culture as there are so many fringe areas. The theme music from the *Harry Potter* films appeared in both the pop music charts and the classical music charts. Serious films such as *The Queen* and *Atonement* have also been

Figure 20.1 The Angel of the North by Antony Gormley, created by a high culture sculptor, but most admired by ordinary people who follow popular culture

hugely popular. Perhaps this is more easily seen in television where traditionally ITV1 is the popular culture channel with BBC2, BBC4 and Channel 4 seen as the high culture channels, but it is ITV1 which screens *The South Bank Show*, a programme all about high culture. The differences between high and popular culture (and the fact that high culture can only survive through subsidies from the taxes of people who do not like it) are dealt with at greater length in Unit 19.

Activities

1. Interview people of a variety of ages and social situations to discover what they consider to be the key features of British culture.

2. Use the Internet to discover the main features of popular culture.

3. Listen to 30 minutes of Classic FM, 30 minutes of Radio 1 and 30 minutes of an Asian radio programme. Decide whether the music played on Classic FM or the Asian station has most in common with the music of Radio 1 and why.

4. Make a list of the arguments for and against western culture being adopted throughout the world.

EXAM QUESTION

This is an A2 essay question taken from Section B of the Unit 3 Specimen Paper in 2007.

'High culture is more valuable and important than popular entertainment.'

Discuss the validity of this statement.

(25 marks)

EXAMINER'S ADVICE

- This is a standard A2 essay question on a central topic in General Studies concerned with the appreciation and evaluation of the arts in their various forms. The question requires an assessment of the relative merits of what are stereotypically known as 'high culture/art' and 'popular culture/entertainment' and therefore you need to show that you have a clear idea of what these terms represent. Popular entertainment should, in the context of this unit and question, be understood to refer to broadly artistic areas and not sport.

- What are the real differences between 'classical' and 'popular' music, or between a Shakespeare play and *EastEnders*, for example? You should think about this in artistic rather more than in social/cultural/class terms.

- You will also usefully seek to define the two other keys terms in the statement of what might be meant by 'valuable' and 'important', e.g. valuable and important for what reasons? To whom? And why? Clearly there is a great deal of subjective judgement in the statement as well as cultural conditioning. Should the question really be about 'good' and 'not so good' art? What characteristics help to define 'good' and 'bad' in the arts?

- Overall you would be expected to provide a balanced discussion which examines the rival claims of various forms of artistic activity to be superior, perhaps for different reasons, or essentially the same, although there would be no harm in showing that you have personal preferences, as long as you clearly justify them with illustrations/actual examples.

- Use the discussion in this unit and the previous one to build up your arguments and compile some illustrations which will support them. This is not a topic where the examiner is expecting a single right answer and you are well within your rights to argue both sides.

- When you have thought about the topic and assembled some material for your answer, spend no more than 30–40 minutes writing it out. Then compare your ideas with the notes on page 278.

Creativity and innovation

Creativity can have many meanings. There is a sense in which everyone is creative. Anyone who has written a letter, decorated a room or planted a garden has been creative. However, calling someone creative is usually taken to mean more than this – it is used to refer to people who write books, paint pictures or create designer gardens.

Innovation is more clearcut. To count as an innovation, what is created must be different from what has gone before. It must break new ground, by starting a new school of art as the Impressionists Renoir and Degas did, developing the form of the symphony as Beethoven did, or, like the Beatles, changing the direction of popular music.

Creativity and ordinary people

Many experts believe that all human beings have a creative urge and so they believe that education should give people the opportunity to develop that creativity. The purpose of art, music, cookery, woodwork, metalwork, needlework, drama, and design lessons at school is to encourage creativity, and also to give young people the opportunity to discover whether they have particular creative gifts and to give them the skills to use their gifts. It is often argued that many great artists will never be able to reveal their creative gifts if they are not given skills and opportunities in creative subjects. In just the same way that Shakespeare could not have written his plays if he had not been taught to read and write, likewise no one can become a great violinist if they never have the chance to learn to play a violin or become a great designer if they are not given the necessary basic skills. This is seen very clearly in the case of Sir Paul McCartney, who composed all the music for his classical piece *Standing Stones*, but had to have expert help to write it into an orchestral score because he had never actually been taught musical composition.

It is also argued that those who take part in the arts, in even the most basic way, are more able to appreciate them than those who only go to watch. Someone who has played in a school orchestra knows how hard it is to get a group of musicians to play correctly. They also have some understanding of musical forms, and so are more able to appreciate great music. Someone who has tried to paint or sculpt is likely to have far more appreciation of a painting or sculpture than someone who has not, because they are aware of the technical problems involved. Likewise, people who have sung in choirs or acted in school plays are likely to have a better appreciation of choral music or theatre than someone who has not.

However, it can also be argued that anyone who has creative urges and skills will be driven to use them. Sir Paul McCartney may not have written and performed great pop music if he had been trained in music. It can be argued that if he had been trained, he would not have had the originality or the desire to perform that a great pop musician needs. He has been a great musician without training. In the same way, artists like van Gogh and Gauguin had no formal art training, but felt a compelling urge to paint. Very few novelists have any formal training in literature.

In the same way, it is possible that music lessons and art lessons put many young people off the arts in the same way that teaching Shakespeare, rather than going to see performances of his plays, puts young people off Shakespeare for life.

Le Corbusier and modern architecture

Charles Jeanneret (1887–1965), who adopted the pseudonym Le Corbusier (the name of one of his ancestors) when he started writing, was the most famous of a group of artists and architects who wanted to break away from traditional forms. In *Towards a New Architecture*, Le Corbusier put forward the view that architecture should be functional, rather than decorated – 'A house is a machine for living in', 'a curved street is a donkey track, a straight street, a road for men'. Le Corbusier utilised the new invention of reinforced concrete to build a shell of concrete floors resting on steel girders so that the outside of his buildings could be of any material – he most often used glass – that would keep plain vertical and horizontal lines. He also believed that the city of the future would be full of green areas and parks with all the living spaces and offices being in skyscrapers.

Le Corbusier found it difficult to get his designs built (a workers' city he built in Pessac, France, in 1926, was so hated by the local authority that it refused to pipe water to it), but his books illustrated with his designs had a tremendous impact on young and trainee architects. By 1950, his ideas had become so influential that he was

Figure 21.1 A building by Le Corbusier

able to design a complex of housing and shops for 1800 people in Marseilles. In 1951, he was made architectural adviser for the construction of Chandigarh, the brand new capital of the Punjab Province of India. His use of unfinished concrete for the principal buildings of the city had an immediate impact on architecture around the world. What is often called 'modern architecture', high rise, straight line, functional buildings using concrete and glass, is the result of Le Corbusier's successful fight against the conservative forces of architecture.

Monet and Impressionism

Claude Monet (1840–1926) was the son of a successful grocer and ship's chandler in Le Havre. He began painting in his mid-teens, and, though he went to Paris, he refused the formal art training his father wanted to pay for, preferring to work with artists. Throughout his life Monet was fascinated by the *effects of light* on how objects are perceived. Oil painted landscapes were painted in studios after remembrances or sketches of the real thing. Monet insisted on painting his landscapes outdoors so that the perception could be put onto canvas immediately.

In 1869, Monet went to La Grenouillère, a resort on the Seine, to paint with Renoir. Together they painted what were to be regarded as the first Impressionist paintings, recording on the spot the impression of a scene rather than a detailed study. This was done by interpreting the light and movement by *rapid, short strokes and fairly vivid colours*. It was Monet's painting, *Impression: Sunrise*, shown at an exhibition in Paris in 1874, which led the critics to call this school of painting 'Impressionism'. Other famous painters worked in the same style and exhibited with Monet and Renoir (for example Degas, Pissarro, Cezanne). However, the artists gradually drew apart and began to develop different styles. The last Impressionist exhibition was held in 1886.

Monet himself continued to paint in his impressionistic style through paintings that studied a single subject through varying lights. As he became more famous, he used the money to develop a garden at his new home in Giverny (now a French national monument), which he painted in his later years. Between 1906 and 1926 he painted a series called *Water Lilies*, in which the actual features become more and more indistinct, with just a shimmering series of colours giving the overall impression of sunlight playing on a lily pond.

Monet was not only an innovative creator – his ideas have had an influence on all the modern schools of art. The exhibition of his paintings at London's Royal Academy in 1999 was a sell-out, the most successful art exhibition ever held in London.

Modern art

Innovation and creativity is particularly concerned with what is termed 'modern art'. This was most connected with abstract art when artists like Wassily Kandinsky and Jackson Pollock began to paint pictures whose content was shapes and colour rather than anything which could be directly connected with the 'real world'. However,

Activities

1. Think of any creative activity you have ever been involved in (especially to do with music, art or drama – remember what you did at Junior School) and try to analyse its good and bad effects on you.

2. Find examples of the work of either Le Corbusier or Monet and use the criteria from Unit 19 ('Aesthetic evaluation') and the knowledge from this unit to assess their greatness.

3. Work out the arguments for and against giving every school child the right to learn a musical instrument.

4. 'Only those who have participated in the arts can understand the arts.' To what extent do you agree with this statement?

5. Many works of art (novels, films, plays, paintings, etc.) are created as vehicles for political, social and/or moral comment. Choose any one work of art that has influenced your thinking about life and society, and explain its purposes and impact on you.

abstract artists had to have considerable artistic skill in terms of the 'form' of aesthetic evaluation. Moreover, modern artists like Pablo Picasso and David Hockney often moved between representational and abstract art.

A major issue in the contemporary art world is whether 'conceptual installation art' is art at all. This type of art has featured in the Turner Prize and is typified by: Tracey Emin's unmade bed; Martin Creed's empty room with the lights going on and off; Damien Hirst's dead sheep in a glass case filled with formaldehyde. Many people argue that such things are not art at all. The 81-year-old-Welsh painter, Sir Kyffin Williams, has said, 'Much of modern art is totally unbelievable . . . Conceptual installation art is worthless and people don't want it.' (BBC News, 14 January 2004)

However, a very different view is given by *The Guardian*'s art critic, Adrian Searle, 'Maybe Creed wanted to give us a prolonged moment of expectation (in the empty room with the lights going on and off) . . . The more I thought about them (Tom Friedman's empty cups) the more associations piled up: from the manufacture of the cups themselves; to the water cooler culture of the office; the fact that the ring of cups on the floor was more beautiful and shimmering than I would have thought possible; that it looked like a sci-fi halo . . . Some people are undoubtedly afraid – both of the feelings art provokes and of having their preconceptions of what art ought to be upset. They want meaning on a plate, served up the way it always has been.' (*The Guardian*, 11 December 2001)

EXAM QUESTION

Study Extracts A and B on Modern Art and then answer Questions 1 and 2. Use your own words, rather than simply repeating those used in the sources, to show your understanding of the points being made.

Source analysis and evaluation question on *The Turner Prize*

Extract A

In 2001 a piece of work entitled 'The Lights Going On and Off' won the Turner Prize – one of the most controversial and sought-after awards in contemporary art.

The minimalist artist Martin Creed collected £20,000 for his installation, which centres around an empty gallery with a pair of flashing lights.

The organisers said that the competition is not designed to show the best artists, but the art that is most interesting at the time.

The winning artist said of his work: 'I think people can make of it what they like. I don't think it is for me to explain it.'

Extract B

Four comments on the Turner Prize:

(a) I wasn't going to bother venturing an opinion on this until I saw a suggestion that we should take this 'art' seriously. The Turner Prize has as much relevance to art as the contents of my dustbin. It is simply a device for selling the artefacts of the untalented poor to the gullible rich. Nobody with the slightest taste would touch this junk with a bargepole.

Andrew, UK

(b) Even I, as a former art student, was sceptical about Martin Creed's installation, but the *Times* art critic explained it in a way that must, I feel, be considered. He said you really have to be there and experience it to appreciate it and that the experience was oddly disquieting. For any installation to have an effect on someone like that totally legitimises it in my eyes, although I won't pass personal judgement until I'm able to experience it for myself.

LD, Cambridge, UK

(c) Art is essentially a subjective matter. It's amazing how many people equate their opinion with fact. I happen to think that the works of Turner, Constable and their ilk are not particularly 'good art' but I cannot claim that view to be fact! I also happen to think that the winner of this year's Turner prize is not 'good art' though I have enjoyed the work of other recent winners. Whatever we think, the Turner Prize has once again achieved its aim, which is to encourage debate and raise the profile of modern art.

John, UK

Source: Adapted from http://news.bbc.co.tik/l/hi/talking_point/1701556.stm

(d) Occasionally one is bowled over by the beauty of something. I recently saw a piece in Paris which was basically an environment of changing light, and intensity of light, and hues of light, and it was just extraordinarily beautiful. And it persuaded me that the artist who can make this must be a significant mind and artist.

But there have been plenty of cases when I don't respond to a work, so I meet with friends afterwards and we have a debate and thrash it out. We hardly ever use the word 'rubbish'. It is just not an appropriate word to use about a work of art.

The Turner Prize was established in part to provoke discussion of contemporary art and it has been very successful. But there is the slight danger that, as in other areas of life, the media feeds off itself and the reactions of others, as much as off the art itself.

Sir Nicholas Serota

Source: based on the words of SIR NICHOLAS SEROTA, Director of the Tate galleries published in *The Financial Times*, 1 February 2003

1 Assess the strengths and weaknesses of each of the four comments about the Turner prize.

(12 marks)

2 To what extent do you consider such contemporary works to be valid and worthwhile forms of art?

(8 marks)

EXAMINER'S ADVICE

- This is an example of a new type of question taken from Section A of the A2 Unit 3 Specimen Paper in 2007. (See page 1 for a summary of the full contents of the Unit 3 test). It is an exercise in source evaluation. In the first question you are asked to assess the appropriateness and quality of a range of expressions of opinion on a topic related to Culture and Society and in the second question to give your own opinion.

- A good answer to the first question will provide a sustained appraisal of each of the four comments, with the best offering some comparison and contrast between them. You should include references to style, content and the origin of the sources, including comments on the authors' overall approaches and positions in relation to the topic. You may choose to deal with each of the comments in turn, or approach the task in a more integrated and comparative manner. Either approach is acceptable, but the latter might indicate a greater degree of understanding and grasp of issues which the comments raise.

- Note that there are 12 marks in total for this question, so you might usefully seek to provide at least three observations on each comment. As always you will be given credit for supporting your points with appropriate examples/evidence. Which of the comments do you think is the most convincing and speaks with the most authority, and why? At this stage you should evaluate the comments objectively, disregarding whether you agree with them or not.

- The second question is an open one and you may express your own opinions here, positive or negative. Say what you consider most appropriate according to your own understanding and appreciation of contemporary art. You might legitimately raise the question of what exactly is meant by 'such contemporary works', as they may be regarded as difficult/impossible to categorise. In this context however it should be recognised that the discussion is mostly about pieces of 'conceptual' or 'installation art' of an abstract kind, as reflected in the Turner Prize. As always you will gain marks for the overall quality of your ideas/arguments/ opinions supported by appropriate known examples and references.

- Note also that it is another 'to what extent question' so you don't have to come down or one side or another and there may be more to be gained from offering a balanced response, as reflected in some of the comments in the passage above and also in this study unit.

- You have approximately 40 minutes to complete your answers to this section in the exam and you should spend your time on each question according to the number of marks, i.e. 25 minutes and 15 minutes respectively. When you have written your responses, compare them with the possible points suggested on pages 278–279.

The media

The word 'media' relates to any form of communication between a small group and a larger group. It is usually thought of in terms of the mass media, i.e. communication with a mass audience. The most important forms of mass media are: the press (newspapers), radio and television. However, it is important to remember that cinema, magazines and books are also part of the media. The most important recent addition to mass media is the Internet, which enables individuals anywhere in the world to communicate with a worldwide mass audience (see Unit 11, 'Computers').

The press

In the UK, the press is dominated by the national press. There are regional daily morning newspapers such as the *Northern Echo* and the *Yorkshire Post* and regional evening papers such as the *Manchester Evening News*, but over 90 per cent of the morning newspaper market belongs to the nationals.

The national press is traditionally divided into 'popular' and 'quality'. The popular press aims at a large circulation (85 per cent of sales go to the popular press). The popular press is largely represented by *The Sun*, *The Daily Mirror*, *The Daily Star*, *The Express* and *The Daily Mail*, although the latter two regard themselves as in between popular and quality and are aimed at a more educated and discerning reader than the

Figure 22.1 Miss Middleton complained to the Press Complaints Commission after the publication of a paparazzi picture of her going to work

other three. Sometimes the popular press is called the 'gutter press' because of its tendency to publish sensational stories about the private lives of the rich and famous.

The quality press is represented by *The Times*, *The Guardian*, *The Daily Telegraph*, *The Independent*, and *The Financial Times*. These newspapers are aimed at an educated, middle class market. They have more news content, especially political and world news, than the popular press. They also have less sensationalism and show business gossip. They rely heavily on advertising for their income (as does the popular press, but to a lesser extent). The quality press used to be called broadsheet because of the size of the papers, but only *The Daily Telegraph* and *The Financial Times* have stayed at broadsheet size.

Newspapers as we know them began in the seventeenth century and the first English newspaper was *The Weekly Newes*, which appeared in 1622. Although gimmicks and sensational reporting are generally thought of as something new, they are not. (In 1890, *The Daily Mail* offered £1 a week for life to any reader who could guess the value of the gold in the Bank of England.) However, all journalists see that the press has an important role to play in informing the public and in ensuring that the government and political parties are subjected to regular scrutiny.

The press is controlled by the Press Complaints Council (run by the press itself), D-notices and the laws of libel (see Unit 23, 'Censorship').

Radio

Radio in the UK is divided into those stations funded by the BBC (through money raised by the television licence) and independent stations funded by advertising. Both BBC and independent radio are also divided into national and local stations. The BBC's national stations are Radio 1 (mainly popular music), Radio 2 (light music and entertainment), Radio 3 (classical music and cultural programmes), Radio 4 (news and spoken word programmes) and Radio 5 (sport and current affairs). The BBC's 30 local radio stations use Radio 2 or 4 when not broadcasting their own programmes.

There are over 50 local independent FM radio stations, and two national independent FM stations – Virgin Radio and Classic FM (Britain's first national independent radio station and now the largest classical music radio station in the world).

Digital radio (DAB) began in 1999 and now covers 80 per cent of the country (as well as being available via digital television and worldwide through radio station websites). As well as the BBC stations, DAB has several national stations – Prime Time, Talk Sport, Life, Planet Rock, One Word, Core – as well as Virgin Radio and Classic FM. DAB requires no tuning, has a much clearer signal and can be paused and replayed. Interactivity is a future possibility.

Both BBC and Independent Radio can have their licences revoked by the government, so it can be claimed they are not completely free (see Unit 23).

Television

Television is the most rapidly expanding form of the media. In the UK, the most watched television is still provided by the terrestrial stations (the BBC provides

Channels 1 and 2 from the licence fee, independent regionally based stations provide ITV, and Channels 4 and 5 are both separate national independent stations). However, the growth of satellite, cable and digital broadcasting has led to many more stations being available and also to links between television and the Internet. The Independent Television Commission (ITC) is responsible for licensing all independent television stations, including cable and satellite. It awards licences to the regional ITV companies on the basis of their past record, their proposed schedules and the amount of revenue they intend to give to the government. The ITC is responsible for the content of the programmes and advertising put out by ITV, Channel 4 and 5 and enforces government codes on advertising and violence. The terrestrial independent stations are funded solely from revenue from advertising during 'natural breaks', whereas cable and satellite are funded from a mixture of advertising and subscription.

Fifty-five per cent of households now have digital television and this has led to a great growth in channels. The BBC has introduced BBC 3 and 4 and other new channels. Programmes and films can be bought by using a digital handset, the Internet can be accessed and e-mails sent, Sky Plus allows recording while watching, pausing and a whole range of facilities to put the viewer in charge. These changes, plus the huge increase in channels, have led to a great change in viewing habits. Twenty years ago it was normal for a popular BBC 1 or ITV programme to attract twenty million viewers, now an audience of ten million is regarded as exceptional. Moreover, the BBC's entry into digital, cable and satellite television means it is gaining money from subscriptions as well as the licence fee, leading recent reports to suggest scrapping the licence fee so putting the BBC on a similar footing to the other television companies.

Both the BBC and ITC have to produce a mixture of types of programme. Figure 22.2 shows the BBC hours of output of different types of programme for 2006/7. Can you work out the percentage of output for each different type?

> **DID YOU KNOW?**
>
> **Good news**
> The first great example of investigative journalism occurred in Britain in *The Pall Mall Gazette* in 1884, when the editor, W. T. Stead, showed that there were young girls being used as prostitutes in London by procuring one himself. Stead was charged by the police and served a term in prison. However, his news story led to the passing of the Criminal Law Amendment Act of 1885, which improved the protection of children. This case is used by journalists to illustrate the role and power of the press. They feel that it is the duty of the press to expose behaviour that is unacceptable to society and that, in a democratic society, the press has the power to hurt the rich and powerful if they are behaving in unacceptable ways.

	2006/2007
First Transmission: Originated programmes Network BBC 1 and BBC 2	
Factual and learning	1,728
Education for children	57
News and weather	3,019
Current affairs	411
Entertainment	610
Sport	1,419
Children's	452
Drama	541
Music and arts	245
Film	6
Religion	115
Subtotal	**8,603**

Figure 22.2 BBC Television hours of output by origin
(*Source*: Table 7, BBC Annual Report and Accounts, 2006/2007)

The influence of the media

Some sociologists believe that the media are used by the Establishment to influence people's behaviour. They claim that almost everyone in the top positions in the media belong to the ruling group. They went to public schools and pass on to the public the ideals of a bourgeois society through the media. The media encourage people to follow certain ways of life and to buy certain goods. Capitalist society is always portrayed in a good light, even in programmes such as soaps and sitcoms.

Other people believe that the media's use of sex and violence has an influence on behaviour. Some psychologists have claimed that the rise in sex crimes and crimes of violence can be directly linked to the rise in the portrayal of sex and violence in the media. (For example, the young boy killers of James Bulger were alleged to have been watching, and possibly copying, a very violent film.)

However, others believe that although the media clearly have some influence, otherwise advertisers would not use them, the audience has just as much effect on the media as the media have on the audience. *The Simpsons* is one of the most popular shows worldwide, but it makes fun of capitalist society. Television and newspapers are in competition and need to keep their viewers and readers. If a programme does not attract viewers, it will be dropped, showing that it has not had the intended influence on the audience. *The Sun* had supported the Conservatives until 1996, when it saw that most people were now supporting Labour. It changed its support to Labour to keep its readers, rather than to influence them. In the same way, *The Sun* adopted 'Page 3 girls' to attract a mass male readership, but is beginning to change this due to fears that 'Page 3' might now lose readers for the paper.

You should also be aware that TV and newspapers have been responsible for uncovering lots of things the government and capitalists would like to keep secret such as whether there were weapons of mass destruction in Iraq.

Some experts feel that there are now so many different elements to the media that the audience can pick and choose, so that they have more influence on the media than the media have on them.

Bias in the media

It is often argued that the media are biased, an issue closely connected to the media's influence. Most newspapers have a particular political bias (i.e. they support one of the political parties). It is also claimed that certain television programmes are biased for or against a political party (for example, that *Panorama* is biased against the Conservatives and *Today* on Radio 4 is biased against Labour).

'Bias' means a prejudiced view. In the media, it occurs when one side of an argument or one point of view is given an unfair advantage by lots of coverage or ignoring its bad points. Bias can be very difficult to uncover, but a typical example is the word 'terrorist' compared with 'freedom fighter'. If a newspaper calls someone a terrorist, this predisposes the reader to think that their cause is wrong, whereas calling them a freedom fighter predisposes the reader to think that they are right.

Media ownership

Many people are worried that the ownership of the media is in the hands of too few. Rupert Murdoch, through his News International Corporation, owns *The Sun*, *The Times* and BSkyB, as well as newspapers and television stations in Australia and the USA. This is now a typical situation as communications multinational companies develop. People think that someone like Murdoch must be able to manipulate public opinion and that he is too powerful to be opposed by governments. He was regularly consulted by the Conservative Prime Minister, Mrs Thatcher, and Tony Blair was criticised in 1999 for discussing Murdoch's commercial interests in Italy with the Italian Prime Minister.

However, Murdoch was banned by the ITC from making a bid for Channel 5, and when he refused to publish a book on China (because it was critical of the Chinese Government and his companies were just about to sign a deal with China), it provoked an outcry and was criticised not only in the rest of the media, but also by *The Times*, which Murdoch owns. The UK does have monopoly laws that prevent any one company owning too much of the media, but the arrival of the Internet is going to make it much more difficult for any group to manipulate people through the media.

Activities

1. Use the Internet to discover the names of the Sunday national papers, their circulation figures, their owners and what other papers they own.

2. Use the Internet to discover the ITV TV stations, who owns them and how near their owners are to the legal limit of 25 per cent of ITV advertising revenue ownable by any one company.

3. Use the Internet to find one recent case referred to the Press Complaints Council, why it was referred and what was done about it.

4. Record the news on BBC 1, BBC 2, ITV, Channel 4 and Channel 5 on the same night. Watch them, noting the differences in coverage of the same story and stories carried by some channels but not others, and suggest reasons to explain the differences.

5. Try to find any notes you have on media bias from your GCSE English course.

EXAM QUESTIONS

Read the passage below about privacy and the press and answer the multiple choice questions which follow.

Intrude at your peril

(1) Talking to two national newspaper editors this week, I heard each confess that the decisions that bring them most anguish and that most upset readers are almost always about photographs that seem to intrude into private grief. That is why I was surprised – as, anecdotally, were many readers – by *The Daily Telegraph*'s weepy, tabloidesque front page on Tuesday featuring the photograph of Gordon and Sarah Brown leaving Edinburgh Royal Infirmary after the death of their daughter, Jennifer Jane, and its headline: 'Jennifer dies in their arms'.

(2) After a debate with senior executives, Simon Kelner, the editor of *The Independent*, also decided to use the photograph, although it was, he says, a 'hairline' decision. Next morning he was a troubled man. Both *The Times* and *The Guardian*, which deal with the same constituency of readers had shunned the picture. A decision which to Kelner had seemed right the night before did not seem quite so right twelve hours later.

(3) Kelner deserves sympathy. Editors have to make quick decisions on important issues and cannot always get them right. Nor did any of the tabloids have any qualms. Readers of the *Financial Times*, which also used the picture inside, have an obvious interest in the life of the chancellor as Sarah Sands (the deputy editor of *The Daily Telegraph*) says, it illustrated a heart-wrenching story – and it was a story, as readers' letters in *The Sun* demonstrated, in which the whole nation shared the Browns' anguish.

(4) Yet there is a danger that since the death of Diana, Princess of Wales, we have become desensitised to intrusion into obvious private grief. Editors have lost a sense of discretion. There is no mercy. Instead, in the case of the Browns, there is a gnawing sense of shame (as Jonathan Freedland wrote in *The Guardian*) at being in a room where we do not belong. And there is also, if we are honest, hypocrisy. We cannot help but look, said Freedland, but we want to turn away just as quickly.

(5) That is why the treatment of the Browns' bereavement, and stories over the past three weeks about the actress Amanda Holden, Leo and Euan Blair, and Prince William have raised in sharp focus an issue – privacy – that will worry editors increasingly. Three clauses in the Press Complaints Commission (PCC) Code of Conduct are relevant to all the cases. Their import is that everyone is entitled to respect for their private and family life; that news and pictures must not be obtained by intimidation, harassment or persistent pursuit; and that in cases involving grief or shock, inquiries must be carried out with sympathy and discretion.

(6) Defining privacy nevertheless usually boils down to an instinct. Unlike most of my friends, but in common with many young mothers and the *Daily Mail*, I do want to know if Tony Blair's baby, Leo, has been given the MMR vaccine – although the Prime Minister believes the question is a 'horrible and unjustified' invasion of his family's privacy. I am also fascinated to know if Euan Blair is on his way to Oxford, but unlike *The Daily Telegraph* and *The Spectator's* Stephen Glover, I believe that in this case he has a right to privacy. Blair has made a complaint to the PCC using the section of the code which says that young people should be free to complete their time at school without unnecessary intrusion (now extended, in the case of Prince William, to university as well).

(7) Illogical? Maybe, but the question in both cases is whether the child is at the centre of a news story for good reason. How baby Leo has been vaccinated involves a public and controversial policy of the Blair Government. It is a matter of public interest to know if the Blairs have ignored the Government's advice. But Euan Blair is not public property simply because he is the Blairs' son and, unlike Prince William, he won't be the son of a public figure when his father ceases to be Prime Minister.

Source: adapted from "Paper Round" by Brian MacArthur, *The Times*, 11 January 2002

For the questions which follow, choose the answer A, B, C or D which you think fits best. Each of the questions is worth one mark.

1 The author's reaction to the photograph in *The Daily Telegraph* (paragraph 1) is best described as
 A sympathetic to the subject.
 B taken aback by the newspaper's stance.
 C ambivalent about the story.
 D angry at its inclusion.

2 'anecdotally' (paragraph 1) means
 A a researched finding.
 B an unpublished impression.
 C supported by known facts.
 D a finding of *The Daily Telegraph*.

3 Which of the following might describe a 'tabloidesque front page' as mentioned in paragraph 1?
 1 in poor taste
 2 thought provoking
 3 sensationalist
 4 attention grabbing

 Answer
 A if 1 and 2 only are correct.
 B if 1, 2 and 3 only are correct.
 C if 1, 3 and 4 only are correct.
 D if 2, 3 and 4 only are correct.

4 According to the author, Kelner's decision discussed in paragraph 3 could be defended for each of the following reasons **except**
 A the story was of genuine interest to readers.
 B this was not the only broadsheet newspaper to show the picture.
 C the decision to print had to be made quickly.
 D the tabloids could not be allowed exclusive coverage.

5 'hypocrisy' (paragraph 4) implies that newspaper readers
 A read articles that they think should not have been published.
 B oppose press intrusion into the lives of celebrities.
 C lack sympathy for the suffering of others.
 D want to read more articles about the sufferings of celebrities.

6 When the author states in paragraph 6 that 'Defining privacy nevertheless usually boils down to an

instinct', he is suggesting that it
 A is impossible for everyone to agree.
 B is easy to recognise, but hard to define.
 C is impossible to define.
 D does not need to be defined.

7 The use of inverted commas for 'horrible and unjustified' in paragraph 6 is to signify that the words are
 A a deliberate exaggeration.
 B the Prime Minister's own words.
 C a paraphrase of the actual words used.
 D a quotation from someone other than the Prime Minister.

8 The distinction which the author draws between the cases concerning Leo and Euan Blair in paragraphs 6 and 7 is based on
 A the issues involved.
 B their age difference.
 C personal preference.
 D the importance of their father.

9 Which of the following does the author put forward in paragraphs 6 and 7 as criteria which should be used by editors in deciding what is private and what is not?
 1 the attitude of other editors.
 2 the public's right to know.
 3 an instinctive sense of right and wrong.
 4 the age of the subject of the story.

 Answer
 A if 1 and 2 only are correct.
 B if 1 and 3 only are correct.
 C if 2 and 3 only are correct.
 D if 3 and 4 only are correct.

10 In writing this article the author is most concerned to highlight the problems of
 A editors.
 B celebrities.
 C bereaved families.
 D politicians.

EXAMINER'S ADVICE
The passage and questions are taken from the AQA AS Unit 1 test set in May 2005. Remember the detailed advice given on tackling these Unit 1 multiple choice questions in previous units of the book. The answers can be found on page 279.

23

Censorship

Forms of censorship

When westerners think of censorship, they tend to think of the type of censorship that once existed in the Soviet Union and still exists, to a certain extent, in countries such as the People's Republic of China. Under such governments, the media are owned by the government and only publish the views of the government. Plays and books have to be submitted to a government censor prior to publication.

The justification for such a form of censorship is to protect the state from being weakened, either by hostile powers being given access to its secrets, or by its institutions being weakened by criticism. If you believe that your form of government and its institutions are the best (as most communist or totalitarian governments do), then you will believe that they should not be weakened in any way. Such governments also feel that the people who live in their society should be protected from the misinformation that capitalist societies try to feed to them in order to bring them back under the control of capitalism. Non-communist governments opposed to freedom of information and so imposing media censorship may do so because they think their people should be protected from lies. A fundamentalist Muslim government may feel that anything not based on the *Qur'an* is untrue and that the citizens should be protected from it.

The United States Constitution states that there should be a right to freedom of speech and freedom of the press, and this is why all societies with democratic forms of government (as in western society) claim to believe in freedom of expression. In order for democracy to work, the electorate has to be able to make informed choices before they vote. For this, they need a free press so that they can know what is going on in the world and in their own country and can work out which political party will deal best with the problems of the country and the world.

Even so, most democracies have forms of censorship in certain areas.

Censorship and the press

In some countries, especially France, there are privacy laws preventing the press from publishing any stories that infringe upon an individual's right to privacy. It is sometimes claimed that this law is the reason why French politicians are not as worried by the press as British politicians. In Britain there are three forms of press censorship.

- *D-notices.* The government can issue the press with a D-notice under the Official Secrets Act to prevent them from publishing anything classed as an official secret. There have been a few occasions when a newspaper has ignored a D-notice in the public interest, for example when a civil servant has leaked a piece of information showing the government to be breaking the law.
- *Obscene Publications Act.* Under this act, a newspaper or publisher can be charged with a criminal offence if they publish something that is obscene. The definition of

'obscene' varies, from the 1868 British definition – 'whatever has a tendency to deprave and corrupt those whose minds are open to such immoral influences' – to the 1973 American definition – 'works which portray sexual conduct in a patently offensive way, and which, taken as a whole, do not have serious literary, artistic, political or scientific value'.

- *Defamation of character* (libel when written, slander when spoken). If the press publishes an article defaming someone's character, and it is untrue, then they can be sued for damages. The damages can be huge (Jeffrey Archer received £500,000 damages and £700,000 costs from the *Daily Star* when they could not prove their story about him and a prostitute. They then claimed it back when he was proven to have lied in court about his alibi and was sent to jail for perjury).

Censorship and television

Television is covered by all the same censorship regulations as the press, but has some additional regulations.

The 'watershed' is a voluntary code of practice under which the television companies agree only to screen programmes of 'a family nature' before 9.00 p.m. This is self-censorship, aimed at the protection of children.

In addition, there are extra requirements for the self-censorship of ITV. The Broadcasting Act requires the Independent Television Committee (ITC) to ensure that nothing is included in programmes that 'offends against good taste or decency'. The ITC's own code of conduct requires that there should be no abusive treatment of religious views or beliefs and no 'improper exploitation of any susceptibilities of those watching programmes'. Furthermore, the ITC requires that any adverts shown on television must be 'legal, decent, honest and truthful' and that companies sponsoring programmes must be suitable for the subject content of the programme.

The BBC is controlled by its charter, which requires it to produce a range of programmes that uphold the standards of public decency. After the 1990 Broadcasting Act, which established the ITC, the BBC set up its own Programme Complaints Unit, to which the public can complain if they think programmes have offended standards of decency or have been biased. The BBC has also published a set of *Producers' Guidelines* showing how producers are prevented from producing programmes which give an unbalanced view of a political issue or offend public decency.

Censorship and the arts

The Lord Chamberlain's Office used to view all theatre productions and censor them for obscenity, until this was ended by the Labour Government of 1966–70. Today, the theatre is only censored by the same obscenity and defamation laws as the press and television. However, many theatres operate a voluntary policy of indicating to the public if a performance may cause offence or is unsuitable for children.

All films must be submitted to the British Board of Film Classification for a viewing category. The categories must be enforced by cinema owners who can be prosecuted if

DID YOU KNOW?

Have you heard this one?

- 'Blue jokes', meaning jokes with sexual innuendo, originate from the days of theatre censorship, when the Lord Chamberlain's Office would put a blue line through scripts or jokes with sexual innuendo.

- Sir Karl Popper, one of the greatest twentieth-century philosophers, argued that freedom of expression is essential in order for human societies to make progress. He claimed that it is no accident that the most advanced societies also have the greatest freedom for their citizens. According to Popper, progress is made by subjecting all ideas, policies, etc. to scrutiny, discovering what is false in them and then putting forward a new form without the false elements. This can only happen if, for example, government policies can be investigated by a free press, opposition parties, trades unions, employers, etc.

under-age children are watching '12', '15' or '18' films. The Board can also cut scenes from films if it considers that they are too graphic in their portrayal of sex or violence. It is also possible for the Board to refuse to grant a certificate to a film, and local councils can refuse permission for such films to be shown in their area. The Board used to justify its work in terms of 'preserving public decency', but now justifies it in terms of the guidance its categories give to parents and cinema owners.

In a question on censorship in the arts, the information on television could also be used.

The case for censorship

The amount of censorship currently existing in the UK is usually justified by some or all of the following arguments:

- Children have a right to be protected from adult material. There is evidence of children being influenced by what they see because they are too young and inexperienced to have worked out their own ideas and opinions on adult issues. (You could quote the James Bulger case or the Helen Mirren film *Killing Mrs Tingle*, which was banned in Germany after children plotted to kill their teachers when they received low grades, like the children in the film.)
- People have a right not to have their sensibilities offended. So, people have a right not to be confronted by graphic sex scenes, obscene language, etc. on their televisions; members of religions have a right not to see their beliefs ridiculed, etc. People who argue for censorship in this way claim that there is a difference between 'free-to-air' television, radio and the Internet, where people have no control over what is on and 'pay-to-view' television and the theatre, where subscribers only see what they have paid to see. They argue that there is much less need for censorship when there is no free access.
- Film and television directors, newspaper publishers, etc. are motivated by greed and profit and should not be able to make money by gratifying people's baser desires.
- The press needs to be prevented from intruding on people's privacy. Famous people should have a right to a private life and the *paparazzi* should be banned from taking photographs without permission. In the same way, people should have a right to freedom from press intrusion in moments of family crisis, such as after a murder or a plane crash.

The case against censorship

Those who argue against censorship are often in favour of a system such as film categories in order to protect children and people's sensibilities. They also accept the need for defamation laws to protect people from untrue things being published about them. However, they would oppose all other forms of censorship, including the Official Secrets Act. They hold the following views:

- Any democracy needs freedom of information. How can voters make informed decisions in elections and referenda if facts are kept from them?
- Who decides what needs to be kept secret or what needs to be censored, and, perhaps even more importantly, who is there to check that their decision is correct?
- If obscenity and violence are corrupting, then the censors, who spend their lives watching such things to decide that other people cannot see them ought to be very corrupt.
- Censorship has always been impossible to impose completely. The rich and powerful have always been able to gain access to what was denied to the mass of the population. Nowadays, with new technology and the advent of the Internet, effective censorship is impossible.
- Privacy laws can be, and have been, used by the powerful to cover up their misdeeds. Who is to decide whether a politician having an affair is in the public interest, other than the press?

Is it censorship?

Not everything that happens reaches the pages of the newspapers or the screens of our televisions. Someone has to decide which of the many items are to be published and in what prominence. Local newspapers, for example, attend the Magistrates Courts, but only a fraction of the cases reach the pages of the local newspaper. First the journalist, then the sub-editors and finally the editor decide which cases are newsworthy and which are not. However, is it censorship if the case of shop-lifting by the editor's mother-in-law is not reported, while the case of under-age drinking by youths from the local council estate is?

Experts in Communications and Cultural Studies have called this selection of news 'gatekeeping' and the people doing the selecting 'gatekeepers'. Of course, there are many more gatekeepers than newspaper journalists and editors:

- Laws passed by the government, the EU and the UN can prevent some news stories from being published. For example, privacy laws meant that newspapers did not report on David Blunkett's affair in 2004 until he went to court to gain access to his son, thus ending his right to privacy.
- Libel laws can make it difficult for newspapers to publish stories unless they can prove them to be true without any doubt, for example the *Daily Telegraph* and George Galloway in 2004, over alleged receipt of 'oil money' from Iraq.
- Pressure groups can affect news organisations and broadcasters. For example, The National Viewers and Listeners Association can make television companies reluctant to screen programmes with sex and violence; animal rights groups can make journalists reluctant to report on animal experiments which might reveal the identities or addresses of scientists.

The question is whether gatekeeping is censorship or just an inevitable feature of living in a society.

Activities

1. Read some tabloid newspapers to find a scandal story about a famous person. Investigate the story and work out which public interests were served by publishing the story and what the effects of not publishing the story might have been.

2. Make a list of the problems parents might encounter in trying to ensure that a child does not see or read anything offensive until they are 15.

3. Discuss the problems the Internet poses for censorship, e.g. scandal, obscene publications, private activities of famous/powerful people, mis-information.

4. Use the Internet to discover freedom of information laws in the USA and the UK. Make a list of the differences and explain which system you would prefer.

Activities

5. Blasphemy against the Christian religion is still a criminal offence. It is rarely used and some members of ethnic communities have suggested that it should be extended to make it an offence to denigrate any religion. What problems can you see in trying to impose such a law in a multifaith community?

6. Interview people from varying age groups to see what they would regard as a programme which 'offended public decency'.

Often connected with gatekeeping is 'government spin'. If the government publishes a decision to end free school meals on the same day that it publishes its decision to abolish the House of Lords, is that a form of censorship, because the free school meals will get little media attention compared with the abolition of the House of Lords? The Hutton Inquiry into the death of Dr Kelly revealed a large amount of gatekeeping by both the BBC and the government.

EXAM QUESTION

This is a typical A2 essay question from Section C of the Unit 3 test. It is central to the main theme of this unit.

To what extent is freedom of expression more important than the privacy of the individual? Discuss what limits should apply to freedom of expression both in the news media and the arts generally.

(25 marks)

EXAMINER'S ADVICE

- There are two substantial questions here, and both must be addressed for a good answer. The second of the two questions might be expected to require more detail, particularly if you choose to develop different points to cover the news as opposed to the arts.

- In response to the first question you might consider the tension between the two 'rights' under discussion, i.e. how one may conflict with the other. You do not have to produce a definite conclusion – awareness of the issues is what you need to show. A challenge to or rejection of the question in its existing form might be a good sign – is one more important than the other?

- All 'rights' are matched by 'responsibilities', and if you wish your rights to be respected, you also have to respect those of others. This is what the second question is partly about: how freedom of expression and individual privacy can co-exist in practice. Think of some examples where the two might come into conflict and how you might resolve the conflict, for example details of the private life of the Prime Minister and his/her family, or the use of images which might easily shock or offend in the news or in a play or film.

- Some further notes are given on page 279. Remind yourself how A2 essays are marked on page 270.

Society, Politics and the Economy

The nature of society

The *Oxford English Dictionary* has eight different definitions of 'society', showing how difficult it is to define the nature of society exactly. The study of the nature of society (how society originated, what it is for and how it works) is called 'sociology'. Auguste Comte first used this word in 1834 to describe the 'science of society'. He thought that this science would discover the social laws controlling the development of the human race, in the same way that the physical sciences discover the physical laws controlling the development of the earth.

Some sociologists follow Comte and believe that sociology is a science. They claim that by applying scientific methods of observation, theory and experiment to society, it is possible to discover social laws. Such sociologists are called positivists because they think of society as an objective fact, like a rock or a plant.

Other sociologists believe that sociology is about discovering how people interpret the world and how people interact with each other to form social groups. This is called 'phenomenology'.

The nature of society according to positivists

Some positivists are known as *functionalists*. They believe that each area or institution within society (such things as education, the family, and the legal system) has a function in relation to the whole of society. They often compare society to the human body and institutions to the parts of the body. Just as the heart maintains the body by pumping blood round, so the family maintains society by training children to become members of society (socialisation). The function of an institution is to contribute to the maintenance of society and to provide some of what society needs to keep it going (see Figure 24.1 on page 185).

Society's needs include such things as shelter, food, socialisation and value consensus, which are often called 'functional prerequisites'. 'Value consensus' means a general agreement about what the values of society are. For example, in western society there is a value consensus that everyone should have a good supply of material goods, so the economic institutions provide a large range of goods and the family is organised to buy increasing numbers of those goods (for example CD players, camcorders, fitted kitchens).

Any society needs its members and institutions to be integrated if it is to flourish. Functionalists think that value consensus is the main means of social integration, but this is backed up by social control. Society controls the behaviour of its members by norms, which can be either formal or informal. Formal norms are the rules and the method of imposing the rules, often involving rewards or positive sanctions (for example promotion at work) and punishment or negative sanctions (for example imprisonment). Informal norms are such things as dress codes (wearing different types of clothes for work on a building site from work in an office), which are imposed by informal sanctions (smiles, frowns or comments).

Functionalists accept that there can be conflicts between different groups in society, but feel that the institutions of an effective society will soon settle these, because social groups have more in common than they have differences. This is why some people claim that civil wars are only likely to happen in the less materially advanced countries, because even the poorest people in an advanced society have an interest in maintaining the electricity supply, the water supply, television broadcasts, etc.

However, there are other positivist sociologists who take a different view of society. *Marxists* believe that society is based on conflict rather than value consensus. Karl Marx believed that the history of society is based on one group being in control until their control is challenged by another group. Marx claimed that in industrial society, the controlling group is the *bourgeoisie* (the owners of the means of production), which is trying to control the *proletariat* (the workers) to keep it from taking control. Marx claimed that society is based on economics, especially the 'forces of production' (the technology, raw materials, etc. involved in producing food, clothes, cars, etc.). The ruling class is always concerned to own the means of production. Marx was an economist and political philosopher rather than a sociologist, but Marxist sociologists have used his theories as a basis for their 'conflict theory of society'.

Marxist sociologists claim that the social institutions of society (what they call the superstructure) are used by the ruling class to keep the proletariat from revolting and taking control. They reflect the interests of the rulers rather than the workers and so there is a basic conflict. For example, educational institutions teach the ideology of the rulers and prepare children to perform the functions that will make money for the ruling class. The law is designed to protect the interests of the ruling class. For example, the laws on property usually protect the owners of property more than the interests of groups such as ramblers. Such sociologists explain value consensus in society by the idea of 'false consciousness'. This means that the ruling class is able to use such things as education and the family to make workers believe the ideology of the rulers (for example getting a mortgage and a car to give profits to the banks and car makers), when it is really in their interests to reject the ruling ideology and adopt a Marxist ideology (see 'Key terms').

The nature of society according to phenomenologists

Most phenomenologists are called *interactionists*. Functionalism and Marxism may have differences, but they agree that society is made up not only of people, but also of institutions and systems, which have a great impact on the behaviour of individuals. Interactionism is completely different in that it claims that society is made up of individuals who work out their role in society through interaction with other individuals rather than being forced into roles through institutions such as the family and education. Consequently, society for interactionists is always changing, as people negotiate their role in society.

Alienation feeling yourself no longer a part of society

Anomie not sure what the norms of society are and so feeling unhappy and lost

Bureaucracy an organisation (especially government) whose operations are full of written rules and a hierarchy of officers

Capitalism an economic system in which the means of production are privately owned

Cycle of deprivation where the social problems of one generation are passed onto the next through the family

Demography study of population changes

Dysfunctional family a family which is not working in the way society expects it to (e.g. mother and father pursuing their own lives and not providing material or emotional care for their children)

Hegemony where one class or group controls another, e.g. bourgeois hegemony

Homogeneity where all parts of society are of the same kind

Labelling connected with stereotyping, it claims that people label others into certain groups on the basis of such things as appearance

Marxist ideology the belief that capitalists will try to increase their profits by paying low wages until the workers revolt and form a workers' state

Means testing only giving benefits after assessing the income and wealth of the person applying for the benefit

Monogamy the practice of only being married to one person at a time

Peer group a group of similar age and social characteristics

Secularisation the decline in importance of religion, with political and social institutions taking on the importance formerly given to religious institutions

The nature of society according to philosophers

Philosophers would agree with interactionists that society is made up of individuals living and working together. However, they believe that any society needs laws so that people can live and work in peace. Once this happens, social institutions will be formed and society becomes a mixture of individuals and institutions. Clearly, the institutions will have functions because that is why they arose, and there is a sense in which the institution is greater than its members (your school or college was there before you started and will still be there when you leave). However, individuals do have choices about their roles, and society and its institutions change through individuals changing their roles.

So, philosophers would see society as a mixture of functionalism and interactionism, but would tend to reject Marxism because, since individuals changed society's institutions into more democratic forms, there are lots of ways in which society can be changed without conflict.

How sociologists discover facts about society

Sociologists use a variety of tools to study society.

Social surveys

These are usually conducted either by questionnaire or interview. To be absolutely accurate they would have to survey everyone in the population, but as this is impossible they should use either random sampling (which requires a large sample to make sure that all opinions are covered) or quota sampling (where the census figures are used to work out how many people in the population are in certain groups – 40–50-year-old male working class, for example – and the relevant representative quota is interviewed). Surveys have many problems, not only concerning the numbers of people interviewed (mathematicians claim that the minimum is 11 per 100,000 of population), but also in the avoidance of bias in the questions or the interviewers.

Statistical studies

These include census records and *Social Trends* (an annual publication of government figures on such things as marriages, births, employment – see Figure 24.1). Though these are more accurate than surveys, they cannot be accepted without question because there may still be some bias, for example when suicide was a crime many suicides were not recorded as suicide to save hurting the family.

Observation

Some sociologists research by studying a small group intensively over a period of time (this method is also known as ethnography). It is typically used when investigating small communities, gangs, firms, institutions etc. The researcher usually negotiates with the group to establish their credentials and to outline how the research will be done, and how the results will be used. This type of research uses informal interviews

Marriages and divorces

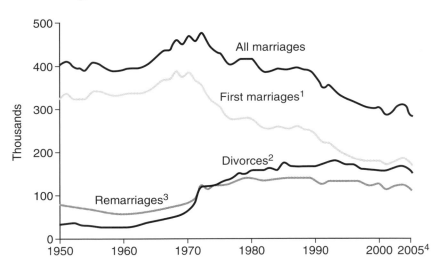

Figure 24.1 Marriage and divorce trends in the United Kingdom

1 For both partners.
2 Includes annulments. Data for 1950 to 1970 for Great Britain only.
   Divorce was permitted in Northern Ireland from 1969.
3 For one or both partners.
4 Data for 2005 are provisional. Final figures are likely to be higher.

Source: Office for National Statistics; General Registar Office for Scotland;
Northern Ireland Statistics and Research Agency

Source: Figure 2.9, Social Trends 37

with members of the group, participation by the researcher in the activities of the group, observation of key events/issues in the life of the group. The data is then written up in a long account which is usually qualitative rather than quantitative. Occasionally, researchers join the group without declaring their identity in the hope of their research being more objective as the members of the group do not know they are being researched.

Critics of this method claim that the data is unreliable because: either the groups know they are being studied and so behave differently, the researcher gets too close to the group and so becomes biased, the researcher tends to see causes and motives without explaining his/her reasons for doing so, and/or there is no criteria of proof for claims made from the research. Proponents say it provides a depth of insight which other methods cannot hope to achieve, especially when deviant groups such as young hooligans, drug addicts, etc. are being researched.

For the next examination question go to the end of Unit 25.

Activities

1. Imagine you have been asked by the government to investigate the effects of poverty on family life. How would you carry out the research and what methods would you use?

2. By questionnaires or discussion, investigate whether there is a value consensus among people you know about an issue such as car ownership versus public transport.

3. Do you think that married couples should be given greater tax benefits than single people? You should think about the importance of the family in society and use information from Unit 33 ('Economic theories') on taxation.

25 Social change

Social change means the ways in which society has and is changing, and also what possibilities there are for change in a society. Many types of social change are dealt with in other units. This unit will look at social change in terms of the family, social class, ethnicity, gender and demography.

Demographic trends in the UK

Demography is concerned with the statistics of births, deaths and population changes. When the first official census was taken in 1801, the population of the United Kingdom was 12 million, in 2002, it had risen to 59,228,900 and has recently passed 60 million.

The UK's population grew rapidly in the nineteenth century, but slowed down in the 1920s and 1930s, perhaps because of a combination of economic depression and the new availability of contraception. After the Second World War there was a 'baby boom', but by the 1980s the UK's birth rate had fallen more quickly than the death rate, so that the population was only increasing very slightly (indeed between 1974 and 1978 the population actually fell). Today the birth rate has begun to increase and it is now expected that births will exceed deaths up to 2031.

As the birth rate has fallen, so the death rate has declined. This means that the number of under-16s in the population has fallen (25 per cent in 1961, 20 per cent in 2002), but the number of over-65s has risen (12 per cent in 1961, 18 per cent in 2002). Life expectancy has risen from 45 for men and 47 for women in 1901 to 76 for men and 81 for women in 2002.

Another trend has been for the population to move southwards. In the Industrial Revolution, it was the North of England which recorded big increases in population. However, since the collapse of heavy industry in the 1970s and 1980s, the South of England has experienced big population growth as people moved to jobs in the high-tech sector. This has been even more marked in Scotland (population 5,054,800 in 2002), Wales (population 2,918,700 in 2002) and Northern Ireland (population 1,696,600 in 2002). In 2002, 84 per cent of the UK's population lived in England and about 70 per cent of that lives south of the Wash.

As the population has moved southwards, it has also moved out of the cities. Although the population of the South East has risen fantastically in the past 30 years, the population of London has actually fallen. People have moved into the countryside in search of better living conditions. This trend was initiated by the government after the Second World War, when a New Towns policy was begun to build integrated living and work areas using the latest designs and ideas. The largest of the New Towns is Milton Keynes in Northamptonshire, which was built to take in people from London.

In the nineteenth century, the UK had more people immigrating than emigrating as there was a great demand for workers, and Britain had a tradition of taking in religious and political refugees. Between 1890 and 1955, the UK was a net exporter of people as economic problems led to massive migrations to the USA, Australia, New Zealand and Canada. In the 1950s, a shortage of labour for British industry led to workers being recruited from the new Commonwealth countries (India, Pakistan, Bangladesh, West Africa and the Caribbean). Many of these workers had fought for the UK in the Second World War (there were more people from the Commonwealth than from the UK in the British Armed Forces in the Second World War). As these workers have settled, the UK has become a multi-ethnic society. Even so, in the 2001 Census, only 7.9 per cent of the UK's population came from ethnic minorities. Since the 2001 census, the accession of several Eastern European states to the EU has led to a large increase in immigration from these countries which have high unemployment to supply shortages of labour (especially in the services industries) in the UK.

The implications of these trends

Demographic trends have major implications, especially in terms of government policies. The ageing population trend has implications for the National Health Service (NHS). An ageing population is going to require the NHS to take a greater proportion of government spending. There are also major implications for the Social Security budget. If people live for longer after they retire, this means that there will be more pensioners in relation to the working population. This may mean that there will be insufficient working people to pay the pensions. This is connected with the current trend of reducing the age of the workforce by giving workers early retirement. Pensions have to be worked out on the basis of how long the pensioner is expected to live. If pensioners are living five years longer, then it may be sensible to require people to retire at 65, or even 70. There are also housing and social service issues when seaside resorts on the South Coast consist of almost 50 per cent of people over the age of 65.

The southward drift has major implications for housing and transport. More houses will need to be built in the South, putting pressure on the Green Belt. Greater numbers of people will also lead to much more transport congestion, leading to the issue of whether to increase public transport or to build new roads. Further implications are that schools and hospitals in the South are likely to be overcrowded, whereas those in the North will have surplus places. Government policies aimed at

DID YOU KNOW?

Family first
In a 1997 government questionnaire about attitudes to the family, 88 per cent of people agreed that children should expect help from their parents even after they have left home; 70 per cent agreed that people should keep in touch with close family members even if they have little in common; 56 per cent agreed that people should keep in touch with other relatives such as aunts, uncles and cousins; 48 per cent agreed that people should turn to their family for help before going to the state.

Do you feel British?
This question was asked to 300,000 people in a Labour Force Survey in 2003. The percentage answering yes were:

White British	100 per cent
Mixed	85 per cent
Black Caribbean	80 per cent
Other Black	80 per cent
Pakistani	78 per cent
Indian	75 per cent
Bangladeshi	75 per cent
Chinese	60 per cent
Black African	55 per cent
Other white	40 per cent
Other ethnic groups	38 per cent

Source: Office for National Statistics

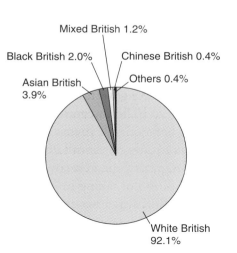

Mixed British 1.2%
Black British 2.0%
Chinese British 0.4%
Asian British 3.9%
Others 0.4%
White British 92.1%

Figure 25.1 Ethnicity of UK population, Census 2001

Baby boomers people born in the period 1946–53, when there was a very rapid rise in the number of births

Bourgeois members of the middle class and/or property owners

IMR infant morality rate – the number of babies who die before the age of one year per thousand births

High-rise housing blocks of flats which are many storeys high

Intergenerational mobility children moving social class compared with their parents

Intragenerational mobility people moving social class through their working life

Meritocracy a system where the top jobs are given to people on the basis of their talents and qualifications (merits) rather than their birth, wealth or the school they attended

Official census a survey of the whole of the UK's population carried out by the government every 10 years (1991, 2001) – every household has to fill in a questionnaire

Proletariat the working class

Reclaiming the inner city the practice of building new middle-class housing, shops, etc. in the inner-city so that it is no longer a slum for problem families between the CBD (Central Business District) and the suburbs

Registrar-General the civil servant in charge of the official census

Social class there are many views of social class from the basic upper, middle and working classes to the Registrar General's social classes 1–5. This classifies class 1 as professional, e.g. doctors and accountants; class 2 as intermediate, e.g. policemen, nurses; class 3 (a) as skilled non-manual, e.g. office workers; class 3 (b) as skilled manual workers, e.g. plumbers; class 4 as semi-skilled, e.g. postmen and bus drivers and class 5 as unskilled.

encouraging businesses to move away from the South are already in place and may have slowed down the drift.

The rural drift also has implications. People moving into the countryside are likely either to commute to work in towns or to be retired, but wealthy. This pushes up house prices, causing another drift away from the rural areas by people born in those areas who do not have high paying jobs. There are problems of rural deprivation as the newcomers are likely to drive to town supermarkets, doctors, etc. so that the less well-off living in rural areas suffer depleted facilities as village shops and schools close down.

The development of the UK as a multi-ethnic community has many implications because it is so varied. Although only 7.9 per cent of the UK's population is made up of ethnic minorities, there is not an even spread of ethnic minorities across the country. The immigrants of the 1950s settled where the jobs were, and where they were able to obtain housing. Consequently there are areas with very high percentages of ethnic minorities. Recent immigrants tend to settle in areas where they have contacts who provided them with details of job and housing opportunities in the UK. So there are now areas with high concentrations of Poles, Hungarians, etc.

Racism cannot be allowed in a multi-ethnic society as it is likely to destabilise the society. Successive British governments have tried to deal with this leading to the Race Relations Act and the Commission for Racial Equality both of which aim to remove racism from the UK and give all citizens an equal chance.

Other social trends

One major trend of the twentieth century was for women to have greater participation in work and politics and for men and women to have equal rights and status. It was not until 1928 that women gained the same rights as men in voting and becoming MPs; it was 1970 before women had the right to the same pay as men for the same work; it was 1975 before it was made illegal to discriminate against people on grounds of sex. As a result of these changes, the gender pay gap was at its narrowest in 2007 – in median hourly pay the gap was 12.6 per cent. Such changes also have implications in terms of childcare and the nature of the family.

The nature of the family has been another area of social change. Marriage has become less popular (there were 405,000 marriages in 1971 and only 283,730 in 2005) whilst divorce has become more popular (25,400 1961, 148,141 in 2005). The number of households made up of cohabiting couples accounted for around 10 per cent of households in 2001, compared with just over one in 20 (5.5 per cent) households in 1991. In 2006, 43.5 per cent of babies were born outside marriage. Some sociologists and moral experts have used these figures to suggest that the family, as it had been known during the twentieth century, will almost disappear in the twenty-first century.

The development of a classless society has also been a feature of the twentieth century. The introduction of the Welfare State (pensions, sick pay, unemployment pay, free education and equal access to examinations and higher education, the National

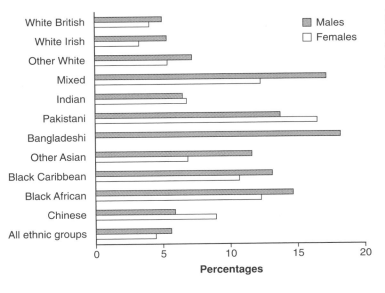

Figure 25.2 UK unemployment rates by ethnic group 2002–3 (Source: *Social Trends 32*)

KEY TERMS

Social mobility movement from one social class, or group, to another

Suburbanisation the extension of suburbs (areas of domestic housing on the edges of towns) further and further into the countryside

Health Service) by the Liberal governments of 1906–14 and the Labour government of 1945–51 removed absolute poverty and led to the rise of a meritocracy. The restriction of the power of the House of Lords in 1911 (the Lords had prevented independence for Ireland on several occasions between 1884 and 1911), the reform of the Lords in 1999, and various policies between 1945 and 1999, led to a reduction of the power and influence of the aristocracy at the same time that the media revolutions led to the rise of the new aristocracy of pop stars, TV and film stars and sports stars.

How equal is British society?

At first sight it might appear that major changes have been made. In 1911, 5 per cent of the population owned 87 per cent of the nation's wealth; by 1990, that figure had reduced to 40 per cent of the nation's wealth. However, that is still a large imbalance, which may be increasing due to changes in capital transfer tax and inheritance tax making it possible for people to hand down more of their wealth to their children. *Social Trends 29* (published by HMSO) compares the average gross income of the UK's population for 1996/97 in fifths and shows that the average gross income for the bottom fifth was £7080, while that for the top fifth was £45,870.

There is evidence from the latest government statistics that people from the lowest two-fifths of the income divide are much more likely to have lower educational qualifications, more health problems and lower life expectancy. A government report published in 1999 also showed wide regional variations not only in income and house prices, but also in education, health and life expectancy (income in London was 23 per cent above the average GDP, while in Northern Ireland it was 19 per cent below). There is also evidence that black people are more likely to be in the bottom two-fifths, are more likely to be arrested and are more likely to be sent to prison if they are convicted.

Activities

1. Use the Internet to find the latest figures on births, marriages and deaths in the UK.

2. Interview people from different age groups and educational backgrounds to discover what they feel about social class in the UK.

3. Research cases such as the Stephen Lawrence inquiry to discover background material on attitudes to race in the UK.

4. To what extent would you agree that the UK is an equal opportunities society?

EXAM QUESTION (1)

Study the following text and figures, and then answer the question which follows.

Extract from a case study on *Changes in the family*

Data on households and families

In 2004, the population of the United Kingdom was estimated to be 58.1 million. In 1901, it was 38.2 million. Over the same period, the number of households increased from approximately 8.3 million to an estimated 24.1 million. In 1901, about one in 20 households comprised one person living alone; this increased to just under one in three in 2004.

A household is defined as one person living alone, or a group of people at the same address who share living arrangements. Families are defined as a married or cohabiting couple with or without their never-married children who have no children of their own, or a lone parent with such children. Most household surveys do not consider a person living alone to form a family. A household can contain one or more families and also members other than those belonging to a nuclear family.

	Percentages					
	1961	1971	1981	1991	2001	2004
One person						
Under pensionable age	4	6	8	11	14	14
Over pensionable age	7	12	14	16	15	15
Two or more unrelated adults	5	4	5	3	3	3
One family households						
Couple						
No children	26	27	26	28	29	29
1–2 dependent children	30	26	25	20	19	18
3 or more dependent children	8	9	6	5	4	4
Non-dependent children only	10	8	8	8	6	6
Lone parent						
Dependent children	2	3	5	6	7	7
Non-dependent children only	4	4	4	4	3	3
Multi-family households	3	1	1	1	1	1
All households						
(millions) (=100 per cent)	16.3	18.6	20.2	22.4	23.8	24.1

Figure 25.3 Households: by type of household and family

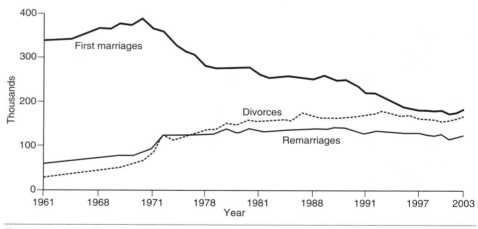

Figure 25.4 Marriages and divorces

Source: adapted from *Social Trends 2005*

What do the data and figures tell us about changes in the family in the United Kingdom?

(11 marks)

EXAMINER'S ADVICE

- The data and figures here are examples of a larger set of documents and data for the Unit 4 test which you are given to study several weeks in advance of the examination. General advice on how to prepare the material for the test is also given on pages 267–268. You should read this before you attempt the question.
- The question above is very typical of the first of the four case study questions. It is basically asking you to interpret the data and highlight the key features and trends. Sometimes it may ask you to discuss the implications of the data or the issues which they raise. Sometimes it may ask you to relate the data to themes or issues in the other documents.
- Here it is simply asking for key features and trends. There are eleven marks allocated to the question, so you should try to make eleven clear points from the text and figures. In particular look for changes (in proportions) over time and suggest what these indicate/mean. It will help to start with a broad overview of the changes relating to both figures and any links you can see between them. Then to go on to comment on detailed points from each. Be careful to distinguish between proportions/percentages (in Figure 25.3) and numbers (Figure 25.4).
- You should write your answer in continuous prose and **not** use bullet points. The test is partly about how you are able to link ideas together, even though the first written question in each of these tests tends to be about identifying and outlining key points. Expect to write at least a page for a decent mark, but once you have studied the material and made some notes, you should attempt to write your answer in no more than 15 minutes.
- The points you might be expected to make are given on page 279.

EXAM QUESTION (2)

This is an A2 essay question from January 2004. This topic would now be set in Section C of Unit 3.

> **How successful do you think Equal Opportunities legislation and targets have been in addressing issues of ethnicity, gender, disability and class?**
>
> Choose **two or more of these areas** and discuss to what extent 'positive discrimination' should be used to help address these problems in education, the workplace and public life.

(25 marks)

EXAMINER'S ADVICE

- This question is quite complex but has plenty of scope provided that you have sufficient knowledge on the topic. Use the material and activities in this unit (plus perhaps an Internet search) to help with this.
- The main knowledge required focuses on EO legislation (some going back to the 1960s and 1970s), e.g. Equal Pay, Maternity Rights, various Discrimination Acts, and targets which have been used subsequently to improve such things as the representation of minority groups in the work place, e.g. more women managers, more black police officers, etc.
- The second key bit of knowledge is that you understand fully what 'positive discrimination' is and how it might operate in various spheres, e.g. all-female shortlists for vacant parliamentary seats, or reserving a proportion of higher education places for pupils with slightly lower A level grades from lower performing schools. These are two topical examples. What do you think of ideas like these?
- **'Choose two or more'** in the question means that you must refer to **at least two** and either concentrate in detail on these, or you may take the issues of legislation, targets and positive discrimination more broadly and discuss how successful/effective these have been in more than two of the areas. You might take the view, for example, that more visible progress has been made in reducing sex discrimination than say, race or disability, but you may have a different view to support. The important thing is that you produce some arguments and evidence to support your ideas and opinions.
- Attempt to write your answer in no more than 40 minutes. Some further notes are given on page 280.

Crime and deviance

Despite the huge amount of research, there does not appear to be a consensus of opinion about the most effective way of deterring crime or about which causal factors are most influential. Some people believe that the primary causes of crime are deep psychological states over which the criminal has no control, so that he/she cannot be held responsible or punished for his/her actions. On the other hand, the fact that many poor, unemployed, badly housed people do not commit crimes does not lead to the conclusion that these factors have no bearing on why some people become criminals.

Why do prisons fail in their aim to help offenders to return to and cope with society?

Despite the popular conception of prisons as becoming more and more like 'rest-cures' or 'holiday-camps', recent reports have described many prisons as seriously overcrowded, inhumane and uncivilised places, with insensitive and destructive regimes. If 70 to 80 per cent of offenders return to prison, then prisons obviously fail, except in the areas of revenge and protection of society. Many sociologists and criminologists have argued that prisons are the breeding grounds of criminals – universities of crime, where offenders have their self-image of deviancy reinforced and where the possibility of reform is virtually impossible. Prisons often reinforce the criminal behaviour they are designed to punish or inhibit by gathering together in tightly segregated and alienated groups those who already feel marginalised, and giving them the opportunities to teach one another the skills and attitudes of a criminal career. This is particularly true of young offenders, who may find themselves mixing with hardened criminals.

What is deviancy?

In general, what is described as deviant behaviour is decided by society itself. The American sociologist Marshall Culinary defined deviance as 'behaviour which is in a disapproved direction'. This means that behaviour acceptable in one society may not be so in another. For example, drinking alcohol is regarded as a serious offence in strict Muslim countries but is acceptable in others. Also, ideas about acceptable behaviour change over time. For example, attitudes to homosexuality changed during the twentieth century among large sections of society. Also most definitions of deviance relate to laws drawn up by only certain sections of society, i.e. powerful middle-class groups. Their norms of behaviour (table manners, for example) may be alien to other sub-cultures in society and hence are not universally agreed. Once we have labelled certain actions and those that carry them out as deviant we develop stereotypes, reinforced by the media, by which we categorise individuals. The effect of this is often to change the self-image of the criminal so that he/she is forced into the role created by society.

Physiological explanations for deviancy

These types of theory tend to assume that criminals indulge in deviant or abnormal behaviour, which can harm individuals and be socially disruptive. Since their behaviour is abnormal, they must be sick and the solution to their problem lies in diagnosing their illness. It has been suggested, for example, that stocky, well-rounded individuals tend to be particularly active and aggressive and therefore more likely to commit crimes. Other evidence suggests that a statistically significant number of violent antisocial men have an extra Y chromosome instead of the usual XY combination. Similarly, too much sugar in the blood – *hyperglycaemia* – may lead to criminal behaviour. Of course, it does not follow that everyone suffering from any of these conditions will necessarily become a criminal, but only that there is a disposition that may encourage deviancy.

Structuralism

Some sociologists argue that many criminals develop their deviant behaviour because of the way in which society is structured. Some young people belong to *sub-cultures*, which have developed different values from mainstream society. These values can develop because of educational, employment and financial deprivation and can result in people using criminal means by which to achieve high social and financial status.

Such situations could include:

- Young men who steal and joyride expensive cars in order to bolster their own status in the eyes of their peers.
- Persistent stealing to enhance the image of the thieves in the eyes of their own sub-culture – the 'respect' earned is far more important than the value of the goods stolen.

Recent trends in youth crime

The life-time likelihood of acquiring at least one criminal conviction is greater than commonly realised. Four in ten males and one in ten females are likely to be found guilty or cautioned for an indictable offence at some point during their lives. However, it is also true that a comparatively small proportion of the population – about five per cent of males – are chronic offenders who account for about half of all known offending.

Official records and 'self-report' studies also show that individuals more often break the law when they are young. The 'peak' ages at which they are most likely to be found guilty or cautioned are between 15 and 19. Criminal involvement typically starts before the age of 15, but declines markedly once young people reach their twenties. However, young people who become involved in crime at the earliest ages – before they are 14 – tend to become the most persistent offenders, with longer criminal careers.

Young offenders tend to be versatile and rarely specialise in particular types of crime, including violence. Recent research has identified features in the childhood and adult lives of violent offenders and non-violent persistent offenders that are very similar, suggesting that violent offenders are essentially frequent offenders. Studies have also found that young offenders are versatile in committing other types of antisocial behaviour, including heavy drinking, drug-taking, dangerous driving and promiscuous sex. Delinquency is, therefore, only one element in a much larger syndrome of antisocial behaviour.

Interviews with young offenders, meanwhile, suggest that their crimes are most commonly committed for material gain. However, a minority of offences, especially vandalism and taking vehicles without the owner's consent, are committed for excitement, enjoyment or to relieve boredom.

Recent statistics show that ten per cent of 11–12-year-old boys have carried a knife, and this rises to 24 per cent by the age of 16.

Gang culture

During the last decade, there has been a large increase in the number of young people joining gangs. This often involves carrying imitation or real firearms and knives, both for protection and as part of their image.

The shooting of Charlene Ellis and Letisha Shakespeare in Aston in 2003 received a huge amount of media attention and increased public concern about the escalating problems relating to gangs, violence and drugs that are prevalent across some of our most deprived inner city neighbourhoods such as parts of Manchester and Liverpool.

As categorised by the Jill Dando Institute (JDI) in 2005, the 'gangs' fall into three groups or hierarchies:

- *Peer groups* – small unorganised groups who share the same space and a common history. Their involvement in crime will mostly be at a low level and will not be important to the identity of the group.
- *Gangs* – mostly comprised of street based groups of young people for whom crime and violence is an essential part of the group's identity. Groups tend to have a name.
- *Organised criminal groups* – groups of individuals for whom involvement in crime is for personal gain, and is probably their main occupation. These groups operate in the illegal marketplace.

Street gangs are typically made up of males in their teens to early twenties, whilst females tend to follow gangs without becoming as heavily engaged in activity as their male counterparts. The JDI study suggests that females are more involved in peer groups than street gangs. They often share an identity based either on age, location, ethnicity, peer networks or blood relationships and tend to be hierarchical communities with common interests and shared purposes. Gangs may also form due

<aside>
KEY TERMS

Crime an activity that breaks the law of the land and is subject to official punishment

Delinquency acts committed by young people, which are considered as antisocial or criminal

Deterrence the view that people will be put off committing crimes if the punishments are harsh enough

Deviance actions or attitudes that do not follow the norms and expectations of a particular social group

Rehabilitation the view that many criminals are 'sick', and therefore need therapeutic treatment rather than punishment

Retribution the theory that criminals are responsible for their actions and should be appropriately punished

Subculture certain norms, attitudes and values distinctive to a group and different to those of society as a whole
</aside>

to social exclusion and discrimination – people come together for a sense of safety and belonging. Immigrant populations, those excluded from education or people who have engaged in criminal activities from an early age are particularly at risk of gang involvement. Others may join a gang simply for something to do, seeking protection in numbers, or for reasons of status and peer pressure.

Once someone is a member of a gang it can be extremely difficult for them to leave, particularly when the gang feels that ex-members may divulge gang secrets or provide evidence against them to the police. Loyalty within a gang is so strong that members thought to have been disloyal are at risk of violence – even being killed.

There are a number of interventions that have been launched across the UK to divert young people away from gang activity, and to help those wanting to leave gangs. One such initiative is a radio project set up in Aston in September 2004, offering young people a supportive and attractive alternative to gang culture which is still credible amongst their peers. Through formal training the project has helped people develop careers as producers, DJs, presenters and sound engineers. The project also runs an enterprise course to teach people the skills needed to run their own business, and provides alternative role models for young people to look up to.

Understanding and preventing youth crime

The decline in the number of young offenders recorded in criminal justice statistics over the last 15 years is almost certainly illusory and due to changes in the way crimes are now reported, according to a recent MORI report. The report also stated that those people who commit crime from an early age are especially likely to become habitual offenders with long criminal records.

Major background factors associated with and contributing to youth crime include:

*   low income and poor housing
*   living in deteriorated inner city areas
*   a high degree of impulsiveness and hyperactivity
*   low intelligence and low school attainment
*   poor parental supervision and harsh and erratic discipline
*   parental conflict and broken families.

Research suggests that the most promising techniques for reducing the risks of young people's involvement in drug misuse, crime and other antisocial behaviour include:

*   frequent home visiting by health professionals during pregnancy and infancy
*   education in parenting
*   high quality nursery education
*   training children to 'stop and think'.

The most hopeful strategy for reducing youth crime is to identify the main risks and ways of reducing these within a community. This knowledge can be used to apply prevention techniques whose effectiveness has been demonstrated by research. Prevention before a crime is always more effective than punishment after it.

Consider the statistics and article below about recorded crime, and answer the question which follows.

Extract from a case study on *Crime and punishment*

Table 26.1 Crime recorded by police with clear-up rates: England and Wales by type of offence

	Thousands		Percentages
Type of offence	**1999–00**	**2000–01**	**Clear-up rate**
Theft and handling stolen goods	2,223	2,145	17
of which: theft of vehicles	375	339	13
theft from vehicles	669	630	6
Criminal damage	946	960	14
Burglary	906	836	12
Violence against the person	581	601	62
Fraud and forgery	335	319	29
Drugs offences	122	113	95
Robbery	84	95	18
Sexual offences	38	37	53
of which: rape	8	9	46
Other notifiable offences	66	63	73
All notifiable offences	**5,301**	**5,171**	**24**

Source: Office for National Statistics

Robbery statistics inflated by liars

About one in ten robberies reported in yesterday's annual crime figures probably never took place, a police investigation has found.

Officers in Coventry re-examined 72 cases of robbery over a three-month period and found that at least six of the allegations made could be proved to be false and no evidence could be found to support another two. Their findings have been confirmed by senior officers who blame the false reporting on insurance fraud and the need to have a crime number to make a claim.

'It is appalling when you think how many police resources are going into following up robberies that never took place in the first place,' Detective Chief Inspector John Larkin, who led the investigation, said. 'These were serious allegations which were being made and as a result genuine robberies have not been getting as much attention as they deserve.'

Mr Larkin said they had decided to embark upon the survey after anecdotal evidence suggested that a proportion of all robberies could not be substantiated. Officers examined closed-circuit television footage from places where offences were supposed to have occurred and then re-interviewed complainants. 'We would play the CCTV footage from the time and place where they said they were robbed and could find nothing to substantiate it. That was when we re-interviewed people.' In one case a teenager who claimed that he had been robbed actually named his 'attacker'. But he later admitted to police that he had invented the incident as revenge for a long-running argument.

Once a crime is recorded by police it does not come off the figures, even if it is later proved to be false. Although offenders could be prosecuted for perverting the course of justice, such prosecutions are rarely brought.

Source: The Times, 12 July 2002

26 Crime and deviance

Using the source, and your own knowledge, explain why statistics on crime should be treated with caution.

(14 marks)

EXAMINER'S ADVICE
- This kind of source analysis question is set in Section B of AS Unit 1 as either Question 3 or 4. It will appear as the second or third of three compulsory source analysis questions in this section of the test.
- It is important to question the validity, reliability and representative nature of any set of statistics, the claims based upon them and any conclusions that you may draw from them. In your answer you should consider what the figures mean in the light of what you have read in this unit about crime and how it is reported and recorded. Also you should consider what you have learned elsewhere about the use of statistics – What is a reliable sample? Who has collected the data and how? Who is making the claims and what do they have to gain or lose from the conclusions?
- Don't fall into the trap of assuming, however, that all statistics collected on behalf of the government are bound to be biased or unreliable. The Office for National Statistics is reasonably independent and prepares data for national use, whichever government is in power. Here the important things are the accuracy of the data, the method of collection and why assumptions and conclusions should be treated with caution.
- For 14 marks you should try and produce up to 7 clear and developed points. Once you have studied the material and made some notes, attempt to write out your answer in no more than 15 minutes.
- A range of appropriate points is given on page 280. Look at these when you have written your answer.

The nature of law

Why do we need laws?

Human beings are social creatures – they tend to live together in groups. During the thousands of years over which societies have developed, human beings have learnt that survival of the group depends on the development of a system of law. Law could be described as a way of structuring the tension between the self-interest of an individual within a group and the interests of the group as a whole. Anthropologists, historians and others who study primitive societies point out that whatever the cultural differences between different groups, they all have laws about such matters as protecting the elderly and weak, bringing up children, marriage, property rights and violence.

In a simple, small society, the population can decide its own laws and pass judgment on its lawbreakers. However, in larger, more complex societies, not only do the laws themselves become more complicated, but politicians have to be appointed to make the law, and lawyers, judges and police are needed to interpret and enforce the law. In this situation, the law is often seen as something imposed by the authorities from 'outside', or from 'above', rather than as a system of rules agreed to by every member of the community. However, most people would agree that, in general, the law provides a secure framework for society, in which human beings can flourish and exercise personal moral choice. Also, the law, in theory at least, protects the weak and vulnerable from those likely to exploit them.

Examples of laws

One of the earliest known systems of laws comes from the reign of Hammurabi, ruler of Babylon in 1790 BCE. One example of his laws is, 'If a man blinds a freeman in one eye, he shall lose his own eye.' At first glance, this law looks like a commendable attempt to deal with violence in a just manner. However, by using the word 'freeman', it implies the existence of slaves. By definition, slaves have no rights. The idea of justice, on the other hand, suggests equality and fairness for everybody. This raises the question of the relationship between law and justice. Also, this law makes no distinction between a deliberate or an accidental act. Laws tend to be very general, as it would be impossible to describe every possible situation in advance. Another issue raised here concerns the problem of violence. Should the state show its disapproval of violence by engaging in further violence? This is an important question when discussing such issues as capital punishment.

Another famous set of laws is The Ten Commandments, which appear in the Old Testament. They are claimed to be of divine origin and probably originate from before 1200 BCE. One of these laws states, 'You shall not kill'. This is obviously an essential requirement for any civilised society, but it raises many problems in interpretation. For example, does it mean that violence is ruled out in all circumstances? Does it rule out defending oneself, one's family or one's country against unprovoked attack? Does it rule out helping an elderly suffering relative who asks voluntarily for euthanasia?

Why obey the law?

Any civilised society needs *civil laws* to decide issues concerning property, taxation, child custody, etc. and *criminal laws* to deal with violence, theft, fraud, etc. Most people recognise that obeying the law produces benefits – settling disputes by non-violent means and providing a clear framework describing how people should behave as members of a civilised society, for example.

Civil disobedience or direct action?

The compulsory wearing of seat belts and the fluoridisation of water supplies are both modern examples of legislation which require individuals to give up their personal right to choose in the interests of society as a whole. However, it is clear that there may be examples of unjust laws, and this raises the issue of whether disobeying the law can ever be justified. The mediaeval theologian, *Thomas Aquinas* (1224–74), argued that an unjust law was not a proper law.

In 399 BCE, the Greek philosopher *Socrates* was unjustly condemned to death by the Athenian council on the grounds that he was subverting the state and corrupting the young with his radical ideas and questions. Despite the attempts of his friends to persuade him to escape from prison, Socrates refused, on the grounds that if one accepted the benefits of the state, so one had to abide by its decisions. Socrates was not against all forms of disobedience, however. He also argued that if someone believed that the laws of a state were corrupt then he had the right to disobey any that affected him.

John Rawls (1962) argued that any system of justice and law is to do with the concept of 'fair play'. If people agree to abide by this and recognise that it is socially necessary for everyone to obey the law, then it is not fair if someone decides to disobey the law because it is to their personal advantage. Provided that the injustice is not too great or unfairly distributed, Rawls argued that we have to accept some unjust laws. According to Rawls, the injustice of a law is not sufficient reason for disobeying it.

Many current-day practitioners of civil disobedience draw heavily on a tradition that goes back to Henry David Thoreau, a nineteenth-century US writer. In 1849, Thoreau published an essay entitled *Civil Disobedience*, where he encouraged US citizens to protest slavery, oppression and the war against Mexico by refusing to pay taxes. Though refusing to pay taxes was not a new idea (it was a tactic used by anti-slavery abolitionists), Thoreau's twist on the tactic was the punishment angle. He saw civil disobedience as an act where the punishment is as important as the act of breaking the law. Punishment, or overcoming the power of punishment, is fundamental to Thoreau's method of civil disobedience.

The *Peace Movement* has also embraced civil disobedience as a method of protest. This movement has defined the word 'civil' to mean the opposite of violence. Their philosophy states that those who are engaging in civil disobedience should do so in a 'civilised' manner, with respect for the opponent or identified target(s). Relying heavily on the teachings and philosophical thought of Mahatma Gandhi (who used the term 'passive resistance') and Martin Luther King, the Peace Movement sees the personal consequences that result from choosing to disobey as an integral component of the action.

Both of these approaches embrace civil disobedience as a tool for dialogue – primarily with the authorities that have created unjust laws – and they assume that there is a general understanding of justice. These philosophies hold that the act of creating or maintaining a conversation about an unjust law is essential to getting that law overturned. Like the actions of the Civil Rights Movement, the appeal is to the society's sense of justice.

Direct action

Direct action means acting for yourself against injustice and oppression. It can, sometimes, involve putting pressure on politicians or companies, for example, to ensure a change in an oppressive law or destructive practices. However, such appeals are direct action simply because they do not assume that the parties in question will act for us – indeed the assumption is that change only occurs when we act to create it. So, direct action is any form of activity which people themselves decide upon and organise themselves, which is based on their own collective strength and does not involve getting intermediaries to act for them. As such, direct action is a natural expression of liberty and of self-government. It is clear that by acting for yourself you are expressing the ability to govern yourself. Thus direct action is a means by which people can take control of their own lives. It is a means of self-empowerment and self-liberation.

Many direct activists had identified the US justice system, for example, as a racist, heterosexist, homophobic and sexist institution, where (at best) dialogue with the authorities has historically and repeatedly lead to misinterpretation or total destruction. US citizens, therefore, decided that they could no longer use the democratic system in which other people acted on their behalf, but would have to act directly to bring about change.

Most direct actions also work indirectly and symbolically. A strong indirect effect is to show what can be/needs to be done. When black slaves escaped from the plantations in the South, they proved that freedom was possible. When activists shut down the World Trade Organisation meetings and disrupt the smooth flow of corporate operations, they show that the empire can be ruffled.

With direct action, the participants do not necessarily welcome the consequences of their action. Unlike civil disobedience, where the resisters generally welcome the punishment as a means of furthering their message and increasing the dialogue, direct actions such as hanging a banner, spray painting a political message on a wall or damaging property are public acts of protest that can be done discreetly and in a non-public manner.

Activities

1. In small groups, describe six serious crimes which have been in the media recently. List them in order of seriousness, giving reasons for the order. What punishment would you consider appropriate for each of these crimes and why?

2. A recent television series showed a fictional group of animal rights protesters who planted bombs that killed two people. Do you think such illegal action can ever be justified and why?

3. Over 60 per cent of first-time offenders return to prison. Do you think prisons should emphasise punishment or rehabilitation and why?

4. List the occasions when you think it would be reasonable to break the law, giving your reasons.

Conclusion

Despite their differences, both civil disobedience and direct action are powerful forms of resistance. They share the common aims of:

- preserving or changing a societal phenomena
- generating public debate
- empowering the practitioners and inspiring others to take action, and
- breaking the law(s), often with serious and unjust consequences for others.

Organisations which have taken part in direct action in recent years include, Greenpeace, CND, animal rights groups and other ecological movements, pro-life organisations and various terrorist groups.

This is an A2 essay question from January 2003. This topic would now be set in Section C of Unit 3.

Pressure groups sometimes take 'direct action' in order to make their case known. To what lengths should protestors be prepared to go to 'promote their cause'?

Are illegal actions ever justified? Refer in your answer to the aims and methods of a range of activist groups.

(25 marks)

EXAMINER'S ADVICE

- There are two basic questions here: 'How far should you go in taking direct action?' and 'Are illegal actions justifiable?' The issues are about activities within and outside the law. There are some legal rights to peaceful protest and you should know and state what these and their limits are.
- You need to think of some circumstances where there are strong arguments to support protest (e.g. perhaps the right of workers 'to strike' in the face of unfair treatment from their employer). Are there other different examples you can think of? Is the nature of the activity being protested against also a relevant factor (e.g. tests on animals)?
- You also need to consider carefully and specify in what circumstances it could be 'right' to break the law – this implies a 'moral' right or imperative to break an 'unjust' law. Again can you think of some appropriate examples? The wording of the question implies some balanced argument supported by a good range of actual examples and perhaps some hypothetical considerations.
- Some further suggestions are given on page 280. You should allow yourself 40 minutes to write your answer.

28 Rights and responsibilities

Rights

According to the *Oxford English Dictionary*, the word 'right', means 'a justifiable claim on legal or moral grounds to have or obtain something or to act in a certain way'. The question of rights can be interpreted in different ways and can be analysed from a philosophical, moral, legal or political point of view.

Many modern discussions of rights and responsibilities are a response to political situations where human rights appear to be absent. These include:

- *minority rights* – concerned with the way religious or ethnic groups are treated
- *gay rights* – concerned with discrimination against homosexuals
- *women's rights* – concerned with the role and rights of women in society, particularly in relation to less developed countries
- *animal rights* – concerned with the treatment of animals, particularly in relation to hunting, conservation and animal experimentation.

The issue of rights only arises because human beings tend to live in communities and there are often conflicts between the interests of individuals. On a desert island with only one human being present, there are no such conflicts. The status of rights is often categorised as one of the following:

- *Legal rights.* An example of a legal right would be the right of ownership to legally acquired property. This type of right can be protected by law. Legal rights also involve the right to behave in a certain way or to expect someone else to do so, such as a legally binding contract requiring someone to supply certain services in exchange for money.
- *Moral rights.* The right of an old person to care and respect is an example of a moral right, although this would not be directly enforceable in law. Similarly, one might argue for the rights of an unborn child and against the rights of the mother to choose in the context of a possible abortion. Whatever the legal status of the act of abortion itself, there is still a further moral discussion about rights involved.
- *Universal rights.* This category would include those rights with a possible moral basis but which are not necessarily legally supported in some countries or societies. For example, most people would argue that no human being should be a slave and that this right of freedom should apply universally, or that people should have the right to free speech, to express their opinions in public without fear of persecution.

In practice, rights often take the form of:

- *claims* – being owed money means that you have a claim on the debtor
- *powers* – the right to distribute your property in your will
- *liberties* – being exempt from giving evidence against a spouse in court
- *immunities* – the right not to be persecuted for joining a trade union.

The origins of human rights

Article 1 of the Universal Declaration of Human Rights produced by the United Nations in 1948 states, 'All human beings are born free and equal in dignity and rights. They are endowed with reason and conscience and should act towards each other in a spirit of brotherhood.' The Declaration goes on to specify a long list of human rights including the rights to life, liberty and security, freedom from slavery and freedom of movement across national borders. Although most civilised societies would agree to this declaration, at least in theory, there have been different views in the history of thought concerning exactly what rights human beings should have, and the basis on which such rights can be justified.

Natural rights and natural law

The phrase 'human rights' is comparatively recent. Traditionally, the phrase 'natural rights' was used, and this was often based on *natural law*. This refers to the idea that all people recognise some moral obligation, leading to generally agreeing moral principles.

- The classical Greek philosophers, *Socrates*, *Plato* and *Aristotle*, all argued that there is a natural justice or a right thing to do.
- In the New Testament, *Paul* spoke of those who obey, by nature, the things of the law, because they have the law written on their conscience (Romans, 11).
- *Thomas Aquinas* (1224–74) linked Christian belief with the idea of natural law in the thirteenth century. He argued that there are certain principles of true morality and justice discernible by human reason without the aid of revelation (even though they are of divine origin). Man-made laws that conflict with these principles are not valid law.
- *Thomas Hobbes* (1588–1679) argued that in its natural state, human life was 'solitary, poor, nasty, brutish and short'. In order to protect people from one another, a 'social contract' was needed, which involved the natural right not to be harmed by another.
- *John Locke* (1632–1704) had a more optimistic view of human nature. Human beings are naturally capable of acting in the interests of others and of recognising a natural law, instituted by God, which says that 'no one should harm another in his life, health, liberty or possessions'.
- The *American Declaration of Independence* (1776) is another example. It claimed to be founded on the self-evident truths that man has a right to life, liberty and the pursuit of happiness.

However, the Utilitarian philosopher, *Jeremy Bentham* (1748–1832), argued that there was no such thing as human rights. His theory was designed to cut through all the confusion and conflicts to which arguing about human rights might lead. He believed that the assertion of natural rights incites 'selfish and dissocial passions', the great enemies of public peace, and so militates against social order and the laws of the land.

DID YOU KNOW?

Moral responsibilities
- At least five different British companies provide electronic torture equipment such as cattle prods to repressive regimes.
- Official Roman Catholic teaching regards contraception as a sin because it is against their understanding of natural law.
- In 1998, at least 5,000 people died in 114 countries from torture or imprisonment.
- During the 1999 World Trade Talks, some less developed countries objected to the idea of abolishing child or slave labour.

KEY TERMS

Amnesty International a voluntary organisation, founded in 1961, which publicises and fights for the freedom of people who are unfairly imprisoned, tortured and otherwise persecuted for speaking out against corruption

Homophobia an extreme aversion to and prejudice against the idea and practice of homosexual relationships of either sex

Justice refers to the idea of fairness and equality for all and to the system of reward and punishment that helps to maintain it

Sexism the view that one sex (usually women) is inferior emotionally, intellectually or physically and the practical application of this attitude in society

Speciesism the view that animals have fewer rights than human beings and could be used for such things as experiments

Human rights were not something to which human beings were entitled by right of being human, but only permissible if they contributed more happiness than unhappiness to society.

Article 18 of the Universal Declaration of Human Rights states that everyone has the 'right to freedom of thought, conscience and religion'. It could be suggested that this is the part of the declaration that has been most flagrantly ignored and contravened since the Second World War. All over the world, the right to express political or religious views contradicting those of the prevailing authorities has been removed and those expressing such views have been imprisoned, expelled, tortured and/or killed. Examples include:

- the murder of thousands of Baha'i (a pacifist religion) in Iran in the 1980s
- the obliteration of Tibetan Buddhist culture after the Chinese invasion
- the torture of men, women and children in Bosnia in the 1990s
- the struggle for independence by the Kurds against, Iraq, Turkey and Russia.

Responsibilities

The idea of responsibility can refer to the idea that people are answerable for their behaviour, implying that they are free to choose their actions and can thus be praised or blamed for what they actually do (see Unit 27, 'The nature of law'). But it can also refer to the idea of 'duty'. Duty can be defined as 'the obligation of an individual to satisfy a claim made upon him by the community or individual or group in order to serve the common good'. In all successful societies, rights and duties have to be balanced against each other. If children have a legal and/or moral right to education, then the parents and the state have a duty to provide it. Another good example of this balance can be seen in the purchase and use of a railway ticket. The railway company has the duty to convey the passenger from one place to another and has the right to be paid for doing so. The passenger has the duty to pay for this ticket and the right to be conveyed to the destination for which they have paid.

This relationship between rights and duties has given rise to the view that all morality depends on a 'social contract'. Individuals agree to perform certain duties in exchange for the acquisition of certain rights. For example, law-abiding citizens agree to respect the property of their neighbours, in exchange for the right to have their own property protected.

What is our duty?

The philosopher *Immanuel Kant* (1724–1804) argued that human beings are rational and have the capacity to work out what their duty is and to do it. For Kant, a good action is one that involves doing what you ought to do, rather than what you want to do. Reason tells you that you ought always to treat people as ends in themselves, rather than as means to an end. This involves always telling the truth and never taking life.

Figure 28.1 Conflict of rights – these protestors feel they have the right to deny homosexuals rights

The Ten Commandments

Some lists of duties such as the Ten Commandments have stood the test of time. Whatever their religious inspiration, they seem to contain basic rules that contribute to the survival of civilised human communities. Basic human rights seem to be protected when people accept the following duties:

- Do not steal.
- Do not commit adultery.
- Do not tell lies.
- Do not kill.
- Honour your father and mother.

The problem with duties

The problem with lists of duties, however, is that they never allow for exceptional circumstances. There are always situations, for example, where one might consider that killing in self-defence or lying about the whereabouts of a relation being pursued by an assassin seems to be the right course of action. However, in general, discussing human behaviour in terms of rights and duties seems to contribute positively towards the preservation of society.

Citizenship

The 2001 General Election produced the lowest turn out of voters since 1918. Less than six out of ten of those people entitled to vote bothered to do so. In 2005, the

28 Rights and responsibilities

Activities

1. Should human rights only be granted to those people who carry out their duties to others? Give examples to support your views.

2. 'Whatever is my right as a man [woman] is also the right of another and it becomes my duty to guarantee as well as to possess' (Thomas Paine). How far do you think that this idea could be used to support the criticism of another country's human rights record and why?

3. What effective measures do you think could be taken by members of a society in order to guarantee and maintain basic human rights?

turnout was 61.36 per cent of the population. This apparent apathy and disinterest in the way democracy operates and the alarming ignorance displayed during recent years regarding the whole machinery of government has led to the introduction of Citizenship as a compulsory part of the National Curriculum in schools and examinable at GCSE. Its introduction, however, has had significant effects on PSHE and Religious Education because of the time constraints already present caused by the demands of the National Curriculum.

The Department for Children, Schools and Families identifies three inter-related components that should run through all education for Citizenship, as shown below:

- *Social and moral responsibility.* Pupils learning from the very beginning of their education, self-confidence and socially and morally responsible behaviour both in and beyond the classroom, towards those in authority and towards each other.
- *Community involvement.* Pupils learning about becoming helpfully involved in the life and concerns of their neighbourhood and communities, including learning through community involvement and service to the community.
- *Political literacy.* Pupils learning about the institutions, problems and practices of our democracy and how to make themselves effective in the life of the nation, locally, regionally and nationally through skills and values as well as knowledge – a concept wider than political knowledge alone.

Pupils develop skills of enquiry, communication, participation and responsible action through learning about and becoming informed and interested citizens. This will be achieved through creating links between pupils' learning in the classroom and activities that take place across the school, in the community and the wider world. The *National Curriculum Handbook* sets out what pupils should learn through citizenship education and there are now a large number of organisations supporting this project. The main emphasis of the course is on the importance of participation in the operation of a community and the development of a sense of responsibility towards the community as a whole. (Source: DfES website)

EXAM QUESTIONS

Consider the source below, and answer the questions which follow. This kind of source analysis question is set in Section B of AS Unit 1. It is similar to the one set at the end of Unit 16 of this book.

Letter on experiments using animals

It was refreshing to read an accurate piece about Huntingdon Life Sciences, and animal experiments in general, rather than hear the same old stories the animals rights movement uses to gain the support of moderate members of society.

Most work at HLS involves testing drugs to satisfy safety regulations. Thalidomide didn't 'pass the safety tests' but did 'go on to kill and maim humans'. Animal rights activists claim to have the support of scientists and doctors, but never quote references from reliable sources. There have been 13 occasions in the past decade when the Advertising Standards Authority has found their claims to be false and misleading. Who would you believe?

Source: Adapted from *The Daily Mail,* 4 October 2000

(a) *In your own words*, give *three* reasons which the author of the source uses to support the work undertaken by Huntingdon Life Sciences.

(4 marks)

(b) *Using your own ideas and knowledge*, give *three* reasons which might be used against conducting experiments on animals.

(4 marks)

EXAMINER'S ADVICE

- Check out the requirements for Section B of AS Unit 1 on page 1. In this section you are required to answer three compulsory source analysis questions each based on a short source for a total of 35 marks and you have about 45 minutes in which to complete them. This first question is the shortest and simplest and is worth 4 marks, which means that you should aim to complete it in no more than 10 minutes.

- As before, Part (a) asks for **three** reasons **from the source**, using your own words. The question is an exercise in quickly picking out key points in a text and communicating them in your own words. You will gain one mark for each valid reason, up to a maximum of three, plus one mark for accurate communication, predominantly in your own words. Here your answer should consist of three simple sentences (ideally one per point) and you should use only points or arguments made in the source.

- Part (b) requires you to think of arguments **against** those made or implied in the source and here you have to use your own ideas and knowledge. Once again your answer should consist of three simple sentences, for which you stand to gain one mark for each valid point made, plus one for clear and accurate communication overall.

- When you have written your answers, compare your points with those given on pages 280–281. There are similar questions to be found at the end of Units 16 and 30.

Power and control

Power can be defined on a personal level as the ability to get one's own way, even when others are opposed to one's wishes. From a wider perspective, power is about who has the authority and the capacity to change states of affairs in a society. Politics is often defined as the struggle to acquire and exercise such power. Sociologists often distinguish between two forms of power – authority and coercion:

- *Authority* refers to the exercise of legitimate power, which is accepted by everyone as right and just. For example, parliamentary decisions are accepted as lawful by members of society because they accept parliament as having legitimate authority.
- *Coercion* refers to the exercise of power that is not regarded as legitimate by those subject to it. Members of the Republican Movement in Northern Ireland, for example, did not accept the authority of the British Government and so regard the exercise of their power as coercion. Coercion may involve the use of force to overcome opposition.

The sociologist Max Weber suggested that there were three types of authority:

- *Charismatic authority* derives from those exceptional qualities displayed by some leaders which enables them to produce intense loyalty, admiration and obedience in their followers. Examples of such powerful leaders include Alexander the Great and Napoleon.
- *Traditional authority* refers to the acceptance of certain customs and traditions which have been long established. Accepting the authority of a reigning monarch because of his/her inherited status would be an example of this.
- *Rational/legal authority* is based on the fact that all the members of society accept a legal framework with a particular shared end in view. In general, people accept the authority of the legal system because they realise that it serves the goal of justice.

There is also what might be referred to as the *authority of expertise*. We tend to accept the authority of those whose expertise we recognise – doctors, teachers, solicitors, etc. Accepting their authority often means accepting their right to give us instructions.

Why do we need power?

Human beings tend to be gregarious (inclined to live in groups). The fact that virtually everyone lives together in groups immediately raises problems about how such groups should be organised. For example, the idea of 'government' usually implies either a group or an individual who is in control of the affairs of a nation. However, the way this control is exercised has profound effects on the lives of the population. Under some forms of dictatorship, a 'political discussion' might take the form of indoctrination, which justifies the authority of those in power and stifles opposition. On the other hand, you might argue that although in a democracy everyone has the right to express their views, the complicated nature of the democratic process itself prevents people's views from being heard.

Important questions raised by the discussion of power include the following:

- Who should govern and by what means?
- By what right do they exercise authority and control?
- What activities should governments be involved in?

What is a government?

A government is an organisation that has the authority to make and enforce rules and laws about important and extensive areas of human life. However, it is only a legitimate government if its authority is accepted by everybody. A government that makes laws that no one accepts, but which forces people to obey it through military might, is not a proper government because its right to enforce laws is not recognised by society. Many other organisations, such as labour unions, large corporations, religious institutions and schools, etc. exercise authority over sections of society, but what makes governments significant is the extent of their authority. This may include such areas as law and order, education, social welfare, defence, taxation, and immigration.

The purpose of government

Most political thinkers agree that some form of government is necessary and preferable to a state of *anarchy* in which there is no institutional government whatsoever. The justification for needing some form of government includes the following reasons:

- *To serve the interests of the most powerful.* This is the cynical view that government is just an organised form of domination. The most powerful group uses government agencies as a means of serving its own interests.
- *To protect people from one another.* This is the most common theory about the purpose of government. Without laws and the means to enforce them, some people would treat other people very badly and subject them to theft, personal violence and other forms of abuse. Governments exist to construct and establish a legal and social system that will provide a secure environment in which economic production and culture can flourish.
- *To promote God's will.* This ancient theory argues that governments exist to carry out the will of God and their authority consists of the fact that the government is the Earthly representative of God on Earth. This type of view can still be seen in some religiously fundamentalist societies.
- *To develop and control the economy.* This type of theory is particularly associated with *Marxism*. According to Marx, the purpose of government is to promote the

expansion of the forces of production by finding more and more effective ways of producing goods. In the final stages of history, ordinary workers finally own the means of production and control the government so that policies are all aimed towards the general welfare.

- *To bring about equality.* This theory is based on the assumption that people should have equal opportunity and equal status in a society. It is the role of government to prevent artificial social or economic distinctions and to eliminate all inequalities of property, money, achievement or power.

In practice, most governments carry out a range of functions, some of which are conflicting. While most democratic governments try to act in the interests of the general welfare of society, this may involve attacking the rights of some individuals. For example, forcing people to pay taxes or to engage in compulsory military service are attacks on individual freedom which are justified in terms of the good of society as a whole. There is a wide range of political views concerning the extent to which governments should exercise control over people's lives. *Socialist* political thinkers tend to argue that governments should own the agencies that provide education, housing, health, transport, power, etc. because these are all essential to the welfare of human beings. *Free-market/libertarian* thinkers tend to argue that governments should exercise as little control as possible in peoples' lives and that people should provide for their own welfare.

Who should have control?

The most widely accepted view is often referred to as *the consent of the governed*. A government gets its power from the fact that the people of a particular country consent to it acting on their behalf. A range of other views are presented below:

- The *American Declaration of Independence 1776* not only specified the purpose of government as the protection of natural rights and the promotion of people's happiness, but also claimed the right to abolish the authority of a particular government if it was not pursuing those purposes.
- *Thomas Hobbes (1588–1679)* argued that in their natural state, the lives of men were 'solitary, poor, nasty, brutish and short'. In order to avoid a lawless state of nature, people agree to a 'social contract', in which they give the sovereign enough power to control people's lives. This will provide a secure environment in which goods can be produced, and people can be protected from each other. However, once the sovereign has acquired this power, it cannot be claimed back, therefore government is no longer by consent.
- *Jean Jacques Rousseau (1712–78)* argued for a different type of social contract. Rousseau thought that human beings were naturally good and had kindly feelings for each other. However, he suggested that they need to live in society in order to develop their full potential and to do this they should enter into a social contract where they surrender their individual rights to the 'general will'. This is

KEY TERMS

Anarchy a state in which there are no institutional forms of government

Freedom of information the idea that there should be no government secrets

Legal aid a government-financed scheme to pay the legal costs of less well off people so that the rich cannot control the poor in the legal system

Lobby to try to influence a Member of Parliament

Meritocracy a form of government in which a self-appointed elite of the most knowledgeable and capable people rule

Oligarchy a state in which the government is in the hands of a small group

Republic a state without a monarchy

Totalitarianism a type of government that allows no opposition to its policies or the existence of rival parties – found in extreme right- and left-wing countries

Universal suffrage the right of virtually all adults to vote in political elections

concerned with the good of the whole community, and in large communities wise legislators have to be elected to draw up laws and policies in agreement with the general will.

Democracy

Most political thinkers would argue that democracy – rule by the majority or all of a population – is the best form of government. In a democracy, the government is elected by the free choice of the population and can be removed without violence. In a modern democracy, virtually all adults can vote, irrespective of sex or status. The principal advantage of democracy is that people can exercise direct control over their policy makers by voting them out of office. Also, policies tend to reflect the interests of the majority and so receive general support. Disadvantages of democracy include the fact that non-experts often get elected to powerful positions because they are popular. Also, in a system where the majority rules, minority interests and opinions may suffer, although some definitions of democracy include human rights and individual freedom as a part of democracy. Another disadvantage is that in a system where candidates have to appeal directly to the voters, the most charismatic and financially supported public speaker may be elected rather than the most suitable person for a particular post.

Consider the source below, and answer the question which follows.

'I believe we should claim certain rights for children and labour for their universal recognition.'
(Eglantyne Jebb, founder of *Save The Children*, 1923)

Save the Children has a firm commitment to making a reality of children's rights. Eglantyne Jebb recognised that *Save the Children's* practical work on the ground needed to be complemented by the much wider support which could come from a heightened awareness of adult obligations towards children. All of *Save the Children's* work is now centred on its commitment to making a reality of children's rights.

Human rights derive from recognition of the inherent worth and dignity of all human beings. They assert the entitlement of all people to the fundamental conditions necessary for their freedom and well being.

Essentially, human rights allow human beings to make claims on all other people to uphold their rights. For example, every human being has a right not to be tortured. This is asserted both morally and legally within the human rights framework and, therefore, implies obligations upon everyone to both respect this right and offer some protection against the wrongful behaviour of others, especially states.

Source: Save The Children (UK), 2001

Using specific examples from the source, and your own knowledge, examine the difficulties of ensuring that different groups in society have access to the rights to which they might be entitled.

(14 marks)

- This type of source analysis will appear in Section B of Unit 1. It is one of three different compulsory source analysis questions that you have to complete in this section of the test.
- The question is typical of the last of the three questions in the test. It requires much more of your own ideas and opinions as well as your ability to draw points and arguments from the source.
- How difficult is it for a society (through its government, its laws, and through individuals) to guarantee appropriate rights for everybody, minorities as well as majorities? Think of the problems, think of different groups – poverty, health, education, discrimination, for example.
- For 14 marks you should cover at least two or more groups in addition to children's rights and suggest where the difficulties lie in meeting all expectations. A range of points is given on page 281. Look at these when you have made your attempt.

Politics

What is politics?

One useful definition might be, 'Politics is the activity by which groups reach binding collective decisions through attempting to reconcile differences amongst their members.' The Greek philosopher *Aristotle* (384–322 BCE) said that 'man is by nature, a political animal'. Human beings live in groups and they can only resolve their conflicts of interest, make plans and take decisions by engaging in some sort of political activity. In this sense, all rational human beings take part in politics even if they are not professional politicians. Politics is a complex activity, which contains the following elements, to name but a few:

- *Diversity of views.* If there were no differences between people about future plans and methods of achieving them, there would be no need for political activity.
- *Reconciliation.* One of the principal functions of politics is to find an accepted solution to problems caused by major differences of points of view.
- *Decision-making.* Politics involves making decisions about future actions that will be binding on all members of a group and may be backed up with force.

Politics and government

Although some extreme political activists argue for 'anarchy' – the absence of law and government – most people recognise that in large communities individuals and institutions have to be appointed to take decisions and execute policy on their behalf. Collectively, this is referred to as the government. (Different types of government are discussed in detail in Unit 29, 'Power and control'). Governments can loosely be divided into *authoritarian* and *democratic*. Examples of authoritarian governments include the following:

- *Military rule.* In many African, Asian and Latin American countries, military leaders took over governments in response to economic and civil problems. Many of these leaders put down opposition ruthlessly and acted as a dictatorship.
- *Personal dictatorship.* Many African countries replaced colonial powers with 'hero-figures' who had fought against the colonial powers, for example, Jomo Kenyatta, President of Kenya (1962–78), and Kenneth Kaunda, who ran Zambia (1964–91). Both these leaders ended up as very autocratic, resistant to change and responsible for economic decline.
- *Dominant party rule.* Countries such as Singapore and Egypt appear democratic but in reality are run by one very powerful party, which controls the media, the economic resources and has the ability to rig elections.

Politics in Britain

Like most Western European countries, the USA, Australia, New Zealand, etc. the UK is governed as a *liberal democracy*. This can be described as a system where elected politicians act on behalf of those who elect them but within carefully defined limits, so that the rights of minorities and individuals are protected. The most important feature of democracy is the idea of *representative government*. This includes the following characteristics:

- A *Member of Parliament* who represents the interests of their constituents.
- *Freedom of expression*, meaning that people can choose their representatives freely.
- *Sovereignty of the people*, where the will of the general population is paramount.
- *Political equality*, meaning that every person's vote and right to vote is of equal value.

Parliament

In the UK, the representative government is Parliament, which consists of three parts:

- *The Monarch*, who has no real power but presents the current government's future plans in the Queen's Speech at the opening of Parliament.
- *The House of Lords* (in the process of being reformed), which has hereditary peers, life peers, archbishops, bishops, and senior members of the legal system known as Law Lords.
- *The House of Commons*, consisting of 659 elected members. Since 1872, Members of Parliament have been elected by secret ballot. Any member of the public can vote for any candidate without having to reveal their choice. Virtually all members belong to either the Conservative Party or the Labour Party (the two largest), or the Liberal Democrats. Much smaller numbers represent the Ulster Unionists and the Welsh and Scottish Nationalist parties.

The process of government

In practice, the government is made up of the Prime Minister and the Cabinet, which consists of approximately 20 of the Prime Minister's senior colleagues and their assistants who have been appointed as Ministers of State to run various departments such as defence, education, transport, etc. or to represent areas such as Scotland or Wales. This group of ministers is responsible for introducing new policies that they wish to become law. These measures are known as bills until they have passed through Parliament, after which they become *Acts of Parliament* and then law. This whole process of government involves three interlocking areas:

- *Legislature.* This describes the work of Parliament, which has the responsibility to make new laws and to change existing ones.
- *Executive.* This refers to the work of Ministers of State and the civil service departments they run. They are responsible for the execution of the wishes of Parliament, for example producing the detailed administrative framework for a change in the law affecting pensions, or raising the school-leaving age.

- *Judiciary.* This refers to the process by which expert judges settle disputes concerning the interpretation of the law.

Acts of Parliament

In order for a bill to become an Act of Parliament, it has to have three readings. The first introduction is a formality before the second reading, where the general principles of the bill are discussed by those present in the Commons at the time. This is followed by the committee stage, where the details of the bill are examined in depth before it is sent back to the Commons for a third and final debate. Although in theory it can then be held up by the House of Lords, it will eventually become law despite their opposition, as long as a majority vote for it in the Commons. The formal Royal Assent of the sovereign is then required for it to become law. In practice, very few bills introduced by a majority government fail to become law.

Criticisms of the system

Although in theory the political process in the UK appears to be very democratic, various important weaknesses have been highlighted in recent years.

The problem of oligarchy

Oligarchy means 'rule by the few'. In the House of Commons, very few backbench MPs have any influence on government policy or the opportunity to introduce a bill dealing with the interests of their constituents, because of the pressure on parliamentary time. Backbenchers may be appointed to Parliamentary Select Committees to examine various issues, but in general, they are there to vote in accordance with party wishes. This gives the Prime Minister enormous *patronage* (the power to grant favours, including promotion in response to loyalty). Legislation is controlled by the Prime Minister and the Cabinet.

Adversarial politics

In the House of Commons, the government benches face those of the Opposition. Debates in the House tend to emphasise criticism of the other major party, and the manipulation of the process in order to gain narrow political advantage, instead of emphasising important national and social interests. Because of the shortage of parliamentary time, bills can be 'talked out' by opponents using up all the time available to pass a bill through to the next stage, sometimes involving an all-night sitting.

Conflict of interest

Unlike the USA, where the written constitution guarantees a clear distinction between the different processes of government, there has been a tendency for recent British governments to interfere with the judiciary and the executive branches of government. High-ranking members of the civil service, which is supposed to be impartial, have been replaced by people sympathetic towards government policies, and senior civil

Globalisation the process by which social, cultural and economic trends and policies are less dependent on national power and more influenced by worldwide issues, e.g. European currency issues

Referendum a system that allows every elector to vote directly on an important national issue, such as Scottish or Welsh devolution – an example of direct rather than representative democracy

Single transferable vote an electoral system that allows voters to transfer their vote to where it will be most effective after the first ballot – used in Eire

Two-party system the traditional state of affairs in British politics, where Parliament is dominated by two strong parties with far more members than the nearest minority. This would be changed by proportional representation

Activities

1. Read the extract below from Lord Hailsham. What improvements do you think might make the parliamentary system more democratic?

'I have reached the conclusion that our constitution is wearing out. Its central defects are gradually coming to outweigh its merits, and its central defects consist in the absolute powers we confer on our sovereign body [parliament], and the concentration of these powers in an executive government formed out of one party which may not fairly represent the popular will.' (Lord Hailsham, 1976 Dimbleby Lecture)

2. What might be the advantages and disadvantages of closer ties with Europe?

3. Do you think Members of Parliament should be allowed to vote according to their conscience or should they always obey the party line?

4. Do you think the establishment of separate Welsh and Scottish assemblies would divide the UK or help to bring it together?

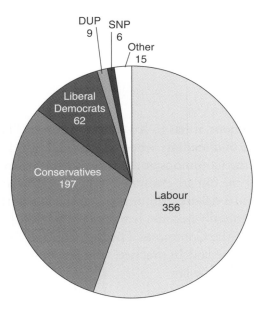

Figure 30.1 Votes and seats in the 2005 election

servants have been overruled by government 'advisers'. The government also has a strong influence in the appointment of bishops and judges.

The electoral system

Proportional representation

Under this system, a large number of candidates would stand in each constituency and, according to a special formula, votes of the least supported candidates would be transferred to stronger ones. This would eventually ensure that members elected represented the number of votes cast and a much wider range of members would be elected. This would be a more representative electoral system, but it might make strong government more difficult because of the reduced possibility of a large majority for any one party and the need to accommodate a wide range of interests when making policy.

First-past-the-post

A democratic electoral system should ensure that the majority rules and that significant minorities are represented. The present system elects the candidate whose voters are in the majority in a particular geographical area. This means that a particular party may become the government because it has the most members returned in a particular election, but does not represent the total numbers of voters nationwide. In the 1987 election, the Conservative Party had a majority of 102 members but had only polled 43.4 per cent of the total vote. Under the first-past-the-post system, the government is formed by the strongest minority rather than a genuine majority. Parties such as the Liberal Democrats are under-represented in Parliament because their support is distributed evenly across the country, but not concentrated in any particular area. This means that they end up with fewer parliamentary seats than they are entitled to by their total vote.

Consider the source below, and answer the questions which follow.

Things are changing fast. The acid dissection of Royal wealth published in 1975 by the republican Labour MP Willie Hamilton made him a hate-figure; today similar points are made on the Tory benches, while a play and a novel about the eviction of the Royal Family to a council estate have become mainstream, uncontroversial mass entertainment. Where will this process end? In a republic?

The idea is slowly gaining ground today and the pace of changing attitudes makes it dangerous for even the most dogmatic royalist to sound wholly robust. A dislike of the whole monarchical business is widespread among young voters. But this is still a nervous and conservative country. A less decisive outcome is still much likelier – a further shaving away of the wealth of less central royals, and perhaps the main ones too, and an assault on the final political powers of the monarchy.

Source: Andrew Marr, *Ruling Britannia* (Michael Joseph), 1995

(a) *Using your own words*, give *three* reasons the author of the source offers as evidence that attitudes to the monarchy in the United Kingdom are changing.

(4 marks)

(b) *Using your own ideas and knowledge*, give *three* reasons for retaining the monarchy in the United Kingdom.

(4 marks)

EXAMINER'S ADVICE

- This question is typical of the first of three source analysis questions in Section B of the AS Unit 1 test and similar questions can be found at the end of Units 16 and 28 in this book.
- The requirements are therefore identical and you should refer back to page 134 to remind yourself of how to approach the answers to these two short questions. A quick look at the relevant sections of the next unit (Unit 31) might also give you some ideas for your answer to Part (b).
- A suggested range of points is given on page 281. Compare these with your own when you have made your attempt.

The British Constitution

It is hard to define the concept of 'constitution' and even harder to define the British Constitution. However, a generally accepted view is that, 'a constitution sets out the formal structure of government, specifying the powers and constitutions of central government, sets out the balance between central and other levels of government and specifies the rights of citizens'.

There are written and unwritten constitutions, with most modern countries having a written constitution. The constitution of the USA is contained in seven pages, while that of India is several hundred pages long. It is usually claimed that the British Constitution is unwritten, but there are several written parts of it:

- *The Bill of Rights, 1689*, is the basis of the British Constitution. It was written to justify the way in which the leaders of Parliament had removed King James II from the throne. By declaring various practices of James II illegal, it made the British monarchy constitutional. It stated that the monarch cannot raise taxes, pass or suspend laws or keep an army without the consent of parliament. It set down rules for the length of parliaments and for free elections to them. It also gave all British people the right to freedom of religion and MPs the right to complete freedom of speech in the House of Commons.
- *Habeas Corpus, 1679*, compels the authorities to bring anyone arrested before the courts, so preventing what is known as 'arbitrary arrest', where people can be arrested and kept in prison without trial.
- Various *Representation of the People Acts* have been passed so that now, by law, everyone over the age of eighteen has the right to vote and parliamentary constituencies are arranged so that a similar number of electors elect each MP.
- *The Act of Settlement, 1701*, stipulates that the monarch and the monarch's spouse must be Protestant (James II was a Catholic). This is a sign of the way in which parliament is in control of the monarchy, but also reflects the fact that the monarch is also the Head of the Church of England, which is Protestant.
- *The Parliament Act of 1911* removed the power of the House of Lords to do anything but delay legislation approved by the House of Commons.

All political power is based on the Prime Minister and the Cabinet. The monarch must act on their advice. The Cabinet controls all the government departments (run by the civil service) and the armed forces. However, the courts are independent of the government (though the Lord Chancellor who selects judges, is a member of the government) and citizens can challenge the government through the courts (including the European Courts) if they believe the government is acting illegally.

There are other checks and balances on the power of the government. If the Prime Minister loses a vote of confidence in the House of Commons, he or she must resign. They must also hold an election at least every five years. The monarch could remove any Prime Minister who refused to do either of these things, and, as the armed forces and the civil service take their oath to the monarch, there would be the power to force their resignation. The monarch also has the final decision as to who to call as Prime Minister if no one party wins a majority in an election – this has never yet happened and no one knows what would happen if it did.

The British Constitution has considerable flexibility as parliament can adjust the constitution if conditions change.

The need for reform of the British Constitution

Many political thinkers believe that the British Constitution is in need of reform. Some feel that there is a need for a complete written constitution in one document, which should also make a clear statement of the rights of individuals. Others think that the position of the monarch needs to be more clearly defined, while others think the idea of hereditary monarchy in a democracy is contradictory and so the monarchy should be abolished. Others feel that too much power is concentrated in the hands of the Prime Minister and the Cabinet and that power should be devolved, firstly to the separate nations of the UK (Northern Ireland, Scotland and Wales), then to the

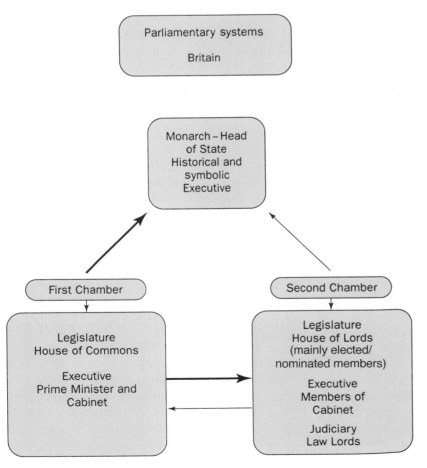

Figure 31.1 The British Constitution (Source: Barrie Axford, *Politics: An Introduction*, Routledge, 1997)

regions. It is also felt that the sovereignty of Parliament requires a second chamber to vet proposed legislation from the Commons, but this cannot be done by a chamber with an inbuilt majority of one political party (until the hereditary peers were reduced from 750 to a maximum of 92 following the *House of Lords Act*, 1999, the Conservatives could win almost any vote in the Lords).

Devolution and the House of Lords are two of the main issues concerning the British Constitution.

Figure 31.2 The House of Lords before reform

Reform of the House of Lords

The UK is the only democracy to have a second chamber where the members are unelected, but it has been difficult to find an acceptable alternative. Labour governments have recognised that while the House of Lords usually has a large Conservative majority, its undemocratic nature has meant that it has no real political authority to challenge legislation produced by a majority in the House of Commons. Replacing it with a large number of elected members would give it more power to resist government policy, while having too many directly appointed members would allow governments to put its own supporters in place. This would continue the political patronage, which appoints a majority of life peers who support the current government. The current debate initiated by the recommendations of the Wakeham Commission (2000) is focused on what proportion should be elected, what proportion should be directly appointed and for how long, how to bring in representatives from social and ethnic minorities, and what the total membership should be.

Devolution

Devolution refers to the process of transferring the power from ministers and Parliament to regional or sub-national bodies, which are subordinate to Parliament but directly elected. Unlike such countries as the USA or Germany, which operate a *federal* system where individual states have guaranteed status, in theory Parliament could abolish the powers of a region. For example, in 1972, the British Government abolished the Northern Ireland Parliament at Stormont.

Devolution has been a political issue since at least 1886, when W.E. Gladstone introduced an unsuccessful bill to give Ireland Home Rule in Dublin. In the late twentieth century, the pressure for devolution in Scotland and Wales was seen in the increased number of Members elected to Parliament representing the Scottish National Party and Plaid Cymru, the Welsh National Party.

However, since 1997 the devolution process has established assemblies in Northern Ireland, Scotland and Wales. These reforms have had far-reaching implications for the politics, policy and society in the UK. Radical institutional change, combined with a fuller capacity to express the UK's distinctive territorial identities, is reshaping the way the UK is governed and opening up new directions of public policy.

The effects of devolution so far

One of the main justifications for devolution has been the view that it might enable a fairer distribution of financial resources. What has actually happened is that there has been a wide variation in the new policies which have been developed, as shown below.

Different public policies in Scotland since devolution include:

* free long-term personal care for the elderly
* abolition of up-front tuition fees for students in higher education
* abolition of fox hunting
* abolition of the ban on 'promoting homosexuality' in schools.

Wales has fewer policy differences. But these include:

- free school milk for all children under seven
- abolition of school league tables
- free medical prescriptions for those under 25 and over 60
- free bus travel for pensioners.

Different public policies in Northern Ireland since devolution include:

- abolition of school league tables
- establishment of a commissioner for children
- free travel for the elderly.

These national differences obviously mean that some people may have financial advantages denied to others depending on where they live. Also, the introduction of some policies directly opposed to recent government legislation has caused some embarrassment and tension, for example the abolition of university fees in Scotland and school league tables in Wales. Variations in policy like this weaken central control from Westminster.

Views on further devolution

Nationalist parties – SNP and Plaid Cymru
These see devolution as a first step to complete independence, which is their ultimate goal. Plaid recognises that this goal will take time as there is considerable resistance to the idea amongst the population.

Labour party
The Labour Party sees devolution as the compromise that was necessary to satisfy demands for self-government but without granting full independence, which it does not believe a majority are in favour of. It remains committed to the UK together but with some devolved power to the regions (this may ultimately include England as well, as the party committed itself to elected regional assemblies in England in its 1997 manifesto).

Conservative party
They are very concerned that devolution will be the 'thin end of the wedge', and that it will fuel, rather than satisfy, demands for greater regional autonomy. They are committed to a unified UK and have opposed the idea of devolution in the past.

Liberal Democrat party
They see devolution as a victory as they had been campaigning for greater decentralisation of decision-making for years. They see a fully federal system as the logical outcome for the UK, with sovereignty devolved.

Regionalism

'Directly elected regional government' was a goal in Labour's 1997 manifesto, but since then the party has retreated somewhat on this issue. However, some steps have been taken already towards decentralising some power in England:

- Setting up of Regional Development Agencies (RDAs). These are unelected quangos, whose purpose is to spearhead regional economic planning and development to rejuvenate the regional economies of England.
- Reform of the voting system for European elections divided the UK into 12 constituencies, and RDAs recognise these boundaries.
- Since 2000, London has directly elected its mayor and a London Assembly. Together they control billions of pounds of funding. The most recent elections for the Mayor of London and members of the London Assembly took place on 10 June 2004. Ken Livingstone, the labour candidate, was re-elected as Mayor of London on a slightly reduced share of the vote compared with the elections in 2000. Turnout was 35.9 per cent, an increase of 2.2 percentage points compared with 2000. These low turnouts throw doubt on mayoral elections as a means of rejuvenating interest in local democracy.
- Reform of local government. The 2000 Local Government Act required local authorities with populations over 85,000 to change their management structures. One option was for a directly elected Mayor (as opposed to a Mayor or Leader chosen by the councillors) with this decision to be made by referendum. In the event, very few areas opted for this choice.

Some English regions exhibit substantial support for their own regional assembly, whilst the issue is dead in others, for example, the North East decisively rejected the idea of a regional assembly.

The general consensus of opinion is that the process of devolution has gone very smoothly so far. This is partly due to Labour's large majority in the House of Commons and partly due to the healthy state of the economy. However, the situation could change quickly if people feel that there has been no change in the financial health of their region/country or that they are still unable to get their grievances heard and dealt with.

Activities

1. In small groups, discuss what features you think are essential in the constitution of a modern democracy. Construct a Bill of Rights that clearly lists these features.

2. Do you think that the advantages of separate Welsh and Scottish Assemblies outweighs the disadvantages and why?

3. Some MPs have been paid to ask particular questions in Parliament by powerful interest groups. Is this practice antidemocractic and why?

EXAM QUESTIONS

Consider the sources below, and answer the questions which follow.

Source analysis and evaluation question on *The monarchy*

Source A

In the first year of the third millennium, Britain still selects its head of state by birth certificate. Are we content with the prospect of having a hereditary monarchy in another 100 years' time? This is not a question that politicians want to address. The ludicrous recent furore when Mo Mowlam mildly wondered whether the Windsors might move into a more modern home is testimony to the neurosis among politicians about any discussion of becoming a republic.

Unlike nearly every other democracy in the world, the British constitution treats us as subjects, not as free, equal and sovereign citizens. Well, who cares? Don't we all know it is a fiction?

The Queen reigns: the Prime Minister rules. The powers are in her name, but they are really wielded by Number 10. Her honours list and her bishops are selected in Downing Street. The monarchy is just a glittering delivery carriage for the decisions of the government.

The monarchy remains symbolic of privilege over people, of chance over endeavour, of being something rather than doing something. We elevate to the apex of our society someone selected not on the basis of talent or achievement, but because of genes. For all the lip-service that politicians of all parties pay to meritocracy, for so long as we have a hereditary monarchy, Britain enthrones and glorifies the exact opposite.

Source: Editorial, *The Observer*, 30 July 2000

Source B

I have read *The Observer* uninterrupted for the best part of 40 years. That relationship is in severe jeopardy if there are any more editorials of last Sunday's kind and hatchet jobs on the Royal Family, as you had the temerity to perpetrate upon Her Majesty Queen Elizabeth, the Queen Mother, a fortnight ago. And I cannot be alone in this view.

If the United Kingdom were to become a presidency next year, the incumbent would be a politician. Which of the current bunch do you suggest would make a suitable president? Better the devil you know than one who is elected because he or she has the most money to spend! I rest my case. Let us have no more of this unutterable nonsense.

Source: Reader's letter in response to the above editorial and an earlier article, *The Observer*, 6 August 2000

Source C

It is very hard for the political nation in Britain to discuss the monarchy in sensible terms. By most people and for much of the time it is accepted as simply being there, somewhat like the weather: rather baffling but a fixture and very much part of the scene, part of the specialness of being British and often a source of self-congratulation verging on the smug.

A decade ago, the journalist Sir Peregrine Worthsthorne could declare: 'These days the only efficient part of the British Constitution is the monarchy' without raising a ripple of dissent from his audience of political scientists. A few months earlier, in July 1984, the historian Lord Blake said: 'No doubt the preservation of monarchy, like that of liberty, requires eternal vigilance, but I see no reasons whatever to believe that this will be kept any less in the future than it has been in the past.'

Ten years on, thanks chiefly to the personal misfortunes of some members of the Royal Family, waves of heated speculation about the durability of the House of Windsor afflicts the press.

Source: Professor Peter Hennessy, *The Hidden Wiring* (Indigo), 1996

1   Assess the strengths and weaknesses of each of *Sources A, B and C*.

    (12 marks)

2   In line 1 of *Source C*, Peter Hennessy states that 'It is very hard for the political
    nation in Britain to discuss the monarchy in sensible terms.' What is he likely to
    mean by this sentence? Why do you think it is so difficult for the nation to have a
    sensible discussion about the monarchy?

    (8 marks)

EXAMINER'S ADVICE

- This is a second example of a type of question that will appear in Section A of the A2 Unit 3 test. (See page 1 for a summary of the full contents of the Unit 3 test and the end of Unit 21 of this book for a further example taken from the Specimen Paper set in 2007). It is an exercise in source evaluation.
- The first question here tests your ability to analyse and compare the quality of the sources and to assess the relative value of their arguments. However, here you are not asked to give your own opinions on the topic. You have to stand back from the issues in an objective way and evaluate the way the three writers express their different opinions.
- Note that there are 12 marks for this question. There are three sources, so you might usefully seek to provide two comments on the strengths and two comments on the weaknesses of each, making a total of 12 points. As always you will be given credit for supporting your points with appropriate examples/evidence. Consider the nature of each source. Which do you think is the most convincing and speaks with the most authority, and why? As

suggested you should evaluate the comments objectively, disregarding whether you agree with them or not.

- The second question goes further and requires interpretation of what the author means and some understanding of different types of knowledge and argument (AO3). For more on this Assessment Objective see pages 2–6. What do you think characterises a 'sensible discussion', or rather a 'less than sensible' one, as the author thinks this is likely to apply to most people (the 'political nation'). Perhaps people don't think too hard about it because the monarchy is part of British tradition and values? Perhaps it is an emotive issue for some, like the letter writer in Source B?
- You have approximately 40 minutes to complete your answers to this section in the exam and you should spend your time on each question according to the number of marks, i.e. 25 minutes and 15 minutes respectively. When you have written your responses, compare them with the possible points suggested on pages 281–282.

Education issues

'Education' is a difficult word to define exactly. Almost the entire population of the UK has been to school and, in a sense, this entitles everyone who has been through the experience to express an opinion. At an individual level, education can refer to the process by which people develop their intellectual, emotional and social skills. It can also refer to the entire system of schooling within a country from nursery to university.

What are schools for?

It is usually agreed that schools have two major functions:

- to educate students in various academic or cognitive skills and knowledge
- to educate students in the personal and social skills necessary to function successfully in society.

In democratic societies, education provides the possibility of equality of opportunity and achievement. However, educational thinkers are often divided into those who think that education should serve the needs of the individual and those who think that it should serve the needs of society. Private fee-paying schools have tended to encourage individualism while, in the past, state education for the masses has emphasised the need for well-trained workers with skills relevant to the industrial demands of society.

Some important views on education

In his influential books, *The Republic* and *The Laws*, Plato (427–348 BCE) argued that philosophers should be kings. In a turbulent and unstable historical context, Plato was trying to produce a blueprint for a stable, well-ordered society in which people fulfilled the roles and functions for which they were most suited. Only those capable of understanding and discovering the real truth about things and distinguishing true knowledge from opinion and illusion should be rulers or guardians of society. However, as the development of this ability depended on a rigorous and demanding intellectual training, only a few would be successful and the rest would occupy lower but nonetheless important positions in society. Plato's views have been very influential in the history of western education. Many education systems still reflect the views that:

- Intellectual pursuits are somehow superior to practical and technical ones.
- Education should involve such processes as selection, segregation, assessment and rejection, in order to sort out potential leaders and followers.

John Locke (1632–1704) argued that the mind was like a blank sheet of paper at birth, 'a tabula rasa', devoid of innate ideas, which would acquire knowledge through experience. He emphasised the qualities of virtue, wisdom and learning amongst others. His view that 'experience' was essential to the educational process has remained very significant. The experiences or learning opportunities pupils are presented with at school may have a significant influence on their future success or failure.

In *Emile*, published in 1762, Jean-Jacques Rousseau (1712–78) argued for a much more natural type of education. Rousseau was not impressed by the values of the civilised society in which he lived. He wanted an education system that valued and enhanced 'natural' qualities such as spontaneity, freedom, subjectivity and

Figure 32.1 A Victorian schoolroom – Shepton Mallet Grammar School, Wiltshire, 1899

simplicity, rather than the cold, impersonal values of scientific objectivity and rationalism. Feeling is much more important than thinking for Rousseau, who objected to the way in which children's development was 'over-intellectualised' at an early age. Rousseau's views have been the foundation of the debate between those *traditionalists* who argue for reason, discipline and authority in education and those *progressives* who want a system more sensitive to the idea of individual growth and development.

Karl Marx (1818–83), together with Freidrich Engels, argued that many human beings were alienated and dehumanised by the fact that the ruling classes owned the means of material production, even though it was the workers who created the wealth. Marx emphasised that the economic dimension of life was primary and that religious, political and educational values reflected the values of the ruling class. Marx wanted an education system that would produce responsible and autonomous persons who would work towards the idea of 'community' through social relationships. Marx had a vision of a system that would develop the idea that the interests of the individual and those of society are the same. However, many of his educational ideas have been distorted by Marxist or Communist societies, which have produced education systems that indoctrinate their students to accept the ideas of those in power without question and which discourage freedom of thought.

The transmission of values and beliefs and culture

Schools are often described by sociologists as 'agents of cultural transmission'. All schools transmit to their pupils, whether deliberately or not, some sense of what is acceptable in terms of behaviour and attitudes. Schools emphasise the idea of achievement through personal effort and perseverance and also community values, such as honesty and consideration for others. In some education systems, the prevailing religious beliefs of the country are built into the curriculum. There has been a strong Catholic emphasis in Irish schools in the past, and religious education with a strong Christian emphasis is compulsory by law in the UK. On the other hand, in France and the USA, for example, religious teaching is forbidden. Recently, some school boards in religiously conservative parts of the USA refused to allow the use of textbooks that taught Darwin's theory of evolution on the grounds that it contradicted the account of creation in the book of Genesis. However, many school systems encourage patriotic feelings and emphasise democracy.

Preparation for life

Traditionally, one of the most important functions of schools has been to prepare its students for a place in society. Modern governments are concerned to produce a work force with relevant and up-to-date skills so that the country can compete economically in the international marketplace. This requirement has resulted in different ways of organising schools and in legislation to ensure that all children receive some education. In the UK, for example, most local authorities operate a system that involves primary education until the age of 11, followed by non-selective comprehensive education until the age of at least 16. This may be followed by voluntary post-16 education either in a school sixth form, a purpose-built sixth form college or further education college, or as a preparation for university. A few local authorities still retain selective grammar schools (where the children sit an exam at eleven to decide whether they are clever enough to go to grammar school) and others operate a three-tier system, where children move from first school to middle school and on to secondary school at the age of 13. New specialist schools have also been introduced. These have a special focus on their chosen subject area but must meet the National Curriculum requirements and deliver a broad and balanced education to all pupils. Any maintained secondary school in England can apply to be designated as a specialist school in one of ten specialist areas: arts, business and enterprise, engineering, humanities, language, mathematics and computing, music, science, sports, and technology.

Recent important education debates

The gender gap

During the past few years the increasing gap in academic attainment between boys and girls has become of increasing concern and a focus for government educational initiatives. Nationally, girl's results have been improving faster than boys. In 2004, for example, 62.4 per cent of girls' exam entries achieved A*–C grade as opposed to 53.4 per cent of boys'. Various reasons have been given for this gap such as:

- Extensive use of coursework in GCSE. This is commonly thought to be a major reason for the gender divide as it rewards hard work and consistent application, which girls seem to be more content to do than boys.
- The anti-learning laddish culture.

A recent Ofsted report identified the following factors, amongst others, as significant in boys' success at school:

- Ongoing assessment procedures which value work and give clear advice on how to improve.
- A school environment where pupils and staff show respect for each other, which offers plenty of extra-curricular activities and a place where boys feel they belong.
- Teaching styles which set shorter, more frequent deadlines and encourage students to reflect on their answers and break down long written tasks into shorter sections.

The use of 'boy friendly' texts and strategies (charts, data, graphs) as well as the recruitment of male teachers have been suggested as remedies to the problem of boys' underachievement in literacy. However, while these factors do help, they do not provide a complete answer, and risk over-simplifying a very complex problem.

Research done in 2004 has found that gender gaps in performance are significantly large in virtually every country (50 researched) between boys and girls aged between nine and 15. It is felt that the change in teaching methods when children are learning to read is causing the ever-increasing gender divide in reading ability. Boys have a

---

DID YOU KNOW?

Schooldays
The 1988 *Education Act* initiated the following changes:
- Regular school inspections
- Qualifications and Curriculum Authority to oversee national examinations and the curriculum
- The extension of parents' right to choose schools
- The freedom of schools to 'opt out' of local authority control.

Deschooling society. In the 1970s a series of educational thinkers argued that most education systems were a waste of time. Most pupils leave school uneducated and resentful. Schools are a type of prison, operating on the assumption that education can only take place inside mass institutions and adults assume that they know what is best for young people.

Formula funding. Money for schools is based on the number of pupils enrolled. An increase/decrease of 20–30 pupils can mean the addition or loss of one teacher.

---

different timetable of brain development to girls. For example, the neural networks connecting the two halves of the brain develop more slowly in boys, and the implementation of more appropriate teaching methods, particularly in the area of literacy has produced significant improvements in boys' performance, both in SATs and at GCSE level.

However, while girls consistently do better at school than boys, this is not reflected in their future earnings or employment status. This is clearly a social issue rather than an educational one.

Fees in higher education

There has been much recent debate over the government's introduction of fees for students in full-time higher education.

Following the recommendations of the Dearing Committee appointed in 1996 to examine the future structure of funding in Higher Education and the passing of the Higher Education Act 2004, the government has allowed Universities to charge up to £3,000 per year for any particular course from 2006, and established a maintenance grant of up to £2,700 per year for students from lower-income households. A recent National Union of Students survey showed that many students were incurring debts up to £20,000. A similar survey showed that those students most opposed to the idea of debt came from those socio-economic groups which produced the lowest number of entrants.

Some of the arguments for and against tuition fees

For

A university education is a valuable and expensive privilege. Why should something that is so rewarding and costly be free? It is equitable for students to make a financial contribution to their degree teaching. They stand to gain financially from a degree. Education is an investment and it is rational for students to borrow at this stage of their life cycle to finance such investment. It is rational to forgo current earnings in return for higher future earnings.

Tuition fees provide extra finance for facilities, teaching and research, allowing the government to fund an expansion of the number of students able to enter higher education thus promoting wider access. New entrants into universities under the new scheme may be drawn mainly from lower-income households as students are means-tested on what they need to pay.

Fees will encourage students to be more selective in the courses they choose and will stimulate an improvement in teaching quality of universities.

Against

It is a tax on learning.

Only seven per cent of children from families in the lowest social class currently go to university. Tuition fees will make it harder for relatively poor families to fund a degree. This will widen educational inequality and create a further widening of the two-tier education system.

Student debt may deter poorer students. Tuition fees will lead to a huge surge in student debt and hardship which in turn will have negative economic and social consequences in the long run. Seeking to expand higher education too much may work against the best interests of the economy because the graduate market may become over-crowded.

Conclusion

Applications to university have increased steadily in spite of the financial cost of being a student and the spectre of debt. The market has changed and the number of places in higher education is increasingly demand-led rather than supply-led. Applicants have realised that higher education offers significant advantages and that the converse, not going into higher education, keeps many employment doors permanently closed.

In the face of these facts, it is important that everyone who could benefit from higher education has equal access to it. This is not only about social justice but also about making sure we get the very best graduates for the benefit of our country. So far, the increase in applications has come predominantly from the wealthier part of society.

This increase in applications has precipitated two key questions: how is university expansion and the maintenance of quality to be funded and how do we ensure all members of society get a fair bite at the cherry? There are some points on which all parties appear to agree: the UK currently has world-class higher education and we must increase investment in it if it is to continue to perform at that level. Where opinions differ is over the question of where that extra investment should come from, the state or the individual. (Vice-Chancellor of Bristol University Address)

Activities

1. A school with poor examination results is a bad school. What reasons would you use to either support or oppose this statement. What other information would you need to know about the school?

2. Which of the following is the most important part of school and why: the child; the curriculum; assessment?

EXAM QUESTION

Read the source below and answer the question that follows. *Use your own words to show you understand the arguments.*

Wide-ranging action to tackle the culture in schools and workplaces that create job segregation and leave women lagging behind men in the pay stakes is proposed in a ground-breaking report, *Shaping a Fairer Future*. Proposals include setting up a national World of Work programme to improve vocational training, provide work taster days for primary school pupils, work experience to encourage girls to think about non-traditional jobs and apprenticeships for women. Increasing women's employment and ending the gender segregation where women are concentrated in the five Cs – the caring, cashier, clerical, cleaning and catering sectors – would benefit the economy by as much as £23 billion.

Commission chair Margaret Prosser said: 'Many women are working far below their abilities and this waste of talent is an outrage when the UK is facing competition in the global market and for those women personally. We all recognise that the gender pay gap is complex. There is no one solution but if we do not make the fundamental change necessary to our school and workplace cultures women will continue to lose out.'

Source: Adapted from 'Radical programme to end decades of jobs and pay unfairness for women', *Women and Work Commission*, February 2006

Using evidence from the source, and your own knowledge, discuss how the main issues raised concerning females and work might best be addressed.

(14 marks)

EXAMINER'S ADVICE
- This source analysis question is taken from Section B of the AS Unit 1 Specimen test. It is the third of the three source-based questions for extended writing in this section of the test (see page 1 for a summary of the whole test).
- First of all, you should use the source to identify the main issues raised. There are about five or six suggested by the source and the first paragraph highlights three alone. To start you off these are 'school and workplace culture', 'job segregation' and 'the pay gap'. You should develop each of these a little more by explaining what they mean.
- When you have identified as many issues as you can, you have to discuss ways in which they might be tackled. Again there are at least two ways suggested by the source which involve some changes to the education system. What other aspects of society could change (or are changing) to help address the problems of women and work? For the rest it is up to you to develop any knowledge and ideas of your own into a coherent response.
- You have approximately 15 minutes to complete this question in the exam. When you have written your answer, compare your points with those given on page 282.

Economic theories

According to the *Oxford English Dictionary*, 'economics' is 'the science of the production and distribution of wealth'.

If human beings were self-sufficient, there would be no need for economics, but as soon as a farmer could produce more food than he needed, and another farmer, who made pots, discovered that people wanted the pots he made, economics was needed so that the potter-farmer could become a full-time potter. Specialisation or division of labour (certain people producing certain goods rather than each person producing everything they needed for themselves) is one of the bases of economics. Although economics in the form of the production and distribution of wealth has been around since the beginning of society, theories of economics did not develop until the eighteenth century.

Adam Smith (Professor of Moral Philosophy at Edinburgh University) wrote *The Wealth of Nations* in 1776, in which he worked out how the human desire for self-betterment will lead to changes in society and a gradual increase in wealth. Although written over 200 years ago, Smith's book contains most of the economic theories now accepted by the vast majority of economists.

Money and exchange rates

In the early stages of human development, specialisation was needed for civilisation to occur. However, there was then the problem of how the potter and the farmer were to exchange their surplus products. At first this was done by *bartering* (I will give you 'x' beans and 'y' chickens for 'x' plates). However, as society became more complex (it is difficult for people like teachers and poets to barter), some other system was needed. Money was developed as a system, which gave an external value to bartering.

Money has no *intrinsic value* (a pound coin has no value in itself, unlike a plate) but is based on the value or resources of the government or bank that issues the money. These resources must have intrinsic value and if that value goes down, the value of the money will go down. Money works on the law of supply and demand, so that a currency in high demand will have a high value, and one in low demand, a low value.

This can be seen clearly in the exchange rate of a currency. The exchange rate is the value given on the world markets to one currency in terms of another currency (the exchange rates of the world currencies in terms of sterling – the British pound – are on the business pages of newspapers every day). Until 1972 there were fixed exchange rates made under the Bretton Woods Agreement, 1944. This meant that everyone knew the value of goods worldwide and manufacturers exporting goods knew exactly what their profits would be. However, the drawback was that if a country was not doing as well as expected, it would have to *devalue* its currency by negotiating a new exchange rate. Since 1972, there has been a *floating exchange rate*, where the market decides the value of a currency.

If the value of a currency goes up, this means you can buy more with it abroad, but manufacturers will find it more difficult to sell abroad as their products will be more expensive. However, imports will be much cheaper (if the value of the pound against the euro increases by 10 per cent, a French car that cost £10,000 in Britain will now cost £9000, but a British car of the same value will now cost £11,000 in France).

The law of supply and demand

This says that if there is a low supply of a product and a high demand, the price will rise. Conversely, if there is a high supply and a low demand, the price will fall. This is why brain surgeons are paid more than factory workers (there is a high demand and a low supply of brain surgeons; there is a low demand and a high supply of factory workers, who require less training and intelligence than brain surgeons).

Economists believe that the forces of supply and demand create an equilibrium (where supply and demand are mainly equal) through the price people are prepared to pay meeting the price for which the supplier is prepared to sell.

Market forces

Closely connected with supply and demand are market forces. The market means the place where consumers and suppliers meet. A supplier can keep the price of a product artificially high by restricting the supply, or by creating a *monopoly* (a market where there is only one supplier). However, in a *free market*, it will always be possible for another supplier to come along and offer the product at a lower price. This is competition, and is associated with a theory of economics known, from Adam Smith, as *laissez-faire economics*, where the role of a government is to prevent monopolies occurring so that market forces can determine prices and wages and what is produced.

There are lots of market forces that can affect the basic law of supply and demand:

- Changes in income (if wages or taxes fall or rise, people will have less or more money to spend and so demand will fall or rise).
- Changes in price of connected goods (if the cost of CD players falls, the demand for CDs will rise).
- Taste and fashion (BSE caused a fall in demand for British beef; the introduction of mountain bikes caused a fall in demand for ordinary bikes).
- Competition (a new firm producing the same product will increase the supply and reduce the price).
- Population changes (as people live longer, and there are more people over the age of 65 in the population, there will be a rise in demand for Saga holidays and pensions).

Competition Commission

In 1999 the Competition Commission replaced the Monopolies and Mergers Commission. It is the duty of the Commission to implement the Enterprise Act of 2002 to ensure that mergers and markets in the UK remain fair and competitive. Members are appointed by the Secretary of State for Trade and Industry for an eight-year term on the basis of their experience, ability and diversity of background. There are special committees for utilities, telecommunications, water and newspapers. When a merger or takeover is announced which might lead to unfair competition, the Chairman of the Commission appoints a special committee from the members to make a decision. For example, when Morrisons supermarkets wanted to take over Safeway supermarkets, the Competition Commission had to decide whether this would be in the public interest and, in allowing the Morrison bid to go ahead, it stipulated that Morrisons must sell certain Safeway stores where Morrisons already had a number of stores. The Commission was making sure that the demise of Safeway was used to increase competition in the supermarket business rather than reduce it.

Consumerism

This is the word used to describe the economic conditions which encourage people to buy things so that the economy thrives. Clearly if everyone was a miser spending (consuming) as little as possible and saving as much as possible, then money (and the savings) would become worthless. If people do not buy goods, firms cannot sell goods and so they have to make their workforce redundant. If firms do not sell anything, their shares become worthless and if all the firms in a country do not sell anything, then the country's money becomes worthless. This means it is important for a country to make sure that consumers have sufficient money to consume goods.

In modern western society, consumers have much more choice and therefore can be more discriminating in their choices. One of the main consumer changes in the last 15 years has been the rise of ethical consumerism. This means buying products which were ethically produced and/or which are not harmful to the environment and society. It can be buying free-range eggs produced by hens that live a normal life, rather than those produced by battery hens (the market for battery eggs in supermarkets has virtually died out in the last five years). It can be refusing to buy goods which have been produced by child labour (a much more complex process – do you know where your trainers were produced and whether they used child-labour?). The Ethical Consumer Research Association publishes details of ethical and non-ethical goods in its magazine and on its website. Its major success was in virtually ending the sale of GM foods in the UK. However, although 35 per cent of the UK population claim to be concerned about ethical consumption, only three per cent of the UK market is devoted to the production of ethical goods.

Keynesianism

This is an economic theory based on the ideas of J.M. Keynes (1883–1946), who claimed that Smith's ideas on market forces producing full employment were wrong. He said that in times of high unemployment, the government should increase spending to increase national output and so increase employment. In times of full employment and inflation, governments should reduce expenditure. This was the economic theory behind Roosevelt's New Deal in America, which led to the recovery

KEY TERMS

Anti-competitive anything like price-fixing, creating a monopoly, etc. which stops there being fair competition

Assets things that you own – fixed assets are things such as buildings and machinery, current assets are things you can quickly sell for cash

Break-even point the point where the amount of goods sold equals the costs so that a profit is made after this point

Diseconomies of scale where a company has become so large that it is inefficient

Economic constraints any economic issues that might hold back a company's actions/profits e.g. taxation, transport costs

Economies of scale where a company has become so large that it can save a lot of money by bulk buying, borrowing money cheaply, etc.

Equity capital the value of the shares in a company at the price they were first sold at (what a company owes its shareholders)

Free enterprise private ownership of capital, the market economy

Industrial democracy the practice of allowing all parts of the workforce to be involved in major company decisions

Liquidity when a company has more current assets than current debts

Monopoly when there is only one producer or provider of a product

Remuneration usually wages, but whatever you are paid for providing a service

Turnover the amount a company receives for selling its products (this takes no account of costs and so is much higher than the profit)

Activities

1. Follow the exchange rate of the dollar, the euro and the yen against the pound for a period of four weeks to see whether the value of the pound is rising or falling. Establish reasons for the trend.

2. Discuss why computer firms in the South East of England may have to pay higher wages to their staff than the same firms in the North East of England.

3. To what extent do you think that people of high ability deserve higher rates of pay? Should there be a maximum as well as a minimum wage? What overall principles should determine the financial rewards for the work people do?

of the American economy after the Wall Street Crash of 1929 and the Depression of the 1930s.

Monetarism

This is an economic theory connected with the American economist Milton Friedman, who claims that any economic problems such as inflation or unemployment are caused by the government producing too much money (the *money supply*), and that by restricting the money supply, firms will have to lower wages and cut staff to become more productive. This will eventually lead to greater profits and so there will be more resources and the money supply can be increased.

Often connected with monetarism is the concept of *privatisation*. This is the idea that industries run by the government (nationalised industries) are not as efficient as private industries. In the 1980s, the Conservative monetarist government led by Mrs Thatcher privatised water, electricity, gas, telephones, railways and buses. There is evidence both for and against whether this was effective. Although gas, water and electricity might be slightly cheaper than they would otherwise have been, there are problems with the number of power stations and the ease of reducing pollution in the power industries when dealing with several private companies. Some people feel that these utility industries are so important to the nation that they should be in national control (see also Unit 10 for issues involved in the privatisation of transport).

Figure 33.1 Mrs Thatcher, Conservative Prime Minister, 1979–92, claimed to be using the principles of monetarism and market forces to reduce the power of trade unions

Consider the statistics and article below about rates of pay, and answer the question which follows.

Extract from a case study on
Earnings, wealth distribution and poverty

Highest and lowest paid occupations: Great Britain, April 2000	
	Average gross weekly pay (£)
Highest paid	
Treasurers and company financial managers	1059
Medical practitioners	964
Organisation and methods and work study managers	813
Management consultants, business analysts	812
Underwriters, claims assessors, brokers, investment analysts	775
Police officers (inspector or above)	766
Computer systems and data processing managers	757
Solicitors	748
Marketing and sales managers	719
Advertising and public relations managers	690
Lowest paid	
Educational assistants	212
Other childcare and related occupations	205
Counterhands, catering assistants	196
Launderers, dry cleaners, pressers	196
Hairdressers, barbers	190
Waiters, waitresses	189
Petrol pump, forecourt attendants	189
Retail cash desk and check-out operators	185
Bar staff	184
Kitchen porters, hands	184

Perks that go too far

One of the most extraordinary features of the modern chief executive's remuneration is not the huge amounts of money and share options, but the extras that go with them.

That companies should pay chief executives' relocation expenses is understandable, but why should they pay for their apartments? Why can't people who earn that much pay their own rent? And why should chief executives who retire or are sacked continue to have the use of those apartments, together with company-funded country club memberships, cars, drivers, secretaries, laptops and tickets to Wimbledon?

A common answer is that these perks are negotiated when chief executives are recruited. Why chief executives demand what they could so easily afford themselves is a complex question that these typically unreflective people would find difficult to answer. One reason they may demand them is that when the financial rewards are so high they lose all meaning, chief executives look for other, more concrete proofs that the companies they are joining value them. Another is that the headhunters tell them that everyone else gets these benefits and anyone who doesn't is a sucker.

Why do companies agree to such extravagances? Because they are convinced chief executives are hard to find, that the number of people who can run large companies is small and that analysts, investors and the business press set huge store by their appointment. If the recruitment of a star chief executive is going to add 15 per cent to the share price, why deny shareholders the benefit for the sake of a box at the opera?

But as Rakesh Khurana of Harvard Business School points out, the superstar chief executive is a new phenomenon. Until the 1980s, Mr Khurana says in the September issue of the *Harvard Business Review*, the typical chief executive was an insider who worked his way up the ranks and 'was no better known to the general public than his secretary'. Falling corporate profits led to disillusionment with these 'organisation men'. The growth of mutual funds and equity-related pensions led to a demand for corporate leaders who could deliver a better return.

Lee Iacocca, who became chief executive of Chrysler in 1979, was the first of the celebrity bosses, but there were many more to come. They led the US to new heights of innovation and competitiveness, but the signs are everywhere that their time is past, except that the perks continue.

Source: adapted from an article by Michael Skapinker, *Financial Times*, 25 September 2002

What reasons exist for different levels of pay? To what extent do you think they are justified?

(12 marks)

EXAMINER'S ADVICE

- These extracts are taken from the A2 case study set in January 2004. The question is one of four questions based on the case study material in Unit 4 and a substantial proportion of the assessment focuses on Assessment Objective 3 (different types of knowledge and their limitations). If necessary see pages 267–268 for more details on the case study exercise itself and pages 2–6 on AO3.

- The question is a mini-essay in itself, but once you have studied the extract, you should attempt to answer it in no more than 20 minutes and a page and half of writing. This is all the time you will have in the test. Use the material in the unit you have just read and the extract to give yourself some ideas about as wide a range of reasons as possible, and then consider how acceptable/justifiable you think these are. Note these down, as if you were preparing in advance for the test, then write out your answer in no more than 20 minutes.

- A standard range of reasons is given on pages 282–283. When you have made your attempt, look at these to see how your answer matches up.

Economic issues

Economic issues are problems or arguments about issues concerning money or the state of the economy. The main ones you are likely to be asked questions about are covered in this unit.

Taxation

In any country, the government requires money to provide services. This money is raised by levying taxes on the population.

In the UK in 2004–05, the government expected to spend £455 billion (around £5900 for each person in the country – see Figures 34.1 and 34.2).

Total managed expenditure: £488 billion

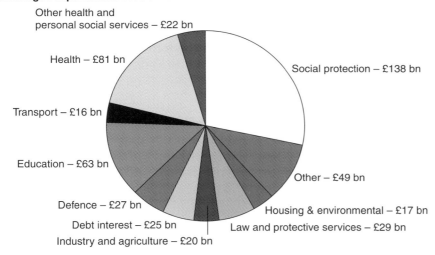

Figure 34.1 Government spending by function

Total receipts: £455 billion

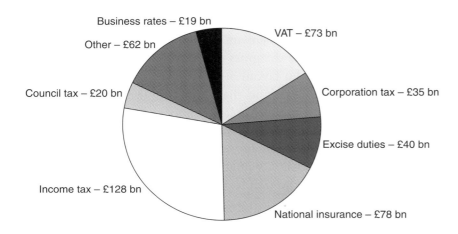

Figure 34.2 Government receipts

Arguments about taxation come in three forms:

1. *Whether the taxes are being spent in the right way.* One of the main debates between political parties is how much money should be spent on *social security.* The reforms of disability allowance and the work of the Child Support Agency are aimed at reducing the amount spent on social security. Any changes in employment will affect the social security spending (the more people who are unemployed, the more benefits have to be paid out). Changes in the population can also affect the budget (an increase in the number of old people will increase expenditure on pensions and health, a decrease in children will reduce expenditure on child benefit and education).

    There are also arguments about whether more or less should be spent on defence than education, etc. Any political party that suggests that there should be more police on the streets is also suggesting that the amount of taxation spent on law and order should be increased, which will mean either increasing taxes or reducing the amount spent in some other area.

2. *Whether taxation should be direct or indirect. Direct taxes* are those collected directly by the government. Income tax is a direct tax, which the Inland Revenue collects from every adult. It is *means tested* (the more you earn, the more you pay) and is a percentage of your earnings, capital gains and interest from savings above a certain allowance. *National insurance* and *corporation tax* are also direct taxes collected by the government. Council tax and business rates are direct taxes collected by the local council.

    Indirect taxes are often called hidden taxes. They are a percentage of the cost of various goods, which are collected by shopkeepers, etc. and then paid to the government. *Value added tax* (VAT) is 17.5 per cent of all goods sold in shops except food, newspapers and books. *Excise duties* are paid on petrol, alcohol, tobacco and are much more than 17.5 per cent.

    Some people claim that indirect taxes are unfair because everyone pays the same amount whatever they earn. Other people claim that indirect taxes are the fairest taxes because rich people can find ways of not paying direct taxes (some of the richest people in the country pay no direct taxes). There is no way of avoiding indirect taxes, but the rich spend more than the poor, so they will pay more taxes.

3. *What the level of taxation should be.* There are many arguments between politicians as to what percentage of the gross domestic product (GDP) should be paid to the government. Those who favour a free market approach believe that the percentage should be much lower and that most people should have to pay for such things as their own health and education needs. Those who believe in a mixed economy (see below) would be happy to see taxation at between 35 and 40 per cent of GDP because of the benefits of giving everyone the same opportunities and care. Some socialists would want much higher taxation in order to redistribute wealth from the rich to the poor, but many economists believe that if taxation is too high, people stop doing any extra work and the economy slows down.

Inflation

Inflation is the rising of prices. It is measured by the Retail Price Index (RPI), where a representative sample of things people have to buy is measured on a baseline of a particular year. This can give an annual inflation rate (the percentage by which prices have risen over 1 year).

Inflation is caused by:

- the value of the currency falling
- pay rises not being supported by increases in productivity
- demand for goods being greater than the supply.

The effects of inflation are:

- a rise in interest rates
- businesses going bankrupt because they cannot afford the interest, or their customers cannot afford the much higher prices they have to charge
- people's standard of living going down because their wages have not increased as much as the prices
- people saving more because the interest rates are high, so they do not buy goods, so firms cannot sell goods and have to sack workers, thereby increasing unemployment.

Governments try to reduce inflation by reducing demand. They may do this by *monetary policy* (restricting credit and increasing interest rates) or *fiscal policy* (increasing taxes and reducing government spending).

Although all economists agree that high inflation is bad for the economy, some economists believe that a medium rate of inflation is better than high unemployment and lower living standards.

Types of economy

In any society there are scarce goods and scarce resources and there has to be a mechanism for allocating them.

In a *market economy*, the scarcities are allocated by market forces. The price mechanism of supply and demand is regarded as sufficient to run the economy. The market economy is favoured by right-wing political parties who claim it is the most efficient way of producing and allocating goods and gives the consumer greater power.

The disadvantages are that social costs are ignored and poor people get no help. If there is no public sector health, education, etc. everything has to be paid for by the private individual buying from the private sector.

Left-wing parties tend to favour the *command economy*, where all production is in the hands of the state (private companies are nationalised). They claim that this is more efficient because people can be given what they need, income can be distributed fairly and industry can be made to be aware of social costs, for example by reducing pollution. The disadvantage is that by ignoring the laws of supply and demand and keeping all decisions in the hands of the government, massive mistakes can be made (for example, making shoes that no one wants to buy) – the Soviet Union had a command economy that collapsed, leading to the collapse of the Soviet Union itself.

Centre parties usually operate a *mixed economy*, where there is a public and a private sector. In many ways, this is a market economy that is controlled by the government to remove the disadvantages. Public goods such as health and education are provided by the state. A 'safety net' is run by the state to provide money for those who are unwanted by the market (the old, the unemployed, the sick and the young). The government also forces firms to pay attention to the social costs of their production.

Industrial location

There are many factors involved in a company deciding where to build its business. Clearly it depends on the type of business:

- A distribution centre needs to be close to the motorway network and probably in the North Midlands for national coverage.
- Some firms need access to raw materials, for example Bird's Eye is located in East Anglia for the fish and vegetables to be frozen immediately.
- Some firms locate in particular areas because of the availability of a skilled workforce, for example computer industries in the Thames Valley M4 corridor.
- Some firms need to locate near their market (market gardeners) or near a port (for example Nissan Sunderland to export to Europe).
- The availability and cost of land will affect the choice of a new site. Sometimes a firm may prefer to take over an existing factory/warehouse because this will be a quicker move, whereas other firms may want empty land because they want the building and facilities to be exactly to their specifications.
- Government or EU policies may affect their location, for example if grants are being offered to locate in areas of high unemployment.
- If a firm is thinking of re-locating to a new area, they will have to make sure that any essential staff who need to move with them are happy to re-locate.
- Many larger companies have moved their manufacturing and even service sectors, overseas because of much cheaper labour costs.

Employment and unemployment

During the 1980s and early 1990s, unemployment was a major issue in the UK as around 12 per cent of the workforce was without work. A variety of issues arise when there is a high rate of unemployment:

- Many people are living on state benefits and so are living close to the poverty line.
- Those who are in work have to pay higher taxes to pay for the benefits of the unemployed.
- Social tensions arise between the employed who can have a good lifestyle and the unemployed who face the prospect of life with few, if any, luxuries.

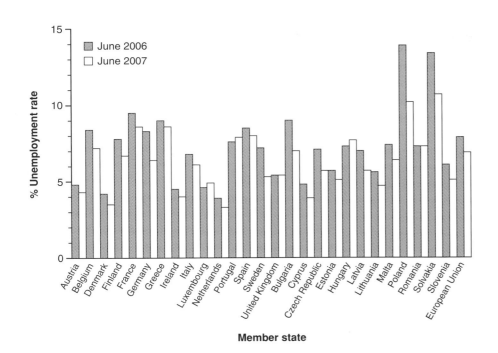

Figure 34.3 Unemployment rate in all EU member states, June 2007 with comparison to June 2006

- Wages tend to be kept low because employers can always find people to fill job vacancies.
- Young people see little point in gaining qualifications when there are no jobs at the end of the training.
- Young people who do gain qualifications will be tempted to leave the country to find work.

The UK unemployment rate has fallen since 1997 and is now one of the lowest in Europe at 4.5 per cent. Many economists believe that this is because business rules and opportunities are more flexible in the United Kingdom (for example, longer hours can be worked). However, having a low rate of unemployment also brings problems:

- There is likely to be a shortage of skilled labour as the unemployed tend to be those who have no skills to offer an employer (the UK is dealing with this problem by increased levels of immigration, especially from Eastern Europe).
- Wages may have to rise in certain firms to keep workers or attract new ones.
- Young people may be less inclined to undergo extensive training if they know they can get a job without it.
- Prices may rise because people have more money to spend so there may be a greater demand for the same supply of goods (though often low unemployment leads to an increase of production as more people have more money to buy the goods).

For comparison, the figure for the USA is 5.5 per cent and for Japan 4.7 per cent.

DID YOU KNOW?

Who wants to be a millionaire?
Hyperinflation is when inflation becomes so high that it has to be calculated on a daily rather than a yearly basis, and the government has to issue larger denomination notes weekly. For example, during the Yugoslavian Civil War in 1993 the daily rate of inflation in Serbia became 50 per cent (something costing £1 on Monday cost £1.50 on Tuesday). In eight weeks, one million dinar notes had become 50 million dinar notes.

Rural development issues

Demographic and economic changes have led to rural problems in the United Kingdom. The fact that better roads and the Internet have made working from home possible, have led to the urban middle-class moving into the countryside, this has driven up the price of housing in the countryside so that people in lower paid jobs (especially young people) cannot find affordable housing. Many young families have migrated to the towns so that there are insufficient school-age children to keep village schools open. The reliance of the farming community on EU subsidies (Common Agricultural Policy) and the EU's attempts to reduce the subsidies have led to business and economic problems in the countryside.

Defra (the Department for Environment, Farming and Rural Affairs) has established the England Rural Development Programme (ERDP), a programme which will provide £1.6 billion of government and EU money from 2000 to 2006 and €14 billion per year throughout the EU from 2007 to 2013 for rural development. The programme provides:

- Hill Farm Allowance for beef and sheep farmers in difficult farming areas in recognition of their vital role in maintaining the landscape and rural communities of the uplands.
- The Organic Farming Scheme provides funding to convert to organic farming methods which are more environmentally friendly and provide higher returns from shops.
- Farm Woodland Schemes encourage farmers to change farmland to woodland for both commercial and environmental purposes.
- The Countryside Stewardship Scheme is the government's main scheme. It pays grants to farmers to follow more traditional farming methods that enhance the landscape, encourage wildlife and protect historical features. Over 1000 miles of dry stone walls, 9000 miles of hedgerow and 16,500 miles of grass margins in intensive arable farming areas have led to an increase in a variety of bird species (for example bittern, lapwing, wagtail) that were in serious decline.
- The Environmentally Sensitive Areas Scheme gives grants to farmers to manage areas of the countryside where the landscape, wildlife or historic interest is of national importance (a quarter of the South Downs is now in the scheme).
- The Vocational Training Scheme offers grants of up to 75 per cent of the costs of improving the skills of those involved in forestry and farming activities.
- The Energy Crops Scheme provides grants for farmers to grow coppice and miscanthus which are carbon neutral producers of heat or energy so reducing greenhouse emissions.
- The Rural Enterprise Scheme provides assistance in setting up new businesses to help farmers diversify (for example turning a piggery into a nursery).

There are arguments within the rural communities as to whether these measures are the right ones.

Marketing and advertising

In a consumer society, businesses have to make sure that the consumer buys their products rather than those of a rival. They also have to make sure that the consumer knows about any new products they want to bring onto the market. Achieving these things is known as marketing. Marketing has two processes:

1. *Market research* to determine what consumers want so that the firm makes a product that will sell. Connected with this will be determining the design and packaging of the product so that it has maximum saleability.
2. *Promotion* to: increase sales of existing products; introduce a new product onto the market; maintain or increase market share; and improve the image of the company. Promotion includes what is called 'below-the-line promotion', for example free samples, special offers, premium offers (collecting labels to get gifts), competitions, point of sale advertising (special displays of a product in a shop). However, the best known, and most argued about promotion method, is advertising. When a firm decides to advertise, it has to decide on a form to choose:

Figure 34.4 Gordon Brown was the longest serving Chancellor of the Exchequer for over 200 years before becoming Prime Minster in 2007. He delivered nine budgets (the government's statement on what it will spend and what taxation will be for the coming year)

- Television provides mass coverage, but it is expensive and digital television and video machines are making it easier to avoid the adverts.
- Radio also provides mass coverage (especially during the day) but is also expensive and the adverts are very temporary.
- Newspapers and magazines have a more permanent nature, allow coverage of selected markets (for example, certain social classes read *The Times*, certain interest groups read *Cricket Monthly*) and are less expensive, but lack the impact of sound, vision and movement.
- Posters give mass coverage, but may not really target vehicle drivers.
- Cinema advertising is less expensive and can use the same film as the television adverts.
- Mail shots (junk mail) reach a mass audience but can be ignored easily by the recipient throwing them in the bin.

Many people argue that advertising is manipulating consumers (especially groups like children) and makes unfair claims which consumers cannot verify. But advertising is checked by the Advertising Standards Authority and it provides the service of not only letting us know what products are on offer, but also of allowing us to have a wide range of television, radio, newspapers and magazines which would otherwise be financially unviable.

EXAM QUESTION

This A2 essay question is taken from Section B of the Unit 4 Specimen Paper set in 2007. It is a typical General Studies essay question in so far as it encompasses several themes, some of them economic from this unit of the book and some social, discussed in Units 25 and 26.

A report in 2006 titled *Freedom's Orphans* showed a widening gulf between the experience of more affluent and poorer families in socialising their children, with many of the latter being left behind.

Explain why socialisation appears to be a problem for some families.

Discuss the claim that, for most families, poverty is an insurmountable barrier to achieving social mobility and success.

(25 marks)

EXAMINER'S ADVICE

- This is a wide-ranging and demanding question. You should go back and refresh your knowledge and ideas about socialisation from the early units in the Society section of the book and then link them with relevant content from the Economics section.
- There are three parts to the question: the first is the context that suggests that poorer members of our society are getting increasingly left behind, economically, educationally and socially ('the poor are getting poorer'); the second is for you to explore the difficulties which can arise in the socialisation (bringing/growing up) of children in modern society; and thirdly the extent to which it is possible to overcome economic and social disadvantage.
- To begin with, you will need to show that you understand what is meant by the process of socialisation (i.e. the way in which people learn codes of behaviour and develop their values). Parents, relations, the media, teachers, peer groups and work colleagues, can all be influential.
- Also poverty has an 'official' definition based primarily on income levels; the distinction between 'absolute' and 'relative' poverty continues to have some importance. Poverty though is not, in itself, necessarily an insurmountable barrier to social mobility (i.e. the ability to move up the socio-economic scale). However *Freedom's Orphans* indicates that social mobility has weakened dramatically in recent years (e.g. there was an 84 per cent chance that a child born into the richest 25 per cent of the population in 1958 would no longer have been in that position by their early 30s, but there is only a 50 per cent chance of that happening to those born in 1970).
- Finally the word 'success' is certainly open to exploration. Should success always be defined in material terms? Are other factors just as, if not more important, like security, happiness?
- There is a lot to think about here. When you have assembled your ideas you should allow yourself no more than 40 minutes to write your answer. When you have finished the essay, compare your effort with the points suggested on page 283.

The European Union

In the first half of the twentieth century, Europe was the cause of two world wars, which killed millions of people and weakened European economies. After the Second World War, European leaders met to work out ways of preventing Europe ever again going to war against itself. Out of the various options, West Germany, France, Italy, The Netherlands, Belgium and Luxembourg signed the Treaty of Rome in 1957 to form the European Economic Community (EEC). The aims of the EEC as expressed in the Treaty were to:

- remove barriers to trade among member nations
- establish a single commercial policy towards non-member countries
- co-ordinate members' general economic and agricultural policies
- co-ordinate member states' transport systems
- remove all national barriers to free trade and competition
- establish free movement of labour and capital throughout the EEC.

The first successful policies were concerned with the removal of tariffs and quotas between members, with the result that between 1957 and 1968, trade between the member states quadrupled. Indeed, the EEC was so successful that in 1973, the UK, Ireland and Denmark also joined. Greece joined in 1981, followed by Spain and Portugal in 1986. East Germany entered as part of the re-unification of Germany in 1990 and Austria, Finland and Sweden joined in 1995. These 15 states were joined in May 2004 by Cyprus, the Czech Republic, Estonia, Hungary, Latvia, Lithuania, Malta, Poland, Slovakia and Slovenia, followed in January 2007 by Bulgaria and Romania. The community is now known as the European Union.

Any new countries wishing to join the EU must fulfil the following conditions:

- have a stable democracy
- have a free market economy
- be prepared to accept all the EU laws.

How the EU is organised

Ultimate power in the EU lies with the *Council of Ministers*, which consists of a representative from each member government, and can be called for meetings at any time to make a decision. The European Council, by contrast, meets three times every year and is made up of the heads of governments of the member states. The system is set up to ensure that no member state can be forced to do things it does not agree with, as each member has a right of veto in the Council of Ministers (though there was some agreement at the meeting in Finland in December 1999 for limited areas where majority voting would be introduced).

Decisions made by the Council of Ministers are implemented by the *European Commission*. This is the EU civil service. The President and Commissioners (each responsible for a policy area, for example Peter Mandelson is responsible for trade) are selected by the Council of Ministers for a four-year term and no more than two may be of the same nationality. It is the role of the Commission to ensure that the policies of the Council of Ministers are put into practice. They also award EU grants to member states and draw up acts for the European Parliament or the Council of Ministers to debate.

The *European Parliament* has 500 members, with each member state having its number of MEPs determined by its population as a proportion of the total EU population. All MEPs have to be elected by proportional representation and the election of 1998 was the first proportional representation (PR) election in the UK. (This system is different from most other elections in the UK which are based on political party rather than personalities – see Unit 30, 'Politics' and Unit 31, 'The British Constitution'.) The Parliament has 12 one-week sessions during the year, but members are also expected to serve on standing committees responsible for checking the work of the Commissioners. The Council of Ministers has to consult the Parliament on various matters, but the Parliament's main function and importance is to keep democratic control of the European Commission. It has to approve the Budget of the EU and can force the resignation of commission members if they have behaved improperly (Jaques Santer, a President of the Commission, was forced to resign by the European Parliament).

The *European Court of Justice* has 11 judges appointed by the consent of all the members states for a period of six years. There are many situations where EU law overrules national law and there have been several instances where individual UK citizens have taken the UK government to the European Court of Justice and the government has been forced to change policy (for example, homosexuals being allowed to serve in the Armed Forces, men having the same rights as women to cold weather payments over the age of 60).

Main EU policy areas

When the EEC was established, all the member states supported agriculture, but in different ways. The first major success was to bring all national agriculture policies into the *Common Agricultural Policy* (CAP). This bans all tariffs and quota restrictions between member states and a common tariff system is applied to agricultural products from non-member countries. An EU price is set for all agricultural products and if the market price falls below this, the EU buys from the farmers at the EU price. Although this policy was a major success, and made the EU agriculturally self-sufficient, it also led to huge surpluses (as farmers produced more when the price was high) which are often referred to as butter mountains and wine lakes. It has also led to conflict between countries such as the UK and Germany, which are net importers of food (and so pay into CAP much more than they receive) and Italy and France which are net exporters (and so receive much more from CAP than they pay in). One of the provisions of the *Maastricht Treaty,* 1991, was the reform of CAP and the reduction of both subsidies and surpluses. This is a major area of concern in the EU.

Another area of concern has been that of *foreign policy*. If the EU has common economic and agricultural policies, it should have a common foreign policy. Matters of foreign policy are regularly debated at the Council of Ministers, and the Kosovo intervention in 1999 showed that it is possible for all the member states to work together on foreign policy. It would seem impossible now for EU members to take different sides in a war, but without any machinery for a common foreign policy, this is still possible in theory. Several decisions were made in 1999 by the Council of Ministers that make a common foreign policy more likely.

In the same way, *defence* should be a common matter. Most, but not all, of the EU states are members of NATO, a common defence group between Europe and North America. It would appear that the EU should have a common defence policy and an agreement to defend any member state that is attacked. The Maastricht Treaty committed the EU to formulating a common foreign and security policy, but by the end of the 1990s, little had been done. The Kosovo intervention in 1999 showed the need for this and there were subsequent agreements for member states to contribute forces to a European rapid deployment force. The European defence industries now work together to produce European fighter aircraft, tanks, etc.

The *Single Market* was established by the Maastricht Treaty. This treaty established the *Single European Act* and changed the law so that all citizens of member states became European Union citizens. All restrictions on mobility of labour, exchange controls, Europe-wide banking and other financial services were outlawed.

The EU Constitution

In June 2004 the member states of the EU agreed a treaty establishing a Constitution for the EU. According to the leaders, the Constitution would not alter the relationships between the member states, rather it was intended to clarify the present complex structure of laws and treaties agreed at different times during the EU's history to 'make its institutions more transparent, more accountable, more efficient and better able to meet the challenges of the 21st century' (British Government statement). This Constitution was rejected by the French and Dutch in the referendums they held and the Constitution was dropped.

In June 2007 The EU leaders agreed to a Reform Treaty to cope with the much enlarged nature of the EU without adopting a new constitution. The constitution would have created an entirely new legal order for the EU, sweeping away earlier treaties, whereas the Reform Treaty merely amends them. It also drops references to the EU flag and anthem. The main terms of the Treaty are:

- A new post of President of the Council of the European Union (this has been held by a member state not a person), but the post has no executive powers.

- A new post of High Representative of the EU for Foreign Affairs and Security Policy who will implement policies that member states have agreed unanimously.
- Decisions currently taken only by means of a unanimous vote, can in future be taken by a majority vote.
- National parliaments will have to be informed of proposed changes to legislation and to be given a chance to challenge legislation.
- The UK has a special clause which says no EU court can rule that the 'laws, regulations or administrative provisions, practices or action' of the UK are inconsistent with the principles laid down in the charter.
- The European Court is given more powers but Denmark and the UK negotiated an opt-out so that the Court would only have jurisdiction over EU legislation the UK agreed to.

The Conservative Party and UKIP feel that the Reform Treaty hands too much British sovereignty to the EU and is the same as the Constitution on which the Labour Party promised a referendum. They claim that there should be a referendum in the UK on whether to sign up to the Reform Treaty.

The euro

A *European monetary system* was begun in 1979 to avoid day-to-day fluctuations in the money markets affecting trade between member states. This was based on the value of the German Mark and meant that members had to make sure (by interest rates, taxation, etc. – see Unit 33, 'Economic theories', and Unit 34, 'Economic issues') that the value of their currencies stayed within a percentage band of the mark. This system was known as the ERM (exchange rate mechanism) and the UK initially took part in it. However, the value of the pound declined rapidly in 1992 and the UK was forced to withdraw from the ERM.

Maastricht had set 1999 as the deadline for introducing the euro. In order for the euro to work, interest rates, inflation rates and public sector borrowing rate (PSBR – the difference between what a government receives in taxes and spends) in states joining the euro had to be equalised (as well as the currencies being in their correct band in ERM). Those members who met the criteria and wanted to join locked their currencies into fixed parities on 31 December 1998, and on the first of January 1999, Austria, Belgium, Finland, France, Germany, Ireland, Italy, Luxembourg, the Netherlands, Portugal and Spain became part of the European Monetary Union (Eurozone). The European Central Bank took over the functions of the national banks to control the exchange rate and interest rates.

The strict rules for the EMU on interest rates, tax and spending have led the euro to increase in value compared with the dollar, the pound and the yen, but this has also led to low growth and high unemployment in many of the countries in the Eurozone.

The UK has not yet joined the euro. The Labour Government set out five tests which must be met before the UK could join:

35 The European Union

Activities

1. Read as much as you can in the newspapers, or use the Internet, to discover more detailed information on the arguments for and against the euro.

2. Consult the Business Studies Department to find out the effects of EC legislation on business.

3. Consult the Health and Safety Committee to discover the effects of the EC on Health and Safety legislation.

4. 'Being part of a European Federal State would be better than being dependent on American multi-nationals.' Examine the arguments for and against this view.

1. Are the business cycles and economic structures compatible so that the UK could live with euro interest rates? (UK interest rates tend to be higher than the Eurozone because the UK has a much larger private housing market and if interest rates go too low the cost of houses rises – very fast.)

2. If problems emerge is there sufficient flexibility to deal with them? (The British labour market is much more flexible than the Eurozone's, making the UK's unemployment rate far lower than the Eurozone's.)

3. Would joining the euro make firms more likely to make long-term investments in the UK? (This is the easiest test to say yes to as several multi-nationals have decided not to invest in the UK because it is outside the huge market of the Eurozone.)

4. What impact would joining the euro have on the UK's financial services industry? (The UK has the strongest financial services industry in Europe and it is now reckoned to be so strong that joining the euro would have little effect.)

5. Will joining the euro promote higher growth, stability and a lasting increase in jobs? (This is likely to remain an issue whilst the UK's growth rate is much higher than that of the Eurozone.)

Tests 1, 2, and 5 are the strongest factors keeping the UK outside the Eurozone, but there are many in Britain (such as UKIP) who would oppose joining the euro even if it brought great financial benefits to the UK because they see the pound as the final sign of national sovereignty.

EXAM QUESTION

This A2 Unit 4 essay question from June 2004 accompanied a case study based on the theme of *The European Union*.

Discuss the arguments for and against the United Kingdom joining the single European currency and explain your preference.

(25 marks)

EXAMINER'S ADVICE

- The question requires both arguments for **and** against and for you to indicate your own views. Use the material and activities in this unit (plus perhaps your own opinions gained from reading or watching reviews in newspapers or on television) to help with this. You should think in terms of both economic and political arguments.
- In the first part there are extensive arguments on both sides which you should be able to reflect in your answer, even though at this stage you may not necessarily agree with all of them.
- In the second part, although you are asked to indicate your preferences, the issue is a big and complex one on which many people are genuinely undecided. If this is your position too, there is no harm in saying that, as long as you explain why.
- When you have thought about the question, write your answer in no more than 35 minutes. Some extensive notes are given on pages 283–284.

Rich world, poor world

In 1980, world leaders expressed their concern about the growing division between the rich countries of the mainly northern hemisphere and the poor countries of the southern hemisphere. The *Brandt Report* (named after the former chancellor of West Germany, who was its chairman), identified the difference in living standards between countries. For example, in North America living standards are 40 times higher than in many parts of India and Africa. These countries are often referred to as *less economically developed countries* or *LEDCs* because they have not benefited from the effects of technology and the Industrial Revolution in the same way as the more developed countries in the North.

Poverty

The most important characteristic of LEDCs is *poverty*. It has been argued by many voluntary and United Nations aid agencies that poverty is the fundamental cause of many other problems. Poverty traps millions of people in a cycle of malnutrition, disease, illiteracy, large families, etc. often limiting their capacity to work hard enough to grow enough food to live on or to earn sufficient wages. Poverty produces powerlessness so that people are incapable of removing themselves from this cycle of deprivation (see Figure 36.1). For example, many southern hemisphere farmers only grow enough food to feed their own families. If the crop fails, they either starve or have to borrow the cost of new seed from money lenders at exorbitant rates of interest. Farmers who operate at this level of *subsistence farming*, often because they are using pre-industrial technology, such as mule-drawn wooden ploughs, and planting low-yield, disease-susceptible and unfertilised crops, never produce a surplus that they can convert into cash in order to buy more modern farming technology.

Definitions of poverty

a) Absolute and relative poverty

Although the most severe poverty is in the developing world, there is evidence of poverty in every region. In developed countries, this condition results in wandering homeless people and poor suburbs and ghettos. Poverty may be seen as the collective condition of poor people, or of poor groups, and in this sense entire nation-states are sometimes regarded as poor. To avoid stigma these nations are usually called developing nations. When measured, poverty may be absolute or relative poverty.

Absolute poverty refers to a set standard which is consistent over time and between countries. An example of an absolute measurement would be the percentage of the population eating less food than is required to sustain the human body (approximately 2000–2500 kilocalories per day).

Relative poverty, in contrast, views poverty as socially defined and dependent on social context. One relative measurement would be to compare the total wealth of the poorest one-third of the population with the total wealth of richest one per cent of the population. In this case, the number of people counted as poor could increase while their income rises.

The main poverty line used in the OECD (Organisation for Economic Co-operation and Development) and the European Union is a *relative poverty* measure based on 'economic distance', a level of income set at 50 per cent of the median household income. The United States, in contrast, uses an *absolute poverty* measure. The US poverty line was created in 1963–64 and was based on the U.S. Department of Agriculture's 'economy food plan' multiplied by a factor of three. The multiplier was based on research showing that food costs then accounted for about one third of the total money income. This one-time calculation has since been annually updated for inflation. The US line has been criticised as being too high, in that it takes into account something other than true poverty. For example, some people object to the fact that, according to the U.S. Census Bureau, 46 per cent of those in 'poverty' in the U.S. own their own home (with the average poor person's home having three bedrooms, with one and a half baths, and a garage).

Both absolute and relative poverty measures are usually based on a person's yearly income and frequently take no account of total wealth. Some people argue that this ignores the key component of economic well-being.

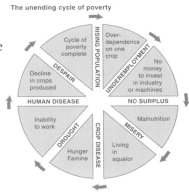

Figure 36.1 The unending cycle of poverty

The effects of poverty

There are many conditions associated with absolute poverty that affect the lives of about 300 million people worldwide:

- *Malnutrition and hunger.* Many people live on the edge of starvation and do not have properly balanced diets, lacking protein in particular.
- *Disease.* Poor diet and bad water contribute to the many diseases associated with poverty. Diseases such as malaria, sleeping sickness, river-blindness and bilharzia, etc. affect 200 million people annually. It is estimated that 20,000 children die every day from diarrhoea.
- *Mortality rates.* The average age of death in LEDCs is between 40 and 50. (In Britain, it is about 76.) This is caused by a high infant mortality rate and the effects of endemic diseases on many adults.
- *Environment.* Many people live in slums in vast urbanised areas such as the shanty towns of Manila in the Philippines, Mexico City and Calcutta. Most of these areas lack clean drinking water, proper sanitation, power for heating, cooking and lighting and community health care or leisure facilities.
- *Illiteracy.* Across the world, 800 million people worldwide can neither read nor write. Many poor countries cannot afford to build schools or pay teachers, but they cannot increase their wealth without a more skilled work force.

Figure 36.2 Starving children

The causes of poverty

Physical causes

- *Heat.* Many LEDCs have extremely hot, humid climates which not only make it impossible to work efficiently in the daytime heat but also encourage diseases such as malaria.
- *Desertification.* Due to climatic changes, extensive deforestation of land and other land mismanagement, huge areas of once-fertile land are becoming desert. (The Sahel region in North Africa is a good example of this.) This reduces the food-growing and wealth-producing capacity of a particular country. Although other parts of the world also suffer from the climatic and physical conditions described below, the difference lies in the economic capacity to cope with such conditions. Rich countries cope much better with flood, drought, earthquake, crop failure and the effects of typhoons because they can store or buy in food and technology to reconstruct their society.
- *Lack of natural resources.* Some poor countries not only have the problems of a subsistence level and unmechanised agricultural system, but they have no other natural resources such as oil or other valuable minerals, such as rare metals or coal. (Japan's enormous development with no natural resources is an exception).
- *The population explosion.* One of the most serious problems facing not just poor countries but the world as a whole, is the problem of increasing population. One million people are added to the population every five days and the current total figure is six billion. This is not just a cause of poverty but also a result of it. Poor families tend to have the largest number of children, partly because they lack access to family planning information and also because high infant mortality rates encourage the need for several children, so that there is someone to look after the parents when they are old. However, in many developed countries such as Sweden, Switzerland and Japan, there has been a drastic decline in the birth rate, raising concerns about their future capacity to generate enough wealth to maintain current standards of living.
- *Distribution of wealth and resources.* One of the major causes of poverty is the unfair distribution of wealth. Poor countries are often exploited by richer countries who pay very low prices for exports of raw materials and set up unreasonable tariffs to make manufactured goods produced by LEDCs,

uncompetitive in price. Powerful multinational companies have engaged in economic *neo-colonialism* by controlling what poorer countries produce and paying very low wages to people desperate for work. International banks have also contributed to the continuing poverty of many LEDCs by lending them vast sums of money, the interest payments on which are quite beyond the capacity of the country to pay. Thus, no spare capital is generated for development. Unfair distribution also applies to crucial resources such as food. Despite the increases in population, there is enough food to go round but it is unfairly distributed. The rich northern hemisphere, for example, has only 25 per cent of the world's population but consumes over 70 per cent of the world's resources (see also Unit 7 'Agriculture and food production').

Possible solutions

Current trends

a) Economic growth

The World Bank defines poverty in absolute terms. The bank defines *extreme poverty* as living on less than US$1 per day, and *moderate poverty* as less than $2 a day. It has been estimated that in 2001, 1.1 billion people had consumption levels below $1 a day and 2.7 billion lived on less than $2 a day. The proportion of the developing world's population living in extreme economic poverty has fallen from 28 per cent in 1990 to 21 per cent in 2001. Much of the improvement has occurred in East and South Asia. Other regions have seen little or no change. Life expectancy has greatly increased in the developing world since the Second World War and is starting to close the gap to the developed world where the improvement has been smaller. Even in Sub-Saharan Africa, the least developed region, life expectancy increased from 30 years before the Second World War to a peak of about 50 years before the HIV pandemic and other diseases started to force it down to the current level of 47 years. Child mortality has decreased in every developing region of the world. The proportion of the world's population living in countries where per-capita food supplies are less than 2,200 calories (9,200 kilojoules) per day decreased from 56 per cent in the mid-1960s to below 10 per cent by the 1990s. Between 1950 and 1999, global literacy increased from 52 per cent to 81 per cent of the world. Women made up much of the gap: female literacy as a percentage of male literacy has increased from 59 per cent in 1970 to 80 per cent in 2000. The percentage of children not in the labour force has also risen to over 90 per cent in 2000 from 76 per cent in 1960. There are similar trends for electric power, cars, radios, and telephones per capita, as well as the proportion of the population with access to clean water. Income inequality for the world as a whole is diminishing, although this statistic is driven mainly, but not fully, by the extraordinary growth rate of the incomes of 1.2 billion Chinese citizens.

DID YOU KNOW?

Rich and poor
- Japan contributes a greater percentage of its GDP to foreign aid than any other country.
- During the past six years, more people have died of hunger than died in two world wars.
- Developed countries spend 20 times as much on arms as they do on aid.
- Total global military expenditure is £1.5 million per minute.
- The world population doubles every 35 years.
- LEDCs now owe £1.4 trillion in international loans and pay back three times more in interest than is lent in aid annually.

b) Areas where poverty has increased

Even if poverty may be lessening for the world as a whole, it continues to be an enormous problem. Despite the emphases by major conferences and other related organisations such as the Brandt Report, United Nations Agencies and the World Bank since the 1980s on the need for:

- the removal of crushing international debt;
- the re-organisation of the international trading system so that it treats LEDCs more favourably;
- the redirection of the huge amounts of money spent on arms towards health and clean water supplies, for example;
- major expenditure on agricultural research to improve and strengthen crop yields;
- more effective strategies to make sure that the results of globalisation (the integration of world economies), are more widely felt, etc.;

most peoples' lives are affected by poverty.

What poverty means

Three billion people live on less than two dollars a day.

1. The GDP (Gross Domestic Product) of the poorest 48 nations (i.e. a quarter of the world's countries) is less than the wealth of the world's three richest people combined.
2. Nearly a billion people entered the 21st century unable to read a book or sign their names.
3. Less than one per cent of what the world spent every year on weapons was needed to put every child into school by the year 2000 and yet it didn't happen.
4. The wealthiest nation on Earth has the widest gap between rich and poor of any industrialised nations.
5. Twenty per cent of the population in the developed nations, consume 86 per cent of the world's goods.
6. The lives of 1.7 million children will be needlessly lost this year because world governments have failed to reduce poverty levels.
7. A few hundred millionaires now own as much wealth as the world's poorest 2.5 billion people.
8. Approximately 790 million people in the developing world are still chronically undernourished, almost two-thirds of whom reside in Asia and the Pacific.
9. According to UNICEF, 30,000 children die each day due to poverty. And they 'die quietly in some of the poorest villages on earth, far removed from the scrutiny and the conscience of the world. Being meek and weak in life makes these dying multitudes even more invisible in death.'

The global economy

Is globalisation benefiting the poor?

Economic experts and some political leaders have been calling for radical changes in the direction of world economic policy to overcome the negative effects of globalisation. Major changes in trade and immigration policy are needed if the world's poor are to share in the benefits of globalisation, according to a recent UN report.

The report says that only a dozen developing countries have benefited from the increasing integration of the world economy. Those who have lost out include the poor, the asset-less, illiterate and unskilled workers, and indigenous peoples. Income per person in the world's 20 poorest countries has barely changed in the last 40 years, from $212 in 1960–62 to $267 in 2000–02, while income in the richest 20 nations has tripled, from $11,417 to $32,339. The report said globalisation's 'potential for good is immense', but 'the advantages are too distant for too many, while the risks are all too real'.

The president of Tanzania and co-chair of the report, Benjamin Mkapa, said the situation was 'untenable' and that 'countries with impoverished, disadvantaged and desperate populations are breeding grounds for present and future terrorists'.

Important changes called for are:

- An international agreement on migration.
- Fairer trade agreements that open Western markets to agricultural and textile products from developing countries.
- An agreement on a 'balanced framework' for foreign direct investment that will ensure that developing countries benefit.
- Enforcement of labour laws and trade union rights especially in export processing zones.
- Better coordination between world institutions like the IMF, World Bank, ILO, and World Trade Organisation in ensuring that job creation is the central economic policy goal.

The report also says that the fundamental problem is that 'global markets have grown rapidly without the parallel development of economic and social institutions necessary for their smooth and effective functioning'.

The distribution of wealth in Britain

We tend to assume that inequality of wealth distribution is a function of less developed countries. However, according to some expert observers, including the journalist Polly Toynbee, Britain has one of the world's worst distributions of wealth. Income inequality in Britain is the worst in Europe and the minimum wage virtually the lowest (£5.52 in 2007). The argument against raising the minimum wage is fear of job loss. All predictions about job losses when the minimum wage was introduced turned out to be wrong. The lowest paid jobs tend to be in the service industries and there is an argument that this is because women traditionally fulfil these roles (such as catering, caring or cleaning).

EXAM QUESTION

Consider the article below about global politics, and answer the question which follows.

Extracts from a case study on *Global politics*

Globalisation crucial to creation of a just world

by Niall FitzGerald

THE dreadful events of September 11 are a defining moment for our world. This was terror on a catastrophic scale, a strike against freedom and democracy itself. For humanity's sake, we must draw together and focus on the universal values that decent people everywhere seek. Freedom. Dignity. Tolerance. Sustainable livelihoods. The opportunity to prosper.

These universal values hold the key to defeating terror. They reflect the aspirations of billions of people and they transcend divisions between 'the West' and 'the rest'. They are the foundation stones for globalisation that creates a better world.

Since September 11 there have been many calls to tackle terrorism's 'root causes'. The international community must contribute to ending the causes, political and economic, of the anger and despair that leads wider numbers of ordinary people to cheer for those who resort to terror. This involves a complex mix of issues arising from entrenched poverty and governance problems, as well as struggles over land and self-determination.

We need to sustain a vision of inclusion, economic growth and good governance. There is no shortage of initiatives; what is needed is action that focuses on priorities that will have the greatest impact. These include domestic governance, trade and market access, investment and business capacity-building, access to basic health care and information networks.

Fostering economic growth – and no society has overcome entrenched poverty without it – will require more trade and investment, not less. The record shows that communities that trade on global markets are more stable and prosperous than those that don't.

The reinforcement of economic interdependence within a truly global marketplace will help to ensure stability and security, whether political and economic, whether social and cultural.

The last world trade round was estimated to have added at least $350 billion annually to world income.

Among developing countries it is those with the most open markets and dynamic education systems, such as Hong Kong, Singapore and South Korea, that have advanced most rapidly. A generation or so ago they were as poor as some African countries. For a new trade round, the Tinbergen Institute has estimated that another 50 per cent cut in world trade barriers would be worth at least $150 billion to developing countries, about four times their current aid receipts.

Those in whom we have trusted responsibility should adopt a negotiating agenda designed to:

- Fundamentally reform rich countries' agricultural policies, as these contribute directly to the loss of domestic and overseas markets for developing country farmers.
- Redesign farm subsidies to encourage developing country agricultural capacity and de-link environmental and social subsidies from production.
- Promote greater services trade in key sectors such as financial, transport, telecom and energy services.
- Remove high tariffs on processed goods from developing countries to encourage investment and job creation.
- Examine WTO agreements that impose significant administrative costs on small developing countries.
- Examine whether there is a substantive case for WTO rules on foreign direct investment and competition policy.
- Establish a standalone negotiation on actual and potential clashes between WTO rules and global environment treaties to facilitate coexistence.

It is legitimate for France to defend its farmers or India to focus on unfinished business from the last round. But not to the extent that the world's poor pay the price of an aborted trade round. The greatest responsibility rests with the EU and USA. They must lead by example. Agree today the opening up of their markets to stimulate growth in developing economies. Defer and seek a more appropriate forum for discussions about environmental and labour standards.

The author is chairman and chief executive of Unilever

Source: The Times, 12 November 2001

What steps do you think should be taken by business and governments to create a fairer, more sustainable world?

(12 marks)

EXAMINER'S ADVICE

- This extract is taken from the A2 case study of January 2003. The question is the last of the four questions set on the case study material in Unit 4 but it focuses fairly specifically on points made in this article (as well as some of the others in the same set). If you have done your preparation of the case study properly you will know where to go to find the points. In this instance, use the article and other relevant material in the unit to frame your answer.

- The question is a mini-essay in itself, but once you have studied the extract and the rest of the unit, you should attempt to answer it in no more than 20 minutes and a page and half of writing. This is all the time you will have in the test.

- Use the key terms in the question to develop your ideas and points and as a structure for your answer, i.e. 'steps . . . by **business** and **governments**' (to what extent do they have different roles and responsibilities?), and '**fairer**' and 'more **sustainable**'.

- Some points are given on page 285. When you have made your attempt, look at these to see how your answer matches up.

Procedures for tackling exam questions

Multiple choice/comprehension questions (Units 1 and 2)

- Scan all the material relating to the test as a whole, including the questions, so that you gain a quick idea of what the content is about.
- Read all the stimulus material carefully, trying to work out what the text is covering and the main points conveyed. At this stage you should be focusing on the key points and the main thread of the arguments. Underline what appear to be the key points or topic sentence(s) in each section as you go.
- Work through each of the questions in turn. Think through your answer before you indicate what you consider to be the correct response.
- Speed and decisiveness are essential. Objective or multiple choice tests are designed to cover a lot of ground in a short period of time. The questions are worth only one mark whether they are easy or difficult. In the tests you have about 45 minutes for each section, so this means that you should spend the first ten minutes or so on the first two bullet points above. You then have approximately one minute to spend on each of the questions with five minutes to review your answers at the end.
- Do not expect to get all the questions right, even if you are aiming at a Grade A. Pass quickly over those items which leave you 'floored', and concentrate on the ones which you feel you ought to be able to get right.
- Concentrate hard but briefly on the question in hand. If the question points you to a particular part of a passage, this is where the answer will be. Do not become distracted by the questions you have passed over or have not yet done. Do not panic. Some of the questions are designed to be beyond all but the best candidates. Be decisive, and try not to change your mind. If you are unsure, go with the answer you first thought was right.
- Return to the more difficult items at the end and try to eliminate the less likely alternatives. Use your deductive powers to reduce the element of guesswork.
- ***Answer all the questions***. Marks are not deducted for incorrect answers, so you have nothing to lose, if all else has failed, by resorting to guesswork. Despite this, every year there are some candidates who fail to attempt some of these questions.

Preparation for Unit 4

The emphasis in the Unit 4 test is on how you respond to stimulus material, so the best preparation in General Studies is developing general awareness of what is going on in society and political life, and practising the analytical, summarising and evaluation skills which will be tested in the case study.

For the Unit 4 test, you are issued in advance with a collection of articles and some data on one or more broad themes relevant to Science and Society. This will contain

- material from different sources (most commonly newspapers)
- representing different dimensions and viewpoints
- including some statistics/tables of data.

It is *issued up to twelve weeks before* the written test (i.e. any time after 1 November for the January test and 1 April for June) to allow you sufficient time to become acquainted with the material and the broader issues that it raises. Typically you will receive between 4 and 6 extracts to study and you are allowed to discuss these freely with your teacher(s) or anyone else you choose. You may make notes and prepare answers to possible questions, but you will not be allowed to take these into the exam.

When you come to the exam you will be provided with a further copy of the sources plus one or two additional extracts which you will not have seen in advance to complete the set on which the questions will be based.

You should spend at least *three hours* studying the material prior to the test, and this should be sufficient for you to become familiar with the detail and main thrust and points of each source. In your preparation you should:

- know and understand thoroughly the contents of each source
- ensure that you understand key vocabulary, terms and concepts
- summarise for yourself, in your own words, the main themes and arguments of each source
- draw points together from the different sources and make connections and comparisons between them
- make sure you know which points come from where and why
- study the data to establish what they reveal in their own right
- consider the extent to which the data support ideas and arguments presented in the sources
- evaluate the contribution each piece of information makes to the larger picture.

In the test you are required to:

- read the additional extract(s)
- show your broad understanding of the detail of the material
- be able to summarise the points and arguments contained within the sources
- recognise the connections between the different elements of the topic
- identify the different standpoints and values represented, and
- exercise your own judgements and knowledge on the nature of the arguments and problems.

Questions relating to statistical data are to test your:

- appreciation of their use in the broader context
- understanding of what they reveal in terms of issues raised and support for arguments presented, and
- evaluation of the conclusions that may be drawn.

There are typically *four compulsory questions* on the case study itself, and they are likely to widen in scope from fairly close comment on particular themes in the documents to broader issues raised by the case study. In this section the answers are not expected to be essays, but they must be written in continuous prose and for the highest level marks must demonstrate a sense of overall understanding and present an overview of the key issues under discussion.

- Make sure you answer *all* the case study questions (a lot of marks are lost by candidates who fail to do this) and answer only *one* essay.
- Typically 45 marks are allocated to the case study questions (eleven or twelve marks for each) and 25 marks for the essay.
- Aim to spend about 20 minutes on each of the case study questions and 40 minutes on the essay. Some of this should be thinking and planning time.

You will not be able to achieve this unless you have prepared the case study material thoroughly in advance.

Mark scheme for AS written answers (Units 1 and 2)

Level of response	Mark ranges	Criteria and descriptors for Assessment Objectives
LEVEL 3	UNIT 1 11–14 UNIT 2 13–18	**Good response to question** Good to comprehensive knowledge, understanding and approach demonstrating overall grasp of the range and nature of issues (AO1). Capacity to interpret evidence and sustained ability to present relevant arguments, analysis and exemplification, focusing on the main points of the question (AO2). Shows some understanding of different types of knowledge, with some appreciation of their limitation in seeking to reach a reasoned and logical conclusion (AO3). Ability to communicate clearly and accurately in a fluent and organised manner (AO4).
LEVEL 2	UNIT 1 6–10 UNIT 2 7–12	**Reasonable attempt to answer question** Modest to quite good knowledge and understanding approach demonstrating some grasp of the nature of some key issues (AO1). Moderate range of arguments, analysis and exemplification covering some of the main points of the question (AO2). Limited understanding of different types of knowledge but some ability to work towards or achieve a reasoned conclusion (AO3). Mostly clear and accurate communication and organisation (AO4).
LEVEL 1	UNIT 1 1–5 UNIT 2 1–6	**Limited response to the question** Restricted/narrow knowledge and understanding of key issues (AO1). Simple, perhaps mostly unexplained points – or very narrow range – with limited interpretation or analysis and exemplification (AO2). Lacking in understanding of different types of knowledge with little or no evidence of ability to work towards a conclusion (AO3). Variable levels of communication and organisation (AO4).
LEVEL 0	0	**No valid response or relevance to question**

Mark scheme for A2 essays (Units 3 and 4)

The essay questions in AQA General Studies A are designed to test the four assessment objectives (see Introduction page 3) as follows:

AO1 – 8 marks   AO2 – 7 marks   AO3 – 5 marks   AO4 – 5 marks   Total – 25 marks

Level of response	Mark range	Criteria and descriptors: knowledge, understanding, argument, evaluation, communication
LEVEL 5	21–25 (5)	**Very good to excellent treatment of the question:** comprehensive knowledge of topic (AO1); extensive range of convincing arguments and supporting illustrations, effective conclusion and overall grasp (AO2); clear understanding and appreciation of material, nature of knowledge involved and related issues (AO3); well structured, accurately and fluently expressed (AO4).
LEVEL 4	16–20 (5)	**Good response to the demands of the question:** sound knowledge of topic (AO1); fair range of valid arguments and appropriate illustrations, reasonable conclusions (AO2); reasonable understanding and appreciation of material, nature of knowledge involved and related issues (AO3); coherent structure, accurate expression (AO4).
LEVEL 3	11–15 (5)	**Competent attempt at answering the question:** some relevant knowledge of topic (AO1); modest range of arguments and illustrations, attempt at conclusion (AO2); some understanding and appreciation of material, nature of knowledge involved and related issues (AO3); some coherence and structure, reasonably accurate expression (AO4).
LEVEL 2	6–10 (5)	**Limited to basic response to the demands of the question:** limited/basic knowledge of topic (AO1); vague argument and sparse illustration, lacking conclusion and overall grasp (AO2); limited understanding and appreciation of material, nature of knowledge involved and related issues (AO3); weak structure and errors in expression (AO4).
LEVEL 1	1–5 (5)	**Inadequate attempt to deal with the question:** very limited knowledge (AO1); little or no justification or illustration, no overall grasp or coherence (AO2); little understanding and appreciation of material, nature of knowledge involved and related issues (AO3); no structure and weak expression (AO4).
LEVEL 0	0	**No response or relevance to the question**

Answers to examination questions

Unit 1
1-C, 2-D, 3-B, 4-C, 5-A, 6-B, 7-A, 8-A, 9-D, 10-B

Unit 2
1-C, 2-B, 3-D, 4-B, 5-C, 6-C, 7-C, 8-C, 9-D, 10-B

Unit 3
Supporting information and ideas:
- Creationism claims a fairly literal interpretation of Genesis in the Bible, whereby the world and humanity were created by a supernatural creator not more than 6000 years ago. After a study of biblical chronologies in 1654, Archbishop Ussher declared 23 October 4004 BC as the first day of creation.
- However, the discovery of fossils had already thrown doubt on the Bible's account of how the Earth was created. A pioneering eighteenth-century geologist, James Hutton, showed that the Earth is renewed as well as worn away by geological processes. He influenced the later work of another geologist, Charles Lyell, a friend of Darwin, who is credited with making Darwin aware of the large timescales associated with the Earth's age and which underpin the Theory of Evolution.
- Evolution is about the slow process of change from one form to another. Darwin assigned the major role in evolutionary change to natural selection acting on naturally occurring variations. Natural selection occurs because those individuals better adapted to their environment reproduce more effectively, thus contributing their genes to future generations.
- Both Galileo and Darwin used 'the scientific cycle'. They attempted to provide systematic, justifiable explanations of natural phenomena. An experiment was performed, observations were made. (Galileo looked upon the moons of Jupiter with his telescope. Darwin made his observations and had his thoughts on them whilst on *The Beagle*.) A hypothesis is produced and predictions are based on it. Further experiment and observation then test the truth of these predictions. As evidence builds up to confirm the hypothesis, it may become a theory, which is a verified and established explanation fitting known facts or phenomena and which holds good until it can be disproved.
- Science is generally highly regarded for adopting careful and detailed study before reaching defensible conclusions. The adjective 'scientific' means that there is a reliability about a line of reasoning or a piece of research. Generally speaking, science has been a highly fruitful activity responsible for greater understanding of universal matter, the natural world and the place of humankind within it.

Unit 5
1-C, 2-C, 3-C, 4-D, 5-D, 6-C, 7-B, 8-B, 9-B, 10-D, 11-A, 12-D, 13-B, 14-D, 15-A, 16-D, 17-C, 18-A, 19-D, 20-D

Unit 6
Background information and ideas:
- In January 2001, a consortium of scientists led by Panaylotis Zavos and the Italian Severino Antinori said they planned to clone a human in the next two years. At the same time, an American couple were willing to pay half a million dollars to Las Vegas-based Clonaid for a clone of their deceased daughter from preserved skin cells. In January 2003, the Realian sect in the USA claimed to have produced a clone – still not proved!
- Two types of cloning produce complete genetically identical animals. **Blastomere separation** (sometimes called twinning after the naturally occurring process that creates identical twins) involves splitting a developing embryo to give rise to two or more embryos.
- Dolly the sheep however, carries the DNA of only one parent – **somatic cell nuclear transfer** was used. The nucleus from an adult sheep's udder cell was transferred to an egg whose nucleus had been removed. The embryo formed was placed in a surrogate mother through IVF who gave birth at the

end of a normal gestation period. The success rate is about one or two in a hundred. It took 277 attempts to create Dolly. This is the process that scientists are intending to use for human cloning.

- **Therapeutic cloning** is the process by which a person's DNA is used to grow an embryonic clone. However, instead of inserting this embryo into a surrogate mother, its cells are used to grow **stem cells**. These may be used as human repair kit. They can grow replacement organs such as hearts, livers and skin. They can also be used to grow neurons to cure those who suffer from Alzheimer's, Parkinson's or Rett Syndrome. Cloning can also be used to help couples with **infertility problems** but who want a child with at least one parent's biological attributes.
- Another use for cloning could be to bring **deceased relatives back to life**. Imagine using a piece of your great grandmother's DNA to create a clone of her. In a sense you would be the parent of your great grandmother. This opens a door to many ethical problems!
- The FDA has said that anyone in the USA attempting cloning must first get its permission. In Japan, human cloning is a crime punishable with up to ten years in prison. In Britain, cloning of human embryos is allowed but a ban on total human cloning is expected. Ninety-eight per cent of clones end in failure. The embryos are either not suitable for implanting into the uterus or they die during gestation or shortly after birth. Clones that do survive suffer from genetic abnormalities. Some clones have been born with defective hearts, lung problems, diabetes, blood vessel problems and malfunctioning immune systems. Even Dolly, the first successful cloned mammal, died quite young and had arthritic problems whilst alive. With animals, the defectives are not as significant as they would be with humans. Advocates reason that defective embryos will be spotted before implantation.

Three major grounds for objections:
- **Making a copy of someone is a criminal offence**. However, an exact copy is unlikely to ever happen because of the infinite number of permutations that come into play in the development of each individual, so cloning is no overwhelming threat to unique personhood.
- **Cloning is 'playing God' and evil in nature**. In a *Time/CNN* 1997 poll in the USA, 75 per cent

thought that it was against God's will to clone human beings. Maybe the idea is still unfamiliar compared to IVF and embryo transfer.
- **It is against human rights and dignity**, as embodied in the Roman Catholic Church's official statement against cloning, in that it denies 'the dignity of human procreation and of the conjugal union'. Opponents argue that clones are no more alike than twins raised in separate environments and no one is suggesting that twins do not have rights or dignity or that they should be banned. (See www.newscientist.com for more information.)

Unit 7

Background information and ideas:
- Genetic engineers may try to change the way genes work in a given plant or animal or try to transfer genes from one species to another. This may result in improved nutritional value, visual appeal, processing potential, resistance to disease/pesticides/herbicides or longer shelf life, e.g. BST hormone improving milk yields, Flavr Savr tomato, insect-proof crops.

From a political point of view:
- The UK government's strategy unit reported in July 2003 that GM crops offer little economic value – there is little point in farmers growing them if the public carries on refusing to buy them. The government, on the one hand, risks a potential transatlantic trade war if they do not lift their effective ban on GM and are likely to find inward investment drying up if they appear to be hostile to science-based companies. On the other hand, there is an alliance of anti-GM groups whose views hold sway over a sceptical electorate.

From a scientific point of view:

Is it safe in health terms?
- Arpad Pusztai lost his job in 2000 at the Rowett Research Institute in Aberdeen when he claimed that rats fed with GM potatoes had damaged stomach linings – a report rebuffed by other scientists. A huge unofficial experiment is going on in the USA where millions of meals containing GM foods have been eaten since 1995 – with no apparent problems. The only apparent hint of danger was in 2001, when a type of GM maize approved only for animal food, because it contained a potentially allergy-inducing

protein, got mixed up with normal maize and turned up in tacos across the US. Some people complained of a range of ailments but the FDA failed to establish whether the GM maize was to blame.

Higher yields from GM crops?
- Several studies have shown yield improvement, especially if resistant to pests. One study shows that pest-resistant GM corn increased yields in America by the equivalent of 500,000 hectares a year.

Does it affect organic farming?
- Because GM crops are capable of crossing with non-GM varieties, there is a worry that the purity of organic produce is threatened. Pollen from oilseed rape can travel up to 3 km on the wind.

Does it affect farmland wildlife?
- GM crops are often used with broad-spectrum herbicides, i.e. they wipe out everything. If used carelessly, such herbicides could turn farmlands into almost lifeless wastelands. There is evidence of damage to Monarch butterfly larvae which ate large amounts of Bt maize (modified to be resistant to the bug *Bacillus thuringiensis*) in the laboratory.

GM crops lead to superweeds?
- The vast majority of available GM crops are either resistant to certain herbicides or produce toxins that kill pests. Some GM crops have the potential to give rise to superweeds if they cross with other plants. In the UK the only crop that is likely to cross with wild relatives is oilseed rape.

Are herbicides used with GM crops better than traditional herbicides?
- Modern broad spectrum herbicides do appear to be more environmentally friendly. Their effects depend largely on how responsible farmers are in their usage. Some GM crops could be farmed with less tilling saving energy and soil (from wind loss).

Will we get pesticide-resistant insects?
- This is likely but a minimal risk in Britain – it is more likely in places with lots of crops and pests.

Can GM food be identified?
- Simple labelling is the main tool but there are tensions in the US where labelling is not compulsory. In Europe, there is a mandatory requirement for labelling of any food containing more than 0.9 per cent GM ingredients.

Unit 8

(a) Social/scientific reasons for a varied/balanced diet: Nutritionists have identified almost 50 essential nutrients, chemical substances such as vitamins, amino acids, minerals and essential fatty acids that the human body needs but cannot synthesise itself. A varied diet might include a broad selection of foods across traditional groups such as fruits, vegetables, cereals, meat, fish and dairy products. A balanced diet might include carbohydrates, protein, non-saturated fats, fibre, vitamins, minerals and the consumption of water/fruit juice. The specific balance depends on individuals and factors such as their age.
- A varied and balanced diet will help to balance positive and negative interactions among food components.
- Balance might include carbohydrates (for energy), fat (energy efficient), proteins (for metabolic tasks), calcium (teeth and bones), fibre (digestive system), etc. All contribute to healthier individuals, perhaps with higher self-esteem.
- 2006 government report indicated that, on current trends, >1 million U16s in Britain will be classed as obese by 2010 (22 per cent of girls and 19 per cent of boys). Levels of obesity in children aged 2–10 have increased from 10 per cent in 1995 to >14 per cent in 2004. Britain currently has the highest obesity rates in the EU. Headlines such as 'the fat man of Europe', 'junk food generation' and 'epidemic of obesity'.
- Balanced and varied diet, especially in conjunction with exercise, can reduce calories going in and increase those coming out. People often feel better both physically and mentally and have higher self-esteem.
- Childhood obesity can contribute to diabetes and have longer term impact on illnesses such as cardiovascular disease, high blood pressure and high cholesterol levels with implications for individual life expectancy and healthcare costs.
- Variety seems to protect against onset of Type 2 diabetes, some cancers and cardiovascular disease.
- Higher survival rates among those consuming food from a greater variety of food groups. (Lower life expectancy in north of England where there are more overweight people. Death rates from heart disease,

stroke and related illnesses are 25 per cent higher in the north west than the south east.)

- Eating a variety of nutrient-rich, low energy foods like vegetables and fruit, helps in weight control.
- Balanced diet requires moderation and this might discourage dangerous habits like binge drinking.

(b) Difficulties in achieving this aim:
- Formidable (if increasingly regulated) role of television advertising aimed at young people.
- Preferences of the 'fast food' generation. How much should be left to individual choice?
- Question of responsibility. Government can help to educate but can't force people to change dietary habits.
- Restrictions planned/implemented for school vending machines. Too little, too late or should we be making longer-term judgements?
- Jamie Oliver's school meals campaign and new government regulation on content. Too early to judge impact – much expected but minimal funds available to school caterers and early evidence of some significant falls in take-up of school meals. What of nearby shops selling fat-filled burgers or fizzy drinks or indulgent parents packing lunch box with items high in sugar, salt and saturated fats?
- Inertia and cultural factors? Difficult to change attitudes? 'It won't happen to me' factor common amongst young people.
- Do major retailers like supermarkets or McDonalds do enough to promote healthy eating among the young?
- Limited and often expensive health and fitness facilities, especially in inner city and rural areas.
- School sport/PE not popular among many young people. Not always given much curriculum time or priority.
- Far fewer children walk or cycle to school.
- Lifestyle of young people often based on more sedentary interests. Exercise means effort and commitment.

Unit 9

Medical/scientific:
- Doctors are often anxious to secure transplants for patients who might quickly die without them. However, this is a highly sensitive area. The UK transplant code of 1979 states that two doctors (independent of the transplant team and each other) must certify that the donor is brain dead before organ removal. The 2006 Human Tissue Act makes it more difficult for relatives to override the wishes of someone who has previously signed the Organ Donor Register.
- Face transplants involve an exceptionally complex surgical procedure involving hours of micro-surgery. The first 48 hours after surgery are critical and typical complications include blockage of the blood supply, infection and rejection. The Royal College of Surgeons say there is little evidence that Butler's plans would work, that the risks of rejection are too great and that the general population is not ready for face transplants.
- Doctors have to consider the opportunity costs of transplants. Is it worth spending so much on a face transplant when there are people who cannot get cancer drugs (the 'postcode lottery') because of the cost to the NHS?
- If face transplants are successful would people, in a few years' time seek face transplants for cosmetic reasons? Already there is a shortage of transplant surgeons and nurses. Surgeons are increasingly examining the possibilities of xenotransplantation (organs from animals to humans). There may be objections from some religious groups and vegetarians.
- Increasingly, efforts are being made to develop forms of stem cell research based on embryos – a highly contentious area in both religious and ethical terms.

Donor/recipient:
- Organ transplants are often for life-saving purposes. However, the antigens of the graft are recognised by the body as 'foreign' and the recipient's immune system produces antibodies that target the graft which is then destroyed by white blood cells. Transplant patients will need to take immunosuppressive drugs for life. Regimes are very demanding for both the recipients and their families.
- Dependency on immunosuppressant drugs can increase the risk of a range of health problems, including heart disease and cancer. Would recipients really wish to face the demand of another major illness?
- A major factor in face transplants is the psychological impact – both on the patient and the donor's family. Face visibility and facial expressions may have a considerable effect on human behaviour.

- Often those in need of transplants are very severely disfigured, depend on life-restricting and expensive methods like kidney dialysis, or face imminent death without a newly-transplanted organ.
- The death of a loved one is a very sensitive and emotional time for families – a time when it is very difficult to make a decision about donating organs for others. 40 per cent of families approached refuse permission for organ removal.
- Potential organ donors, or their families, may feel 'pressured' against their wishes. Some people may feel uneasy that organs from one person are transplanted into another person. Potential use of organs from animals may be even more problematic.
- Increasing pressure from many quarters for a law to 'presumed consent' (meaning that people would have to opt out of being an organ donor).
- Donor shortages have opened up a black market in organs. Outright purchase/sale for profit is banned by the 1989 Human Organ Transplant Act but many stories circulate about sales to desperate recipients (not least of the sale of organs of executed Chinese prisoners).

Unit 10

Possible points include:
- electric car (heavy, slow and limited distance before re-charging required)
- hybrid petrol/electric car (slow, with inadequate infrastructure to maintain it)
- natural gas (limited supply and fossil fuel source)
- fuel cell (expensive, more suitable for commercial vehicles)
- more efficient and 'cleaner' engines using current fuels (have to be replaced sooner or later)
- road charging (untried technology).
- Are these likely to solve the problem of congestion caused by too many vehicles?
- Alternatives to the car need to be made more attractive to change people's habits and transport choices.
- More effective solutions might be greater investment in public transport and other options (walking, cycling, car clubs).

Unit 11

Contribution of technology to 'a surveillance society':
- The sciences of biometrics, intelligent photography and data processing have all come together at great speed.

- The refinement of information handling can mean that every habit can be targeted, analysed and pored over by an unseen and unknown number of people. The Data Protection Act offers only limited safeguards.
- CCTV cameras are a relatively recent innovation but are now widely used, particularly in town centres, principally to counter criminal activity such as shoplifting, vandalism and terrorism.
- Future plans might include microchip implants to identify and track individuals, facial recognition cameras fitted into lampposts, and unmanned surveillance aircraft.
- The NHS is seeking to computerise all patient records and has spent large sums commissioning IT firms to do this. Millions of patient records are to be uploaded, irrespective of individual wishes, and may be made available to the security services. Despite the advances in computer technology the plans are well behind schedule because of the technical difficulties involved.
- Genetic science is at an early stage and we cannot predict who will one day use the database and what conclusion future scientists will draw from profiles.
- Workplace monitoring of personal use of e-mails and the Internet through keystroke monitors increasingly takes place, partly to ensure that employees focus on work-related activities and partly to monitor activities such as harassment, bullying or incursions into areas like pornography.
- Other possible areas for comment are tagging, scanning at airports, road speed and number recognition cameras, supermarket loyalty cards, bank and telephone company records, global satellite navigation.

Extent to which technology is beneficial or excessively intrusive:
- Often, the presence of a battery of surveillance techniques suggests we are not trusted or permanently under suspicion. Used to excess, it can compromise individual anonymity and privacy and we often do not have the right to opt out.
- Often surveillance can take place without any form of parliamentary sanction or effective redress if mistakes are made.
- Many people do not realise how much they are being watched because surveillance is often invisible/discreet. Unseen, uncontrolled or excessive surveillance can foster a climate of suspicion and undermine trust.

- Mori polls suggest that most people believe surveillance is a significant factor in the fight against terrorism and violent crime. Necessary to safeguard law and order or growing evidence of an authoritarian society, perhaps characterised by plans for a biometric ID card which may include finger prints and iris scans – linked to a database of personal information.
- It can help to improve entitlement and access to public services and computerised patient records can improve health care.
- To refuse to use technology for fear of some future malevolent government is almost certainly misguided and conspiracy theory might best be left to writers of 'thrillers'.
- Mistakes can easily be made with serious consequences – false matches and other cases of mistaken identity, inaccurate facts and inferences, suspicions taken as reality, and breaches of security.
- How far does the growing gathering and processing of personal data suggest this is vital to contemporary living?

Unit 12
1-D, 2-B, 3-C, 4-C, 5-A, 6-C, 7-A, 8-C, 9-C, 10-B, 11-D, 12-C

Unit 13
1-C, 2-C, 3-B, 4-A, 5-C, 6-D, 7-B, 8-B

Unit 14
(a) Reasons for increase in the number of people working from home:
- Almost certainly the key factor has been the change in ICT which has helped to facilitate working from home making work far less location-specific. Word processing replaced typing and the home computer market has been revolutionised not least with the move from dial-up to high-speed broadband technology. Software packages like Microsoft Office Vista allow for collaborative IT working. Laptops can be linked to work bases and the Internet can be used to access information and provide telephone services. Phone prices are increasingly cheaper. Similarly there are far better printers, scanners, etc. and online monitoring tools for employers.
- For self-employed people who want to work from home, start-up is fairly easy and costs are relatively low.

- Adaptive technologies such as single-handed keyboards, tracking balls and IBM's voice recognition scheme have helped disabled workers to adapt.
- For many workers, transport has become more difficult as both costs and congestion have risen. Working at home is likely to be less stressful and saves time.
- Working at home offers workers more flexibility which may be particularly helpful if there are childminding responsibilities and is often good for morale. (The Flexible Working Regulations of 2003 allow parents with children under six the right to request work flexibility including working from home.)
- No boss or anyone else looking over your shoulder.
- Many employers prefer some homeworking because it helps to defray some of their capital costs. Worker productivity can be higher and high calibre staff who do not wish to work at the office can be retained. Employers may benefit from less absenteeism or days off due to sickness.

(b) Potential disadvantages of this form of work for some individuals:
- Not every employee is suited to flexible working. Individuals need to be self-motivated, disciplined and well-organised to work from home. It is easy to put off doing the work and people who fail to organise effectively may not succeed.
- Work is often an essentially social activity. Some homeworkers complain that they miss the buzz of office social life and banter. They can become rather lonely and isolated, missing the social interaction and gossip.
- Many people still see 'working at home' as something for the lazy and equate it with 'skiving'.
- Not all jobs can be done at home. Colleagues unable to work at home might become resentful.
- Not being in the office can affect promotion opportunities.
- Facilities for homeworking vary. This can make the house crowded if space is limited.
- Need to separate home and work life – can put strain on relationships with spouse/children if work element becomes intrusive.
- Danger of a 24-hour work culture. Someone at

home is almost deemed to be 'permanently available'.
- Computer security (access to a company intranet) might be compromised. (Need for firewalls, anti-virus software, content-filtering and encryption technology.)
- IT systems can break down and maintenance may be difficult/expensive.
- Specialist home-working insurance may be needed and some HSE regulations apply to homeworking, which may or may not be ignored.

Unit 15
1-A, 2-C, 3-B, 4-C, 5-D, 6-A, 7-C, 8-B, 9-D, 10-B

Unit 16
(a) Reasons in favour of removing religious veils:
- Behaviour which is generally understood to be socially acceptable ('social etiquette'/'good manners').
- Wearing veils as a religious symbol might conflict with rules for school uniform/dress.
- Candidates seeking to be an MP need to appear visually on equal terms with men/more balanced gender representation in parliament requires men and women to be seen in equal terms by voters.
- If women wish to compete equally in society it will be harder to do so when the veil creates a barrier between them and men.

(b) Reasons against removing religious veils:
- Wearing the veil is an important symbol and required by some branches of a particular faith.
- Wearing the veil is a matter of personal preference/freedom/entitlement.
- Tolerance/recognition of cultural diversity is an important feature of a free society.
- Retaining the veil in the presence of a male preserves a sense of modesty.

Unit 17
Two useful definitions might be:
- *An organised system of violence and intimidation, especially for political ends; the state of fear and submission caused by this.* (Chambers 1993)
- *Terrorism involves the creation of fear in selected populations – frequently civilian populations. This is done through seemingly random attacks on symbolic targets.* (Guardian 23/3/04)

- In both these definitions the creation of fear is the essence, and what distinguishes terrorism from, say, guerrilla warfare.

Can terrorism ever be justified?
Some of the issues which could be credited are:
- What kind of struggle is waged by terrorists? What political or religious systems lead people to become terrorists? What frustrations lead people to commit violent acts? Is terrorism always a last resort?
- Do the ends ever justify the means? There can be different perceptions of terrorist acts. Freedom-fighters for some are terrorists for others.
- Is terrorism always aimed at ensuring political, social and religious freedoms? Can terrorism be regarded as anti-freedom? Does terrorism carried out in the name of religion lead to political freedom or religious oppression? What freedom is offered to innocent casualties of such acts? What moral or ethical codes or circumstances can consider a cause appropriate/important/desperate enough to kill or die for?

These questions should be discussed within a framework of 'recent or ongoing conflicts'.
- Examples might include Iraq, Northern Ireland, the Basque region, South Africa, other African states, the Balkans, Israel and the Palestinians, Afghanistan, Pakistan and Kashmir, China and Tibet.
- Examples of terrorists who become the establishment (Israel and South Africa are the most obvious examples – cases may be made for Northern Ireland too).

Unit 18
Never justified:
- religious and humanitarian grounds (e.g. Ten Commandments)
- should 'turn the other cheek' and forgive rather than retaliate
- wars involve innocent victims, incite further hatred and anger
- mistakes can be made with capital punishment and euthanasia.

Justified:
- prevention of further death, evil, injustice, random acts of terrorism
- need for self defence, individually or as a nation
- need for justice to be done and seen to be done

- prevention of pain and suffering in case of euthanasia.

Difficult questions:
- Is abortion justified to save the life of another?
- How easy might it be to bend or transgress the law in euthanasia cases?

Unit 19
1-C, 2-B, 3-D, 4-A, 5-A, 6-D, 7-C, 8-B, 9-B, 10-B

Unit 20
High culture:
- Generally defined as the greatest artistic, musical and literary achievements of a society. Works of art accepted as having more 'depth' than others – possibly a variety of levels of meaning. Cultural forms such as opera, classical music and the literary works of Shakespeare, for example, can be characterised as high culture.
- Appropriate criteria might be accepted qualitative judgements of refinement, complexity, intention, skilled artistic content and execution, longevity and approval by expert critics and these might well outweigh the simple counter-arguments of elitism, limited appeal and social class.

Popular entertainment:
- Undemanding works of a superficial or ephemeral (= temporary/passing) nature? Genres might include pop music, comics, soap operas and reality shows designed for mass appeal.
- Does the largely ephemeral nature or popular appeal necessarily make it worth less than something more 'heavy' or 'worthy' which connects with few people? Is popular entertainment necessarily shoddy compared to more serious art? Is the purpose of art to entertain or to instruct; to titillate or to improve?

Meaning of 'valuable and important':
- Various possible strands are the contribution of certain works of art to extending human cultural and spiritual experiences and the sharing of these, developing understanding of ourselves and our emotions (the human condition), responding to the creative and expressive urge and giving enjoyment to others.

Unit 21
1   Points that might be made about each of the comments:

Comment (a)
- strongly worded, sweeping criticism of all works associated with the Turner Prize
- only offers opinion and insults, e.g. references to 'dustbin', 'untalented', 'gullible', 'junk', rather than specific evidence to support the claims
- throws concepts of 'class', 'wealth' and 'taste' fairly gratuitously into the argument
- many people would agree with such an assessment.

Comment (b)
- adopts a more open-minded approach to the issue and gives benefit of doubt about its value
- prepared to consider judgement of the *Times* critic as valid and worthwhile justification
- regards it as important not to pass personal judgement until work seen for oneself
- sustains a reasonably argued position throughout.

Comment (c)
- altogether more objective and measured stance ('art is essentially a subjective matter')
- argues that judgements on works of art can ultimately only ever be opinions
- claims to have reasons for not liking accepted artists' work any more than Turner prize winners, but these are not explained
- ascribes own particular value and justification to Turner Prize ('to encourage debate and raise the profile of modern art').

Comment (d)
- also a measured and balanced argument ('there have been occasions when I don't respond')
- given by one of the most authoritative and influential figures in the world of contemporary art
- provides an example of how works of art can be appreciated and affect the viewer
- promotes the value of discussion and debate in the evaluation of works of art
- points to the role of the media in stirring up controversy as much for its own ends as that of serving art and art appreciation.

2   Points that might be made:
Valid and worthwhile
- they can provide a thought provoking comment on the nature of material world or human condition
- may simply amuse onlooker or challenge their preconceptions
- may provide a stimulating sensory experience

- may demonstrate clever or subtle compositional skills.

Of little value
- often dependent upon a very simple, single idea or concept
- may have little obvious meaning or capacity for development
- may demonstrate little artistic skill or craft.

Unit 22
1-B, 2-B, 3-C, 4-D, 5-A, 6-B, 7-B, 8-A, 9-C, 10-A

Unit 23
Points about the rights may include:
- Both are important rights and freedom of speech is essential in a democratic society.
- The right to respect for your own beliefs and values is important, as long as this does not have an adverse impact on the rights of others ('I abhor what you say, but will defend to the death your right to say it' – Voltaire).
- Free media must be allowed to report on those in positions of power and authority, ultimately to expose and help prevent abuse.
- In such cases (e.g. illegal or improper conduct), the right to privacy should be forfeited.
- On that basis, the right to freedom of speech might be argued to have primacy.
- However, freedom of speech should not be completely unfettered, as this would be a form of abuse of power of its own.

Such an argument would lead naturally into the second part of the question and the limits discussed might include:
- the right to privacy in your personal life, to hold your own personal beliefs and values, and to go about your own lawful business without hindrance
- the right not to be slandered or libelled by untrue accusations and the right to gain redress
- there cannot be an absolute 'free-for-all' in what is presented because of the need to have some controls to eliminate harm
- the right not to be confronted by or exposed to material you do not wish to see, and might regard as offensive or harmful
- some individuals and groups may be particularly vulnerable, and susceptible to influence, and require

special protection, e.g. young people without well-formed sensibilities, values and opinions require some protection until they are old and experienced enough to make judgements for themselves
- old people may be easily shocked or offended, and deserve not to have sensibilities assaulted unduly, the same may apply to other vulnerable individuals and groups
- the need to recognise the particular sensitivity of some issues, e.g. those concerning race, religion, minority groups
- what comes directly into people's homes via domestic TV and radio should be treated differently from material that has to be purchased on a one-off basis, e.g. cinema, theatre, books
- restrictions that are currently applied to domestic 'free-to-air' TV, e.g. the 9.00pm 'watershed'
- films and video recordings that are classified according to their content for restricted access
- warning announcements that are made in advance of TV showings.

Unit 25 (1)
Overall points might include:
- rise in the number of households relative to the population
- dramatic rise in the number and proportion of single person households – many more people, both younger and older, are living on their own
- corresponds to a significant fall in the number of people getting married (half what it was in 1971).

Figure 25.3:
- reduction in proportion of households comprising married couples with children since 1961
- corresponding rise in proportion of couples without children
- reduction in numbers of children and size of families
- corresponding rise in lone parents with dependent children
- reduction in multi-family households, i.e. families sharing.

Figure 25.4:
- (as well as fall in number of marriages noted earlier) rise in number of divorces since changes in the law making these easier to obtain came into force in 1971
- rise in number of re-marriages, apparently linked to number of divorces, but both have tailed off since 1970s despite a recent upturn.

Unit 25 (2)

Further questions to consider might be:

- Can legislation and setting targets act as an effective agent of social change? What evidence is there?
- Have conditions for disadvantaged and minority groups improved? Have some areas been more successful than others?
- Some government departments and employers use targets to monitor progress and this puts pressure on to improve representation. Do you think this works? Is it right?
- Do the weaknesses highlighted by the Stephen Lawrence enquiry or the more recent racial disturbances in northern towns and cities mean that no progress has been made on race? Or despite these setbacks, have improvements been made on a broader front in education, awareness of rights, representation in employment, the media and cultural pressure groups, as a result of the attention paid to specific Equal Opportunities.
- How effective is positive discrimination as a means of addressing inequalities? It means giving preference to individuals on the basis of their group being under-represented. What are the positive and negative arguments for this?

Unit 26

Crime statistics or people's use of them may not be wholly reliable for a variety of reasons:

- As argued in the article, people may not always tell the truth and may be seeking to make a false insurance claim.
- The sample on which the Coventry police's argument is based is very small and may not be reliable on this basis. This could be a good example of how statistics may be (ab)used for partial reasons – in this case to suggest that actual crime rates can be overstated. The police might well have an interest in playing down the amount of crime committed in their area.
- Crime recorded by the police is estimated to be only a fraction (claimed to be 60 per cent) of actual crime committed, as many crimes are not reported to the police.
- Methods of counting and recording crime change from time to time. A major revision took place in 1998, for example, in the recording of violent crime focusing on the victim rather than the offender, with the result that the number of recorded incidents virtually doubled in one year.
- There are alternative national statistics based on

British Crime Survey data rather than crime recorded by the police. These show much higher rates of crime, of the order suggested above.

- Policy on pursuing particular offences may change according to local targets and/or political imperatives, e.g. reduced use of stop and search powers.
- Both the press and politicians may have an interest in 'talking up' or 'playing down' the significance of crime figures for particular purposes.

Unit 27

- Protest might be defended as a basic right and a necessary antidote to injustice and harmful actions.
- Some alternative processes for peaceful protest are: argument and persuasion directly or through the media, lobbying, petitioning, legal action. Should these be pursued first?
- Is the frustration of failure to succeed with legal protest sufficient justification for then turning to undemocratic means?
- How far can protest go before it becomes immoral or illegal? Strongly held views can lead to what the majority of society considers to be extremism.
- When does the exercise of individual rights and freedoms for some become an infringement upon the liberties of others?
- Can the end justify the means or when do certain more extreme forms of action become counter-productive and lose public sympathy?
- The more detailed the discussion of a range of examples you can provide the better. What about anti-war protests, anti-capitalist demonstrations, road and airport building, lorry drivers, hunting with dogs, divorced fathers, etc?

Unit 28

(a) Reasons given by the author:
- inaccurate claims often made against HLS
- importance of testing drugs to satisfy safety regulations
- animal rights activists do not back up claims with reliable sources
- critics frequently mislead and fail to give a truthful picture.

(b) Possible arguments against animal testing:
- natural concern/compassion for animals/animal rights
- unnecessary cruelty towards and abuse of other sentient (= feeling) beings

- alternative testing methods are available in many cases
- animals do not necessarily respond to treatments as humans.

Unit 29

Possible problems/groups:
- mass poverty, access to health care and education provision, particularly in LEDCs
- democratic rights, discrimination against minorities (race, gender, disability), animal rights.

Difficulties identified will depend on the groups chosen, but general problems might be:
- securing laws that apply to particular groups
- obstacles which may impede the operation/effectiveness of laws
- historical/cultural obstacles
- prejudice and discriminatory practices
- enforcement across states/in other countries
- numbers involved/majority and minority views
- cost
- lack of consensus
- existence/effectiveness of pressure groups
- ability to generate favourable publicity.

Unit 30

(a) Evidence offered includes:
- criticisms of the Royal Family which used to be rare and deemed to be worthy of censure are now more common and more readily accepted
- even traditional defenders of the monarchy ('the Tory benches') are critical in a way they never used to be
- media irreverence towards royals is now quite acceptable/normal
- royalist views are more likely to be challenged
- younger voters are less supportive of the monarchy.

(b) Possible reasons might include:
- oldest political institution of government
- fulfils necessary constitutional role above parliament (would republic/elected president be any better?)
- authority of monarch helps to protect from revolution, civil war, dictatorship, constitutional breakdown
- visible symbol of tradition that people can identify with

- ceremonial function that would also need to be replaced.

Unit 31

1   Source A – Strengths:
- from a reputable broadsheet newspaper, raises an issue for debate in the light of social change
- challenges anomaly of retaining hereditary system in a democracy, realistic assessment of where power really lies
- captures changing public mood (less deferential attitudes to monarchy).

Source A – Weaknesses:
- strongly opinionated, makes exaggerated claims
- one-sided/heavily biased against the monarchy, politically motivated (typical journalism of a left-of-centre newspaper?)
- relies on rhetoric, uses emotive language.

Source B – Strengths:
- speaks for many (particulary older?) people
- readers (through their letters) are sometimes better barometers of public opinion than editors
- identifies key issues of who/what would replace the monarchy and its role in political life.

Source B – Weaknesses:
- uninformed view of unidentified member of public, no evidence that he/she 'cannot be alone in this view'
- expresses a reactionary and old-fashioned view, out of touch with changing public opinion
- relies far more on emotion than reason, uses emotive language.

Source C – Strengths:
- extract from published book by established political analyst and academic
- stands back from issues to some extent, gives objective/analytical view of scene over time
- uses actual quotes from authoritative figures to illustrate point in second paragraph.

Source C – Weaknesses:
- rather forthright and sweeping judgement about British attitude to monarchy
- gratuitously (= for no essential reason) critical of British values at end of first paragraph

- conclusion is brief and extract is too short to evaluate fully.

2   Relevant points:
- Hennessy does not make clear what he means either by 'the political nation in Britain' or by discussing the issue of the monarchy 'in sensible terms'.
- He certainly implies that more people are inclined to view the monarchy in less flattering/deferential terms. In that sense, the political nation could be anyone who is part of the electorate or those who have more specialist knowledge.
- Typically, we are likely to associate certain characteristics with 'sensible terms'. Those who are well-informed make clear, rational points which are supported by knowledge.
- Such people seek to be 'detached' and, though opinions are likely to play a part in the discussion, emotions are less evident, and the case is dependent on the quality of arguments.
- In reality, the subject generates strong feelings (pro-monarchists v. anti-monarchists) and this often varies according to age, background and the strength of one's political viewpoint.
- Many people do not always respond to political issues rationally or logically. We are all subject to particular beliefs and values which influence our views and judgments.
- Emotions, bias and prejudices are likely to make it quite difficult to have a 'sensible' discussion of such a potentially controversial topic.

Unit 32

Issues raised:
- enduring culture in schools and workplaces that females are more suited to certain kinds of work ('the five Cs – caring, cashier, clerical, cleaning and catering')
- job segregation still exists, contributing to unequal pay (gender pay gap described as 'complex' with 'no one solution')
- women may often be working well below their abilities which is a waste of talent and worsens Britain's position in a competitive global market
- women may be personally unfulfilled if they work below their capabilities.

Tackling issues:
- 'Fundamental change necessary to our school and workplace cultures'.

- Need for programmes to improve vocational training, work-tasting for primary school pupils, more varied work experience in non-traditional areas and apprenticeships for women.
- Need to focus change on schools and changes in thinking (probably from an early age) with perhaps more attention in curriculum being given to non-traditional subjects.
- Must be recognised that some women are more likely to choose certain kinds of work/working patterns for family reasons.
- Some members of both sexes might find comfort and reassurance in reaffirming and supporting traditional stereotypes in choosing certain kinds of work. People do not always like to be seen as 'different'.
- Trade unions might do more to recruit female members and to give them better protection at work.
- Improved child care facilities would help many women.
- More emphasis on female role models in different areas of life (beyond celebrity culture).
- The law appears to give women considerable protection in the workplace but it needs more effective enforcement. Redress can be a long and complicated process and penalties for discrimination are not always sufficient to act as a deterrent.
- Politicians do not always give a positive lead. Change takes time and it usually takes place incrementally with values shifting slowly over generations.

Unit 33

Reasons for different levels of pay may include:
- supply of and demand for labour
- market price and profitability of product/industry, 'marginal revenue product' of employee
- employee characteristics, e.g. education, training, experience, expertise, ability (age, sex, ethnic background may also enter into equation)
- employer characteristics, e.g. public (state), private, self (trade unions), 'monopsonist'/monopoly supplier
- employment characteristics, e.g. responsibility, risk, (un)pleasant/(un)popular work, security, geographical position
- determination to preserve differentials and status.

It may be argued that these details in themselves offer adequate justification as they obey 'natural' economic laws and the differences reflect the value of an employee to an employer, for example. On the other hand, the passage raises the question of the fairness and the need for such differentials and whether the scale of them can be justified in ethical terms, independent of economic theory. Some may argue that all jobs are functionally important and that workers should be rewarded equally, but is this realistic in an 'imperfect labour market'?

Unit 34

Socialisation

- This is seen primarily (but not exclusively) as a function of the family and changing family structures and the difficulties that some groups face (e.g. poorer single mothers) no doubt have their effects.
- Southern Europe and some Asian and Afro-Caribbean communities have sometimes stronger family, community and religious bonds. This is less evident in northern European countries.
- Peoples' beliefs, values and moral codes are developed in a wider context – socialisation also takes place through the immediate social and cultural environment, peer group influence.
- Education clearly plays its part and there can be little doubt that the affluent have more choice when it comes to their children's education. Those from socially disadvantaged areas may have low achieving schools. Similarly, the better off may have access to richer and more fulfilling activities.
- Schooling has changed and some may question how much time is available for social development when so much emphasis is placed on training to pass exams.
- Cycle of deprivation may play a part – limited employment opportunities, inadequate housing, crime, drugs, anti-social behaviour.
- Children from affluent households will have more material resources, better housing, space, perhaps a different cultural outlook but their socialisation is not necessarily going to be more successful.
- Socialisation difficulties are not necessarily confined to poorer families. Drug taking, binge drinking and anti-social behaviour are certainly not confined to poorer people and less affluent areas.
- Children from poorer backgrounds may well have limited horizons and ambition. People from all backgrounds may be curious and intelligent but lack the support and environment to capitalise on this.
- Equality of opportunity exists in theory but, in reality, this may be heavily restricted and early disadvantage may be quickly compounded.

- State might intervene via initiatives like Sure Start nurseries to provide infants with more stimulation but such initiatives are often viewed with suspicion in the communities concerned.

Insurmountable barrier

- Do we live in an increasingly 'classless' society? As a concept, social class is rarely debated today in the way it was in the 1960s and 1970s, yet social class seems still to matter.
- One of the *Freedom's Orphans* main findings is that personal and social skills such as self-control, self-motivation and an ability to get on with others have become more and more important in helping to determine future success.
- Poverty certainly makes life difficult especially in areas of high unemployment/low wages and it may be very difficult for most to escape from the cycle of deprivation. Debts build up quickly, credit is non-existent or expensive, dependency on cigarettes, drugs and alcohol may be high and living standards may be very low.
- Poverty is not, though, necessarily an insurmountable barrier. There are high achieving state schools in poorer areas and, whatever might be argued about the class system and its inbuilt advantages, it is not entirely rigid.
- Scope for social mobility, perhaps via higher education, or the development of particular skills in terms of employment potential.
- Personal qualities – drive, ambition, determination all matter and not all successful careers are confined primarily to the middle classes (professional football being one major example).
- Many different forms of success possible (although it might be argued that most depend on at least some degree of financial security).

Unit 35

Opinion polls currently show that a majority of British adults do not want to join the euro. The arguments against are:

- **Transition costs.** Consumers and workers will suffer because they will have to learn to think about transactions in a new currency. Businesses will have to update software, change counter tills and vending machines and reprint price lists. The one-off costs will run into billions of pounds and prices are likely to rise.
- **Sovereignty.** Joining the euro will further increase

the powers of the EU and diminish the powers of national government. Many voters have a deep mistrust of the EU and its competency.

- **One rate for all**. Inevitably, the central bank of a monetary union has to set a monetary policy which it believes is in the best interests of the majority. However, it may be inappropriate for some regions. For instance, in 2000 Ireland was enjoying what some argued was an unsustainable boom, with above-average inflation. Interest rates in Ireland would probably have been much higher to counter the inflation threat if Ireland had had independent control of its monetary policy. Within a UK context, it is often argued that a tight monetary policy, appropriate for a booming London and the South East, is harmful to areas such as Wales or Northern Ireland where there is above-average unemployment.

- **Exchange rate**. The rate at which the UK enters the euro is crucial. The very high value of the pound against the euro in 1998–2000 was the wrong exchange rate to use, according to most exporting businesses. A high exchange rate would be likely to lead to large current account deficits. So a much lower exchange rate is needed, perhaps even lower than the current rate of €1.40.

- **Not necessary**. Many argue that the UK doesn't need to be part of the euro-zone to benefit from it. For instance, although foreign businesses complained about the high value of the pound, the UK saw record levels of inward investment in 1999. So long as the pound doesn't fluctuate wildly against the euro, the UK can get benefits without membership.

Those arguing in favour of the joining the euro say that any potential drawbacks are outweighed by the benefits:

- **No exchange costs**. Individuals and firms will not have to pay fees and commissions to exchange UK currency for EU currencies. This reduces costs and encourages trade.

- **Exchange rate uncertainty**. This will be abolished in the area which accounts for 60 per cent of our foreign trade. Importers and exporters will know how much they will be charged when dealing with each other. This too will reduce costs and encourage trade.

- **Standard prices**. Consumers should benefit because there will be greater price transparency. Firms will find it more difficult to segment markets in Europe and charge higher prices for goods in, say, the UK than in Belgium.

- **Genuine single market**. Monetary union is a further step towards creating a wholly single market in Europe. Single markets, like the United States, allow firms to exploit economies of scale and this reduces prices to consumers.

- **Influence in EU affairs**. By staying out of monetary union, the UK is losing its ability to influence how the EU is run and how it should develop. This is against the long-term interests of the UK.

Overall, perhaps, the main argument of the anti-euro lobby is a **political** one, centred around the issue of sovereignty and who should control British affairs. On **economic** grounds, there are strong arguments both for and against entry. Most economists agree that the exchange rate at which the UK enters the euro, if and when it does, will be crucial in determining whether the UK benefits or suffers in the short term from entry. They also agree that the UK should be at roughly the same point in the trade cycle as Europe to prevent the European Central Bank from setting interest rates which are either too high or too low for the best interests of the UK. The Chancellor of the Exchequer has identified **five tests** to determine whether it is in the UK's best economic interest to join the euro and all of these must be met before the proposal is put to the electorate in a promised referendum. These tests are:

- Are business cycles and economic structures compatible so that we and others could live comfortably with euro interest rates on a permanent basis?
- If problems emerge is there sufficient flexibility to deal with them?
- Would joining EMU create better conditions for firms making long-term decisions to invest in Britain?
- What impact would entry into EMU have on the competitive position of the UK's financial services industry, particularly the City's wholesale markets?
- In summary, will joining EMU promote higher growth, stability and a lasting increase in jobs?

In the long term, with the euro-zone being such an important trading partner for the UK, some argue that it is difficult to see how the UK could stay out of monetary union forever. On the other hand, if put to the electorate in a referendum with a recommendation to join, the majority, encouraged by a largely anti-euro press, would most likely vote against, as in Sweden in September 2003.

Unit 36

Fairer world:
- increased trade between the rich and the developing world, removal of tariffs on processed goods
- increased investment by rich countries in industry and services, rescheduling of foreign debts
- reform of agricultural policies and farm subsidies to aid developing countries, stop dumping of agricultural surpluses
- assistance to improve governance, education and healthcare in developing countries
- greater willingness on part of EU and USA to impose more rigorous standards and controls on multinational companies.

More sustainable:
- greater investment in alternative, cleaner and renewable energy sources
- increased energy efficiency
- greater emphasis on recycling of products and reduction of packaging
- much higher levels of environmental controls and reduced pollution
- greater investment in technological solutions to energy and pollution problems.

Businesses:
- operate fair and ethical practices
- pay economic price to commodity producers
- contribute to local infrastructure and educational standards.

Governments:
- remove barriers to free trade
- greater controls on conservation and environmental pollution provide incentives to develop sustainable technologies.

Index